Expert .NET Delivery Using NAnt and CruiseControl.NET

MARC HOLMES

Apress®

Expert .NET Delivery Using NAnt and CruiseControl.NET

Copyright © 2005 by Marc Holmes

Lead Editor: Ewan Buckingham
Technical Reviewer: Brian Nantz
Editorial Board: Steve Anglin, Dan Appleman, Ewan Buckingham, Gary Cornell, Tony Davis,
    Jason Gilmore, Jonathan Hassell, Chris Mills, Dominic Shakeshaft, Jim Sumser
Assistant Publisher: Grace Wong
Project Managers: Tracy Brown-Collins and Beth Christmas
Copy Manager: Nicole LeClerc
Copy Editor: Liz Welch
Production Manager: Kari Brooks-Copony
Production Editor: Katie Stence
Compositor: Dina Quan
Proofreader: Elizabeth Berry
Indexer: Carol Burbo
Artist: Kinetic Publishing Services, LLC
Cover Designer: Kurt Krames
Manufacturing Manager: Tom Debolski

Library of Congress Cataloging-in-Publication Data

Holmes, Marc.
 Expert .NET delivery using NAnt and CruiseControl.NET / Marc Holmes.
   p. cm.
 Includes index.
 ISBN 1-59059-485-1 (pbk. : alk. paper)
 1. Install programs (Computer programs) 2. Computer software--Development. 3. Computer software--
Testing. I. Title.
 QA76.76.I55H6 2005
 005.1--dc22

                        2005008428

Printed and bound in the United States of America 9 8 7 6 5 4 3 2 1

Trademarked names may appear in this book. Rather than use a trademark symbol with every occurrence
of a trademarked name, we use the names only in an editorial fashion and to the benefit of the trademark
owner, with no intention of infringement of the trademark.

Distributed to the book trade in the United States by Springer-Verlag New York, Inc., 233 Spring Street,
6th Floor, New York, NY 10013, and outside the United States by Springer-Verlag GmbH & Co. KG,
Tiergartenstr. 17, 69112 Heidelberg, Germany.

In the United States: phone 1-800-SPRINGER, fax 201-348-4505, e-mail orders@springer-ny.com, or visit
http://www.springer-ny.com. Outside the United States: fax +49 6221 345229, e-mail orders@springer.de,
or visit http://www.springer.de.

For information on translations, please contact Apress directly at 2560 Ninth Street, Suite 219, Berkeley,
CA 94710. Phone 510-549-5930, fax 510-549-5939, e-mail info@apress.com, or visit http://www.apress.com.

The information in this book is distributed on an "as is" basis, without warranty. Although every precau-
tion has been taken in the preparation of this work, neither the author(s) nor Apress shall have any
liability to any person or entity with respect to any loss or damage caused or alleged to be caused directly
or indirectly by the information contained in this work.

The source code for this book is available to readers at http://www.apress.com in the Downloads section.

For Helen

Contents at a Glance

Foreword xv

About the Author xvii

About the Technical Reviewer xix

Acknowledgments xxi

Introduction xxiii

CHAPTER 1   A Context for Delivery 1

CHAPTER 2   Dissecting NAnt 25

CHAPTER 3   Important NAnt Tasks 59

CHAPTER 4   A Simple Case Study 91

CHAPTER 5   Process Standards 135

CHAPTER 6   Continuous Integration 167

CHAPTER 7   Extending NAnt 199

CHAPTER 8   Database Integration 225

CHAPTER 9   Code Generation 279

CHAPTER 10   Closing Thoughts 319

APPENDIX A   A Fistful of Tools 337

APPENDIX B   NAnt Sweeper 349

INDEX 355

Contents

Foreword xv

About the Author xvii

About the Technical Reviewer xix

Acknowledgments xxi

Introduction xxiii

■CHAPTER 1   **A Context for Delivery** 1

Why Delivery Processes Are Needed 1

The Etomic Situation 2

Potential Processes 4

    Simple Delivery 4

    Segregated Delivery 6

    Automated Delivery 6

Thoughts on Delivery 9

    The Environment 9

    Configuration Management 12

    Planning 14

A Solution for Delivery 16

    Automation 16

    Design to Deliver 17

A Delivery Process for Etomic 21

    The Build Process 21

    The Deployment Process 22

A Glossary for Delivery 23

Summary 23

    Further Reading 24

■CHAPTER 2   **Dissecting NAnt** 25

All About NAnt 25

    What Does NAnt Do? 26

    Why Choose NAnt? 26

    NAnt Nomenclature 27

Basic Anatomy of a Build File 28
    A "Hello World" Example 28
The NAnt Executable 29
    Command-Line Options 29
The Build File 41
    The Project 42
    The Target 42
Properties 46
    Built-in Properties 50
A Build Process for Etomic 52
    The Build Skeleton 53
    The Deploy Skeleton 56
Summary 58
    Further Reading 58

■CHAPTER 3   **Important NAnt Tasks** 59

There Is More Than One Way to Do It 60
General Task Features 60
    Using Attributes 61
    Using Nested Elements 62
Structural Tasks 64
    <call> [NAnt] 65
    <nant> [NAnt] 67
    <loadtasks> [NAnt] 68
Conditional Tasks 69
    <foreach> [NAnt] 70
    <fail> [NAnt] 70
    <if> [NAnt] and <ifnot> [NAnt] 70
File Tasks 71
    <attrib> [NAnt] 71
    <copy> [NAnt], <delete> [NAnt], and <move> [NAnt] 71
    <mkdir> [NAnt] 73
    <get> [NAnt] 74
Build Tasks 74
    <asminfo> [NAnt] 74
    <exec> [NAnt] 76
    <mkiisdir> [NAntContrib] 76
    <ndoc> [NAnt] 76

<nunit2> [NAnt] 78

<solution> [NAnt] 78

<csc> [NAnt] 80

Utility Tasks 81

<echo> [NAnt] 81

<style> [NAnt] 81

<zip> [NAnt] and <unzip> [NAnt] 81

<xmlpeek> [NAnt] and <xmlpoke> [NAnt] 82

Source Control Tasks 83

<vssget> [NAntContrib] 84

<vsscheckin> [NAntContrib] and <vsscheckout>
[NAntContrib] 84

<vsslabel> [NAntContrib] 84

<vssundocheckout> [NAntContrib] 85

Special NAnt Tasks 85

NAnt Functions 85

Script Tasks 86

Summary 89

■CHAPTER 4   **A Simple Case Study** 91

Examining the Application 91

What Does It Do? 92

Use Cases 96

Organizing the Environment 98

Visual SourceSafe 99

Build Folders 99

Creating the Build File 100

Error Handling in NAnt 101

Clean 103

Checkout/Get 104

Version 105

Build 110

Test 111

document 116

publish 117

notify 118

fail 118

Examining the Output 119

Opportunities for Refactoring 127

    Refactoring Settings 128

Creating the Deploy File 128

    Core Settings 129

    selectversion 129

    get 130

    selectenvironments 130

    createenvironments 130

    position 130

    configure 131

    notify 131

    fail 131

    help 131

Examining the Output 132

Summary 133

    Further Reading 133

▮**CHAPTER 5**   **Process Standards** 135

Another Case Study 135

Considering the Delivery Scenario 136

    The Solutions 137

    The Build Process 137

    The Deploy Process 137

Consideration of Standards 138

    Naming Conventions 138

    Source Control Organization 139

    VS .NET Settings 140

    Third-Party Components 142

    Tools and Support Organization 144

Creating the Build Files 145

    What Has Changed? 145

    Comparing the Build Files 146

    Refactoring the Build Files 148

    Further Refactoring 150

Creating the Deploy Files 152

    Etomic.Library.Transformer.Deploy.xml 153

    Etomic.Transformer.Win.Deploy.xml 155

    Etomic.Transformer.Web.Deploy.xml 156

Observations 157

A More Complex Scenario 157
    VSSManager 158
Summary 166
    Further Reading 166

CHAPTER 6 **Continuous Integration** 167

What Is Continuous Integration? 167
    Opportunities 169
    Threats 170
Technical Options 170
    CruiseControl.NET 171
    Draco.NET 172
    Hippo.NET 172
Implementing CI for the Sample Applications 172
    Examining CCNet 172
    Basic Configuration 175
    Configuring the Server 177
    Amending the Build.Core.Xml File 183
    Amending the Deploy Scripts 186
    Creating a Startup Script for the Server 186
    Examining the Dashboard 187
    Examining the cctray application 189
    Examining the State File 190
    Testing the multi Source Control 190
Enhancing CCNet 194
Summary 196
    Further Reading 196

CHAPTER 7 **Extending NAnt** 199

NAnt Functionality 199
Investigating NAnt Tasks: <mkdir> 202
    A Look at <mkdir> 202
    A Look at <copy> 203
    A Look at <version> 205
    A Look at <exec> 206
Creating a NAnt Task: <fxcop> 208
    FxCop Task Requirements 208
    <fxcop> Task Usage 209

Creating the Visual Studio Project 210
Implementing the <fxcop>Task 210
Testing the Task 214
Adding the Solution to the Build Process 216
Using the Task 221
Summary 223

■CHAPTER 8   Database Integration 225

The Problems with the Database 225
Database Scenarios 226
Planning the Database Tasks 228
Control Task 228
Analyze Task 229
Integrate Task 229
Configure Task 229
The Impact on Continuous Integration 229
Implementing the Database Tasks 231
Manual SQL Script Processing Task 231
Automated Integration Task 237
Thinking about Data Synchronization 250
A Process for Database Integration 251
Control and Configure Tasks 251
Deployment Considerations 252
Implementing Database Integration 254
The Build Script 255
The Deploy Script with Database Deployment 263
Considering DTS Packages 273
Organization 274
Load XML File Task 274
Set Variables Task 276
Summary 277
Further Reading 277

■CHAPTER 9   Code Generation 279

Why Use Code Generation? 279
Tools for the Task 281
Basic File Manipulation 281
XSLT 281
CodeSmith 281

Investigating CodeSmith 282
    Using Properties 283
    Generating Multiple Files 288
Investigating XSLT 292
    Generating Multiple Output Files with XSLT 292
Targets for Generation 296
    CruiseControl Configuration Files 296
    Build Files 304
    Deployment Files 310
Managing Generation Automatically 313
    A New CruiseControl Instance 315
Summary 318
    Further Reading 318

█CHAPTER 10   **Closing Thoughts** 319

What Have We Done? 319
    The Problem 319
    The Solution Proposal: Design to Deliver 320
    The Solution Definition 323
    The Solution Implementation 325
Best Practices 327
    Process 327
    Standards 328
    NAnt 328
    CruiseControl.NET 329
    Other Factors 329
Closing Comments 330
    Tool Selection 330
    It Is All About the Standards 330
    Start Small and Work Under a Banner 331
    Refactoring to Efficiency 332
    Complex Scenarios 332
Views on the Future 333
    Regarding MSBuild 333
    Other Directions 334
Conclusion 335

■APPENDIX A   A Fistful of Tools 337

Software Dependencies 337
Tool Organization 338
Automating the Organization 339
Core Tools 343
Script Editing 344
Other Tools 346

■APPENDIX B   NAnt Sweeper 349

Playing NAnt Sweeper 350

■INDEX 355

Foreword

The success of any open source project is contingent on the strength of its user community. On the CruiseControl.NET project, we have been fortunate to have a strong community of users. As one of the authors of CCNet, I can honestly say that the formation of this community has had relatively little to do with us; it has been built up and fostered primarily by the efforts of its members. These days most of the enhancements, feature requests, and email traffic are driven not by the committers, but by the community at large. The level of activity is such that the committers have a hard time keeping up with all the submitted patches.

It is in this spirit that I view Marc's book: it is an example of how community members support and give back to the community. This book is an effort to help fellow users of CruiseControl.NET and NAnt set up, understand, and get the most out of their tools. It is a comprehensive overview of both tools and is full of practical advice for applying them to your project. Through the use of a detailed case study, Marc demonstrates how to build up a foundation for automating a project's build and deployment process.

The goal of any software development project is to deliver valuable, working software into the hands of its users. This is the guiding principle behind Marc's "Design to Deliver" approach, and it is the objective that led to the creation of both CruiseControl.NET and NAnt. I hope that you find both the book and these tools useful in helping to achieve this end.

Owen Rogers
Author of CruiseControl.NET

About the Author

MARC HOLMES is one of the lucky ones—he was born into a generation of home computing. His first computer, acquired at age ten, was a Commodore Vic-20. This was followed up with a Commodore 64 and Marc's first programming project: "SpaceBats." He has willingly been chained to a computer since then.

Having studied computer science and artificial intelligence at university, he has devoted his time to working and developing technology in various industries, including retail, semi-conductors, and media. As a developer, he has written numerous systems, from WAP-based "m-commerce" applications to media management systems.

Since the dotcom era, Marc has concentrated on software design and engineering processes, following closely the introduction of the .NET platform. This focus currently forms the basis of his day-to-day activities. Passionate about the provision of software engineering processes as the glue that binds and industrializes software development, he is a firm believer in software as a commodity.

Currently, Marc is head of application development at a global media corporation. He and the development team oversee dozens of systems, from small "brochureware" sites to significant enterprise systems for human resources, customer relationship management, and logistics operations. He can also be found participating in the "blogosphere" and in various newsgroups and discussion groups. And in his spare time, he enjoys cooking, fine wine, and occasional interaction with other humans.

About the Technical Reviewer

 **BRIAN NANTZ** is currently employed with Cornerstone Consulting. He has developed Microsoft solutions for companies in both the medical and security industries. Brian has written various .NET books, including *Expert Web Services Security in the .NET Platform* (Apress, 2004) and *Open Source .NET Development: Programming with NAnt, NUnit, NDoc, and More* (Addison-Wesley Professional, 2004). He lives with his wife and three children in the Milwaukee, Wisconsin area.

Acknowledgments

There was a time when I thought, "You know, I could write one of these books—can't be too hard."

I guess I was both right and wrong: I have done it, but it was hard. In fact, it would have been impossible without the help of a whole bunch of people.

I'd like to say thanks to the gang at Apress: Gary Cornell for the deal; Ewan Buckingham for listening to my idea and believing in it; Beth Christmas for her guidance, counsel, and always positive attitude; Liz Welch for making sense of my words jumbled; Katie Stence and Dina Quan for making it all look great; Beckie, Tina, Glenn, and everyone else who helped me out.

I need to say a big thank you to my colleagues at BBC Worldwide who offered continuous support and interest. You're a great bunch of people. In particular, thanks to Ben Lovell for his efforts with the source code and for convincing me that I could actually do this. Also thanks to Alex Hildyard for his feedback and for NAnt Sweeper—the oddest version of that game I've seen.

There were many others who played their part too. Most important are the creators of the tools that have inspired me to write this book. By doing what they do in the selfless way they do it, these folks benefit the development community through their brilliance. I can't list all of the contributors here—thanks to you all—but in particular significant thanks is given to Owen Rogers for his efforts with CruiseControl.NET, Gert Driesen for his unceasing attention to NAnt, and Bart Read and Neil Davidson at Red Gate Software Ltd. for their invaluable help and feedback.

Finally, a huge thanks to Brian Nantz (which is the most appropriate name I can imagine!), who has provided great feedback and wisdom throughout the whole process as the technical reviewer.

Introduction

Delivering software? If you have bought this book, or grabbed it from a colleague's desk, or even found it in the street and are looking at it with some interest, then I think it is quite likely that you have been struggling with the same problems as I have for some time.

Successful build and release processes seem to be easy when given some casual thought. In principle, moving and configuring a Windows or web application from development through testing and staging environments ultimately to production is quite straightforward.

In practice, though—as I am sure you have found—the process can be considerably more complex.

An application can have many aspects that require configuration as well as many assets to move around and store. A developer can easily miss these aspects. These factors can also go unnoticed for some time, and only cause a problem when the assets are needed "right now."

Builds and releases can take an extended amount of time. They will not usually "fail" in the sense that a piece of software is not delivered to the customer, but they will fail in various other ways. They may gradually add risk and complexity to the processes and reduce confidence in the platform. For example, they may rely on Bob being available because only he knows the configuration file.

I am constantly disappointed by projects where difficulties are introduced by failing to look at these processes, among others. Some developers do not see these aspects of work as core to their role. Teams may produce excellent code and present some clever innovation in the software, only to find out that the development platform contains hundreds of zip files named things like "DontDeleteRegressionJustInCase" or a dozen SQL databases with dates appended to their name on a virtual server that now cannot be rebuilt because these assets have become an integral part of the system. And no one can be sure that they *are* an integral part of the system—Bob is on leave!

Success came to my own delivery processes through the use of two fundamental tools: NAnt and CruiseControl.NET. I was introduced to both through murmurings on the Internet and one or two searches for specific issues. Since discovering and learning how to use and develop both tools, I have started to think that even the ugliest of delivery problems can be solved.

NAnt is a tool that has me marveling at the beauty and simplicity of programming. Something so seemingly simple can do an amazing amount of work, and can do it in a countless number of ways. One of the core aims of this book is not to present every available option—which I could not do if I wanted to—but to describe some methods that have worked for me and for teams I am associated with. You may find that they work equally well for you, you may find they do not, or you may find you have stumbled across a much better way of doing things (if so, please share!). My main hope is that this book gives you some ideas for pushing forward your own successful processes.

CruiseControl.NET is also an excellent system. The framework and utility it provides to a collection of NAnt-based projects gives the user a benefit that cannot be underestimated. The promise of continuous integration is a bold one, but the tool enables centralized control of delivery processes quickly and relatively satisfactorily. It will only get better, too.

Aside from the actual processes, I hope that you gain some theoretical and practical knowledge of the toolsets utilized in this book. It has been a pleasant struggle to implement these practices, and as you will see there are still questions left unanswered.

The Aims of the Book

I want to point out the purpose of the book so that it is clear from the outset. The book is about providing ideas, practices, and a platform for standardizing approaches to build and deploy processes.

It is not supposed to be a comprehensive guide to NAnt, or CruiseControl.NET, or even any aspects of the .NET platform. NAnt and Cruise Control.NET have not matured fully yet—they are not even considered version 1 releases by their authors—and will undoubtedly see significant changes. They have even seen some changes during the writing of this book.

At the same time, this book is not about being exceptionally clever with coding/scripting techniques in a "cunning algorithm" kind of way. If you master the tools, then you will be able to do so with your scripts as the inspiration hits you. Rather, this book emphasizes being clever enough to complete the specified process *across many projects in the same way*. It is about introducing standards for solution architectures that can be applied successfully without being too onerous.

Above all, this book offers a practical approach to the problems involved in delivering software. We look at actual applicable solutions. Sometimes they may be best, and sometimes not, but the solutions are always practical.

A Note on Organization

Using NAnt, and scripting languages in general, introduces a lot of, well, scripts into your environment. All of this is great as long as you are organizing your scripts effectively. The success of many of the practical implementations I have experienced has hinged on the organization of scripts and assets to support the process.

I have attempted to ensure that the organization of the book code is such that you will be able to use it on your own system with minimum changes. However, since there are a lot of software dependencies—some deliberate, some as side effects—then some configuration work may be necessary. This is also true if you are adopting the tools yourself. I strongly urge you to consider careful organization of tools and storage for your own processes to facilitate successful development. Appendix A discusses this a little further.

A Note on Open Source Software

I am a huge proponent of any kind of open source activity.

Apart from my .NET hat, I work with a team responsible for developing a Java/J2EE-based application sitting on Solaris and Linux platforms. Sometimes I gaze with a little jealousy at the fantastic freely available open source widgets they get to use. The world certainly appears to be their oyster. (Sometimes I just press F5 and think about how good Visual Studio .NET is and smile to myself.) There are many tools of this kind for .NET now and surely they will only increase in number over time. Naturally, I will be using some of these tools over the course of this book.

There is always a snag, or at least a potential snag, though. Popular software of this kind is developed continuously and released often. In principle, and sometimes in practice, this is great as new features are added and bugs fixed promptly. If you get yourself involved, you could contribute even if it is just an idea.

The flip side to this is that sometimes the software does not go where you want it to, or it is not stable enough to make you feel comfortable using it and knowing it. It can be easy to feel as though you need the latest build or you are somehow missing out. I certainly started out in this way.

To allay this fear, I tend to concentrate on one version of a piece of software as long as it suits my needs. This approach allows me to ensure that my own work with it is stable and that I understand the tool fully.

The upshot of this is that by the time you read this book versions of the software will have moved on and will be doing new things. In lots of ways, I hope this is so, because it will save you from having to do some of the "hacking" described in the book. On the other hand, the tools might not be helping any more, something might have taken their place, or new issues might be introduced. Tool version x does not work with other tool version y, and so on.

So the solutions, practices, and framework laid out here are based on a point in time in a fairly fast-moving environment. I suggest that you do the same thing, whether or not it is at the same point in time. You can always be mindful of changes and remain involved in a research and development sense, but you must ensure that at some point there is some stability and utility to your efforts in this area—which is surely the purpose of the activity.

A Note on Technology

Deciding on the technologies to use for the book was actually quite easy: I use what I am experienced with and what is and has been applicable in environments I've been involved in. The book therefore concentrates on the following areas:

.NET using C#. The example projects for delivery and the extensions to NAnt and the like are written in C# through the use of Visual Studio .NET.

Visual SourceSafe. This is probably a more controversial choice. Visual SourceSafe is usually criticized for various features, or more accurately the lack of them. Generally, though, I have worked in teams using Visual SourceSafe more often than not. Changing source control systems to others supported by NAnt and CruiseControl.NET should not be a problem as there are no real Visual SourceSafe–specific features in the examples.

NAnt. NAnt is my preferred tool for the automation of delivery—you may already have guessed this. Bear in mind that other options are out there. It is unlikely that this text will help you with those, however. I started with 0.84 and then moved to 0.85 RC1 and various nightly builds of NAnt. Again, because we stick to core NAnt features most of the time, changes to scripts as future releases arrive should be minimal.

CruiseControl.NET. To deliver continuous integration I have chosen to use CruiseControl.NET. Again, other options are available. Many of these also harness NAnt, and so if you do choose a different solution, much of this text will still be applicable with some adapting.

More specifically, Table 1 shows the versions of technologies I use throughout the book.

Table 1. *Technology Versions*

Technology	Version
Visual Studio .NET	2003 (and therefore .NET Framework version 1.1)
Visual SourceSafe	6.0d
NAnt	0.85 RC2
NAntContrib	0.85 RC2
CruiseControl.NET	0.8
Red Gate SQL Bundle	3.3
CodeSmith	2.6 (studio version)

Additionally, many other pieces of software are used to handle various aspects of the process, or as productivity aids. Appendix A in this book covers the majority of these products.

What Does the Book Cover?

Deciding on the order of things I wanted to cover has been one of the most difficult aspects of writing this book. When I was working on these processes I had a fairly clear, if slightly abstract, end goal: improve confidence, speed, and reliability of the build and release processes. I am sure you probably have something similar in mind. The devil is in the details, though.

Therefore, I have tried to describe a scenario similar to those I have faced. Elements that needed tackling are combined into one story. From there I have taken the book on a journey to look at solutions to the issues raised in the scenario.

The first three chapters are used to consider the needs and practicalities for the introduction of automated delivery processes. We also get a chance to study NAnt in a little detail so that we understand how it can be utilized in the final processes.

Chapter 1, "A Context for Delivery": Here we set out the initial processes Etomic (our fictitious development company) use for development—specifically build and deploy—and we discuss the successes and failures they have suffered. We will see how Etomic has tackled the issues, and we join them as they are about to move to automation for build and deploy processes. From there we will identify some areas for attention and then plan how to attack these. We will use these requirements as a basis for discussion throughout the book.

Chapter 2, "Dissecting NAnt": With a context in place, we can begin looking at NAnt as a suitable tool to handle build and deploy activities for Etomic. We discuss how NAnt scripts work, describe the core features and fundamental structures of a script, and outline a potential framework for scripts to apply to the applications used by Etomic. We will also touch on some possibilities for more advanced use of NAnt later on.

Chapter 3, "Important NAnt Tasks": Having considered the activities for build and deploy, and proposed a skeleton script for both, we now take a look at the variety of NAnt and NAntContrib tasks that are available for use. We split these tasks into a few categories and consider some practical examples of the application of these tasks.

Once we understand what we have set out to do, and have organized the tools we will use to do it, the next three chapters describe actually implementing the processes. In these chapters we start with a simple example and then move on to more complex and more general scenarios, considering how the practical implementation needs to extend. Here we also utilize CruiseControl.NET to provide continuous integration.

Chapter 4, "A Simple Case Study": Now that we are fully versed in NAnt, in this chapter we take a simple application and implement a build file for it. We flesh out the framework described in Chapter 2 using the tasks described in Chapter 3 to implement the identified steps. At the end of this chapter, we are left with a crude but effective build process with some successes but also some issues to build on.

Chapter 5, "Process Standards": If only it was as easy as the example in Chapter 4! Here we look at another application and we apply the same process to this solution in addition to the deploy script. We then refactor the scripts for the applications we have looked at to provide some common functions in the process that we can harness later on. We look at some of the features a solution should contain, and examine some useful features of the development environment to ensure that we can feasibly maintain an automated process that works across multiple solutions.

Chapter 6, "Continuous Integration": Although we now have a process defined by a script outline and some refactored examples, it all feels a bit loose. This chapter looks at the use of CruiseControl.NET to implement continuous integration. We expand on our earlier discussions of this area and consider the consequences of such an activity.

Having successfully introduced automated delivery processes, the remainder of the book looks at some individual aspects of the tools, some complex parts of the process, and suggestions for enhancements to gain further efficiency and coverage of automated delivery processes.

Chapter 7, "Extending NAnt": This chapter explores a little of the source code for NAnt and describes how you can create your own NAnt tasks. We take a look at some features of current NAnt tasks to get a feel for coding, and then we build a task for use in our own scripts to solve problems we discovered in Chapter 4. We build more in later chapters.

Chapter 8, "Database Integration": This chapter looks at what may be the most complex activity for automation, an area we have until now studiously avoided: the database. We take a look at a potential process to at least partially solve the issues in this area, as well as specific tools to handle the task for us. We then create a NAnt task and consider solution standards we can use in our scripts to facilitate this part of the process. We also take a look at standards for DTS packages.

Chapter 9, "Code Generation": We have now covered a considerable amount of work for handling build and deploy processes, but there are further efficiencies to be made. In a world that is handled via XML, code generation can be very useful indeed. This chapter looks at some candidate areas for automation, and the benefits automation can provide. We then look at code-generation techniques and add them to our process.

Chapter 10, "Closing Thoughts": This chapter takes everything we have worked with so far and recaps this work, considering what we have and have not covered. I then speculate on a wish list for delivery processes in relation to those subjects and themes.

Finally, there are two appendixes, the first one containing additional information on tools and the organization of those tools, and the second one describing a "fun" project with NAnt.

Appendix A, "A Fistful of Tools": This appendix covers the organization and dependencies of the tools used throughout the book to aid the implementation of your own build processes.

Appendix B, "NAnt Sweeper": Just in case you thought NAnt was all about work and no play, an entirely inappropriate but amusing example of its utility may make you think otherwise.

Just Before We Begin

It has been tough to consider all of the options for delivery processes and at times difficult to describe these options adequately and concisely on paper. Nevertheless, writing this book has been a lot of fun and has helped the processes in my own teams significantly.

I hope you find the same utility and fun from this book's exploration of the tools, techniques, and processes for software delivery.

Whether you agree or disagree with my thoughts, I am always happy to hear other views, and you can share these by contacting me through my blog: `http://bitarray.co.uk/marc`.

Happy software delivery-ing!

CHAPTER 1

A Context for Delivery

The introduction of sound delivery processes can be a complex and confusing affair. Occasionally, some parts of the process seem impossible and other times they seem impossibly easy. Just when you think you have cracked an area of difficulty, another issue raises its head. It is a long journey to achieve a smooth and reliable process—and when considered as a whole, it is quite unpalatable. In this book, we will aim to tackle it piece by piece and issue by issue until we are satisfied we have a solution, or a framework, or even an idea of how to provide benefit through delivery processes.

For that reason, I think it is important to have a context for the areas of build and deploy processes we will address throughout the rest of the book. It is important because otherwise these efforts are the kind that may never have an endpoint. There will always be one more tweak, one restructure, one bit of coding wizardry that can be applied to make things just a bit better. In the real world, this is not usually an option; work must reap practical rewards in the short term. This is the usual problem facing development teams today: the need for scaffolding to improve development effort is not encouraged by management teams who need to be making maximum external/customer charges with the available development resource. To compound this, the very people who understand why the scaffolding and processes are a good idea—the developers—are the very people who probably will not make a good job of expressing the idea by way of cost benefits and so on to the management teams. The result can be inertia in the environment and processes to begin with, but ultimately the result can be increased costs for the same work.

To begin with, and to ensure that we are all facing the same direction, we will look at the situation and goals of a fictitious development company in terms of its aims for delivery. Then we will look at a variety of processes and problems for consideration for planning. We will come up with a plan for "delivering on delivery processes" and assess the practical benefits of such a plan. This plan may have an end goal that is utopian in vision too, but at the least it will include milestones and deliverables that can provide focus and measurement to our efforts.

It is this plan that will form the cornerstone for our efforts throughout the rest of the book.

Why Delivery Processes Are Needed

The short answer to this question is obvious: hiring a new person to handle delivery for every x system is too expensive to maintain, and untenable for a development team going forward. Maintaining a knowledgebase on the individual delivery of dozens of individual systems going forward is equally untenable, as is maintaining an individual development and delivery environment for dozens of systems going forward.

The common factor in this answer is "individual." Development is an individual activity: it is creative, it is based on "knowing" the domain you are in, and it is about craftsmanship rather than commodity (in the main). This is not necessarily a bad thing: the creativity, the skills, and the craft of developers provide us with elegant and innovative solutions to problems. In the development area, these things are in fact a boon. To harness and focus individuality in development, we create processes that ensure there is planning and product from the creative aspects of development work so that the customer and team management can understand what is happening with the money. And then—guess what? We do not quite remove the individuality from the delivery of the product to the customer. The innovative solution is developed on time but cannot be moved from the development area to the production area without a lot of effort, or with any confidence. The perception of the product is spoiled at the point it is at its highest profile to the customer—as delivery begins—and so the credibility of the product for the customer is damaged before they have even worked with it. Even when this works relatively well for a specific product, a development team handling multiple systems and subsystems will be quickly caught up in a never-ending set of issues relating to delivery.

Conversely, removing creativity from the delivery of a product results in a set of known parts to the process. It can be specified, costed, measured, and assessed for success upon completion. Doing this requires defining a process for delivery. To define the processes for delivery, we need an understanding of the issues involved. We will spend the rest of the chapter considering these issues and the process itself. Before we do, consider the differences that a sound delivery process could make for you, your team, or your customers, as shown in Table 1-1.

Table 1-1. *Individual Delivery vs. Delivery Process*

Item	Individual Time/Comment	Process Time/Comment
Delivery effort setup cost	Not done/guessed at 2 days?	3 hrs (with a script by script breakdown)
CM activities	Unknown/ad hoc	2 hrs (aligned to standard)
Availability of system to customer	3 days prior to testing	Upon project commencement
System assets	Most under source control	All assets controlled
Time to perform release	Unknown/2 hrs?	257 seconds
Response time for new release	As per queue	257 seconds

The responses shown in the table are a matter of context for your own team, but these represent the responses from teams I have worked with. The message is clear: delivery processes are required if you want a cost-effective, efficient, and professional software development life cycle. With many systems, the need is further accentuated.

The Etomic Situation

Etomic is a small company that can handle full project life cycles for small to medium (up to around 12 months of development effort) web- and Windows-based applications. Primarily, these projects are web based.

It has approximately 50 projects in-house in various stages of completion and with varying degrees of activity. These projects are handled by a team of 6 project managers, 24 analysts and developers, a handful of graphic designers, and a few system/network administrators.

They are a busy team and have many satisfied customers. In particular:

- They receive considerable repeat business from customers.

- Projects have a tendency to be released on time and on schedule.

- Project life cycles tend to be extended longer than originally envisaged through a program of change initiated by customers.

In short, customers tend to get what they want, and as a result, Etomic is a good place to work and has expanded significantly.

Behind the scenes, though, lurk some problems. These problems have been brought on in many cases as a result of business successes. Only five years ago, it was a much smaller, five-person operation operating in a "boutique" style. Projects could be worked in a "handcrafted" style, and indeed they were. There was little concern as to the broader implications of handcrafting and the attention this needed.

On the other hand, if every time an application is produced risk and complexity are added to the overall operation, then a number of things are occurring:

More staff are required to administer the day-to-day activities, because everything begins to take time.

More mistakes are made during routine operations such as development, archiving, bug fixing, building, and releasing.

More pressure is placed on those striving to meet the same levels of customer satisfaction that have been previously achieved.

There is a high risk that, ultimately, something will go wrong with an application that will be difficult to recover from. This could manifest itself in a number of ways:

Estimates are too short and deadlines are missed as change takes a lot longer than originally thought. This could be owing to difficulty in obtaining assets, constructing environments, or maybe just the coding. The result is either an upset customer, or absorption of incurred cost, or quite possibly both. The stress on the team cannot be underestimated either, potentially leading to the loss of team members.

A development server crashes and a backup is not available. Not every asset is stored in source control. The 30 projects that were on that server are in trouble. The result is serious stress for the team, and perhaps multiple instances of estimates being too short and deadlines being missed.

Bob leaves. Oh dear. Bob's application only ran properly on his laptop, but he used to come in on a Sunday to handle live releases. No one is sure what he used to do. The result is more stress, and more estimation and cost problems. Once this sort of malaise is prevalent among the team, it can be hard to overcome.

One day, the team will not be able to account for, or fix, one of these problems. At that point, Etomic may be in some trouble. We cannot account for every problem of this kind with the processes we seek to address and develop with our efforts, but we will be helping to remove the risk from the overall scenario.

Currently, work arrives thick and fast. Projects represent significant commitment to the team. Each handcrafted solution reduces the flexibility of the team, reducing operational capacity as more time is spent in the intervening processes and management of the projects than actually in development.

Of course, as the team has grown, there have been some general gains in terms of process and of course Etomic has been unable to keep functioning as a boutique. But at the same time it has not developed processes to "industrialize" the life cycle.

■**Note** When you are engrossed in these techniques and tools, it is easy to assume that everyone knows something about them. The truth can be very different. I would say that in my experience of recruiting developers, most are unaware of good configuration management and good development processes even if they are quite gifted in terms of general development skills.

As a business, Etomic has a broad aim of improving its capability to deliver. In particular it wants processes that

Cut down on effort and administration at the point of delivery

Reduce overall project risks and improve confidence in delivery

Ensure that mundane, but important, delivery tasks are completed

Introduce standards/frameworks for the development team to adhere to

These are aims with which we can all identify. You may have guessed from the title of the book that we are going to be looking at automation as the key facilitator to these aims. Automation comes with its own baggage, though, and we will quickly see that automation requires more effort than simply coding until a goal is achieved.

Potential Processes

Let us take a look at some activities and processes that may constitute delivery processes in development teams such as Etomic. Actual scenarios will differ for a variety of reasons—there are always business-related hoops that have to be jumped through, the balance of work type may differ, and so on. But I think you will find some common ground in some of these descriptions.

Simple Delivery

This is about as simple as it can get: one developer, one system, one single-minded approach to "getting the system released." It is a poor approach, even though it may in fact contain many of the correct steps needed to ensure a successful delivery. The main problem is the single point of failure: the sole developer. Without standardization, without checking and controls through the use of standards to control the team overall and then tools to control the delivery, we run the risk of being lost in the mind of the developer—the embodiment of the "Bob Leaves!" scenario described earlier.

Note You may scoff and consider yourself to be better than this. My suggestion is to try it; I have, on several pet projects. Despite my focus, I found it very easy to forget about delivery from time to time. If you had picked any point of time for me to hand my project to someone else, I think that there is a good chance they would have had a hard time taking it on. Delivery is in many ways like other "agile" techniques. They work great if you are disciplined and are working to strong principles, but they can fall apart quickly if the reverse is true. This is why pair programming is a crucial aspect of successful agile implementations. In the same way, checkpoints and standards become crucial for delivery.

Figure 1-1 demonstrates the simple activities occurring in the process. Note that the "Run Tests" step encompasses a few potential activities that may occur during delivery.

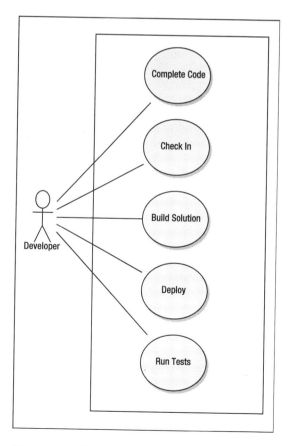

Figure 1-1. *A simple delivery process*

Segregated Delivery

This is a better delivery process than the Lone Ranger approach just described. Although the practices remain similar, we now have a series of checkpoints to move through where various roles can identify issues and thus take remedial action. Everyone would have to be complicit for delivery to be poor. Figure 1-2 demonstrates the separation of activities.

The problem here may be fairly clear from the additional activities and roles involved in the process. That is, it seems quite time consuming.

In practice, it does not have to be. A well-designed, or relatively simple, system may mean that these activities are very straightforward and can be completed quickly. Unfortunately, this may not be the case all of the time. Moreover, we are considering the delivery of 50 systems, not of one or two. Twenty percent of these systems may be in the process of development, and therefore integrated, tested, staged, and deployed at any one time. This puts pressure on the roles involved in this process.

Another issue crops up in this scenario as well. We can see that by giving responsibility to the Operations team to build the software, thus reducing the risk of a developer becoming the point of failure for a system, we have introduced the risk of Operations accessing source control and performing the wrong actions: building and deploying the wrong version, damaging source control, not understanding source control, and so on. Additionally, we may be overloading the Operations team with mundane activities such as documentation production. The risk here is that in an effort to provide a better managed process, we now have people completing tasks inappropriate to their role.

Automated Delivery

To improve upon segregated delivery, we can provide automation to various activities that are required for success but that are actually quite mundane—or at least they should be mundane. Much of the work in this book involves ensuring that the activities we have proposed to automate are indeed mundane prior to automation.

In this process, several activities are the responsibility of the automation agent. These include items such as the actual build and distribution of the system given the correct inputs by the Operations team.

This process removes the risk of developers and operators being the points of failure for delivery of a system, and has also kept the roles of each within expected norms.

The core issue introduced with this process is as you might expect: how do you automate this process and these activities? This is the question we will be answering in the rest of the book. This supposes, therefore, that the question can be answered satisfactorily. If that is the case, then the issue for this kind of delivery is one of standardization and discipline. Automation will only succeed across multiple systems if they are broadly comparable. Specific activities within the process will only succeed if exact standards are followed. Figure 1-3 demonstrates an automated process.

Simply automating a delivery on an individual basis is not such a good principle. This is effectively "Bob Leaves!" except that Bob left behind some scripts. And then Alice leaves and also leaves behind some scripts, and so on.

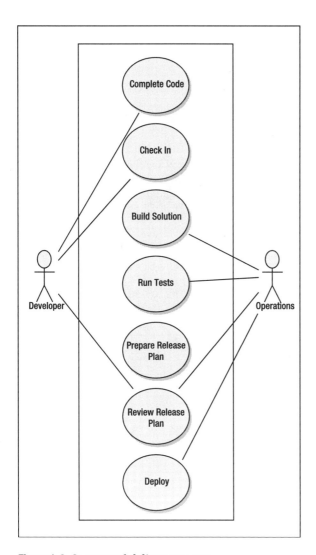

Figure 1-2. *Segregated delivery process*

■**Note** Whether or not you see this as an issue comes down to mind-set. In a busy team responsible for the production of scores of systems, it makes a huge amount of sense. If you have a team or teams producing very different software, it may not seem so viable to have rigorous standards for delivery. We will see what form these standards take in Chapter 5.

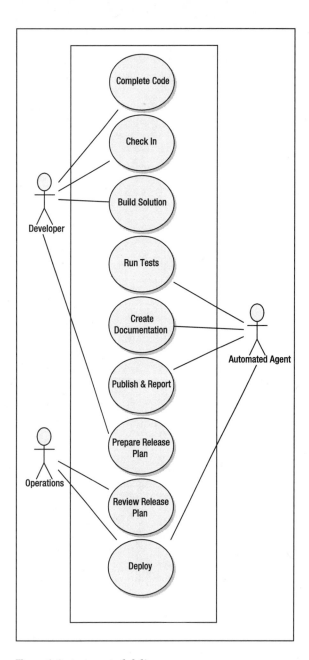

Figure 1-3. *Automated delivery process*

Later, we will also look at continuous integration (CI) as a potential process. As its name suggests, CI provides integration as required. Using CI can provide additional structure to the automatic delivery process because it includes a set of feedback and measures. Perhaps CI can be thought of as a goal for our processes.

CI itself has issues. We will look at these in Chapter 6 when we consider the principles, techniques, and tools in more detail. The primary issue is that it cannot necessarily go far enough to provide a full delivery process. This is simply because you would not want it to: automating production releases is dangerous and could lead to a great deal of trouble, perhaps even in nonproduction environments. It is best to have a human in the way as a final safeguard.

Thus CI is a goal for building and integration only—or so it seems. Perhaps the true point of CI is that you can build and integrate when you want. In that case, we want to be able to do the same thing with deployment, but just not continuously. The purpose of CI is to reduce integration problems through a reproducible build, and therefore this purpose is aligned with reducing deployment problems through a reproducible release.

Thoughts on Delivery

Apart from process problems, a variety of problems from other sources cause headaches for delivery. Once again, on the face of it each problem may not seem very significant, or at least a solution might be obvious. But in a real situation, these problems can be difficult to solve owing to the fluid nature of the business. As we have seen with the Etomic scenario, the situation has developed over time: small-scale decisions have led to situations that are difficult to clarify. We can explore the form these take here. The majority of these issues relate to server-based projects representing the bread and butter of Etomic, although some are applicable to any piece of software.

The Environment

The environment is a core aspect for a successful, standard, automated delivery process. The environment affects the individual coding effort, the testing capabilities, and the manner in which a system is deployed and stored. The core problem with the environment is that the less effort that is put into "doing it well" will directly translate as more coding, scripting, and process effort because of the variety of environmental workarounds that will present themselves. The risk is that this list will become unwieldy and in fact mean that there is no standard way of automating the process. The efforts are then back to square one. It is worth trying to get the environment right.

Standardization

Standardization is going to be crucial for all of the work to provide a satisfactory process and capability for volumes of applications. Although I have placed standardization within environmental concerns, it equally applies to all considerations for our efforts.

Standards within the environment matter to ensure several things:

They ensure that the same mechanisms can be used across many systems to move and deploy assets.

They ensure that the environment remains the same when a system is moved or deployed into a different location.

They provide a mechanism for checking and enforcing that standard practices are being used within the environment: it becomes more obvious when something is amiss.

Providing standardization can be a significant issue, though. If we think about the desktop environment for a moment, we can consider ourselves very lucky. In the magical .NET world, a significant number of developers are able to use the Visual Studio environment to operate within. It is highly likely that teams will standardize on this platform. In doing so, a small amount of standardization is achieved. But even then, there can be many "power toys" or other widgets with which developers may enhance their desktop environment.

This is no bad thing—we are going to enhance our desktop with NAnt very soon—until a developer loses track of upgrades and updates, tools and widgets, and the web of dependencies that can quickly grow. On the other hand, rigidly controlling available environments is likely to provoke a backlash from a development team and genuine concern over the stifling of creativity could grow.

A middle ground that is a useful approach is the use of virtual environments for development activities. In this way, a developer is free to use widgets and tools providing that

The tool is easily deployed to the environment or other developers and plugs into the automated framework.

It does not impact the operating system configuration. This is controlled by the creators of the virtual environment.

They destroy and re-create their desktop every time a new piece of work is begun.

■Note I have used virtual environments in a team situation. It provides an immediate boon to environmental standards for a team and allows the implementation of various policies and practices—standard network shares and the like—that are usually difficult to enforce to be implemented quite easily.

The use of a standard desktop environment allows the team to become comfortable moving from system to system, and even reviewing another developer's screen. The psychological impact of this kind of organization must not be underestimated either: if it feels more professional, then things might just turn out to be more professional. Practically all developers have a standard set of core tools they are familiar with that can and should be used for a variety of development tasks.

Moving on to the server environment, it should be obvious why standardization matters. Clearly, the progression of a system through the various testing and staging environments relies on server configurations that are the same. In addition to the technology platform, though, other aspects of servers should be the same. For example:

There should be a standard method for accessing a server.

The layout and nomenclature of server storage should be the same.

Where automation is used to move assets and deploy systems, it is important to be able to derive locations and apply logic in the creation of new storage in a simple way. To be effective, this requires a good deal of standardization, which may not be easy to achieve in an environment that has evolved over time.

We will be exploring some specific environmental solutions as we work with NAnt throughout the rest of the book.

Simulation

Apart from the standardization of the environment, some thought needs to be given to the simulation of the production environment within the development and other progression environments.

Issues here are likely to be less significant than wholesale environmental differences, but they can still cause problems. In these days of remoting and web services, it can be a chore to ensure the production environment is fully simulated thanks to the number of boxes, hosts, connections, and compromises that need to be made to achieve the simulation.

The knock-on effect for delivery is an increased risk of failure (as usual) of an individual delivery, and also the branching of the delivery plan: in development do this, in test do that, in staging do something else, and so on. This is a problem for a delivery, because it means that the production delivery is never truly tested.

There are likely always going to be compromises in this area since it can be very hard to truly simulate environments. When considering where to comprise, from a delivery perspective, ensure that the delivery mechanism does not branch.

Rigidity

If the team does not have complete confidence that it can build a system from scratch rather than restoring from a backup (or similar approach), then the result can be a rigid environment incapable of change.

For example, if the database scripts are not up-to-date in the source control repository, or there is no confidence that they are up-to-date, then it is likely that the development database will be left active on a SQL Server. Something similar can occur with other environments too.

After a while it can become unclear which is the "real" database. They may all differ, very slightly. Certainly the loaded reference and test data will be out of sync. The environment then becomes rigid.

Management

Management of the environment can be a concern. Even a bright new shiny environment built entirely to standards to facilitate automated delivery can become a mess very quickly if care is not taken to look after it.

Management of the environment must begin with the denizens of the environment: the developers. Developers need to understand that they are trashing their own house, not someone else's house.

■**Tip** "Clean As You Go" was a mantra I used to hear constantly in my time working in kitchens as a student. There is a lot of strength in this simple principle. Busy kitchens cannot operate if there is mess. Apart from the hygiene issues, there is a lack of equipment and space, and usually an abundance of hungry mouths to feed. I will leave it to you to create your own analogy. My point here is that these simple disciplines can reap significant dividends.

Beyond individual management, controls and processes must be in place to ensure that the environment at large is managed. The processes should cover the following:

Cleaning/archiving the environment. Periodically, the environment should be cleaned up. By this I mean the environment-at-large: the areas used for development, as repositories, and for testing, management of documentation, and delivery of the finished systems are all susceptible to the build-up of waste produced from development. Ideally, this can be automated.

Upgrading components. Ensure that the approved third-party controls and components are available in the correct locations and are up-to-date.

System placement. Decisions on the location of systems in the available development environment should not be arbitrary, but locations should be selected and approved intelligently.

■**Caution**   The first time that during a cleanup of the environment someone says, "Do not delete that, just in case," then the environment is in trouble. Do not ignore this. Act upon it.

Configuration Management

Poor configuration management (CM) can hamper delivery efforts. A lack of quality CM can lead to many of the other problems listed in this chapter. Even with the best of intentions, failing to have a strong CM policy will lead to issues. CM is not easy and there are many books and schools of thought on what CM actually is. It is the sort of subject that people think they understand but generally do not. CM is probably a much more significant subject than, say, the use of a source control database—which may be where most developers' knowledge of CM begins to get a little hazy. Borrowing and paraphrasing from Alexis Leon's book (see Further Reading at the end of this chapter), a definition of CM is as follows:

> *Configuration management is a set of processes to minimize the confusion of a team project. CM is about identification, organization and control of software to maximize productivity by minimizing mistakes.*

As you might see already, an individual's understanding of CM may only extend as far as "control," and even then this may not be a full understanding of control. Broadly then, CM in terms of an activity or process should encompass the following areas:

Configuration identification. Identification is about considering what constitutes a "configuration item." An obvious example is a piece of source code, but what about test data—is this a configuration item? What about the technical specification for a software system? Identification is about considering the criteria for identification, listing and naming the identified configuration items, and then choosing a method for acquiring the configuration items.

Configuration control. Control concerns the processes supporting the need to change a system. Configuration control addresses such questions as: How is change initiated? How is the impact of change evaluated? How is it approved and who approves it? How is change then implemented?

Configuration status control. Status control involves making information available on the status of CM, what this information should be, when it should be available, and to whom it should be available. This also covers information such as release control.

Configuration auditing. Finally, auditing is about ensuring the success of the other areas of CM by evaluating each area to ensure compliance and then performing follow-up activities to ensure compliance in retrospect and/or adjust CM policies.

So there is a bit more to configuration management than using a source control database! Rest assured, configuration management is not easy to do. It requires specialist skills and a lot of effort to comply with the more significant standards—possibly more effort than time allows on fast-moving and cost-conscious development teams, though if a team does not care about its assets, then why should it care about cost could be a reasonable counterargument. By nature, development teams are more concerned about practical activities and so may be uncomfortable with some of the theoretical CM activities themselves. If we play to the strengths of the people we have and translate this into what we need to consider specifically for the delivery process, the areas that we should consider as a priority are as follows.

Assets and Source Control

It is easy for a lack of control of all crucial information and assets to exist. The important word here is *all*. Generally speaking, a development team can be relied on to store core coding assets in the source control database (Visual SourceSafe [VSS] in our case), but that approach can be attributed to the links to Visual Studio as much as it can to the developers' own sense of good CM. VSS can easily become nothing more than a dump for source code.

■ Note It can be easily argued that a system such as VSS does not provide CM in the way that a system such as CVS, or Subversion, or Borland StarTeam does. In many ways, VSS is just a dump for source code. It has some of the features that you would expect from a proper CM system such as branching and merging but nothing like the feature set of some of its cousins. On the other hand, VSS is simple for developers to use. What is possibly worse than poor CM is CM handled incorrectly!

Assets not linked to VSS by a tool such as database scripts can quickly become out-of-date, or fail to make it into VSS. Unfortunately, if one set of key assets is missing, then it does not matter whether or not the others are stored well. It can be a lot riskier for an asset to be present in an out-of-date state than not at all. The upshot, though, is a total lack of confidence in the assets for a system.

Additionally, it can be easy for a team to fail to understand what an asset is and why, or how they should be storing it. As we mentioned earlier, while we may assume that everyone sees the value in these processes, that may not be the case. Guidance needs to be offered to demonstrate a good process in this area. A description of how to organize these assets in a physical sense within the source control environment is also a boon. This enables rapid inspection of assets for a system to ensure general compliance. It also facilitates the introduction of new developers to new systems; they come to expect certain features in much the same way as coding to a standard architecture facilitates the same process.

It is natural that if you cannot be sure that assets will be available, or that the assets available are the correct ones, and if you cannot be sure what represents an asset for the system, then of course you are not likely to trust any kind of process or even the physical assets laid out before you. The danger is that developers then concoct their own ways of handling this uncertainty to cover their own backs. This may work temporarily for a piece of work on a system, but it will not translate across multiple systems, developers, or tasks. The rot has already set in.

Management

Related to the general problems of managing system assets is the management of the overall CM process. If this is a shared responsibility, then it will quickly degrade in much the same way as directories become generally untidy: developers have that hoarding mentality.

Nominating certain team members as responsible for and enforcers of the standards ensures that evaluation and monitoring of the process occurs.

Monitoring and management of source control can be automated if you have the time to invest in, for example, wrapping the Visual SourceSafe API. Some useful management activities for source control include the following:

Access. A single-point method for enabling/disabling access to VSS databases should be in place for developers.

Reporting. Useful reports include checkout reports, maintenance reports, and activity reports.

Backups. Automating backups and archiving of VSS can be valuable for business continuity.

Cleaning. It is useful to be notified of folders that do not comply to a set standard, e.g., someone dumping a database backup in the VSS folder for "safekeeping."

There may be no need to reinvent the wheel here. Many productivity enhancers for VSS, as well as for other source control systems, are available if you look around.

Planning

This type of problem represents the softer side of delivery processes. I have seen many situations where inadequate planning for delivery has led to shortcuts and botched jobs during the implementation of a system. Inevitably this leads to more frequent failures because of the increased risk. The problem of failure at this point is compounded by the fact that the delivery stage is the most visible aspect of development for the customer. The customer's perception of project success can be badly affected by a failure to implement.

Note There is no shame in regression! If a delivery fails, then it can be allowed to fail providing lessons are learned about the reason for failure. I would much rather see a successful regression with minimal loss to the business than a botched delivery.

Consideration

The first problem with planning for delivery is that the delivery mechanism and effort is not properly taken into account at the outset of a system design. There can be considerable focus on the system itself for obvious reasons, and the supporting activities can fall by the wayside quite easily. This is as true of a one-person effort as it is of a team effort.

Where it is easy for a lone developer to lose focus, or become passionately focused on a particular issue and thus lose the impetus to consider delivery, it is true of a team as well. The problem of delivery is in the hands of the delivery team and thus the same impetus does not exist in the planning phase to label it as "someone else's problem."

Through the production of a clear framework, or guidelines, or standards, consideration of delivery is pushed onto the agenda at an early stage. Deliverables are required as part of the system build and they can be estimated in terms of time and cost. A much greater chance exists that delivery requirements will have an impact on the overall system design.

Implementation

Apart from the consideration of delivery, the actual implementation must also be completed. In this instance, a developer may be focused on the delivery, and may have thought it out it appropriately and then, at the last minute—perhaps as the pressure is on to achieve completion—does not actually implement the agreed delivery process.

The .NET platform has eased delivery significantly in various ways and therefore it is usually possible to botch together a release or the like given a little bit of time. If this is not then addressed at a later date, this botch likely becomes more "Technical Debt" (see Further Reading).

This kind of debt is the least likely to be addressed at a later stage, since it is very unlikely the customer will seek to address internal issues of which they are not aware. Therefore, this debt hangs around causing problems for the development team for, perhaps, the rest of the project life cycle.

The problems stemming from implementation details, or a lack thereof, directly create the problems of fear and rigidity.

Fear

Fear is a natural reaction to anything that is unknown. In the world of development, this may be a simple sentiment if a developer cannot figure out how to set up a new development environment for a system on his/her laptop.

Fear manifests itself physically in a number of ways. Fear of an aspect of a system in code terms usually results in development going awry: the developer will code around the feared aspect. This can potentially damage the architecture of an application, or just the code quality. From the point of view of delivery, fear leads to rigidity.

A Solution for Delivery

Delivery is one of those activities with the potential to work very well but that is never easy to address adequately. The result is that delivery will tend to be "brute-forced": in other words, delivery is attempted until something works. Earlier we looked at potential manual processes for delivery. As these become more sophisticated, they create more administrative overhead. The risks are then that there simply is not enough management capacity to enforce and ensure the process, and also that there is not enough understanding among the development team to maintain the process, or to understand the process in the first place.

Much is made of standardization of various aspects of delivery and CM. In later chapters we will see how these approaches are practically applied as we begin to automate delivery. For now, let us consider a general solution: automation.

Automation

The most obvious step-change in delivery process is that of automation.

This is of course a major task for the remainder of the book. Being able to build and rebuild at will means that we can clean and trim the physical environments to only the parts necessary on a day-to-day and month-to-month basis. The effects are the reduction of administration overhead of the environment, the decoupling of a specific physical environment from the system assets, improved chances of the architecture and code quality standing the test of time, and reduced stress on the development team.

Removing the ability of a developer to take part in a system release means that there can be no more last-minute heroic efforts to ensure success. When we are working with a customer deadline, this kind of effort is frequently needed to ensure that the customer perception of product success is positive, but in doing this the team is simply hiding the truth of the situation. The real problem is that this truth is hidden internally as well. By making it more awkward to perform last-minute heroics, we encourage a gradual cultural change to being prepared and consistently successful throughout development.

Note It is easy to reward heroic effort. It is harder to view it as a failure, for that is what it is in the context of confidently delivering multiple systems smoothly. Essentially, I think that this is because there is a very human element to heroic effort: how can you criticize Bob when he pulled a 48-hour shift to ensure the customer deadline was met after the third party widget went belly-up on the production server?

This question has no easy answer. A dissociation needs to exist between the human effort that deserves reward and the circumstances that have led to the troublesome delivery.

The effort involved in automation should not be underestimated. One of the main problems is that simple automation does not require a huge effort and can easily be achieved on a single project; however, this automation does not provide significantly visible results.

■Caution Actually, there is a lot of bravado in that statement. "Simple" problems can quickly escalate and frustrate.

If the results are not significant, then enthusiasm from others to solve the problems and invest the time in cracking the problem can be limited. Unfortunately, as the more significant action items to achieve automation begin to appear you will rely on others to assist or mandate the required actions.

For this reason, we are going to describe our automation efforts under an umbrella initiative. We will describe the initiative in pattern-like terms to achieve a common vocabulary and common understanding of the automation efforts. With this as a basis, everyone affected will at least have heard of the initiative and everyone has the opportunity to understand the mechanics and consequences.

Design to Deliver

My description of the automation effort is "Design to Deliver." It is catchy (perhaps) and also defines the underlying theme of standardization and consideration that form some of the core pillars of success for the automation effort.

We are defining a process pattern to mitigate the risks and address the problems highlighted in our earlier discussions. The pattern does not describe the nitty-gritty mechanics of achieving "better quality of delivery" at this point; in the general manner of patterns, the implementation may vary depending on the circumstances. However, we now have a common vocabulary for the work we are attempting, and a focus for what represents success in this work.

Context

Improving the delivery of a software system by ensuring successful build and deployment features is a focus from the beginning of the coding phase, as is automating these features throughout the system life cycle.

Motivation

For any successful development team involved in medium-sized projects of several months' development, the number of systems to manage will eventually become cumbersome.

Failing to address delivery as a specific, controlled activity leads to a degradation in the delivery processes (whatever form they take) and also increases the risk of failure for a system at a crucial point in its implementation.

Through the implementation of a framework for delivery and the automation of that framework, enabling a confident repeatable delivery process has the potential to

- Improve software quality through increased value to supporting activities such as unit testing

- Improve customer satisfaction through increased levels of delivery success

- Reduce overhead in administration of delivery

Mechanics

The broad mechanics for the implementation of Design to Deliver include the following:

Decide on the desired delivery process for build and deployment. Many things can be covered as part of an automated delivery solution. Listing the initial priorities provides focus for the first attempt. At this point, the automation does not necessarily have to produce a richly developed process. Aiming too high initially does not aid the exploration activities.

Identify the tools to achieve the processes. There are a variety of possibilities for the automation itself and also the technologies used to complete aspects of the automated process. Providing a list of initial tools ensures that, in a world of limitless possibility, a constrained approach is followed to ensure the continued focus and simplicity of the delivery process.

Identify an initial candidate for automation. An ideal candidate is a system that is stand-alone and that does not have too many areas of complexity, such as a database. A good candidate could be a console utility or a shared assembly.

Prototype the process with the candidate. The candidate should then be automated following the steps defined in the initial process. At this point, as more required steps are found, they can be added to the overall process or held over for verification.

Identify more candidates for automation. Following a successful implementation, more candidates can be identified for inclusion in the process. Once more, it is useful to group similar systems to better achieve automation.

Utilize and refactor the initial automation to provide standard scripts. The new candidates should reuse the scripts from the first prototype, but the emphasis should be on refactoring, the reduction of duplicated effort, and the identification of complexity where each project has specific needs not present in the others. Refactoring should also occur in the systems themselves to provide a standard environment and system structure to facilitate the automation; that is, not only should the scripts adapt to the system but also the system should fall into line with requirements.

Publish standards for the up-front implementation of automation. Scripted solutions for problems should be maintained in a library of solutions. Where systems have been amended to facilitate the automation, these amendments and standard requirements should be published and enforced in the development team at large.

All systems need to be brought into line with delivery standards. Now outside of the realm of research and development, the published standards should be introduced as part of all new systems, and at the opportunities that maintenance cycles afford. It is critical to release responsibility for implementation of standards to the development team at a finely balanced point in time as it will then slow down progress on automation as a result of the time taken to implement any new refactorings and standards across multiple systems. At this point, an assessment is needed to determine whether there is scope for a full-time role or roles to handle the ongoing maintenance of this and other CM activities. In my opinion, this role will be needed.

New systems should adhere to delivery standards. All new developments must adhere to set delivery processes. Development teams should begin viewing the constructs for delivery as something that must be treated as a project in itself, to be maintained and developed accordingly.

Consequences

Design to Deliver has several consequences:

(+) **Speed of delivery is improved.** Naturally, if the task is automated it is highly likely to be a lot faster. Significantly, the measurement of time taken could represent a useful metric for success of the initiative: delivery measured in terms of seconds and minutes rather than vaguer notions of hours.

(+) **Confidence in delivery is improved.** The ability to repeat delivery constantly and on demand is a significant boon to the development and operations teams. New doors are opened in terms of team capability, such as daily system releases to customers or project teams.

(+) **Scope of manual delivery activities is reduced.** This is another obvious consequence of automating the process. Importantly, it becomes more likely that some of the supporting processes that do not form a critical path but that are still important, such as the distribution of documentation, notification of support teams, and so on, are guaranteed to occur. The process cannot degrade, and occurs in the same way every time.

(+) **Mundane tasks are automated.** Similarly, these kinds of tasks may be considered mundane in the first place, and thus the effort required in this area is not valued. Here it is removed.

(+) **Quality of the software improves**. A system must conform to the process, forcing the developer to consider and implement delivery features up front, forcing delivery higher up the quality agenda.

(+) **Understanding of delivery improves.** Because there is a framework and stated benefits to the automation of delivery, the reasons for considering and implementing successful delivery on a conceptual basis are clearer to the development team. On a practical basis, the actual implementation requirements for a system are detailed.

(+/−) **Options are limited.** It may not be appropriate to use a solution that would ordinarily be appropriate because of difficulty in implementing the standard process. For example, a useful third-party component may not be easy to deploy and thus hamper automation efforts. We need to decide what is a more important system feature: a useful UI widget or successful delivery. On the other hand, limiting these options may be a good idea with more "innovative" developers in order to maintain a little control over some of the crazier ideas.

(−)**100% success is not guaranteed.** Despite every effort, it is doubtful that all systems and system features can be fully automated for delivery. Therefore, Design to Deliver does not represent a panacea for delivery, but a roadmap for improvements to the delivery process with some significant successes expected along the way.

Resulting Context

We are able to confidently deliver software using a standard process. The length of time, and planning required, for delivery is known and can be predicted. There is no need for rigid development environments to host our software because we are able to quickly build and deploy a required solution. The complexity and risk of delivery is reduced.

The advantages to the implementation of Design to Deliver are as follows:

Developers. The developers have a clear strategy for the delivery of products and a set of defined standards to work within. They understand what is expected of them and how the process operates. They can consider the delivery of a product—how and when it will be done—at the outset of the project rather than toward the point of delivery, a risky activity. Product delivery can, and does, occur at any point in the project, which is a boon to project managers as well. They are freed up to handle true development, which is what they want to do rather than handle mundane tasks. Removing reluctant developers from mundane tasks improves morale and probably improves the quality of the mundane task in itself.

Management. To management, the delivery processes are transparent. Risk is reduced since all systems follow the same overall processes. Standards, and therefore monitoring, are available for the management team. The delivery process encompasses part of an overall configuration management strategy for IT and can work within the confines of an existing process quite easily; it is a practical solution without its own paperwork overhead. Cost benefits can be described to senior management in simple terms since development effort for delivery can be calculated beyond just headcount: ordinarily a team can only speculate effort required to deliver a product and this usually becomes a simple headcount issue ("We need another Ops member because we have more systems"). With automated processes, the effort to align a system to the process can be fully estimated, and the delivery measured. The net effect should be a leveling of headcount required for these processes. The bonus is the additional quality and reduced risk in the same activities *but for fewer people*. Customer response (see the next item) is improved.

Customers. The customer can see the product sooner and almost upon demand since the delivery can occur upon demand. The risk of system problems is reduced during user acceptance testing because defects arising from deployment are less likely and thus scheduled testing time is more likely to be unaffected by such things (development teams sometimes forget that testing software disrupts the business as much as customers not turning up to testing disrupts the development). The support cycle should be reduced; it becomes easier for small support teams to deliver small changes once complete. If deployment is tricky, support teams would tend to "roll up" several bugs into scheduled releases. If deployment is easy, then change can be effected quickly with confidence. This virtuous circle then increases time available for actual development and/or support from the team. Finally, incurred costs from delivery are now transparent; they can be accurately specified and estimated at the project outset. They will also be cheaper as ongoing delivery costs are met through the automated system.

A Delivery Process for Etomic

After all of this discussion, our path is clear. We have considered the problems faced by a team like Etomic. We have defined a set of mechanics and consequences for our automation efforts. The first step on the road to success is the identification of the build and deployment processes to address the stated aims of Etomic and the Design to Deliver initiative.

The Build Process

The first aspect of our delivery process is the build process. In the simplest terms possible, this process must result in the creation of a compiled solution. However, a number of other functions can be performed as part of this compilation.

Help is at hand from Martin Fowler's article on continuous integration (CI). In this article, Fowler describes the principles of CI and the activities that would need to take place as part of CI. We will cover CI and its impact in Chapter 6; the important thing to understand at this point is the activities described in CI, which are broadly as follows:

Check out. This involves physically getting the source code from the source control database to ensure that we can carry out the rest of the process. In fact, we probably will not check out the source code, but will "get" the latest version of it.

Build. This encompasses the compilation steps necessary to build the system successfully. This could consist of several complex and interdependent steps, but in many cases it may be a straightforward compilation of the kind achieved through the Visual Studio environment.

Test. Automated testing is a cornerstone of agile methods and CI is of course no exception. Just because you can physically compile a solution does not mean it is a success. The testing step allows the process to report a success or failure on the basis of the application of unit tests subsequent to compilation.

Publish. The automated publishing of the results and assets is a useful feature of the automated process.

We can round out these with a few additional steps that will be useful to us:

Clean. This is alluded to in most commentary on automated delivery. Here we are specific about ensuring a cleanup of the used environment for delivery to ensure that no problems occur as a result of using incorrect assets and so on.

Version. Providing some automated versioning is a boon when increasing the number of deliveries significantly; it is a consequence of the process we are subscribing to. We will note this as a requirement immediately, since it will undoubtedly cause some consternation.

Document. Apart from testing, we can leverage the process to carry out other useful tasks such as reporting and documentation. This can be another discrete step.

Notify. This could be implied by the Publish step, but we will again define these steps discretely. Notification can let the team know of successes and failures, and perhaps distribute logs and reports.

Bearing in mind all of the steps discussed, the final list and order of activities could therefore be defined as follows:

Clean. We may also repeat this step at the end of the process if required.

Get. Grab the source code.

Version. Apply some versioning to the source code files.

Build. Compile the application.

Test. Apply the unit tests.

Document. Generate documentation and reports.

Publish. Place the compiled assets, reports, etc., in an agreed location.

Notify. Tell everyone of the success (or failure).

The Deployment Process

Deployment is the second stage of our delivery. This is a little trickier since it will differ depending on the kind of system to be delivered. For instance, it is quite trivial to deploy a single .NET component to a network share, though it may be slightly less trivial to ensure that this deployment operates within the constraints of the team development process. On the other hand, deploying a web application with a database, third-party components, and other dependencies is altogether more complicated. Furthermore, deployment will usually occur to a number of different environments.

However, we can establish what kind of application we will be delivering. Broadly, Etomic concentrates on web applications and so we will concentrate on deploying this kind of server-based application.

A possible deployment process may be as follows:

Select version. Inform the rest of the process which version of a system is to be deployed. Our versioning strategy from the build process may be important.

Get assets. Obtain and prepare the required assets from the agreed location. Therefore, how we organize these assets in the Publish step is important.

Select environments. In a similar decision-making step to selecting the version, consider which environment is required for the deployment. This may require various tweaks to the deployed assets.

Create environments. With the knowledge of the prior steps, environments such as databases and web sites can be created.

Position assets. The assets can then be positioned as required within the generated environments. Files can be copied, database scripts run, components registered, and so on.

Apply configuration. Configuration changes can then be applied to ensure that the environments communicate and operate successfully.

Notify. Notify everyone of success or failure.

This process will be complicated by the addition of decision-making steps regarding the differing environments and whether existing assets should be overwritten or backed up, or whether the process should fail if an environment already exists. For now, though, this is a general representation of a deployment.

A Glossary for Delivery

We have described various terms in this first chapter. Captured in Table 1-2 are some of these terms and their definitions.

Table 1-2. *A Glossary for Delivery*

Term	Definition
Build process	This is the process used to compile, analyze, and package a system ready for deployment.
Deploy process	This refers to the process used to position, and configure for use, a system on a specified delivery environment.
Environment	In the context of delivery, an environment is an area for delivery of a product, for example, a system-testing environment, a user-testing environment, or a production/live environment.
Delivery process	This overall process encompasses the build and deploy processes.
Automated *x* process	This refers to using a tool or set of tools to perform the specified process.
Continuous integration	This is a specific branch of delivery made popular through agile/extreme programming and methodologies. CI is the notion that a built system should be available at any time a change occurs to the system. In other words, the build process is performed continuously against some trigger, usually a change to the source code.
Configuration management	This term encompasses processes that minimize the confusion of a team project. CM is about identification, organization, and control of software to maximize productivity by minimizing mistakes.
Source control	This is the control aspect of CM. Source control is about managing the software assets. Usually source control in this context means a source control system such as VSS, Subversion, or CVS.
Design to Deliver	This is the initiative described in this chapter, which provides reasoning and mechanics for the introduction of delivery processes to a team.

Summary

As we end this chapter, we have taken important steps toward improvement of delivery processes. We have looked at the inside of our fictitious development company, Etomic, and we have seen some of the issues they have faced and are facing. We have reviewed a list of aims Etomic has for delivery processes, and discussed the surrounding context for delivery, looking at the problems posed and hinting at potential solutions or methods for the mitigation of risk.

We have also proposed an initiative known as Design to Deliver, which we will use as the basis for delivering improved delivery processes.

Finally, we have taken the first step in this initiative by defining a very broad build and deployment process and have briefly discussed automating these processes.

In the next chapter, we are going to start practical work on the Design to Deliver initiative with a look at NAnt—the tool we will use for build automation. This tool offers a lot of power, and so we will spend some time thinking about how it works but, just as importantly, what we can do with it.

Further Reading

There are a host of worthwhile resources related to a variety of topics touched on in this chapter.

When I am stuck for an argument as to why an initiative is a good idea, it is a good bet that it is covered in *Code Complete: A Practical Handbook of Software Construction* by Steve McConnell (Microsoft Press, 1993).

For excellent commentary and a succinct read on breeding a successful developer, I recommend *Coder to Developer: Tools and Strategies for Delivering Your Software* by Mike Gunderloy (Sybex, 2004). This book also covers a host of tools and topics that I've put to practical use myself, such as virtual environments.

There are quite a lot of places to read about continuous integration. I of course recommend the original article by Martin Fowler at `http://martinfowler.com/articles/continuousintegration.html`.

The following book describes the role of continuous integration in an enlightened software process: *Domain-Driven Design: Tackling Complexity in the Heart of Software* by Eric Evans (Addison-Wesley, 2003).

For a discussion on Technical Debt, refer to *Beyond Software Architecture: Creating and Sustaining Winning Solutions* by Luke Hohmann (Addison-Wesley, 2003).

My handbook for any configuration management concern I have is *A Guide to Software Configuration Management* by Alexis Leon (Artech House, 2000).

Finally, I find a lot of use in *Essential SourceSafe* by Ted Roche (Hentzenwerke Publishing, 2001).

CHAPTER 2

■ ■ ■

Dissecting NAnt

We have defined an outline for our process as described in the Design to Deliver initiative. The next stated mechanic is that of selecting tools to assist with the automation of the process.

In this chapter, we will take a look at NAnt. You will see what it is, what it can do, and how it works. We will examine the key concepts of NAnt and prepare a plan for using NAnt to facilitate automated processes.

We will consider why NAnt is chosen for a particular task, but you should be aware that other options are available. Unfortunately this book will not be able to help you with implementation specifics for other platforms; since we will be focusing on NAnt, I will not spend too long discussing the various platform merits.

The core purpose of this chapter is to gain an insight into how you use this tool to automate our process. NAnt is deceptively simple but has a significant amount of flexibility and options for use. With this flexibility comes decision making and responsibility for choices made that may be difficult to undo at a later point in time. It is therefore important that you understand the tool quite well before imposing standards on development teams.

At the end of the chapter we will turn the processes we described in the previous chapter into skeleton "build files" for NAnt. You will find that even without any discussion of the actual tasks that NAnt can perform—of which there are many—we will have achieved quite a lot, and your mind may well be bursting with ideas, particularly if you have not explored NAnt previously.

All About NAnt

NAnt is a .NET port of the Java build tool Ant, though it has quite a different set of characteristics in parts. It is currently being actively developed, but it has been a useful and relatively stable platform for a significant amount of time.

NAnt allows a process to be defined as an XML file, or as a series of XML files consisting of sections and specific tasks to be carried out. I use the word "process" rather than "build process" because while NAnt's raison d'etre is to assist building and many of the tasks are specifically designed for this purpose, it can be used for many things.

NAnt is an open source project, with a homepage at http://nant.sourceforge.net. There are links to many resources from this page. In particular there is a useful wiki containing help and tips on the use of NAnt and the specific tasks it enables. Additionally, you can sign up or search the archives of the NAnt user and NAnt developer mailing lists.

Additionally, there is an adjunct to NAnt called NAntContrib. It has a homepage at http://nantcontrib.sourceforge.net. This project is for task contributions to NAnt that do not make it into the core NAnt release. Occasionally, tasks in NAntContrib will make the switch to NAnt.

Both of these projects are required for our work. If you take a look at Appendix A, "A Fistful of Tools," you will find more instructions on obtaining NAnt.

■**Note** For the remainder of the text, unless there is a reason to be specific, NAnt should be assumed to mean either NAnt, NAntContrib, or both.

What Does NAnt Do?

In short, NAnt parses XML build files and executes the instructions gained from the file. Generally, a build file will consist of a set of instructions for the build of a .NET solution. Effectively, this is a replacement for the VS .NET builder.

This, however, does not come close to describing the power and flexibility of NAnt. Apart from building a solution, it may also run unit tests, zip up the output, transform XML with Extensible Stylesheet Language Transformations (XSLT), access source control, send an email, and a myriad of other possibilities.

Why Choose NAnt?

To me, NAnt is the tool of choice for the automation of build processes for a few reasons:

First, it can handle things (as described above) that VS .NET simply either cannot handle or cannot handle especially well: activities that support the build process rather than just provide the compilation facilities. A user of VS .NET can make use of postbuild tasks (available in the configuration of a project) to perform some operations like those that NAnt would take care of, but in itself this would not constitute a stand-alone build process—it would be more about a specific project compilation process.

Second, it focuses on handling activities that *should* be automated—those activities that cause constant niggles in your team: accessing source control, storing deliverables, applying version numbers.

Third, the build files are defined as XML, which opens a whole world of flexibility in terms of transforms and process management. Other tools may have more flexibility in terms of scripting languages, but XML is the ideal way to design a flexible process because of these possibilities. Picking up XML directives may also be easier than using proprietary scripting languages or user interfaces (UIs).

Fourth, it is so easily extensible and is a fine piece of source code. If you wish you could write great code, then dig around in the NAnt source code to pick up some tips.

Finally, it is free! The price is most definitely right.

But what can NAnt actually do for you? Quite a bit, as it happens.

You can wrap up an entire process in a NAnt build file. It is possible to refactor a build file to handle multiple solutions, and the benefits for your team could be

Producing a repeatable and documented build process

Ensuring new solutions conform to required standards (organizational conventions, unit testing, etc.)

Increasing confidence and reducing risk in solution deployment

Reducing the amount of effort required for these processes

This sounds very similar to the motivations and consequences of the Design to Deliver initiative. NAnt is a great match for the things we are trying to achieve.

Additionally, the flexibility of NAnt enables you to define the process itself in such a way that

The overall process is broken down into steps that can be selected and applied appropriately per project.

It can be branched conditionally depending on inputs and selections.

Finally, NAnt can be programmatically extended as needed to complete specific tasks that are not included as part of the core NAnt tasks. It is actually quite hard to find specific tasks that are required given the range of "out-of-the-box" features. We will look at this capability in Chapter 6.

Maybe you have gathered that I am quite a fan. But I think that we have extolled the virtues of the product enough and should take a look at the NAnt executable and a build file.

NAnt Nomenclature

Just before we dive in, let us clarify some of the terminology that we will use when discussing NAnt:

NAnt: The physical executable (and the associated tasks) that form the application.

NAnt script/build script/build file: An XML file describing a project comprised of one or more targets and zero or more properties.

Project: The root node of a build script. Each script has one project.

Target: A subdivision of a project. A target is a discrete piece of work that can consist of zero or more tasks. Targets can be dependent on each other.

Task: A task is a defined activity that NAnt will execute; for example, creating a directory or zipping a file. There are many built-in tasks to NAnt, and we will look at the most valuable of these in Chapter 3.

Property: An XML key/value pair that can be used to configure tasks and targets in a more dynamic fashion. Property values can be overridden from the command line.

We will define these terms in much more detail next.

Basic Anatomy of a Build File

NAnt is not much use on its own. It requires an input "build file." By convention, these files tend to be called <name>.build, but in fact the files are just XML files and can be called anything at all.

A "Hello World" Example

Consider the following very simple NAnt script:

```
<?xml version="1.0" encoding="utf-8" ?>
<project name="HelloWorld" default="go">
    <property name="message" value="Hello World!"/>
    <target name="go">
        <echo message="${message}"/>
    </target>
</project>
```

Even without knowing precisely how NAnt works, you can tell what the script intends to do: print "Hello World!" to the console.

Save this script as HelloWorld.build and then do one of two things. Either navigate to the directory in which the file is saved and type

```
nant
```

or use an explicit path to the file at the command prompt such as

```
nant -f:D:\BookCode\Chapter2\HelloWorld.build
```

If the PATH environment variable has been set correctly, then you will see something like the following output:

```
---------- NAnt ----------
NAnt 0.85
Copyright (C) 2001-2003 Gerry Shaw
http://nant.sourceforge.net

Buildfile: file:///HelloWorld.build
Target(s) specified: go

go:
    [echo] Hello World!

BUILD SUCCEEDED
Total time: 0 seconds.
Output completed (0 sec consumed) - Normal Termination
```

Our first, clearly very trivial, NAnt build file is complete. We will be looking at some much more useful and realistic examples soon where we will also see many more complicated actions.

In the meantime, we need to consider what makes up the build script shown here, the available structures of any NAnt script, and the NAnt executable options themselves.

The NAnt Executable

As we have seen, once you have installed NAnt and added the \bin directory to your PATH environment variable, you are able to play with it from the command line via

```
nant
```

Running this command will invoke the NAnt executable. With no arguments, NAnt has the following default behavior:

Invoke a file called *.build in the current working directory.

Invoke the default "target" in this build file.

Handy enough if that is what you want, but there are a variety of other possibilities. If we run the command nant -help we will see a screen similar to that in Figure 2-1.

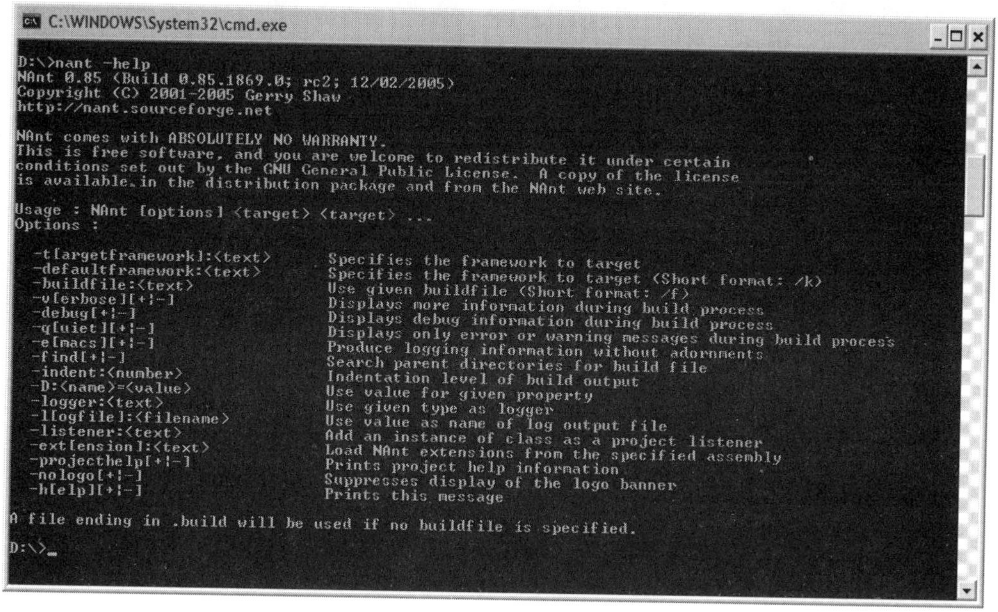

Figure 2-1. *The NAnt executable*

Command-Line Options

NAnt accepts command-line options in the following way:

```
nant [options] <target> <target> ...
```

The options available are shown in Table 2-1.

Table 2-1. *A List of NAnt Command-Line Options*

Option	Description
-defaultframework:<text>	Uses given framework as default (short format: –k)
-buildfile:<text>	Uses given build file (short format: –f)
–v[erbose][+|-]	Displays more information during build process
–debug[+|-]	Displays debug information during build process
–q[uiet][+|-]	Displays only error or warning messages during build process
–find[+|-]	Searches parent directories for build file
–indent:<number>	Indicates indentation level of build output
–D:<text>	Uses value for given property
–logger:<text>	Uses given type as logger
–l[ogfile]:<filename>	Uses value as name of log output file
–listener:<text>	Adds an instance of the class as a project listener
–projecthelp[+|-]	Prints project help information
–nologo[+|-]	Suppresses display of the logo banner
–h[elp][+|-]	Prints a list of these options

Probably the most important of these options are the [target] option, the –f (file) option, and the –D (property override) option. You will tend to find that most command-line NAnt usage will be of the following form:

```
nant -f:mybuild.build -d:myproperty=foo domybuild
```

This command would have the effect of running the mybuild.build build file, invoking target domybuild, and setting the value of myproperty to foo.

Do not worry if you are confused about properties and targets: they are all covered in the next part of this chapter.

The following is a more complete explanation of the options. For the purposes of demonstrating the effects of these options, we will be using the following build file, which is just a slightly more complex variation on the Hello World script:

```
<?xml version="1.0" encoding="utf-8" ?>
<project name="CommandOptions" default="target3">
    <description>A very simple build script</description>

    <property name="message" value="Hello World!"/>

    <echo message="Entering main target..."/>
    <echo message="Exiting main target..."/>

    <target name="target1" description="This is target1">
        <echo message="Entering target1..."/>
        <echo message="Exiting target1..."/>
    </target>
```

```
    <target name="target2" description="This is target2" depends="target1">
        <echo message="Entering target2..."/>
        <echo message="${message}"/>
        <echo message="Exiting target2..."/>
    </target>

    <target name="target3" description="This is target3" depends="target2">
        <echo message="Entering target3..."/>
        <echo message="Exiting target3..."/>
    </target>
</project>
```

Running this script with no options produces the following output:

```
---------- NAnt ----------
NAnt 0.85
Copyright (C) 2001-2003 Gerry Shaw
http://nant.sourceforge.net

Buildfile: file:///CommandOptions.build
Target(s) specified: target3
    [echo] Entering main target...
    [echo] Exiting main target...

target1:
    [echo] Entering target1...
    [echo] Exiting target1...

target2:
    [echo] Entering target2...
    [echo] Hello World!
    [echo] Exiting target2...

target3:
    [echo] Entering target3...
    [echo] Exiting target3...

BUILD SUCCEEDED
Total time: 0.1 seconds.
Output completed (0 sec consumed) - Normal Termination
```

A very brief explanation of the script is as follows. Again, the details of this will be investigated later.

The script contains three subtargets: target1, target2, and target3.

Additionally, it has a task in the main body of the project and so this is executed first when the build file is run.

"Dependencies" have been set between target3 and target2, and between target2 and target1.

The default target for the script is target1.

All of this means that when the script is run, the main tasks in the project are called, followed by target3, which relies on target2, which in turn relies on target1. Hence the output appears in the order above.

A lot of the command-line options have a direct impact on the output, as we will see.

–defaultframework, –k

Using this switch allows NAnt to specify the compiler when actually performing a build with the csc task or the other compiler tasks. Table 2-2 shows the available options for the compiler.

Table 2-2. *NAnt Default Framework Switch Options*

Framework Switch	Description
netcf-1.0	Microsoft .NET Compact Framework 1.0
net-1.1	Microsoft .NET Framework 1.1
net-1.0	Microsoft .NET Framework 1.0

So an example use of this would be

```
nant -k:net-1.0
```

For the purposes of this book, we will be working exclusively with the 1.1 Framework and will not be making use of this switch.

–buildfile, –f

We saw a quick use of this switch in the Hello World example earlier. This simply allows you to specify a path to a particular script and is, of course, extremely useful.

An example use of this would be

```
nant -f:C:\MyBuildFiles\MyBuildFile.build
```

This option can be used similarly to choose a build file in a folder that contains multiple .build files.

–verbose, –v

This switch provides more feedback on the build process, including log messages defined as verbose. The output from using this switch would look like the following:

```
---------- NAnt ----------
NAnt 0.85
Copyright (C) 2001-2003 Gerry Shaw
http://nant.sourceforge.net


Framework net-1.2 is invalid and has not been loaded :
Framework directory C:\WINDOWS\Microsoft.NET\Framework\v1.2.30703 does not exist.
Framework mono-1.0 is invalid and has not been loaded :
Property 'sdkInstallRoot' has not been set.
Framework sscli-1.0 is invalid and has not been loaded :
Framework directory C:\sscli\build\v1.x86fstchk.rotor does not exist.
Buildfile: file:///CommandOptions.build
Base Directory: D:\BookCode\Chapter2.
Target(s) specified: target3
     [echo] Entering main target...
     [echo] Exiting main target...

<snip>
Output completed (0 sec consumed) - Normal Termination
```

As you can see, where additional information is available it is provided by the logger. The information may be helpful for debugging efforts when you are constructing a script. It is also useful when you are constructing your own tasks (see Chapter 6).

–debug

This is another switch for controlling the level of verbosity. This is the most verbose that the output can be. Here, we can see that the same information provided by verbose is provided here, as well as some information regarding target execution information:

```
---------- NAnt ----------
NAnt 0.85
Copyright (C) 2001-2003 Gerry Shaw
http://nant.sourceforge.net


Framework net-1.2 is invalid and has not been loaded :
Framework directory C:\WINDOWS\Microsoft.NET\Framework\v1.2.30703 does not exist.
Framework mono-1.0 is invalid and has not been loaded :
Property 'sdkInstallRoot' has not been set.
Framework sscli-1.0 is invalid and has not been loaded :
Framework directory C:\sscli\build\v1.x86fstchk.rotor does not exist.
Buildfile: file:///CommandOptions.build
Base Directory: D:\BookCode\Chapter2.
Target(s) specified: target3
     [echo] Entering main target...
     [echo] Exiting main target...
```

```
Build sequence for target 'target3' is target1, target2, target3
Complete build sequence is target1, target2, target3

target1:
    [echo] Entering target1...
    [echo] Exiting target1...

<snip>
Output completed (0 sec consumed) - Normal Termination
```

–quiet

This is the last of the verbosity switches. When used -quiet has the effect of showing only warnings and errors in the script. Our output would be as follows:

```
---------- NAnt ----------
NAnt 0.85
Copyright (C) 2001-2003 Gerry Shaw
http://nant.sourceforge.net


Output completed (0 sec consumed) - Normal Termination
```

No snipping of code is needed here! This can be a helpful switch when you do not want to produce huge logs of worthless information when your scripts are running successfully.

–nologo

This switch removes the NAnt copyright information from the output. Using this switch in conjunction with -quiet keeps the output very minimal.

```
---------- NAnt ----------
Output completed (0 sec consumed) - Normal Termination
```

–find

The -find option tells NAnt to search in the directories above the invocation directory for scripts to run. So for example, if CommandOptions.build is held in MyDirectory, and SubDirectory1 is a subdirectory of MyDirectory, then the following call will ensure that NAnt finds the build file in MyDirectory:

```
nant -find
```

It would not, however, find a file in SubDirectory2 where SubDirectory2 is a subdirectory of MyDirectory and therefore a sibling of SubDirectory1. This is better seen in Figure 2-2 than explained.

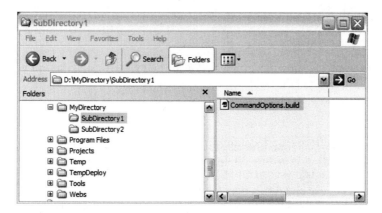

Figure 2-2. *Using –find in NAnt*

–indent

The –indent option is very straightforward to use. By appending a number to indent, you are "tabbing" the output accordingly. For example, the following call would indent the output by two tabs:

```
nant -indent:2
```

–D

This switch is likely to be the one that is used with every call of NAnt that you make by whatever means. It allows a property to be overridden at the command line. This immediately results in a whole bunch of flexibility to the build files. In our sample build file we have only one property. We can change this using

```
nant -D:message="Goodbye World!"
```

The output would now be as follows:

```
---------- NAnt ----------

<snip>

target2:

    [echo] Entering target2...
    [echo] Goodbye World!
    [echo] Exiting target2...

<snip>

Output completed (0 sec consumed) - Normal Termination
```

This option can be applied multiple times:

```
nant -D:property1=foo -D:property2=bar
```

We provide an in-depth discussion of properties a bit later. We are going to be using this information to the max throughout the rest of the book.

–logger, –listener, –logfile, –l

Loggers allow the outputs resulting from the execution of a build file to be logged. If a log file is not specified, then this output will be presented in the standard output window. Listeners will produce the same information but always to the standard output window.

Documentation is light on the use and differences between these switches. The easiest way to delve deeper into what they do is to reflect using Reflector (see Appendix A) over the NAnt.Core.dll assembly and investigate what is happening. Figure 2-3 shows a simplified class view of the loggers and listeners in NAnt that can easily be derived from any investigations with Reflector.

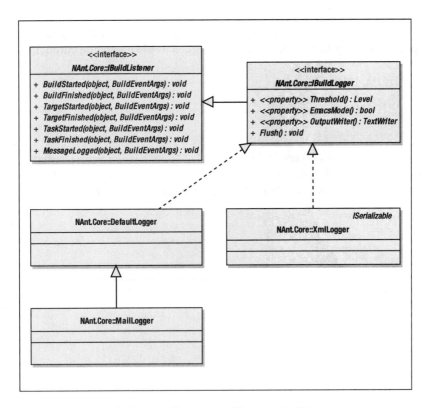

Figure 2-3. *A simplified view of loggers and listeners in NAnt*

We can see from the screen shot that two interfaces are defined: IBuildListener and IBuildLogger. IBuildLogger implements IBuildListener, and in fact all of the available loggers implement IBuildLogger. The most useful options are DefaultLogger and XmlLogger, and it is these options that we will be using.

We have seen DefaultLogger in action with all of our results so far. Here we can see how logging is affected by using the other loggers.

Using XmlLogger requires the following line:

```
nant -logger:NAnt.Core.XmlLogger
```

This produces the following output:

```
---------- NAnt ----------
NAnt 0.85
Copyright (C) 2001-2003 Gerry Shaw
http://nant.sourceforge.net

<buildresults project="HelloWorld">
  <message level="Info"><![CDATA[Buildfile: file:///HelloWorld.build]]></message>
  <message level="Info"><![CDATA[Target(s) specified: go]]></message>
  <task name="property" />
  <target name="go">
    <task name="echo">
      <message level="Info"><![CDATA[Hello World!]]></message>
    </task>
  </target>
</buildresults>
Output completed (2 sec consumed) - Normal Termination
```

As you can see, the logging is now in a much friendlier format for, for example, report production using XSLT or analysis with XPath.

A script can be run with both a logger and a listener defined (but not multiples of either). With the following line, we can use both DefaultLogger and XmlLogger. We will set DefaultLogger to be a listener.

```
nant -logger:NAnt.Core.XmlLogger -listener:NAnt.Core.DefaultLogger
```

This time the output is as follows:

```
---------- NAnt ----------
NAnt 0.85
Copyright (C) 2001-2003 Gerry Shaw
http://nant.sourceforge.net

<buildresults project="HelloWorld">
  <message level="Info"><![CDATA[Buildfile:
    file:///HelloWorld.build]]>
  </message>Buildfile: file:///HelloWorld.build

  <message level="Info">
    <![CDATA[Target(s) specified: go]]>
  </message>Target(s) specified: go
```

```
  <task name="property" />
  <target name="go"
go:

>
    <task name="echo">
      <message level="Info">
          <![CDATA[Hello World!]]>
      </message>
      [echo] Hello World!

    </task>
  </target>
</buildresults>


BUILD SUCCEEDED
Total time: 0.1 seconds.
Output completed (2 sec consumed) - Normal Termination
```

The effect has been to merge both logs into the output window. That certainly is not much use, so of course the effective way to use the logger and listener is to ensure that a log file is defined. The following line is probably the best arrangement:

```
nant -logger:NAnt.Core.XmlLogger -listener:NAnt.Core.DefaultLogger ➡
    -logfile:mylog.xml
```

In the standard output window, the following is shown:

```
---------- NAnt ----------
NAnt 0.85
Copyright (C) 2001-2003 Gerry Shaw
http://nant.sourceforge.net

Buildfile: file:/// HelloWorld.build
Target(s) specified: go

go:
     [echo] Hello World!

BUILD SUCCEEDED
Total time: 0.1 seconds.
Output completed (2 sec consumed) - Normal Termination
```

The mylog.xml file contains the following:

```
<buildresults project="HelloWorld">
  <message level="Info"><![CDATA[Buildfile:
file:///D:/BookCode/Chapter2/HelloWorld.build]]></message>
  <message level="Info"><![CDATA[Target(s) specified: go]]></message>
  <task name="property" />
  <target name="go">
    <task name="echo">
      <message level="Info"><![CDATA[Hello World!]]></message>
    </task>
  </target>
</buildresults>
```

The log file itself has nothing other than XML so it can be transformed or otherwise manipulated directly.

Note NAnt uses the powerful log4net library for logging and, as is typical of NAnt in general, it is easy to extend. For our purposes, console and XML logging will be satisfactory, but you may have a specific need to implement more esoteric solutions.

–projecthelp

This is a very nice switch. When you are confronted with a complex build file (such as the NAnt build file itself), it can be helpful to figure out the available targets that can be run from the build file. Running this against our file produces the following output:

```
---------- NAnt ----------
NAnt 0.85
Copyright (C) 2001-2003 Gerry Shaw
http://nant.sourceforge.net

Default Target:

 target3           This is target3

Main Targets:

 target1           This is target1
 target2           This is target2
 target3           This is target3

Sub Targets:

Output completed (0 sec consumed) - Normal Termination
```

This demonstrates that there are three available targets and that target3 will be called by default if no target is specified. This is very useful when you are first inspecting a complicated or lengthy build file.

In this instance, no subtargets are displayed. It is not obvious from the NAnt documentation what the difference between a main target and a subtarget is. As it turns out, we can use Reflector to investigate Nant.Core.DLL, as shown in Figure 2-4.

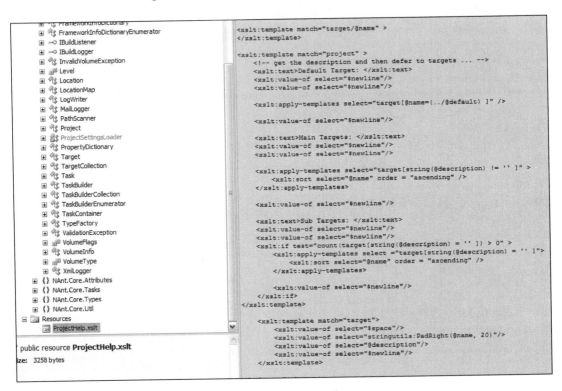

Figure 2-4. *Reflecting over ProjectHelp.xslt*

It turns out that a target is classified as a main target if it has a description, and is classified as a subtarget if it does not have a description. This can be seen at about the halfway point of the XSLT file in Figure 2-4. Simple.

■Caution It can be dangerous to allow the whole script to run if no target is specified. This execution could easily be in error. It should be considered best practice to create an "information only" target as the default. This ensures that actions are always explicitly invoked and provides the author with the option of some improved informational messages.

<target>

This is not a switch in the usual way. NAnt accepts a list of targets as parameters on the command line. These parameters override the default target and represent the actual target(s) to be run. The usual dependencies within the build file apply, though. So, for example, in our test script it is not possible to execute `target2` without executing `target1`, but it is possible to execute `target2` without executing `target3`.

There is no syntax for the switch. The target names are listed by using the names of the targets:

```
nant target2
```

You can place multiple target calls on the command line. NAnt will execute each target and its dependencies in turn. An example of this is

```
nant target1 target2 target3
```

Using this option at the command line can mean that all dependencies can be removed from the NAnt file itself potentially, but this increases the command-line call, which might not be so intuitive for any user.

■Tip If you want to prevent execution of individual targets within a script, then you can prefix the target name with a dash (–). This has the effect of making the NAnt invocation command (`nant -target2`) look as though the target is an argument name, and hence causes an error.

The Build File

We have seen some examples of build files that are not very useful currently. But even so, we can see that there are specific structures and elements to assist in the construction of a build file and therefore the definition of the process for the build. Here we will look at the various opportunities this structure affords us when creating a build file.

You can investigate the allowed structure of a build file through the NAnt XML Schema (XSD file), which comes with the source code for NAnt. Alternatively, the following script will output the XSD to a file of your choosing:

```xml
<?xml version="1.0" encoding="utf-8" ?>
<project name="NAntSchema" default="help">
    <description>Output a copy of the NAnt Schema</description>

    <property name="file" value="NAnt.xsd"/>

    <target name="help" description="About this build file">
        <echo message="This outputs the NAnt XSD to a file."/>
        <echo message="Override the 'file' property to change the location."/>
    </target>
```

```
        <target name="go" description="Create the NAnt Schema XSD file">
            <nantschema output="${file}"/>
        </target>
</project>
```

The Project

The project node is the root node of a build file. This node can contain any number of
<property> nodes, <task> nodes, and <target> nodes. Generally, the rest of the build file is
now defined either as a property, or as a target, or as a task within a target.

The documentation for NAnt describes the project node attributes as shown in Table 2-3.

Table 2-3. *Project Node Attributes*

Attribute	Description	Required
name	The name of the project.	No
default	The default target to use when no target is supplied.	Yes
basedir	The base directory from which all path calculations are done. Current directory is the default.	No

These are quite straightforward options. In fact, NAnt will run fine without the default
attribute, though generally it will not execute anything, of course!

Other points to note regarding the project node are

All properties and tasks that are directly below the project node are executed prior to any
specified target.

All properties and tasks that are directly below the project node are always executed during a build.

Therefore, it makes sense to use the project node to hold global properties for the rest of the
execution. It also makes sense to place tasks inside a target node so that they can be bypassed
when necessary—for example, during testing. The reverse of this statement is also true and
may suit your circumstances.

Apart from these features, the project node is quite dull. Many more exciting things can
be achieved with the target nodes.

The Target

Targets are used to "modularize" the build file. A target contains zero or more tasks to be completed in a sequence.

As we have learned, each project node usually has a default target that will be invoked
when none is specified by the command line. In the Hello World example, the default target
was go.

The documentation for NAnt describes the attributes of a target as shown in Table 2-4.

Table 2-4. *Target Node Attributes*

Attribute	Description	Required?
name	The name of the target	Yes
description	A short description of this target's function	No
depends	A comma-separated list of names of targets on which this depends	No
if	The name of the property that must be set in order for this target to execute	No
unless	The name of the property that must not be set in order for this target to execute	No

When you are constructing a build file, <targets> are excellent ways of organizing your thoughts. We will look at a proposed set of targets at the end of this chapter that can correspond to the defined sections of the processes we have already outlined.

By modularizing tasks in this way, we ensure that individual sections of a build script can be

Tested in isolation by invoking the specific target from the command line (do not forget the -projecthelp switch)

Included in or removed from the process as desired

Segregated along specific lines, such as platform, environment, configuration

Generated for multiple solutions via automated means in itself—such as an XSLT transformation

There is a great deal of strength in the target node, and its attributes are worth considering in more depth.

name

The name attribute is crucial to the target, as the target is invoked by name. Simple as that.

description

The description is shown when the -projecthelp switch is used at the command line, and so can be of some assistance to a user of the build file.

depends

Targets can be made to depend on each other by use of the depends attribute. This attribute takes a comma-delimited list of targets that are to be executed prior to the execution of the target in question. For example:

```
<target name="go" depends="foo, bar"/>
```

This means that target go will not execute until target foo and then target bar have been executed. Additionally, any targets that foo or bar depend on must be executed. You will be pleased to note that NAnt can figure out circular dependencies so that the following build file will not execute:

```
<?xml version="1.0" encoding="utf-8" ?>
<project name="Circular Chaos" default="foo">
    <description>Circular Chaos</description>

    <property name="file" value="NAnt.xsd"/>

    <target name="foo" depends="bar">
        <echo message="Chicken..."/>
    </target>

    <target name="bar" depends="foo">
        <echo message="Egg..."/>
    </target>
</project>
```

The output produced (_nant -quiet -nologo) is as follows:

```
---------- NAnt ----------
BUILD FAILED

Circular dependency: foo <- bar <- foo

Output completed (0 sec consumed) - Normal Termination
```

The depends attribute introduces one of the first main powers of the build script: the chaining of targets, and thus potentially the branching and selection of targets.

It is usually better to create the dependencies in other overarching targets than in the individual targets themselves. If you hard-code the dependencies into the individual targets, then testing aspects of a build file in isolation can be difficult.

For example, you might want to present a build file with multiple targets as

```
<target name="go" depends="action1, action2, action3"/>
<target name="action1">
    <!--Do action 1-->
</target>
<target name="action2">
    <!--Do action 2-->
</target>
<target name="action3">
    <!--Do action 3-->
</target>
```

if and unless

As we will see later, working with conditionals in NAnt can be awkward. Generally, I try to avoid the use of conditionals where possible. My take is that when I have designed a process,

I do not expect to want to bypass aspects of that process. Of course, there is always a good reason to do this in reality, so if, and its counterpart unless, can come in handy.

The if attribute means that a target will execute only if a property has been set to true. Conversely, the unless attribute means that a target will execute only if a property has been set to false. Trying to set properties used by if and unless to anything other than a Boolean will result in an error.

Using these features, we can effectively simulate an if-else scenario using the same property. Consider:

```xml
<?xml version="1.0" encoding="utf-8" ?>
<project name="IfElse" default="go">

    <property name="ifelse" value="true"/>

    <target name="go" depends="if, else"/>

    <target name="if" if="${ifelse}">
        <echo message="Executed if..."/>
    </target>

    <target name="else" unless="${ifelse}">
        <echo message="Executed else..."/>
    </target>
</project>
```

The execution path will ordinarily be via the if target as by default, the ifelse property is set to true, but if this is overridden on the command line (to false) then the else target will be executed. So, for example, executing the line

```
nant -D:ifelse=true
```

will produce the following output:

```
---------- NAnt ----------
NAnt 0.85
Copyright (C) 2001-2004 Gerry Shaw
http://nant.sourceforge.net

Buildfile: file:///IfElse.build
Target(s) specified: go


if:

    [echo] Executed if...

go:
```

```
BUILD SUCCEEDED
Total time: 0 seconds.
Output completed (0 sec consumed) - Normal Termination
```

As you can see, targets are quite flexible. They become even more powerful when combined with properties and attributes. Once we look at some of the specific structural and conditional tasks, we will see that they gain even more flexibility. Before we delve further into that, however, we need to consider properties more fully.

Properties

In the examples used so far, we have seen various properties defined and used. We have also overridden them on the command line. They are the key to making a multipurpose script, though in fact they are simply key/value pairs described in the build file. A property is described in the following way:

```
<property name="foo" value="bar"/>
```

This property can now be accessed by the build script in the following way:

```
<echo message="The value of foo is: ${foo}"/>
```

This will output the message

```
The value of foo is: bar
```

Properties can be combined as follows:

```
<property name="bar" value="${foo}bar"/>
```

So, a similar echo for bar would output the following:

```
The value of bar is: barbar
```

Since you can use properties anywhere in the build script, they are extremely powerful: it is possible to parameterize any attribute.

The NAnt documentation describes the attributes of properties as shown in Table 2-5.

Table 2-5. *Property Task Attributes*

Attribute	Type	Description	Required
name	string	Specifies the name of the NAnt property to set.	True
value	string	Specifies the value to assign to the NAnt property.	True
dynamic	bool	Specifies whether references to other properties should not be expanded when the value of the property is set, but expanded when the property is actually used. The default is false, meaning references to other properties will be expanded when the property value is set.	False
readonly	bool	Specifies whether or not the property is read-only. The default is false.	False

Attribute	Type	Description	Required
failonerror	bool	Determines if task failure stops the build or is just reported. The default is true.	False
if	bool	If set to true, then the task will be executed; otherwise, it will be skipped. The default is true.	False
unless	bool	Opposite of if. If set to false, then the task will be executed; otherwise, it will be skipped. The default is false.	False
verbose	bool	Determines whether the task should report detailed build log messages. The default is false.	False

Clearly, the core requirements are to provide a name and value for a property. The other attributes have some potential uses, though.

dynamic

This can be a little confusing when used in a script, and it is best demonstrated through code. This attribute determines whether the property is expanded at the time it is set, or when it is used. You can see the effects using the following script:

```xml
<?xml version="1.0" encoding="utf-8" ?>
<project name="Dynamic" default="go">

    <property name="one" value="one"/>
    <property name="two" value="two"/>
    <property name="both" value="${one}${two}" dynamic="${dynamic}"/>

    <target name="go" depends="change"/>

    <target name="change">
        <echo message="one=${one}"/>
        <echo message="two=${two}"/>
        <property name="one" value="three"/>
        <echo message="one=${one}"/>
        <echo message="both=${both}"/>
    </target>
</project>
```

We can see the effects of the dynamic switch by calling the script first with the default value, false:

```
nant -D:dynamic=false
```

This produces the following partial output:

```
[echo] one=one
[echo] two=two
[echo] one=three
[echo] both=onetwo
```

Running with the dynamic value set to true produces different output:

```
[echo] one=one
[echo] two=two
[echo] one=three
[echo] both=threetwo
```

We can see that in the first instance, the property had been resolved at the set time because when we adjust the one property later on it has no effect. In the second instance, the property resolves as it is invoked. Subsequently changing the value of one will also be resolved correctly by both.

readonly

Similarly, if a property is marked as readonly, then it cannot be overwritten. Consider a similar build file to the one shown earlier. The effect can be seen here:

```
<?xml version="1.0" encoding="utf-8" ?>
<project name="ReadOnlyProperty" default="go">
    <target name="go">
        <property name="alwaysthesame" value="true" readonly="true"/>
        <echo message="alwaysthesame = ${alwaysthesame}"/>
        <property name="alwaysthesame" value="false"/>
        <echo message="alwaysthesame = ${alwaysthesame}"/>
    </target>
</project>
```

The results are the same, although the reason is different. In this case, the property is readonly so no overwrite is allowed to take place:

```
---------- NAnt ----------
NAnt 0.85
Copyright (C) 2001-2003 Gerry Shaw
http://nant.sourceforge.net

Buildfile: file:///ReadOnlyProperty.build
Target(s) specified: go

go:

    [echo] alwaysthesame = true
    [echo] alwaysthesame = true

BUILD SUCCEEDED
Total time: 0.1 seconds.
Output completed (2 sec consumed) - Normal Termination
```

if and unless

These two attributes give us some control over property settings by allowing the evaluation of a Boolean value, usually a property. In the following example, we can see that usehat will be set to true if raining is true, whereas useumbrella requires raining to be true but windy to be false owing to the unless attribute.

```
<?xml version="1.0" encoding="utf-8" ?>
<project name="IfUnlessProperty" default="go">
    <target name="go">

        <property name="usehat" value="false"/>
        <property name="useumbrella" value="false"/>

        <property name="raining" value="true"/>
        <property name="windy" value="true"/>

        <property name="usehat" value="true" if="${raining}"/>
        <property name="useumbrella" value="true" if="${raining}"➡
            unless="${windy}"/>

        <echo message="usehat = ${usehat}"/>
        <echo message="useumbrella = ${useumbrella}"/>
    </target>
</project>
```

Therefore, the results are that usehat becomes true, but useumbrella remains false:

```
---------- NAnt ----------
NAnt 0.85
Copyright (C) 2001-2003 Gerry Shaw
http://nant.sourceforge.net

Buildfile: file:///IfUnlessProperty.build
Target(s) specified: go

go:

    [echo] usehat = true
    [echo] useumbrella = false

BUILD SUCCEEDED
Total time: 0.1 seconds.
Output completed (2 sec consumed) - Normal Termination
```

verbose

This option enables verbose messages for actions on the property, although in my experience it does not actually provide any utility.

Built-in Properties

NAnt contains several built-in properties that can be useful for builds (depending on the circumstance) and for debugging. They are shown in Table 2-6.

Table 2-6. *Built-in NAnt Properties*

Property	Description
nant.version	The version of NAnt
nant.filename	The full path to the NAnt assembly
nant.location	The base directory of the NAnt assembly
nant.project.basedir	The absolute path of the project's basedir
nant.project.buildfile	The absolute path of the build file
nant.project.name	The name of the project
nant.project.default	The name of the project's default target
nant.onsuccess	The name of a target to be executed when the build succeeds
nant.onfailure	The name of a target to be executed when the build fails
nant.tasks.*	Each task available to nant has a true value.
nant.settings.defaultframework	The default framework as set in nant.exe.config
nant.settings.defaultframework.description	Description of the default framework
nant.settings.defaultframework.frameworkdirectory	The framework directory of the default framework
nant.settings.defaultframework.sdkdirectory	The framework SDK directory of the default framework
nant.settings.defaultframework.frameworkassemblydirectory	The framework assembly directory of the default framework if used
nant.settings.currentframework.*	The same set of properties for the currently selected framework
nant.platform.name	The name of the platform on which NAnt is currently running: either win32 or unix
nant.platform.win32	Holds the value true if NAnt is running on the Windows 32 platform; otherwise, false
nant.platform.unix	Holds the value true if NAnt is running on the Unix platform; otherwise, false

The use of these settings for the diagnosis of problems and for the branching of build files is quite obvious. In the NAnt.exe.config file it is possible to set global properties for use in all scripts. This could be useful for standardizing messages and so on.

Two of the built-in properties—onsuccess and onfailure—merit some additional attention.

nant.onsuccess and nant.onfailure

These useful properties hold the name of a target that should be run when the execution of a build file succeeds or fails. This can be very useful for, say, mail-based notification or other types of notification.

Although I am in danger of "accentuating the negative," I will concentrate on the onfailure property for these examples. Consider the following simple script:

```
<?xml version="1.0" encoding="utf-8" ?>
<project name="FailureTest1" default="go">
    <property name="nant.onfailure" value="fail"/>
    <property name="message" value="Hello again!"/>
    <target name="go">
        <fail />
        <echo message="${message}"/>
    </target>
    <target name="fail">
        <echo message="Oh dear, it has all gone wrong."/>
    </target>
</project>
```

The main points to notice are the addition of the nant.onfailure property and the task to ensure that the go target fails. The output looks like this:

```
---------- NAnt ----------
Buildfile: file:///FailureTest.build
Target(s) specified: go

go:
fail:
    [echo] Oh dear, it has all gone wrong.
BUILD FAILED
No message.
Total time: 0.1 seconds.
Output completed (2 sec consumed) - Normal Termination
```

So the fail target ran when the go target failed. No problem. We can make things a little more dynamic, as the following script shows:

```
<?xml version="1.0" encoding="utf-8" ?>
<project name="FailureTest2" default="go">
    <property name="nant.onfailure" value="fail"/>
    <property name="failed.message" value="Something went wrong."/>
    <property name="message" value="Hello again!"/>

    <target name="go" depends="normal, important"/>
```

```
    <target name="normal">
        <echo message="Normal step OK"/>
    </target>

    <target name="important">
        <property name="failed.message" value="IMPORTANT! World Ending!"/>
        <fail/>
        <echo message="Important step OK"/>
    </target>

    <target name="fail">
        <echo message="${failed.message}"/>
    </target>
</project>
```

This time, we can set an individual message (poor man's debugging!) depending on where the build file fails. The output is as follows:

```
---------- NAnt ----------
Buildfile: file:///HelloWorld.build
Target(s) specified: go

normal:
    [echo] Normal step OK
important:
fail:
    [echo] IMPORTANT! World Ending!

BUILD FAILED
No message.
Total time: 0.1 seconds.
Output completed (2 sec consumed) - Normal Termination
```

This target can be used to carry out corrective action as appropriate to a build file. For example, if a task is to check out a file from source control, manipulate that file, and then check it back into source control, there can be problems if the task fails prior to the check-in but post the checkout. In future runs, the build will fail since the file will already be checked out. An onfailure target could be used to ensure that the file is checked back in, regardless. We will see further discussion of this in Chapter 4.

A Build Process for Etomic

So ends our whirlwind tour of NAnt. Given your knowledge of build scripts now—at least in terms of structure—let us take some time to consider how we would like our core script to look. If we think about the proposed processes in Chapter 1 and some of the practices mentioned throughout this chapter, then we can translate these directly into some script "skeletons."

The Build Skeleton

In this section we can see the code for the build part of the process. This build file is entirely nonfunctional at the moment—we will cover the tasks themselves in the next chapter—but is formed using the good practices we have discussed throughout this chapter.

The build file should be self-explanatory:

```xml
<?xml version="1.0" encoding="utf-8" ?>
<project name="BuildSkeleton" default="help">
    <description>The skeleton file for the build process</description>

    <property name="nant.onfailure" value="fail"/>

    <target name="go"
      description="The main target for full build process execution."
      depends="clean, get, version, build, test, document, publish, notify"/>

    <target name="clean" description="Clean up the build environment.">
        <!--Enter tasks for clean target-->
    </target>

    <target name="get" description="Grab the source code.">
        <!--Enter tasks for get target-->
    </target>

    <target name="version" description="Apply versioning to the source code.">
        <!--Enter tasks for version target-->
    </target>

    <target name="build" description="Compile the application.">
        <!--Enter tasks for build target-->
    </target>

    <target name="test" description="Apply the unit tests.">
        <!--Enter tasks for test target-->
    </target>

    <target name="document" description="Generate documentation and reports.">
        <!--Enter tasks for document target-->
    </target>

    <target name="publish" description="Place the assets in agreed location.">
        <!--Enter tasks for publish target-->
    </target>

    <target name="notify" description="Tell everyone of the success or failure.">
        <!--Enter tasks for notify target-->
    </target>
```

```
    <target name="fail">
        <!--Enter tasks for fail target-->
    </target>

    <target name="help">
        <!--Enter tasks for help target-->
        <echo message="The skeleton file for the build process ➥
is designed to execute the following targets in turn:"/>
        <echo message="-- clean"/>
        <echo message="-- get"/>
        <echo message="-- version"/>
        <echo message="-- build"/>
        <echo message="-- test"/>
        <echo message="-- document"/>
        <echo message="-- publish"/>
        <echo message="-- notify"/>
    </target>

</project>
```

The key points to notice are

All of the targets match the steps defined in Chapter 1. The descriptions may look similar too.

There is one target called go, which has all of the individual target dependencies. This allows us to test individual aspects of the build file independently of the overall process.

The default target is help, which ensures that the process cannot be mistakenly run: go would need to be specified.

The help target outlines the overall process.

The fail target is specified as the default nant.onfailure target.

The output from running the script with no switches is

```
---------- NAnt ----------
NAnt 0.85
Copyright (C) 2001-2003 Gerry Shaw
http://nant.sourceforge.net

Buildfile: file:///BuildSkeleton.build
Target(s) specified: help

help:
```

```
     [echo] The skeleton file for the build process is designed to ➡
execute the following targets in turn:
     [echo] -- clean
     [echo] -- get
     [echo] -- version
     [echo] -- build
     [echo] -- test
     [echo] -- document
     [echo] -- publish
     [echo] -- notify

BUILD SUCCEEDED

Total time: 0.2 seconds.

Output completed (2 sec consumed) - Normal Termination
```

So we receive some useful output, but without the danger of any real execution when we run the script. Listing the targets in order of dependencies is also worthwhile because it allows us to use the built-in projecthelp function to investigate how the script should be used:

nant -projecthelp

This produces the following output:

```
---------- NAnt ----------
NAnt 0.85
Copyright (C) 2001-2003 Gerry Shaw
http://nant.sourceforge.net

Default Target:

 help

Main Targets:

 build           Compile the application.
 clean           Clean up the build environment.
 document        Generate documentation and reports.
 get             Grab the source code.
 go              The main target for full build process execution.
 notify          Tell everyone of the success or failure.
 publish         Place the compiled assets, reports etc. in agreed location.
 test            Apply the unit tests.
 version         Apply versioning to the source code files.
```

```
Sub Targets:

 fail
 help

Output completed (3 sec consumed) - Normal Termination
```

The output from this is useful, but unfortunately it prints the targets in alphabetical order. Now, we could place numbers (for example) in front of target names in order to produce the same effect in this output, but this quickly becomes unmanageable and unwieldy. Finally, we can run the script as intended:

```
nant go
```

This produces the following output:

```
---------- NAnt ----------
NAnt 0.85
Copyright (C) 2001-2003 Gerry Shaw
http://nant.sourceforge.net

Buildfile: file:///BuildSkeleton.build
Target(s) specified: go

clean:
get:
version:
build:
test:
document:
publish:
notify:
go:


BUILD SUCCEEDED
Total time: 0.1 seconds.
Output completed (2 sec consumed) - Normal Termination
```

So at this point, we can see that the script runs successfully, although it is not doing anything. In the next chapter we will examine the various tasks that we can use and combine to complete the activities we have defined. For now, we can be assured that we have started on the correct path.

The Deploy Skeleton

The deploy skeleton is very similar to the build skeleton; once again the steps are defined as we described in Chapter 1.

```xml
<?xml version="1.0" encoding="utf-8" ?>
<project name="DeploySkeleton" default="help">
    <description>The skeleton file for the deploy process</description>

    <property name="nant.onfailure" value="fail"/>

    <target name="go"
       description="The main target for full deploy process execution."
       depends="selectversion, get, selectenvironments, ➡
                createenvironments, position, configure, notify"/>

    <target name="selectversion" description="Selects the correct version.">
        <!--Enter tasks for selectversion target-->
    </target>

    <target name="get" description="Grab the correct assets.">
        <!--Enter tasks for get target-->
    </target>

    <target name="selectenvironments" description="Select the environment.">
        <!--Enter tasks for selectenvironments target-->
    </target>

    <target name="createenvironments" description="Create the environments.">
        <!--Enter tasks for createenvironments target-->
    </target>

    <target name="position" description="Position system assets.
        <!--Enter tasks for position target-->
    </target>

    <target name="configure" description="Make configuration changes.">
        <!--Enter tasks for configure target-->
    </target>

    <target name="notify" description="Tell everyone of the success or failure.">
        <!--Enter tasks for notify target-->
    </target>

    <target name="fail">
        <!--Enter tasks for fail target-->
    </target>

    <target name="help">
    <!--Enter tasks for help target-->
        <echo message="The skeleton file for the deploy process is ➡
```

```
designed to execute the following targets in turn:"/>
        <echo message="-- selectversion"/>
        <echo message="-- get"/>
        <echo message="-- selectenvironments"/>
        <echo message="-- createenvironments"/>
        <echo message="-- position"/>
        <echo message="-- configure"/>
        <echo message="-- notify"/>
    </target>

</project>
```

The outputs using the switches described for the build skeleton are the same but are applied to the specific steps of the deployment skeleton.

Summary

Without even delving into the tasks of NAnt to any great degree, we can see already that there is significant power and flexibility afforded to the erstwhile developer through the configuration and organization possibilities of the build scripts for NAnt.

We can run NAnt scripts with our desired command-line options. We have looked at the core features of a build script and feel confident in meddling with these and applying their various attributes. Additionally, we have looked at two specific tasks that provide significant additional flexibility in script structure. We understand how dependencies between targets work, and how inheritance between build scripts works.

On a practical level, we have considered how we might structure our own build script for our solutions. We have considered the core activities that need to occur as part of our build process and we at least have a "v1" skeleton of the build and deploy files.

Further Reading

As with all open source tools, printed information can become out of date, which is why I have tried to avoid too much in-depth discussion here. The best source for up-to-date information is the wealth of information about NAnt and NAntContrib in the community at large. The first port of call should be the homepage at http://nant.sourceforge.net, which contains links to the latest versions, help, mailing lists, and the NAnt wiki.

For a general discussion of open source tools, I would certainly refer to Brian Nantz's *Open Source .NET Development: Programming with NAnt, NUnit, NDoc, and More* (Addison-Wesley, 2004) in order to better inform my opinion.

Once again, for a good discussion on choices for build tools, refer to *Coder to Developer: Tools and Strategies for Delivering Your Software*, by Mike Gunderloy (Sybex, 2004). There is a good discussion of log4net, the logging tool used by NAnt, as well.

CHAPTER 3

■ ■ ■

Important NAnt Tasks

In the previous chapter, we covered what NAnt is and to some extent how it works. We also saw a considerable number of NAnt scripts that did not really do anything useful but that prepared us for various possibilities. Finally, we saw a proposed outline for our own build file based on a previously designed process.

In the next chapter, we will apply the process fully to a real project, using the skeleton scripts we have outlined. Before we do this, it is useful to explore the various built-in tasks of NAnt and NAntContrib to provide some ideas, and ready-made solutions, to the processes.

Therefore, the purpose of this chapter is to familiarize ourselves with the ways in which NAnt tackles the various tasks required of it. We will also begin stirring the creative juices before we start the real work in Chapter 4 as we tackle a real delivery scenario.

NAnt and NAntContrib contain pretty much every task you need to implement a desired delivery process. Some are more complete than others but largely NAnt and NAntContrib will not be found wanting. Additionally, there are some catchall tasks that allow some additional flexibility without the need for code extensions immediately.

In this chapter, I am not intending to discuss every task, for two reasons:

NAnt is constantly changing, and the best reference for current task capabilities lies on the NAnt homepage rather than in print at this time.

I do not use all of the tasks; many are not appropriate to my needs on a practical level since they relate to a different set of technologies, such as differing source control systems.

With that in mind, we narrowed down the tasks from NAnt and NAntContrib and will present some of them here. We then provide examples of using the tasks with the process and scripts we are trying to create.

We have organized the tasks into categories covering the general kind of work that the tasks handle:

Structural. These tasks can be used to manipulate and structure the NAnt build files and the targets within them in helpful ways to gain efficiencies within scripting structures.

Conditional. Some tasks allow the control of flow within a build file.

File. These "bread and butter" tasks will be used constantly as we manage assets through delivery.

Delivery. This collection of usually quite specific tasks are the kind that will be of use for the specific goals of the delivery processes.

Utility. These tasks are quite specific but not as delivery tasks themselves. They are all very useful within build files, though.

Source control. This category consists of the available wrapped source control functions.

Interestingly, it is NAntContrib that tends to provide more of the specific tasks for the build process. NAnt itself supplies the core tasks and framework that give the whole package its structure and flexibility.

There Is More Than One Way to Do It

If you thought that Chapter 2 demonstrated the significant flexibility available in NAnt, then be prepared for even more. The number of tasks, and the ways in which they can be organized and applied, means that you will constantly see multiple ways to solve a problem.

This is great news when you are problem solving, but as in general coding, without a model to aid the coding process and provide a conceptual framework, it is easy for things to become confusing.

■**Tip** Decide on your general approach and outline the way that you will use tasks in your scripts. Then stick to your approach as long as it is successful. There is no shame in refactoring to a different structure or implementation later on; on the contrary, it is likely to be a positive thing. But when you are planning and executing standard scripts across multiple projects, refactoring should not be taken too lightly and too often. One of the main reasons can be that the solutions themselves require reorganization or refactoring to take advantage of a new build technique, and this can be quite an effort.

General Task Features

We learned about tasks in the previous chapter when we discussed how to get the most out of NAnt. Before we look at the specific tasks we are interested in, let us define in detail what a task is.

A task is an XML tag inside a NAnt build file that instructs the NAnt executable to perform a specific action. For example, you may recognize the following:

```
<echo message="I am an example of a task"/>
```

This task tells NAnt to echo the message to the listener/logger—a very simple example.

We will look at the internals of task construction when we need to build our own task in Chapter 7. For now, it is important to recognize the features of a task. First, each task has a specific tag name rather than an attribute to describe its function (for example, we do not use `<task type="echo"/>`). Second, tasks are customized in two ways: by using attributes and by using nested elements. Let us briefly consider these features.

Using Attributes

Most tasks have individual attributes to provide the level of customization necessary for the specific task. By way of comparison, take a look at the <echo> and <mkiisdir> tasks. Each task has some standard attributes, which are listed in the individual task documentation. We can also see what those tasks are by using Reflector to examine the source code of nant.core.dll. All tasks for NAnt inherit from the Task abstract class. By reflecting over the Task class we can see the code signatures shown in Figure 3-1.

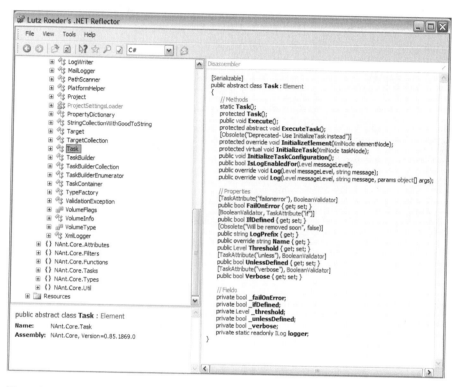

Figure 3-1. *Reflecting over the Task class*

The important features here are the following properties, which directly translate to attributes for the task:

FailOnError. The default of this property is true. The property specifies whether NAnt should halt execution and report a problem if the task fails. This property translates to the failonerror attribute.

IfDefined. The default of this property is true. The property specifies whether the task should execute if the expression in the if attribute evaluates to true. This property translates to the if attribute.

UnlessDefined. This is the reverse of the IfDefined property; its default value is false. The property specifies whether the task should execute if the expression in the unless attribute evaluates to false. This property translates to the unless attribute.

Verbose. The default value of the Verbose property is `false`. This allows us to provide a more verbose description of task execution if the property evaluates to `true`. This property translates to the `verbose` attribute.

All of these properties are marked with the attributes `TaskAttribute` and `BooleanValidator`. We will explore these in Chapter 7 in terms of implementation, but for our current purposes this means that all tasks have these four properties defined and available for use if we apply a Boolean value to them in the task implementation within a build file.

Apart from the documentation for tasks describing the attributes of the task in question, it can be very useful to use Reflector (or open the source code) to examine the behaviors and requirements of task attributes.

Using Nested Elements

A task can also be customized by including support for a variety of nested elements. The set of NAnt tasks contains many useful examples of this.

The available set of nested elements are held in the `NAnt.Core.Types` namespace. Using Reflector, we can see the available types, as shown in Figure 3-2.

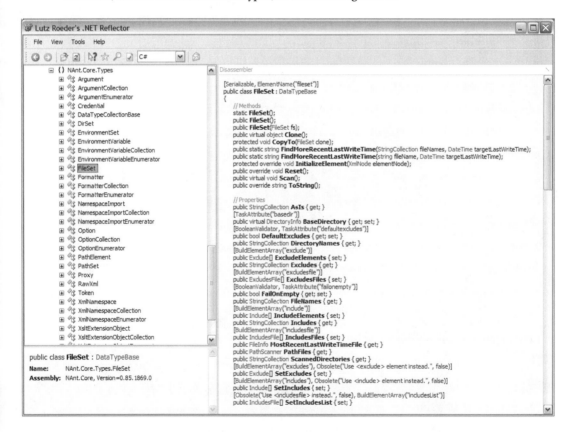

Figure 3-2. *Reflecting over the NAnt.Core.Types namespace*

> **■Caution** Unfortunately, sometimes the types are named differently according to the context of the task. This is a positive thing in terms of understanding the purpose of the element, but when you are approaching the task for the first time, it can be confusing. As a simple example, compare the `<copy>` task to the `<style>` task. `<copy>` uses the name `fileset` as the name of its `fileset` element, which is very simple, but `<style>` uses the name `infiles` to refer to its `fileset` element, which makes it less obvious that the nested element has the same features and behaviors of a regular `fileset` element.

Some tasks contain several structures of this kind. These features are particularly prevalent among the specific tasks that have been used to automate core parts of the process, such as the automation of Visual Studio and the use of NDoc.

Again, we will not go into depth here; the current documentation is a better starting point. However, we will take a look at the most common of these nested elements: the `fileset`.

The fileset

The `fileset` type is one of the most common types used as a nested element by the various NAnt tasks. It has some useful features that are worth bearing in mind.

First, a `fileset` is usually composed of `includes` and `excludes` nodes defining which files we want to include and exclude, respectively, as part of a `fileset`. Here is a simple example:

```
<fileset basedir="D:\MyFolder">
    <include name="myfile.txt"/>
    <exclude name="somefile.txt"/>
</fileset>
```

This `fileset` describes the inclusion of one specific file in the folder `D:\MyFolder`, which means that the `excludes` node is entirely superfluous. The `includes` and `excludes` nodes work well together when we are describing patterns. Table 3-1 shows pattern possibilities.

Table 3-1. *Fileset Pattern Matching*

Symbol	Meaning
?	Match any one character
*	Match any number of characters
**	Match a complete directory tree

Let us look at a practical demonstration. The following `fileset` describes a useful set of `excludes` to walk a set of web files, filtering out all of the superfluous code to be moved to a web server. For example, we do not require the C# source code, or the resources files (as they will be compiled), nor do we require the `.csproj` files or other source control artifacts.

Therefore, to walk a directory tree preserving all other assets such as `.aspx`, `.jpg`, and `.css` files, then the pattern could be described as follows:

```
<fileset basedir="D:\DirtyFolder">
    <include name="**"/>
    <exclude name="**\*.cs"/>
    <exclude name="**\*.resx"/>
    <exclude name="**\*.csproj"/>
    <exclude name="**\*.vspscc"/>
    <exclude name="**\*.scc"/>
</fileset>
```

This has been a brief look at a common structure. Keep in mind that we will come across others.

The filterchain

A `filterchain` is similar in use to a `fileset` in that it involves file manipulation. Effectively, a `filterchain` can be used to handle such tasks as token replacement during file copying and moving. `filterchains` cannot be used with any in-memory file representation and so must be used as a part of a file-manipulation task. Table 3-2 show some possible uses for a `filterchain`.

Table 3-2. *Filterchain Types*

Filter	Summary
expandproperties	Parses NAnt properties and expressions.
replacestring	Replaces all occurrences of a given string with a user-supplied replacement string
replacetokens	Replaces tokens in the original input with user-supplied values
tabstospaces	Converts tabs to spaces

The `filterchain` construct may look like this:

```
<filterchain>
    <replacetokens>
        <token key="DRIVELETTER" value="D" />
    </replacetokens>
</filterchain>
```

This `filterchain` would replace the token `@DRIVELETTER@` with the value D when the file manipulation it was embedded within takes place. The `<copy>` task example later demonstrates this.

Structural Tasks

In this section, we examine tasks that can be used to add flexibility and power to the structure of a build file, thus moving the construction of a build file from a simple linear activity to an activity more akin to coding. The tasks can be used to handle various requirements:

Repeat targets or whole build files with different properties (and therefore outcomes).

Reuse build file solutions and therefore reduce duplication of functionality.

Split build file contents to improve management and understanding through a separation of concerns.

Improve refactoring possibilities and implementation details through the use of the above features.

As powerful as these tasks are, approach with caution. NAnt is generally very linear for two reasons: the way the current engine translates and uses a build file, and the lack of support for parallel execution that is present in NAnt.

A build file can be made relatively complex on its own through the use of conditionals and target dependencies and can be difficult to follow even with debug and verbose switches. Once build files are separated and begin to loop, the flow of the build process becomes even less obvious. As with collections of VBScripts database-stored procedures, XSLT, and other similar scripted code dependencies are not always easy to track and going forward it can be easy to introduce risk and rigidity into the delivery process—which is precisely the situation we were attempting to avoid.

■Tip Start small and refactor. The positive side of collections of scripts and the following tasks is that they can be implemented quickly. In my experience, avoiding a "big design" up front will help the implementation of a delivery process move more quickly, particularly if you are exploring the processes and their possibilities. This is the approach that will be used in the next few chapters.

Now, let us consider the tasks that are helpful structurally and how we are likely to apply them in our process.

<call> [NAnt]

This task can be used to call a target within a build file at any point in a build file. Efficiencies can be gained by calling a target multiple times with a different set of properties, as in this example:

```xml
<?xml version="1.0"?>
<project default="repeater">

    <target name="repeater">
        <property name="myparameter" value="foo" />
        <call target="generaltarget"/>
        <property name="myparameter" value="bar" />
        <call target="generaltarget" />
    </target>
```

```
    <target name="generaltarget">
        <echo message="Doing clever stuff with parameter $(myparameter}" />
    </target>

</project>
```

In practice, the <call> task can be used to recurse over some set of information. In the next example, <call> is used to check each folder within a folder by re-calling the original target until the end of the folder hierarchy is reached.

I would not recommend using this kind of function, but it demonstrates some possibilities:

```
<?xml version="1.0"?>
<project default="folderchecker">
        <property name="foldername" value="D:\dotNetDelivery\Assemblies"/>

        <target name="folderchecker">
            <foreach item="Folder" in="${foldername}" property="foldername">
                <echo message="${foldername}" />
                <call target="folderchecker"/>
            </foreach>
        </target>
</project>
```

Running this task would produce something like the following output, demonstrating the recursive call:

```
---------- NAnt ----------
NAnt 0.85
Copyright (C) 2001-2004 Gerry Shaw
http://nant.sourceforge.net

Buildfile: file:///Folderchecker.build
Target(s) specified: folderchecker

folderchecker:
    [echo] D:\dotNetDelivery\Assemblies\Etomic.Library.Transformer

folderchecker:
    [echo] D:\dotNetDelivery\Assemblies\Etomic.Library.Transformer\Deprecated

folderchecker:
    [echo] D:\dotNetDelivery\Assemblies\Etomic.Library.Transformer\Latest

folderchecker:
    [echo] D:\dotNetDelivery\Assemblies\Etomic.Library.Transformer\Specific

folderchecker:
    [echo] D:\dotNetDelivery\Assemblies\log4net
```

```
folderchecker:
    [echo] D:\dotNetDelivery\Assemblies\log4net\Deprectated

folderchecker:
    [echo] D:\dotNetDelivery\Assemblies\log4net\Latest

folderchecker:
    [echo] D:\dotNetDelivery\Assemblies\log4net\Specific

folderchecker:

BUILD SUCCEEDED
Total time: 0.1 seconds.
Output completed (1 sec consumed) - Normal Termination
```

\<nant> [NAnt]

This task allows the wholesale loading of another build file, and its full execution or the execution of a target or targets as required. Effectively, this task enables a build file to execute the NAnt command line itself.

The advantage of using this task is that the build file which is called can inherit all of the existing properties from the calling build file. This particular ability means that hierarchies of build files can be created and called from a common point. The flexibility here cannot be underestimated.

One practical use for this task is to generate a master NAnt file for a project and use it to set "master properties" for the project that all aspects of the build process might use. This master file would be the only build file to be called, and the parameters used to call it would determine how it would perform from there.

A further step would be to use a build file to maintain common properties across all projects. Here is a trimmed-down version of how this master file might look:

```xml
<?xml version="1.0" encoding="utf-8" ?>
<project name="Build.Master" default="help">

    <property name="core.basedir" value="D:\@Build\" />
    <property name="core.build" value="Build\" />
    <property name="core.distribution" value="Distribution\" />
    <property name="core.logs" value="Logs\" />
    <property name="core.documentation" value="Docs\" />
    <property name="core.source" value="Source\" />
    <!-- etc. a whole bunch of other properties -->

    <target name="build">
        <nant
            buildfile="${project.name}\Build.xml"
            target="go"
            inheritall="true"
```

```
        />
    </target>

    <!-- Other targets snipped -->
</project>
```

From this file, we can now invoke the build file for any of our projects—subject to their adherence to these standards—using this build file and a project name parameter:

```
nant -f:build.master.build -D:project.name=project1
```

This would ensure that the core properties—those used by all builds—are set correctly and that the correct project build is begun. The main advantage here is that changing the base directory for all activities requires a single modification to one file: this one.

In the previous example, I have simply used inheritall to pass the properties from the first script through to the second, but I could also include some other properties since the <nant> task accepts a set of properties as nested elements.

Note The called build file inherits the properties of the caller but cannot itself call any of the targets of the caller. This means that the process is still linear.

<loadtasks> [NAnt]

This task allows a build file to load in an assembly, or set of assemblies, from elsewhere other than the NAnt bin folder in order to execute contained tasks.

Therefore, this task does not affect the structure of the build files themselves but instead affects the structure of the code for NAnt, since different tasks (or versions of tasks) can be accessed from different locations.

In practice, I do not usually use this task because it adds to the overhead and risk of the build file itself. In principle, there is nothing wrong with using <loadtasks> to grab tasks from various locations, but I have a tendency to drop my completed customized assembly into the NAnt bin location instead.

The two uses I would put this task to are as follows:

When you are creating a new customized task, it is easy to use <loadtasks> to grab the Visual Studio–generated assembly each time rather than continuously copy the output to the NAnt bin folder. This is crucial for testing changes to existing tests too.

If I practice what I preach—and I should—then I will deploy my customized tasks to a central repository, where I can load them using <loadtasks> when I need them. This means I can specifically target versions of my customized task as well.

Using <loadtasks> is quite simple. Let us look at three broad options.

Loading a specific assembly such as a debug VS .NET–generated version would look like this:

```
<loadtasks assembly="D:\Projects\CustomSoln\MyTask\bin\debug\MyTask.dll" />
```

Loading a set of assemblies from a particular directory such as the latest versions of all of my custom tasks would look like this:

```
<loadtasks path="P:\Repository\CustomNAntTasks" />
```

Loading a set of specific assemblies such as targeted versions of my custom tasks would look like this (and notice here how <loadtasks> accepts a <fileset> type):

```
<loadtasks>
    <fileset>
        <include name="P:\Repository\CustomNAntTasks\DBTask_v1.dll" />
        <include name="P:\Repository\CustomNAntTasks\FxCopTask_v3.dll" />
    </fileset>
</loadtasks>
```

NAnt will give a response when it has found assemblies and is searching for NAnt tasks within the assembly:

```
---------- NAnt ----------
NAnt 0.85
Copyright (C) 2001-2004 Gerry Shaw
http://nant.sourceforge.net

Buildfile: file:///Loadtasks.build

[loadtasks] Scanning directory "D:\MyTasks\" for extension assemblies.
[loadtasks] Scanning assembly "NAntExtensions" for extensions.

BUILD SUCCEEDED
Total time: 0 seconds.
Output completed (0 sec consumed) - Normal Termination
```

Conditional Tasks

The conditional tasks follow on quite neatly from the structural tasks. Generally, they provide a similar flexibility but on a micro rather than a macro level. That is, conditionals are probably best used to provide flexibility within a target rather than a build file.

Once again, take care when using conditionals as part of the process. The effect of a conditional is to introduce new alternative paths to the process and the use cases comprising the process definition. Because NAnt is not easy to test in terms of process paths, the introduction of too many conditionals could lead to behaviors that are difficult to see during implementation.

■**Tip** I am being cautious about the introduction of conditionals and in fact I actually prefer the structural tasks as part of the overall process. This is mainly because I think that defining a process with too many branches and possibilities represents a weakness in the process itself; perhaps it should be a suite of processes instead.

<foreach> [NAnt]

We saw a useful example of the <foreach> task in our discussion of the <call> task earlier; we used it as part of our recursive call procedure. <foreach> is a useful task but has a limited set of looping possibilities, namely that it operates on a folder, a file, a string, or a line. Essentially this means that loops over files and folders are quite straightforward, but other less obvious loops tend to have to be thought about and managed carefully in order to get the best use out of <foreach>.

The previous example showed a simple implementation of <foreach>, but in fact the construct can be relatively involved because it accepts filesets as input.

<fail> [NAnt]

This is a useful debugging task. I generally would not use it explicitly in a production build file since it is easy enough to make a build file fail in the first place.

On the other hand, you may wish to double-check some important property prior to beginning any build activities and instruct the build to fail if some explicit setting is not present—for example, if no project name is being passed to the master build file. In other words, it simply is not worth continuing until failure if certain conditions are not met. <fail> is a useful task to combine with the <if> and <ifnot> tasks.

<if> [NAnt] and <ifnot> [NAnt]

In addition to <fail>, a useful check in the master build file is as follows:

```
<ifnot test="${property::exists('project.name')}">
    <fail message="Please enter a project.name to run this file." />
</ifnot>
```

This will avoid any unnecessary debugging where a parameter that is required has not been used by the caller of the build file. It can be especially useful when build files are being chained and called by each other.

The code in bold is a slight departure from anything we have seen so far and makes use of built-in functions from NAnt. We will look at these functions later in the chapter. For now, the result of running the previous script (without a project.name property) is as follows:

```
---------- NAnt ----------
NAnt 0.85
Copyright (C) 2001-2004 Gerry Shaw
http://nant.sourceforge.net
```

```
Buildfile: file:///IfNot.build

BUILD FAILED

IfNot.build(4,7):
Please enter a project.name to run this file.

Total time: 0 seconds.
Output completed (0 sec consumed) - Normal Termination
```

File Tasks

Undoubtedly you will not be surprised to learn that the file tasks are among the most popular since they are used across all of the process: creating and cleaning the environment, moving inputs and outputs, assembling structures for distribution, and so on.

File tasks are quite easy to understand; they are largely analogous to the DOS commands of the same or similar names.

■Tip You can really learn to love these tasks. As I became NAnt-infected (to borrow a term) I quickly realized that I could automate many mundane tasks to clean up the environment, gather reports, and so on.

<attrib> [NAnt]

This task allows a build file to change a file attribute, for example, the readonly attribute. The task is useful when you want to manipulate files that have been grabbed from source control. In the next example, we can see that a specific file is made writable in order to manipulate it and then made read-only once the operation is completed. As you might be able to tell from the code, this task might come in useful for versioning.

```
<?xml version="1.0"?>
<project>
    <attrib file="${core.source}\CommonAssemblyInfo.cs" readonly="false" />
        <!--Do some clever things with the now writable file-->
    <attrib file="${core.source}\CommonAssemblyInfo.cs" readonly="true" />
</project>
```

<copy> [NAnt], <delete> [NAnt], and <move> [NAnt]

These tasks represent the core file-manipulation tasks. What more could you want? They generally behave in the same way: they are able to accept a single file for manipulation or they can accept a fileset. Our first example shows a useful function for cleaning up web code and removing all of the unnecessary source and source control material from the web code:

```xml
<?xml version="1.0"?>
<project>
    <copy todir="D:\CleanFolder\">
        <fileset basedir="D:\DirtyFolder">
            <include name="**"/>
            <exclude name="**\*.cs"/>
            <exclude name="**\*.resx"/>
            <exclude name="**\*.csproj"/>
            <exclude name="**\*.vspscc"/>
            <exclude name="**\*.scc"/>
        </fileset>
    </copy>
</project>
```

Remember to look back at the previous descriptions of `fileset` and `filterset` types in this chapter to explain the symbols used here.

The next example shows a simpler use of the `<delete>` task to remove a specific file. In this instance, we are looking to regenerate the CREATE script:

```xml
<?xml version="1.0"?>
<project>
    <delete file="${core.source}DB-Create.sql"/>
</project>
```

The `<copy>` task and the `<move>` task can perform some token replacement using a `filterchain` type. The following simple `<copy>` task demonstrates the use of the `filterchain` described earlier:

```xml
<?xml version="1.0"?>
<project>

<copy file="template.txt" tofile="specific.txt">
    <filterchain>
        <replacetokens>
            <token key="DRIVELETTER" value="D" />
        </replacetokens>
    </filterchain>
</copy>

</project>
```

The file `template.txt` contains the following text:

```
I should be deployed to the @DRIVELETTER@ drive.
```

Although I have used a text file for the sample, this could easily be a build file itself or any other file where the token could be embedded. Running the build file results in the following output:

```
---------- NAnt ----------
NAnt 0.85
Copyright (C) 2001-2004 Gerry Shaw
http://nant.sourceforge.net

Buildfile: file:///CopyFilterchain.build

    [copy] Copying 1 file to 'D:\dotNetDelivery\Chapter3\specific.txt'.

BUILD SUCCEEDED
Total time: 0.1 seconds.
Output completed (1 sec consumed) - Normal Termination
```

A very trivial <copy> task has completed correctly. More importantly, though, the content of the specific.txt file has been updated to read as follows:

```
I should be deployed to the D drive.
```

Filter-chaining is another powerful feature of NAnt when used across many files.

■Tip In Chapter 9, we show how to use code generation to save effort on script maintenance (among other uses). Using filterchains for token replacement is a good first step in the generation effort, though clearly not as sophisticated as XSLT or other full generation techniques.

<mkdir> [NAnt]

An operation missing from our earlier discussion is of course the ability to make folders; the <delete> task handles the reverse.

The following example will in fact create the entire folder tree specified rather than fail if one of the parent folders does not exist:

```xml
<?xml version="1.0"?>
<project>
        <mkdir dir="D:\Folder\SubFolder" />
</project>
```

One way to take advantage of the <mkdir> task is in the initial construction of the build or deploy environment. For this reason, we will sometimes use it with the failonerror switch set to false since in fact we are just checking that the environment exists and, for once, we may not want the build file to produce an error if it does.

<get> [NAnt]

This task is useful for obtaining assets when we begin to deploy the constructed systems. It accepts a URL and a folder destination to move the URL content to. Also included are options for adding proxy and credentials settings to the <get> if required.

```
<?xml version="1.0"?>
<project>
    <target name="getresources">
        <get
            dest="D:\SomeFolder\"
            src="http://someurl.com/myassets.zip"
        />
    </target>
<project>
```

The ability to use <get> to obtain resources guides our hand slightly when considering how best to organize and manage the constructed systems. Of course, a <copy> could also be used if the Web is not to be used for this purpose.

Build Tasks

The build tasks form the kernel of the actual solution for building and deploying. They tend to be very specific and also sometimes quite lengthy to script. This is because the tasks have to adapt to whatever nonautomated solution they come across and so it is not always possible to make this translation concise. Also, the activities themselves may be complex or full of options.

The good news is that once you have mastered how to use these tasks, that is usually that—there are not many other ways to use it, and also the task tends to solve a significant part of a process: building a solution or outputting a set of test cases, for example.

■**Note** I have included the <exec> task in this section as well. I think that in reality this is a utility task because it can be turned to many uses, but in practice it is generally used to execute some specific command-line utility that is required for the core process and so is appropriate to this section.

<asminfo> [NAnt]

The first task in this section is a good example of a specific task. The one clear goal of the <asminfo> task is to generate an assemblyinfo.cs style of file, containing assembly-level attributes.

The following example shows a simple example of the <asminfo> task. Notice how the task is quite involved owing to its specific requirements:

```
<?xml version="1.0"?>
<project>
    <asminfo output="CommonAssemblyInfo.cs" language="CSharp">
        <imports>
```

```
            <import name="System" />
            <import name="System.Reflection"/>
            <import name="System.EnterpriseServices"/>
            <import name="System.Runtime.InteropServices"/>
        </imports>
        <attributes>
            <attribute
                type="AssemblyVersionAttribute" value="1.0.0.0" />
            <attribute
                type="AssemblyProductAttribute" value="MyProduct" />
            <attribute
                type="AssemblyCopyrightAttribute"
                value="Copyright (c) 2005, Etomic Ltd."/>
        </attributes>
        <references>
            <include name="System.EnterpriseServices.dll" />
        </references>
    </asminfo>
</project>
```

Running this task results in the production of a file called CommonAssemblyInfo.cs containing the following code:

```
using System;
using System.Reflection;
using System.EnterpriseServices;
using System.Runtime.InteropServices;


//------------------------------------------------------------------------------
// <autogenerated>
//     This code was generated by a tool.
//     Runtime Version: 1.1.4322.573
//
//     Changes to this file may cause incorrect behavior and will be lost if
//     the code is regenerated.
// </autogenerated>
//------------------------------------------------------------------------------

[assembly: AssemblyVersionAttribute("1.0.0.0")]
[assembly: AssemblyProductAttribute("MyProduct")]
[assembly: AssemblyCopyrightAttribute("Copyright (c) 2005, Etomic Ltd.")]
```

We can use this task to generate version numbers during the build process, and in itself, this task can solve one aspect of the proposed process almost single-handedly.

<exec> [NAnt]

As mentioned earlier, in the event that NAnt does not have an available task to complete a specific action, then the first port of call would be to use the <exec> task. The second approach might be to go right ahead and create a custom task, but this takes a little longer than using a command-line option if it is available.

A good example of using the <exec> task is the automatic production of FxCop (see Appendix A) reports for assemblies. Calling the command line can be done like this:

```
<?xml version="1.0"?>
<project>
    <exec
        program="C:\Program Files\Microsoft FxCop 1.21\FxCopCmd.exe"
        commandline="/f:MyAssembly.dll /o:fxcop.xml /r:D:\MyRules\"
        failonerror="false" />
</project>
```

The effect of this script is to produce an XML-based report called fxcop.xml by reviewing MyAssembly.dll with the rules held in the D:\MyRules folder.

Although the <exec> task fills in a gap, it is not especially pretty or intuitive. Moreover, assembling the command line in a more dynamic fashion may be difficult. In Chapter 7, we will see another way of tackling the FxCop problem, but for the time being, and throughout our work, it is useful to have this option at our disposal.

<mkiisdir> [NAntContrib]

A useful task for solving deployment issues, this task can come in handy when a new virtual directory is required on the web server. A huge number of attributes are available for this task because of the number of options for directory configuration in Internet Information Server (IIS). The simplest example, which can sometimes suffice, is shown here:

```
<?xml version="1.0"?>
<project>
    <mkdir dir="D:\Deploy\MySite"/>
    <mkiisdir
        dirpath="D:\Deploy\MySite"
        vdirname="MySite"/>
</project>
```

Here we have combined the creation of the physical folder with the virtual folder. This task has related siblings: iisdirinfo, which reports on the settings of an IIS virtual directory, and deliisdir, which deletes an IIS virtual directory. Both may also be useful for deployment purposes.

<ndoc> [NAnt]

This is another specific and wordy task, as our next example shows. If you have used the NDoc package as a stand-alone tool, then you will see the similarity to the user interface for NDoc.

If you are unfamiliar with NDoc, you should know that it can be used to create extremely presentable MSDN-style documentation in web or compiled HTML (CHM) formats from the XML documentation capabilities of the C# language. NAnt comes with a version of the core NDoc assembly, and this task can be used to perform the same action:

```
<?xml version="1.0"?>
<project>
    <ndoc>
        <assemblies basedir="D:\MySystem\">
            <includes name="MyAssembly.dll" />
        </assemblies>
        <summaries basedir="D:\MySystem\">
            <includes name="MyAssembly.xml" />
        </summaries>
        <documenters>
            <documenter name="MSDN">
                <property name="OutputDirectory" value="D:\MyDocs\" />
                <property name="HtmlHelpName" value="MyProject" />
                <property
                    name="HtmlHelpCompilerFilename" value="hhc.exe" />
                <property name="IncludeFavorites" value="False" />
                <property name="Title" value="MySystem (NDoc)" />
                <property name="SplitTOCs" value="False" />
                <property name="DefaulTOC" value="" />
                <property name="ShowVisualBasic" value="False" />
                <property name="ShowMissingSummaries" value="True" />
                <property name="ShowMissingRemarks" value="False" />
                <property name="ShowMissingParams" value="True" />
                <property name="ShowMissingReturns" value="True" />
                <property name="ShowMissingValues" value="True" />
                <property name="DocumentInternals" value="True" />
                <property name="DocumentProtected" value="True" />
                <property name="DocumentPrivates" value="False" />
                <property name="DocumentEmptyNamespaces" value="False" />
                <property name="IncludeAssemblyVersion" value="True" />
                <property name="CopyrightText" value="Etomic 2005" />
                <property name="CopyrightHref" value="" />
            </documenter>
        </documenters>
    </ndoc>
</project>
```

The generated documentation can then be distributed or displayed by moving the output appropriately. The clever part about the <ndoc> task is that the XML used in the NAnt task is the same as the relevant part of the NDoc project that can be used through the NDoc graphical user interface (GUI) to produce documentation independently. Of course, this also makes it quite lengthy, but given the context of the required settings, that is probably unavoidable.

<nunit2> [NAnt]

The <nunit2> task is similar to the previous task in the sense that it is specifically included to automate another popular tool: NUnit. The purpose of NUnit is to provide a unit testing execution library and execution environment for the tests. Ordinarily, a developer would use the NUnit GUI or console to run his/her tests. In an automated environment, a different mechanism is needed.

The task generally has the same available options as the command-line facilities of NUnit. The following example shows a common use of the task—to run tests over an assembly and then output the results as an XML file:

```
<?xml version="1.0"?>
<project>
    <nunit2>
        <formatter
            type="Xml"
            usefile="true"
            extension=".xml"
            outputdir="D:\MyTests\" />
        <test assemblyname="MyTestAssembly.dll" />
    </nunit2>
</project>
```

<nunit2> is a good example of a task that could have been run using the <exec> task since NUnit has excellent command-line facilities, but it has been deemed important enough to warrant a specific task. In contrast to the <ndoc> task, the <nunit2> task does not follow the same XML format as an NUnit project.

<solution> [NAnt]

Thank goodness for this task. The <solution> task can accept a solution file as a parameter and then generate and execute the required actions to build the solution according to dependencies, references, and any other support you would expect from the Visual Studio environment itself—in theory, at least. In practice, the <solution> task constantly has problems reported against it. The task has gradually been improving since version 0.84 of NAnt, but it tries to cover a lot of ground and new scenarios appear that it cannot handle.

However, you will find it useful for rapid automation of most solutions, because it will in fact handle most regular scenarios suitably—general projects and dependencies are usually OK. From my own experience I have found that it has had problems with .licx files and Seagate's Crystal Reports. The cause of the issues stem from two areas:

The "unusual" format of .sln files. Unfortunately, VS .NET does not use XML for everything it does, so a judicious use of RegEx parsing and the like has been employed to translate .sln and then .csproj files—the latter does support XML (sort of).

VS .NET appears to help the compiler in various ways so in fact the C# compiler does not behave in precisely the same way that a build through VS .NET would.

Undoubtedly, these problems will be fixed in Visual Studio 2005 since Microsoft is launching its own build tool, MSBuild, but it is worth bearing in mind that <solution> may not be a panacea for compilation.

Another case in which you would not want to use the <solution> task is when you are not using VS .NET and therefore the solution structures do not exist.

Once again, there are a variety of possibilities for the application of this task, but the following are two common examples. The first shows a standard library, console, or Windows solution build:

```
<?xml version="1.0"?>
<project>
    <solution
        solutionfile="MyLibrary.sln"
        configuration="debug"
        outputdir="D:\MyLibrary" />
</project>
```

The task will recognize dependencies and build orders from the solution file and will output the compiled assembly or assemblies in the specified debug configuration to the specified output directory.

Because of the way that Visual Studio handles web projects, using the <solution> task becomes more involved since we need to map the URL of the web project or projects to the physical location. This is shown in the following example:

```
<?xml version="1.0"?>
<project>
    <solution
        solutionfile="MySite.sln"
        configuration="debug"
        outputdir="D:\MySite">
            <webmap>
                <map
                    url="http://localhost/MySite.csproj"
                    path="D:\MySourceCode\MySite\UI.csproj" />
            </webmap>
    </solution>
</project>
```

Regardless of the slight additional complexity, this task saves a significant amount of effort when you are creating a build file. In fact, the actual building of a general system is usually trivial—it is all the supporting activities that seem to take the time!

My advice is to try the <solution> task to see if you can use the available power it has and then move to the <csc> <vbc>, or similar task for other languages as required.

One other issue with using the <solution> task is that some of the required build configuration is moved out of NAnt and into the hands of the solution developer. We will see this in action in Chapters 4 and 5 as we put a build process into practice. We will discuss this issue a little more then, but it is worth raising now.

I do not want to be too critical of this task—I use it constantly—but it is worth understanding the implications. You may find, as I have, that in fact it does the job very nicely for your systems.

\<csc\> [NAnt]

Having just discussed the \<solution\> task, we should also look at the \<csc\> task. Also bear in mind that there are equivalent tasks for Visual Basic .NET (\<vbc\>), C++ (\<cl\>), JScript .NET (\<jsc\>), and J# (\<vjc\>). The \<csc\> task gives you control over the command-line compiler for the .NET language of your choice, removing the VS .NET–introduced extras such as the solution and project constructs, and thus gives us a more controlled build. This, of course, is the compiler option of choice for anyone using open source tools for .NET development but should probably be your choice if you are using VS .NET in any case.

The following \<csc\> code is from the NAnt documentation:

```
<csc target="exe" output="HelloWorld.exe"
    debug="true" doc="HelloWorld.xml">
    <nowarn>
        <!-- do not report warnings for missing XML comments -->
        <warning number="0519" />
    </nowarn>
    <sources>
        <include name="**/*.cs" />
    </sources>
    <resources dynamicprefix="true" prefix="HelloWorld">
        <include name="**/*.resx" />
    </resources>
    <references>
        <include name="System.dll" />
        <include name="System.Data.dll" />
    </references>
</csc>
```

As you can see, there is a considerable amount of XML even for what is presumably a trivial application. However, as we learned earlier when discussing \<solution\>, we now have full control over the compiler.

Additionally, as we discussed, certain solution-specific settings are now controlled within NAnt instead of relying on the VS .NET settings (and therefore the individual developer) to maintain or implement build standards. Examples, which appear in bold in the code, include the documentation output and the warning suppression, and even the name of the output assemblies. Using the \<solution\> task precludes the use and control of these switches.

The downside, as you might expect, is that maintaining the \<csc\> tasks as part of the build process can become onerous for large projects. The rub here is that with Visual Studio .NET 2005, MSBuild will likely seek to remove this shortcoming from its own build process, and so if it wants to continue competing with Microsoft for the build process space, NAnt should do the same. Otherwise, the risk is that NAnt will be confined to open source development because MSBuild is "simpler." This is a one-dimensional argument in this specific context but will become more significant over time.

As you might expect, the <csc> task has many options and arguments for control. We will be focusing on the use of the <solution> task throughout the book, so you will need to explore these for yourself. If you are accustomed to the command-line compiler, then this should not be a problem. You will probably find yourself working with a number of supporting tasks such as <license> and <tlbimp> to better support the command-line compiler options.

Utility Tasks

The utility tasks are a little less specific than build tasks, but they still perform some important functions. The difference is that these tasks can usually have several purposes depending on the context they are applied to in the build file.

■**Tip** These tasks are also really handy for day-to-day automation of activities.

<echo> [NAnt]

We have already covered the <echo> task in detail. Do not forget about this task when creating scripts; often the output to the console or log is the best source of information when things go wrong (or even right).

Apart from simply displaying a message, an <echo> task can have a log level set in the same way as regular log messages. These can be Debug, Verbose, Info, Warning, or Error, with the default being Info.

<style> [NAnt]

This task has a straightforward purpose: it takes an XML and an XSLT file and uses both to produce the relevant output. Some tasks that output XML have an option for performing this action as part of the task, but it is useful to know that this step can be managed independently. The following example shows a typical use:

```
<?xml version="1.0"?>
<project>
    <style
        style="FxCopReport.xsl"
        in="FxCop.xml"
        out="FxCop.html"/>
</project>
```

<zip> [NAnt] and <unzip> [NAnt]

The utility that these tasks provide is quite obvious. As you can imagine, zipping and unzipping of assets is a useful action when we are handling build and deploy processes. These tasks can be managed simply. The <zip> task also accepts a fileset as a more complex activity.

Let us look at a couple of ways you could use these tasks. One is to place assets in a suitable location:

```
<?xml version="1.0"?>
<project>
    <unzip
        zipfile="MyAssets.zip"
        todir="D:\Deploy\"/>
</project>
```

Our second example shows the creation of a zip file with a simple fileset:

```
<?xml version="1.0"?>
<project>
    <zip zipfile="MyAssets.zip">
        <fileset basedir="D:\MyAssets\">
            <include name="**" />
        </fileset>
    </zip>
</project>
```

<xmlpeek> [NAnt] and <xmlpoke> [NAnt]

These tasks accept an XPath query and can retrieve or update the value at the node found by the query.

We can use <xmlpeek> to set initial properties from an XML file rather than from the command line. We can use <xmlpoke> to configure a deployed system, as the following example demonstrates. Given a .config file of this structure:

```
<?xml version="1.0" encoding="utf-8"?>
<configuration>
    <appSettings>
        <add key="MyKey" value="MyValue" />
    </appSettings>
</configuration>
```

the following will update the value of MyKey:

```
<?xml version="1.0"?>
<project>
    <xmlpoke
        file="app.config"
        xpath="/configuration/appSettings/add[@key='MyKey']/@value"
        value="SomeValue" />
</project>
```

The script output looks like this:

```
---------- NAnt ----------
NAnt 0.85
Copyright (C) 2001-2004 Gerry Shaw
http://nant.sourceforge.net

Buildfile: file:///XmlPoke.build

 [xmlpoke] Found '1' nodes matching XPath expression
'/configuration/appSettings/add[@key='MyKey']/@value'.

BUILD SUCCEEDED
Total time: 0.1 seconds.
Output completed (0 sec consumed) - Normal Termination
```

The app.config file now looks like this:

```
<?xml version="1.0" encoding="utf-8"?>
<configuration>
  <appSettings>
    <add key="MyKey" value="SomeValue" />
  </appSettings>
</configuration>
```

To retrieve the new value to a property called xml.property, we can use the following:

```
<?xml version="1.0"?>
<project>
    <xmlpeek
        file="app.config"
        xpath="/configuration/appSettings/add[@key='MyKey']/@value"
        property="xml.property" />
</project>
```

For one or two properties, this can be a very useful technique, but when we have several properties, maintaining the XPath queries may become onerous. We will explore this and other techniques for this kind of work when we consider deployment issues in more depth.

Source Control Tasks

As I mentioned earlier, I use Visual SourceSafe (VSS) in my current role and therefore have much greater experience with VSS than any other source control system. The set of tasks here describe the commands that we can use for VSS, but there are similar tasks for other source control systems in NAnt and NAntContrib. In particular, NAnt and NAntContrib provide tasks analogous to those described here for CVS, Subversion, StarTeam, and other software configuration management systems.

<vssget> [NAntContrib]

This is the first VSS task we will use. It obtains the source code from the VSS database, which is the first step in the proposed build process. As you can see, the task is relatively self-explanatory; in fact, all of the VSS tasks are structured in the same way.

The following example shows a straightforward get of some source code:

```xml
<?xml version="1.0"?>
<project>
    <vssget
        user="builder"
        password="builder"
        localpath="D:\SourceCode"
        recursive="true"
        replace="true"
        dbpath="D:\VSS\srcsafe.ini"
        path="$/MySolution/" />
</project>
```

In this instance, the user `builder` needs only read-only access to the VSS database.

<vsscheckin> [NAntContrib] and <vsscheckout> [NAntContrib]

Although we will make less use of these tasks, they do have their place. Say we want to maintain a copy of the latest database schema for a system as part of the build process. In this case, we may want to check out, regenerate, and check in a file containing the schema. The check-in part of this would look like the following; you can see the similarity to the previous task:

```xml
<?xml version="1.0"?>
<project>
    <vsscheckin
        user="builder"
        password="builder"
        localpath="D:\SourceCode\DB-Create.sql"
        recursive="false"
        dbpath="D:\VSS\srcsafe.ini"
        path="$/MySolution/DB-Create.sql" />
</project>
```

In this instance, the user `builder` needs write access to the VSS database.

<vsslabel> [NAntContrib]

As part of our efforts to provide versioning for a system, the `<vsslabel>` task lets us handle the source control side of the problem. A labeling task implementation may look like this:

```xml
<?xml version="1.0"?>
<project>
    <vsslabel
        user="builder"
```

```
        password="builder"
        dbpath="D:\VSS\srcsafe.ini"
        path="$/"
        comment="Automated Label"
        label="v1.0.0.0" />
</project>
```

<vssundocheckout> [NAntContrib]

As you might recall from our earlier discussion of database scripts, in the event of a failure during the generation of the database script, the consequence for the system is that the DB-Create.sql file will remain checked out in VSS, which in turn means that all subsequent attempts to execute the build file will result in an error since the <vsscheckout> task will fail.

To recover from this, we can use the <vssundocheckout> task to restore the state and try once more.

Special NAnt Tasks

Apart from tasks, NAnt has a couple of other ways of performing actions inside a build script. These methods open up further options for handling certain aspects of the build process.

NAnt Functions

First, NAnt comes with a built-in set of functions to be used in build scripts. We came across an example of a function call in the <ifnot> task example earlier in this chapter. NAnt functions cover a variety of areas, such as date- and time-, folder- and file-, environmental-, and NAnt-specific functions. There are many functions, and the list continues to grow. Table 3-3 shows the list of functions available under the file category.

Table 3-3. *NAnt File Functions*

Function	Description
file::exists	Determines whether the specified file exists
file::get-creation-time	Returns the creation time and date of the specified file
file::get-last-access-time	Returns the date and time the specified file was last accessed
file::get-last-write-time	Returns the date and time the specified file was last written to
file::get-length	Gets the length of the file
file::is-assembly	Checks if a given file is an assembly
file::up-to-date	Determines whether *targetFile* is as up-to-date (or more current) than *sourceFile*

These functions can be used to perform tests as shown in the <ifnot> example, or perhaps to perform tests on the if and unless attributes of properties and tasks. The functions help us carry out decision-making and conditional processing within a NAnt script.

We can revisit the `<ifnot>` task to see how a function is called:

```
<ifnot test="${property::exists('project.name')}">
    <fail message="Please enter a project.name to run this file." />
</ifnot>
```

Within the `test` attribute, the function call must return a Boolean value or the script cannot be processed. Next the `${}` (dollar, curly brace, curly brace) syntax is used to encapsulate the function call with the `::` (colon, colon) notation, differentiating the function type and specific method. Finally, if you are using a property name inside a function call (which is very likely), then the property name should be wrapped in `' '` (single quotes).

Functions also support the use of operators such as equals, less than, add, and subtract. The following function, which must also return a Boolean, is straight from the NAnt documentation and uses three functions to determine whether to call the `<csc>` task. In this case, the criterion for calling the task is whether the assembly has been written to (in other words, generated) in the last hour:

```
<csc target="library" output="out.dll"
    if="${datetime::now() - file::get-last-write-time('out.dll')) > ➡
    timespan::from-hours(1)}">
...
</csc>
```

In this example, the operators are in bold. The NAnt documentation contains up-to-date information on available functions and operators.

Keep in mind, as usual, that the introduction of functions such as these into build scripts imbues the scripts with some domain logic, or basis for decision making, rather than just containing process logic. In fact, there will always be a need to have this sort of functionality, but do be mindful of the complexity, and therefore risk, introduced here.

Script Tasks

In Chapter 7 we will see how NAnt can be extended, and how easy this can be, through the creation of assemblies that NAnt can load and reflect over (using the `<loadtasks>` task). NAnt can also be extended more simply through the use of a script task.

A script task is the embedding of code within a build file using C# or another .NET language (except C++). The code can then be executed as a target or as a function call, depending on the implementation. These two implementation possibilities can be seen in the following Hello World script tasks.

First, we can define a function that returns a string (`"Hello World!"` in this case) within a build file. Consider the following build file:

```
<?xml version="1.0"?>
<project>
    <script language="C#" prefix="etomic" >
    <code><![CDATA[
        [Function("hello-world")]
        public static string HelloWorld()
        {
```

```
            return "Hello World!";
        }
    ]]></code>
    </script>

    <echo message='${etomic::hello-world()}'/>
</project>
```

In this file we create a script block using the `<script>` task, which contains a code element with the actual C# code. In this case we are using a simple method to return a string. We have placed an attribute on the method to make NAnt aware of the function and its name. Additionally, we have included a prefix for the code functions: although there is only one here, the script block could conceivably contain many functions. Therefore, when the function is called in the `<echo>` task, it is called with `prefix::function-name` notation, in other words `etomic::hello-world`.

We have not required any other namespaces, but in fact the `<script>` task supports nested elements for imports and references and by default supports the following namespaces: `System`, `System.Collections`, `System.Collections.Specialized`, `System.IO`, `System.Text`, `System.Text.RegularExpressions`, and `NAnt.Core`.

The output from the execution of the build file is as follows:

```
---------- NAnt ----------
NAnt 0.85
Copyright (C) 2001-2004 Gerry Shaw
http://nant.sourceforge.net

Buildfile: file:///ScriptFunction.build

    [script] Scanning assembly "2qn-tswa" for extensions.
      [echo] Hello World!

BUILD SUCCEEDED
Total time: 0.2 seconds.
Output completed (0 sec consumed) - Normal Termination
```

As the output shows, NAnt compiles the code into a temporary assembly and then loads the assembly for use throughout the build file. You can then see the correct execution of the function as part of the `<echo>` task call.

The next type of script task is the creation of an actual target. This is analogous to the creation of an actual custom task. This time, we need to add a little extra scaffolding to the build script. Consider the following:

```
<?xml version="1.0"?>
<project>
    <target name="HelloWorld">
        <script language="C#">
        <code><![CDATA[
        public static void ScriptMain(Project project)
```

```
    {
        project.Log(Level.Info, "Hello World!");
    }
    ]]></code>
    </script>
</target>
```

```
<call target="HelloWorld"/>
</project>
```

This time we have wrapped the `<script>` task in a `target` element. We have also created a public static void method accepting a `project` type as part of (or in this case as the entirety) of the script. We need this `ScriptMain` method as the main entry point in order for a `<script>` task to be used in this way. Having the `project` type available means that you have access to all the aspects of the current build file.

To invoke the `<script>` task, we simply call the wrapping target.

The output from the execution of this target is as follows:

```
---------- NAnt ----------
NAnt 0.85
Copyright (C) 2001-2004 Gerry Shaw
http://nant.sourceforge.net


Buildfile: file:///ScriptTarget.build


HelloWorld:

    [script] Scanning assembly "zp3qshtq" for extensions.
Hello World!

BUILD SUCCEEDED
Total time: 0.2 seconds.
Output completed (1 sec consumed) - Normal Termination
```

The output is similar, as you might expect, but syntactic and semantic differences exist in the two scenarios that can be used appropriately.

Although the examples here are trivial, very complex tasks can be performed in this way. The main challenge of script tasks involves the debugging of C# in the build file, which is not easy. I recommend that once a script moves beyond anything other than a utility that you compile it into an actual assembly to remove risk and complexity from the build file itself and to enhance the clarity of its purpose.

Tip If you would like to see some serious use of functions and script tasks, turn to Appendix B for some NAntsweeping fun.

Summary

It has taken a little time to examine the features and specifics of NAnt, but you should now be feeling confident with the tool. At this point, you should be capable of producing effective scripts. More important, we hope we have whetted your appetite to tackle the issues our process presents even if you are not quite sure of the exact implementation details.

As far as implementation details, this chapter has explored specific tasks and the basis for simple solutions.

We will now move forward and apply our process to an actual system using NAnt. This approach is aligned with the Design to Deliver initiative that we introduced in Chapter 2; we will identify a suitable simple candidate and implement the process with only this candidate in mind initially.

■■■

CHAPTER 4

A Simple Case Study

At last we can get our teeth into a real-world delivery scenario. We have taken some time to get to this point and now we can reap the benefits.

In this chapter, we will look at a sample application and construct the build and deploy files specifically for this application. We will not focus on core standards at this point, though we will highlight areas that may be worth consideration. (The next chapter investigates these standards in detail.)

To work through the scenario, we will first examine the application that we will apply our scripts to. Then we will develop use cases to build and deploy to ensure that our scripts cover the processes in the way we want. After we have organized some environment issues, we will finally run through the detailed process of creating the required scripts.

At the end of this chapter we will have an application that has been fully automated in terms of simple delivery, precisely as required by the Design to Deliver initiative from Chapter 1.

Examining the Application

The application that we will automate is quite simple and does not contain complicated features, such as a database, that require detailed discussion. It is entirely .NET-based.

Let us imagine for a moment that this is the latest offering from the Etomic workshop. It is possibly too much to imagine that the application will be a true money-spinner(!) for the hardworking development outfit, but regardless, the same effort should be made to ensure efficient delivery of the application.

Note All of the solution-based code for the book is stored in the Visual SourceSafe (VSS) database that comes with the source code for this book. This is because we will integrate with VSS as part of the delivery processes. You can find a copy of the same source code, unbound from the VSS database, in the Projects folder of the source code for this book.

What Does It Do?

The application, called Transformer, is quite straightforward. It accepts some XML and XSLT input and can be used to show the results of the transformation on demand. Additionally, it can save and load the XML and XSLT snippets for later use. Figure 4-1 shows the main form for the application.

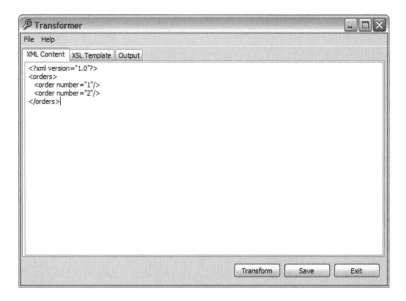

Figure 4-1. *The Transformer application*

The solution itself comprises three projects:

TransformerEngine. This project consists of the actual logic for providing transformation services: it's a very simple service.

TransformerGui. This project provides a Windows Forms GUI for the transformation services and consists of one form and a couple of dialog boxes.

TransformerTests. This project contains the unit tests for the application, focused entirely on unit testing of the TransformerEngine assembly.

So, as we had already mentioned, it is quite a simple application. Aside from the excellent source code that makes up the solution, notice that the developer has taken the time to

Provide unit tests for the solution

Fully utilize the C# XML-commenting capabilities across the solution

Ensure a good degree of FxCop compliancy across the solution

All of these features of the solution are important in terms of fulfilling the requirements of the build process. Since these activities are already completed, or at least under way, our life will be made easier during the scripting process. We will see the outputs of these features using NAnt, but we can also investigate them outside the automated process. This is not an exhaustive list of analytical possibilities by any means, but these are the activities that comply with the requirements of our process. Other possibilities include analysis of software metrics, such as the depth of conditional decision making, and other such measures of complexity, unit testing coverage, and so on.

The best way to see the outputs is to open the solution file and perform a build. Once we do, we can use tools to see the results of the efforts by the developer. A project for NUnit, NDoc, and FxCop is included in the solution items area for this solution.

■**Note** We use the following software: NUnit v2.2, NDoc v1.2, and FxCop v1.30. The source code for the book includes these tools under the `Tools` folder, and they should be ready to use.

The Unit Tests

Providing unit tests for a solution is not a matter of pointing the NUnit GUI at the compiled assembly and hoping for the best; the unit tests must be written by the developer(s) as part of the development of the system. In fact, if you subscribe to the Test-Driven Development concept, then the unit tests become the description of the system in many ways. A unit test for the Transformer application looks like this:

```
[Test]
public void TestGetAll()
{
    DeleteAllTransformations();

    Transformation t = new Transformation();
    t.Output = "aaa";
    t.Title  = "aaa";
    t.Xml  = "aaa";
    t.Xslt  = "aaa";
    t.Save();
    t.Save();
    t.Save();

    ApplicationEngine engine = new ApplicationEngine();
    IList transforms = engine.GetAllTransformations();

    Assert.IsTrue(transforms.Count == 3);
}
```

This code is C#, but by referencing the NUnit framework assembly, we can apply an attribute to the code that allows the NUnit executable to identify the method as a test method. Other attributes exist to identify methods as those that set up a testing scenario, reset a testing scenario, or perform the same actions for groups of tests.

This unit test removes all currently saved transformations from the database and then saves three "garbage" transformations as test data. Then an "assertion" class (provided by NUnit) is used to check that all three transformations are returned when requested, thus proving at least one part of the code—the testing activities—works. Testing the database can be handled in a few ways, and other methods may be more appropriate to your own needs.

There are many nuances to the art of unit testing that are best explained elsewhere and in full. A good source of information can be found in James Newkirk's book *Test-Driven Development in Microsoft .NET* (see Further Reading at the end of this chapter).

Opening up the NUnit project with the NUnit GUI allows us to run the limited unit tests. You should see the screen in Figure 4-2 with all of the lights green when the tests are run.

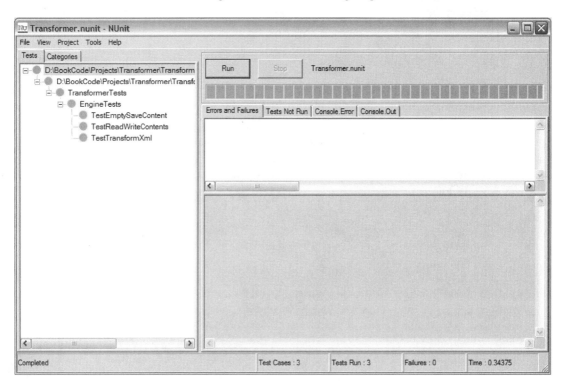

Figure 4-2. *NUnit test results*

Knowing that the current suite of unit tests runs correctly is important because any failures would prevent the build process from completing successfully.

The XML Documentation

We can use NDoc to transform the XML comments made in the code into compiled HTML or other types of documentation. The Transformer.ndoc project demonstrates the settings for NDoc used by the developer. NDoc has many settings and does a great job of ensuring your code documentation looks the way you want it. You can place XML code like the following above a method, class, or other code construct:

```
/// <summary>
/// Gets the XML to be used for the transformation.
/// </summary>
public string Xml
{
    get { return _xml; }
    set { _xml = ReplaceNullString(value); }
}
```

NDoc can transform the XML that is present in the source code (across all of the source code) in the way you choose to describe in NDoc to produce the documentation. The documentation is usually output as HTML but can also be output as the regular Windows Compile HTML (CHM) files you might expect with professional applications.

Opening the project file in NDoc produces output similar to that shown in Figure 4-3. Once again, it is useful to know that no significant problems were encountered with the production of this material.

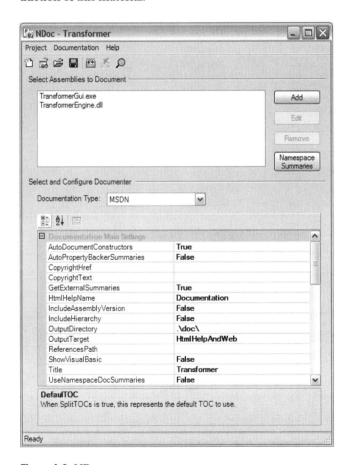

Figure 4-3. *NDoc output*

The FxCop Compliancy

Finally, in terms of additional features that the developer has considered as part of the solution, an FxCop project is provided as well. The developer of this solution has attempted to achieve FxCop compliancy by running checks at various intervals. FxCop checks your compiled assemblies against Microsoft coding standards—that is, the internal standards used by Microsoft developers—rather than more general object-oriented (OO) or stylistic standards. For that reason, some of its rules can seem harsh and overly restrictive, as the tool focuses on very specific uses of the C# language. You may find it is not appropriate to your team on a day-to-day basis, but nevertheless it can identify problems with syntactic technique in your code.

If we run the project using FxCop, we will see the results shown in Figure 4-4. These results are not bad when you consider that FxCop is quite a hard taskmaster.

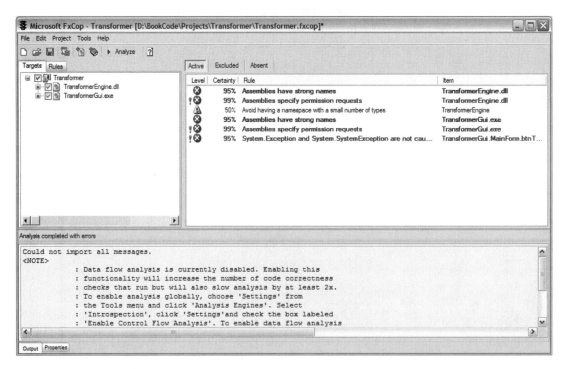

Figure 4-4. *FxCop compliancy*

Use Cases

Although we have a good understanding from prior discussions of the requirements for the delivery process, it is worth formalizing this discussion. Here I have chosen to write simple use cases to describe the two sections of the process. There is a direct correlation between these use cases and the original skeleton scripts we formed during our discussion of NAnt. These use cases are simple but provide a way of measuring success as we construct the build files.

We can expand on the content of the use cases later on when we have a better knowledge of the actual scenario.

Build Use Case

Use Case ID: UC1

Use Case Name: Build System

Description: The user triggers a system build through an application interaction. The application requires no further interaction. The application follows a series of steps to build, test, and publish a system. Once complete, a message is displayed to the user and the built assets are available for use.

Preconditions:

The software is in a state that will compile.

The software is available to the build application.

Postconditions:

The system software is compiled and available in a state that will deploy.

Normal Course:

1. The user triggers the build application to perform a build.

2. The application prepares an environment for performing the build process and publishing results and outputs.

3. The application supplies versioning information applicable to the system for use during compilation, management, and publishing. (See Alternative Course 3.1.)

4. The application compiles the system software.

5. The application performs unit testing and other reports on the status of the software.

6. The application creates documentation based on the output of the software compilation.

7. The application publishes the software system assets in an identifiable package and sends a message to the user.

Alternative Courses:

3.1 Where no versioning is required, then a default version number is used that does not impact the regular versioning system.

Exceptions:

E1. All failures. Process stops immediately and sends message to user. (See Exception E2.)

E2. Unit Testing. Process produces report on failing unit tests and then stops and sends message to user.

Deploy

Use Case ID: UC2

Use Case Name: Deploy System

Description: The user triggers a system deploy through an application interaction. The application requires no further interaction. The application follows a series of steps to perform a deployment of a system based on the assets delivered from UC1. Once complete, a message is displayed to the user and the system is available for use.

Preconditions:

The software system assets are available in an identifiable package resulting from UC1.

Postconditions:

The system is deployed and available for use.

Normal Course:

1. The user triggers the deploy application to perform a deploy.

2. The application selects the correct deployment package. (See Alternative Course 2.1.)

3. The application gets the correct deployment package and unpackages it.

4. The application selects the correct environment information for deployment.

5. The application prepares the environment based on the information in step 4.

6. The application positions the software system assets in the prepared environment.

7. The application performs any additional configuration steps required by the assets and/or the selected environment.

8. The application sends a message to the user.

Alternative Courses:

2.1 Where no versioning is required, a default version number is used that does not impact the regular versioning system.

Exceptions:

E1. All failures. Process stops immediately and sends message to user.

Organizing the Environment

Some final steps are required before we create the build files for the sample application. We need to ensure that VSS is ready to use and that we have developed an appropriate disk area for performing the processes.

Visual SourceSafe

I have set up VSS under D:\dotNetDelivery\VSS. Table 4-1 shows the user accounts in the database.

Table 4-1. *VSS User Accounts*

Username	Password	Notes
Admin	admin	The secret administration account
Marc	marc	My own account for making code changes
Guest	None	A read-only account for viewing source code
Builder	builder	The read-write account we will use in the NAnt build files

The most important account to us at this point is the Builder account. This is the account that NAnt will use to access VSS. For the most part, NAnt does not require read-write access, but as we begin to label the database and perform more complex actions this additional level of access is required.

Standardizing on the Builder account for all VSS databases ensures the same settings will be used for many projects across many build files.

■**Caution** Because the passwords will be stored in plain text inside the build files, security is a concern. Unfortunately, not much can be done about security at this time. However, storing the password to the Builder account is at least preferable to storing the Admin account details.

Build Folders

Now that we have our inputs to the process in the VSS-based information, we need to define locations for the process output. This is not a major headache, but a little thought prior to definition of the file can go a long way. Table 4-2 describes the structures we will use, which are set up under the BuildArea folder of the source code.

Table 4-2. *The Build Area*

Folder	Purpose
Source	Holds the source code retrieved from VSS
Output	Stores the compiled code from the Source folder
Docs	Contains the NDoc-based documentation
Reports	Stores any reporting output such as NUnit and FxCop reports
Distribution	Contains the final assets required for publishing
Publish	Contains actual published assets

These structures are a good starting point for creating and managing assets through the process, and are again similar to the structure of the build file skeleton and the build use case itself.

Now let us move on to the first part of the process: creating the build file.

Creating the Build File

In Chapter 2 we proposed a skeleton for the build file. Using that skeleton, we can make some initial system-specific changes to detail our intent for the build file. Also, we can give the build file a more informative name. In this case, we will call it `Transformer.Build.xml`.

Finally, reviewing the skeleton once more allows us to identify the areas that we need to complete.

■**Note** At this point I have dropped the `.build` extension from the file-naming conventions. This is because we will not always be "building" but perhaps performing other activities. I will use `.xml` for the names from now on (otherwise, `Transformer.Deploy.build` could be a little confusing . . .).

```xml
<?xml version="1.0" encoding="utf-8" ?>
<project name="Transformer" default="help">
    <description>Build file for the Transformer application.</description>

    <property name="nant.onfailure" value="fail"/>

    <target name="go"
        description="The main target for full build process execution."
        depends="clean, get, version, build, test, document, publish, notify"
        />

    <target name="clean" description="Clean up the build environment.">
    </target>

    <target name="get" description="Grab the source code.">
    </target>

    <target name="version"
        description="Apply versioning to the source code files.">
    </target>

    <target name="build" description="Compile the application.">
    </target>

    <target name="test" description="Apply the unit tests.">
    </target>
```

```
<target name="document" description="Generate documentation and reports.">
</target>

<target name="publish"
    description="Place the compiled assets in agreed location.">
</target>

<target name="notify"
    description="Tell everyone of the success or failure.">
</target>

<target name="fail">
</target>

<target name="help">
    <echo message="The skeleton file for the build process ➡
is designed to execute the following targets in turn:"/>
    <echo message="-- clean"/>
    <echo message="-- get"/>
    <echo message="-- version"/>
    <echo message="-- build"/>
    <echo message="-- test"/>
    <echo message="-- document"/>
    <echo message="-- publish"/>
    <echo message="-- notify"/>
</target>
</project>
```

With the specific descriptions of the project in place, we can move on to the details of each target. But before we do, we should consider a very important question: What if it all goes wrong?

Error Handling in NAnt

NAnt was not designed as a robust platform for error handling. It does not have notions of such things as try-catch constructs, though it does have a basic idea of an On Error Goto construct, which may bring a tear to the eye of any VB 6–using reader.

NAnt has two properties (which we discussed briefly in Chapter 2) that can be used to perform actions upon either a successful or failed execution of the build script. These properties are called nant.onsuccess and nant.onfailure, respectively.

In terms of error handling, the property we are interested in is nant.onfailure. This property is set as follows:

```
<property name="nant.onfailure" value="dosomething"/>
```

The value dosomething must be a target of the same name in the current script, or the build script will not execute. Effectively, using this setting means that if the build script fails during execution, the target dosomething will be called before the failure is reported and execution stops. This gives you the opportunity to perform some corrective action or other similar activity, such as a mail task to notify someone of the error. You should be aware of some specific points about this property. Consider the following script:

```
<?xml version="1.0" encoding="utf-8" ?>
<project name="ErrorHandlingExample" default="DoomedToFail">

<target name="DoomedToFail">
    <property name="nant.onfailure" value="GiveUp"/>
    <fail message="This target is not going to work"/>
</target>

<target name="GiveUp">
    <echo message="I give up, I really do."/>
    <call target="CleanUp1"/>
    <call target="CleanUp2"/>
</target>

<target name="CleanUp1">
    <echo message="Doing CleanUp1..."/>
    <property name="nant.onfailure" value="CleanUp2"/>
    <fail/>
</target>

<target name="CleanUp2">
    <echo message="Doing CleanUp2..."/>
</target>

</project>
```

The target DoomedToFail makes use of the onfailure property to target GiveUp to perform corrective action. Immediately afterwards we call the <fail> task to throw a BuildException, which will cause the GiveUp target to be called.

The GiveUp target is then used to call two corrective targets, CleanUp1 and CleanUp2. This is a legal use of the onfailure target.

However, in CleanUp1 we then use the onfailure target again to target CleanUp2 (which will be called anyway by the GiveUp target). Then we cause CleanUp1 to fail. The CleanUp2 target is never called, though. This is because subsequent to the first failure, no other failure can be accounted for and execution halts immediately. It is not possible to "chain" error handling in any way. Therefore, it is important that the corrective steps that you require will not fail themselves, or otherwise the error handling is fairly pointless. The output of running the script is as follows:

```
---------- NAnt ----------
NAnt 0.85
Copyright (C) 2001-2004 Gerry Shaw
http://nant.sourceforge.net
```

```
Buildfile: file:///ErrorHandlingExample.xml
Target(s) specified: DoomedToFail

DoomedToFail:

GiveUp:

    [echo] I give up, I really do.

CleanUp1:

    [echo] Doing CleanUp1...
    [call] ErrorHandlingExample.xml(20,7):
    [call] No message.

BUILD FAILED - 1 non-fatal error(s), 0 warning(s)

ErrorHandlingExample.xml(8,7):
This target is not going to work

Total time: 0 seconds.
Output completed (1 sec consumed) - Normal Termination
```

We can see in the output that following the second failure (in target CleanUp1) halts the script execution immediately; target CleanUp2 is never called.

The net result of this is that there is some utility to the error handling in NAnt—but not to the extent that it provides robust rollbacks, transaction reversals, and so on.

We will see a suitable use of the onfailure property when we look at the testing part of the build script for the Transformer application in just a little while. So, after a pessimistic start to proceedings, let us move on to the real work.

Clean

The first section for attention is the Clean target. In this particular target, we will clean out existing content ready for the execution of the build file. The only folder we want to persist is the publish folder, since this will contain artifacts from prior builds.

After we have removed the old material, we will then set about re-creating the environment as necessary.

These particular actions are quite straightforward. The following code shows the target as required:

```
<target name="clean" description="Clean up the build environment.">
    <delete dir="D:\dotNetDelivery\BuildArea\Source\" failonerror="false"/>
    <delete dir="D:\dotNetDelivery\BuildArea\Output\" failonerror="false"/>
    <delete dir="D:\dotNetDelivery\BuildArea\Docs\" failonerror="false"/>
    <delete dir="D:\dotNetDelivery\BuildArea\Reports\" failonerror="false"/>
    <delete dir="D:\dotNetDelivery\BuildArea\Distribution\" failonerror="false"/>
```

```
<mkdir dir="D:\dotNetDelivery\BuildArea\Source\"/>
<mkdir dir="D:\dotNetDelivery\BuildArea\Output\"/>
<mkdir dir="D:\dotNetDelivery\BuildArea\Docs\"/>
<mkdir dir="D:\dotNetDelivery\BuildArea\Reports\"/>
<mkdir dir="D:\dotNetDelivery\BuildArea\Distribution\"/>
<mkdir dir="D:\dotNetDelivery\BuildArea\Publish\" failonerror="false"/>
</target>
```

The core aspects of this target are as follows:

failonerror. Most of the time it is acceptable, and usually desirable, for a build file to fail when a task fails. In this target, though, this is not the case. We are performing create and delete actions against assets that may not exist. For instance, suppose we were to run the build file for the first time without having created the initial environment; the delete tasks would therefore fail. Or suppose we are not sure that we have created the publish folder (but we *may* have), so we need to make sure that there is no problem in the event the folder does already exist.

publish. We do not attempt to delete the publish folder; we just want to create it in the event it does not already exist.

Running this script should cause no problems and will generate a clean environment ready for use.

Checkout/Get

This particular target takes care of an important task—the retrieval of the source code from the VSS database—in a very simple way. The NAntContrib task <vssget> is all we need to satisfactorily complete this step in the process. The code for the target is as follows:

```
<target name="get" description="Grab the source code.">
    <vssget
        user="builder"
        password="builder"
        localpath="D:\dotNetDelivery\BuildArea\Source\"
        recursive="true"
        replace="true"
        dbpath="D:\dotNetDelivery\VSS\srcsafe.ini"
        path="$/Solutions/Transformer/"
        />
</target>
```

The attribute values for the task are quite self-explanatory. Notice that we use the builder user account to access the VSS database. We then only grab the particular solution we are interested in and place it into the specified source folder of the build area.

In order to use the NAntContrib tasks, we must use the <loadtasks> task to load the NAntContrib tasks as follows:

```
<loadtasks
    assembly="D:\dotNetDelivery\Tools\NAntContrib\0.85rc1\bin\➥
        NAnt.Contrib.Tasks.dll"
/>
<loadtasks
    assembly="D:\dotNetDelivery\Tools\NUnit2Report\1.2.2\bin\➥
        NAnt.NUnit2ReportTasks.dll"
/>
```

I have also included the `<loadtasks>` task for the NUnit2Report that we will use later in the script. Both of these tasks appear in the build script at the beginning of the script following the property declarations. There is no point in processing much of the script only to find that crucial assemblies are missing.

Version

We must provide versioning for the code. Because the version number of an assembly is managed by attributes on the assembly, we need to know the versioning and application of the version number prior to compiling the code. We also need to use the version number again later on in the process.

We will use a combination of tasks to achieve the desired results through a series of steps.

Maintaining a Version Number

Before we apply a version number, we want to be sure that we can adequately maintain version number information.

NAntContrib provides a task specifically for this purpose: `<version>`. This task reads the content of a text file (by default, this file is called `build.number`) and updates the version number based on the strategy marked by the `buildtype` task attribute. Once done, the task sets a property (by default `sys.version`) with the required version number. This can then be used in the build file.

The `<version>` task can use a number of strategies. The one I have selected here is to increment the `build` number of the version number, so that my first build is 1.0.1.0, then 1.0.2.0, and so on. This is achieved with the following code:

```
<version
    buildtype="increment"
    revisiontype="increment"
    path="Transformer.Build.Number"
    />
```

Notice that I have also changed the default file to `Transformer.Build.Number` to improve its identity. This file simply contains the text "1.0.0.0" and will be managed by the process from now on. If we wish to change the numbers—for example, to represent a major or minor release—we will need to edit the file.

Before we move on, we want to make one more point. As we begin the debugging of the build file and attempt to run the process successfully, the build number will be incremented as we hit this target. In some cases, we can test the targets in isolation, but not always. We do not really want to impact the version numbers because of unsuccessful debugging runs.

▪Note This is different from a failed build. It may not be a problem to increment the version when the build itself fails for some reason. I am talking specifically about the construction and debugging phase of the build file.

So, in order to ensure there is no increment during debugging, we can add a test for a debug property setting, and also provide a default debugging value of the sys.version property—in this case I have decided on "0.0.0.0" as a suitable number. The code for this looks like this:

```
<property name="sys.version" value="0.0.0.0"/>
<ifnot test="${debug}">
    <version
        buildtype="increment"
        revisiontype="increment"
        path="Transformer.Build.Number"
        />
</ifnot>
```

We can be sure now that version numbers are incremented only when required. The result of this test is that we need to include a Boolean debug property when running the script. We can enter this information into the help target with the addition of the following messages:

```
<echo message="This file should be run with a Boolean value for 'debug'."/>
<echo message="-- True indicates that no versioning be set (0.0.0.0)."/>
<echo message="-- False indicates that a regular version be set(1.0.x.0)."/>
<echo message="Example: -D:debug=true"/>
```

Versioning the Assemblies

Now that we have the version number, we can apply it to the code for the assemblies we are going to compile. As we know, VS .NET creates a file containing Assembly-level attributes when we create a project in the integrated development environment (IDE). By convention this file is called AssemblyInfo.cs, but of course this is just for organization and convenience. Inside the file are a number of attributes that are ready to be used:

```
[assembly: AssemblyProduct("")]
[assembly: AssemblyCopyright("")]
[assembly: AssemblyVersion("1.0.*")]
```

The last attribute is the one that is of interest to us, though we can make use of the others as well. All we need to do is overwrite the AssemblyVersion attribute with our version number. Fortunately, NAnt provides a task called <asminfo> that can do just that. We just need to point the task to the correct location of the AssemblyInfo.cs file.

The problem with this is that we potentially need to do this several times to update several assemblies. We can use VS .NET to improve this effort.

If we create a file called, say, CommonAssemblyInfo.cs, under Solution Items in VS .NET and then link it to the other projects in the solution, we can achieve the effects of versioning and perform the task only once.

This is done by adding the required attributes to CommonAssemblyInfo.cs and then removing the same attributes from the individual AssemblyInfo.cs files of each project. In the sample application, CommonAssemblyInfo.cs contains the following code:

```
using System;
using System.Reflection;

[assembly: AssemblyProduct("")]
[assembly: AssemblyCopyright("")]
[assembly: AssemblyVersion("1.0.*")]
```

■**Note** We will be replacing this information shortly, so there is no need to worry about the actual settings in the file at this point, as long as the solution actually builds, of course.

The three attributes are removed from each AssemblyInfo.cs file.

Following this, the CommonAssemblyInfo.cs file is linked to the other projects. Figure 4-5 shows how this is done by using the Add Existing option and then the Link File option in the file browser window. On the right you can see how the solution looks after the linking process. Notice the slightly different icons representing the linked CommonAssemblyInfo.cs file.

With the link formed, we need to perform the update to the CommonAssemblyInfo.cs file. The <asminfo> task detail looks like this:

```
<asminfo
    output="D:\dotNetDelivery\BuildArea\Source\CommonAssemblyInfo.cs"
    language="CSharp">
    <imports>
        <import name="System" />
        <import name="System.Reflection"/>
    </imports>
    <attributes>
        <attribute type="AssemblyVersionAttribute" value="${sys.version}"/>
        <attribute type="AssemblyProductAttribute" value="Transformer" />
        <attribute
            type="AssemblyCopyrightAttribute"
            value="Copyright (c) 2005, Etomic Ltd."
            />
    </attributes>
</asminfo>
```

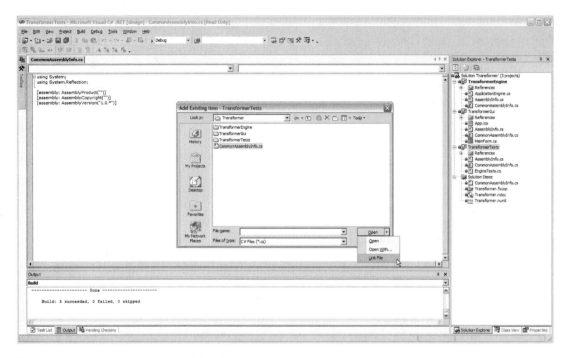

Figure 4-5. *Linking CommonAssemblyInfo.cs*

The structure of this task is reminiscent of the actual code, and in effect all this task is doing is writing out the code declared in the task. Notice that I have used the sys.version property as the value for the assembly version attribute. I have also provided other standard information to the compiled assemblies. Several other options can be found in the NAnt documentation.

Since we have obtained the source code from VSS, the CommonAssemblyInfo.cs file is actually read-only. In order to perform the action described, we must alter the file to read-write and then back again so as not to confuse ourselves (and potentially NAnt). We can use the <attrib> task for this:

```
<attrib
    file="D:\dotNetDelivery\BuildArea\Source\CommonAssemblyInfo.cs"
    readonly="false"
    />

<!-- ASMINFO TASK SNIPPED -->

<attrib
    file="D:\dotNetDelivery\BuildArea\Source\CommonAssemblyInfo.cs"
    readonly="true"
    />
```

Labeling VSS

There are two other aspects to versioning apart from the assemblies themselves. The first is the labeling of the published assets. We will handle this in the Publish step. The second is the labeling of the VSS database.

At this point, we do not perform any other action with VSS, but in future scripts we may want to manipulate assets in VSS later in the process. Therefore, we do not want to update the VSS label until later. We can split the version target into two sections: version1 and version2.

version1 contains all of the work up until this point, such as obtaining a number and rewriting CommonAssemblyInfo.cs. version2 will contain directions for updating the VSS database.

```
<target name="version2">
    <ifnot test="${debug}">
        <vsslabel
            user="builder"
            password="builder"
            dbpath="D:\dotNetDelivery\VSS\srcsafe.ini"
            path="$/Solutions/Transformer/"
            comment="Automated Label"
            label="NAnt - ${sys.version}"
            />
    </ifnot>
</target>
```

The label we want to apply is "NAnt - 1.0.x.0," which corresponds to the version marked on the assemblies and aids the versioning process. I have also included a test for the debug property so that the version 0.0.0.0 is not labeled throughout the VSS database when we are debugging the script, which would also be confusing.

All of this scripting means that the assembly will be versioned as required when the code is compiled in the next step. It has taken longer to explain the necessary steps than it takes to actually implement the solution. The full script for the version1 target follows:

```
<target name="version1" description="Apply versioning to the source code files.">
    <property name="sys.version" value="0.0.0.0"/>
    <ifnot test="${debug}">
        <version
            buildtype="increment"
            revisiontype="increment"
            path="Transformer.Build.Number"
            />
    </ifnot>
    <attrib
        file="D:\dotNetDelivery\BuildArea\Source\CommonAssemblyInfo.cs"
        readonly="false"
        />

    <asminfo
        output="D:\dotNetDelivery\BuildArea\Source\CommonAssemblyInfo.cs"
```

```
            language="CSharp">
                <imports>
                    <import name="System" />
                    <import name="System.Reflection"/>
                </imports>
                <attributes>
                    <attribute
                        type="AssemblyVersionAttribute" value="${sys.version}" />
                    <attribute type="AssemblyProductAttribute" value="Transformer" />
                    <attribute
                        type="AssemblyCopyrightAttribute"
                        value="Copyright (c) 2005, Etomic Ltd."/>
                </attributes>
            </asminfo>
            <attrib
                file="D:\dotNetDelivery\BuildArea\Source\CommonAssemblyInfo.cs"
                readonly="true" />
</target>
```

Because we have added a new target, we must change the go target to account for the new dependency. It should now look like this:

```
<target name="go"
    description="The main target for full build process execution."
    depends="clean, get, version1, version2, build, test, document, publish, notify"
    />
```

Build

As I mentioned earlier, it is the scaffolding of the process that takes the time (the versioning effort is a testament to this!) while the actual compilation activities are quite simple.

This target makes use of the <solution> task to compile the solution file and output the assemblies into the output folder. Since the solution is entirely .NET-based and not complex, there is no need for any pre- or post-compilation activities here.

The target looks like this:

```
<target name="build" description="Compile the application.">
    <solution
        solutionfile="D:\dotNetDelivery\BuildArea\Source\Transformer.sln"
        configuration="Debug"
        outputdir="D:\dotNetDelivery\BuildArea\Output\"
        />
</target>
```

Here I have hard-coded the configuration attribute and I will not address this attribute any further, but of course you may wish to have a conditional (or otherwise) process based on a variety of configuration options.

> **Note** While this target may seem a little disappointing in terms of its complexity, there are many options for compiling assemblies using `<csc>` and other tasks if you prefer a more exotic compilation process. I am thankful for the simplicity!

Test

Now that we have some compiled assets, we can begin finalizing the build process through a series of reporting and management targets. The first of these is the test target, which allows analysis of our choosing to be performed on the compiled assemblies. We will specifically look at NUnit and FxCop, as discussed earlier, but there are many possible options.

The importance of this step in the process is that even if the code has compiled successfully in the previous step, failures here can be set to fail the overall process, which provides excellent standard regression testing before the publishing of "junk" code.

Running NUnit Tests

Once again, NAnt has a specific test for running unit tests on the NUnit framework. We can use this to check the test assembly included with the solution.

The script for this task is quite straightforward:

```
<nunit2>
    <formatter type="Xml" usefile="true" extension=".xml"
        outputdir="D:\dotNetDelivery\BuildArea\Reports\" />
    <test assemblyname="D:\dotNetDelivery\BuildArea\Output\TransformerTests.dll" />
</nunit2>
```

The input is fairly obvious. The output XML file will be named after the assembly with the suffix -results.xml, so in this case the file output into the reports area will be called TransformerTests.dll-results.xml.

Running FxCop Analysis

In this instance, there is no NAnt task for FxCop, so we will use the general-purpose `<exec>` task to execute FxCop at the command line. This makes the task look ugly and introduces a certain amount of rigidity at this point. On the other hand, NAnt at least allows us to use tools that it does not have tasks for, which is a very good thing. In Chapter 6, we will build a specific task for FxCop, but in the meantime the task looks like this:

```
<exec program="D:\Tools\FxCop\1.30\FxCopCmd.exe"
    commandline="/f:D:\dotNetDelivery\BuildArea\Output\TransformerEngine.dll ➥
        /f:D:\dotNetDelivery\BuildArea\Output\TransformerGui.exe ➥
        /o:D:\dotNetDelivery\BuildArea\Reports\fxcop.xml ➥
        /r:D:\dotNetDelivery\Tools\FxCop\1.30\Rules\"
    failonerror="false"
    />
```

Ouch! That is not very pretty at all. I have marked the <exec> task so that it does not fail if there is an error. This is because I do not see this analysis as a reason to fail the build process, though of course I am interested in the results from a quality assurance point of view. As you begin to build up different reports, you may or may not share the same viewpoint depending on the context of the report.

Formatting the NUnit Report

Although we have now successfully reported on the areas required, the reports are in XML format. We can apply some transforms to make the reports readable.

For NUnit, a good independent task is available at http://nunit2report.sourceforge.net/

You can then use <loadtasks> to access the downloaded task or drop the downloaded assemblies into the NAnt bin folder if you are feeling lazy. The task looks like this:

```
<nunit2report out="D:\dotNetDelivery\BuildArea\Reports\NUnit.html">
  <fileset>
    <include
      name="D:\dotNetDelivery\BuildArea\Reports\TransformerTests.dll-results.xml"
    />
  </fileset>
</nunit2report>
```

The output of this is very presentable, as can be seen in Figure 4-6, providing the kind of information you may be interested in.

Introducing the report task has also introduced a problem: if the NUnit testing fails, then the build process itself fails. This is as it should be, but the problem is that the NUnit report will not be generated in this instance, since the task will not be run. Arguably, it is more important to see the report when there are failures rather than when there are not.

We can account for this by using the nant.onfailure property. In this case, we will redirect the property at the beginning of the target, and then redirect to the default once again at the end of the target. We will introduce a new target called fail.test containing the additional actions we need for producing the report.

The script for the property change looks like this:

```
<target name="test" description="Apply the unit tests.">
    <property name="nant.onfailure" value="fail.test"/>

    <!-- REST OF TARGET SNIPPED -->

    <property name="nant.onfailure" value="fail"/>
</target>
```

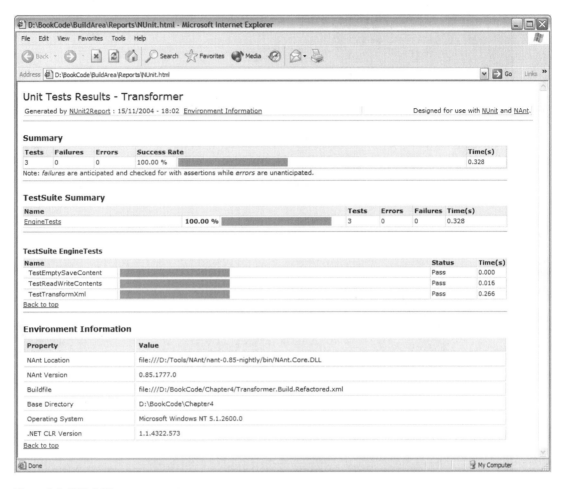

Figure 4-6. *NUnit2Report output*

The fail.test target looks like the following and is just a repeat of the <nunit2report> task from the main test target:

```
<target name="fail.test">
    <nunit2report out="D:\dotNetDelivery\BuildArea\Reports\NUnit.html">
        <fileset>
            <include
name="D:\dotNetDelivery\BuildArea\Reports\TransformerTests.dll-results.xml"/>
        </fileset>
    </nunit2report>
</target>
```

If we now edit the unit tests to produce an error and run the process, we will see a properly transformed report, as shown in Figure 4-7.

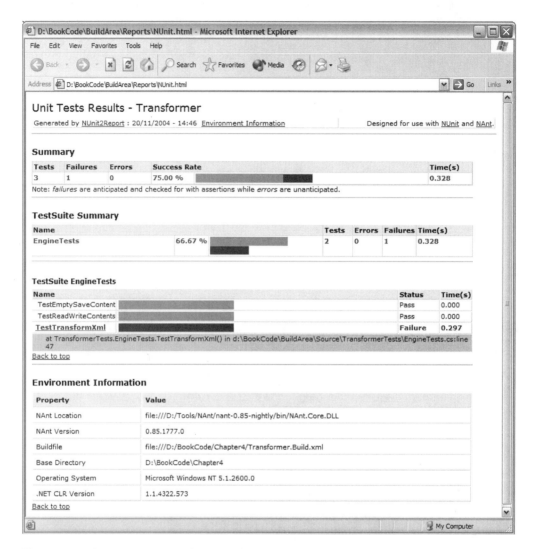

Figure 4-7. *Failing NUnit tests with NUnit2Report*

Using the `onfailure` and `onsuccess` properties in this way can be useful for providing error handling in build scripts where some further work (perhaps a rudimentary rollback mechanism) is required in the event of a failure. Because the properties can be set when required, error handling targets and strategies can be quite fine-grained, even task by task, if so desired, though in this instance I would be concerned about the overall process fragility if that sort of handling was needed.

The environment information displayed at the bottom of the report requires the use of the `<sysinfo>` task. This is an empty task that we can insert in the main body of the file where the property declarations are:

```
<sysinfo/>
```

Formatting the FxCop Report

Formatting the FxCop report is a little more straightforward, since there is no issue with failure. We will use the general-purpose <style> task to apply the required style sheet to the XML report as follows:

```
<style
    style="D:\dotNetDelivery\Tools\FxCop\1.30\Xml\FxCopReport.xsl"
    in="D:\dotNetDelivery\BuildArea\Reports\fxcop.xml"
    out="D:\dotNetDelivery\BuildArea\Reports\fxcop.html"
    />
```

Note Oh dear. Maybe the entire application we are automating could have been handled by NAnt in the first place. We had better not mention this to the Etomic developers.

The full target is shown here:

```
<target name="test" description="Apply the unit tests.">

    <property name="nant.onfailure" value="fail.test"/>

    <nunit2>
        <formatter type="Xml" usefile="true" extension=".xml"
            outputdir="D:\dotNetDelivery\BuildArea\Reports\" />
        <test
assemblyname="D:\dotNetDelivery\BuildArea\Output\TransformerTests.dll"
            />
    </nunit2>

    <nunit2report out="D:\dotNetDelivery\BuildArea\Reports\NUnit.html">
        <fileset>
            <include
name="D:\dotNetDelivery\BuildArea\Reports\TransformerTests.dll-results.xml"/>
        </fileset>
    </nunit2report>

    <exec program="D:\Tools\FxCop\1.30\FxCopCmd.exe"
        commandline="/f:D:\dotNetDelivery\BuildArea\Output\TransformerEngine.dll ➽
        /f:D:\dotNetDelivery\BuildArea\Output\TransformerGui.exe ➽
        /o:D:\dotNetDelivery\BuildArea\Reports\fxcop.xml ➽
        /r:D:\dotNetDeliveryTools\FxCop\1.30\Rules\"
        failonerror="false"
        />

    <style
        style="D:\dotNetDelivery\Tools\FxCop\1.30\Xml\FxCopReport.xsl"
```

```
            in="D:\dotNetDelivery\BuildArea\Reports\fxcop.xml"
            out="D:\dotNetDelivery\BuildArea\Reports\fxcop.html"
            />

        <property name="nant.onfailure" value="fail"/>
</target>
```

document

After another quite involved target, document is handled through the use of one specific task: <ndoc>. As we mentioned earlier, this task mimics the NDoc software in producing documentation based on the XML comments in the source code.

To ensure that the XML comments are being produced by the build process, the configuration information should be entered as shown in Figure 4-8.

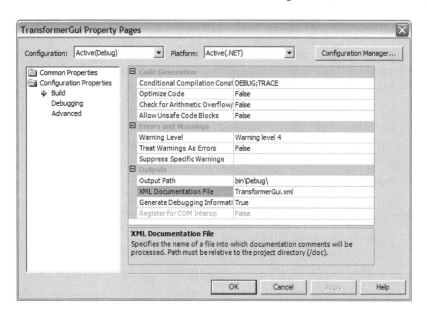

Figure 4-8. *Documentation configuration in VS .NET*

Once the XML documentation is available, the following script allows the generation of the documentation:

```
<target name="document" description="Generate documentation and reports.">
    <ndoc>
        <assemblies basedir="D:\dotNetDelivery\BuildArea\Output\">
            <include name="TransformerEngine.dll" />
            <include name="TransformerGui.dll" />
        </assemblies>
        <summaries basedir="D:\dotNetDelivery\BuildArea\Output\">
            <include name="TransformerEngine.xml" />
            <include name="TransformerGui.xml" />
```

```
            </summaries>
            <documenters>
                <documenter name="MSDN">
                    <property name="OutputDirectory"
                        value="D:\dotNetDelivery\BuildArea\Docs\" />
                    <property name="HtmlHelpName" value="Transformer" />
                    <property name="HtmlHelpCompilerFilename" value="hhc.exe" />
                    <property name="IncludeFavorites" value="False" />
                    <property name="Title" value="Transformer (NDoc)" />
                    <property name="SplitTOCs" value="False" />
                    <property name="DefaulTOC" value="" />
                    <property name="ShowVisualBasic" value="False" />
                    <property name="ShowMissingSummaries" value="True" />
                    <property name="ShowMissingRemarks" value="False" />
                    <property name="ShowMissingParams" value="True" />
                    <property name="ShowMissingReturns" value="True" />
                    <property name="ShowMissingValues" value="True" />
                    <property name="DocumentInternals" value="True" />
                    <property name="DocumentProtected" value="True" />
                    <property name="DocumentPrivates" value="False" />
                    <property name="DocumentEmptyNamespaces" value="False" />
                    <property name="IncludeAssemblyVersion" value="True" />
                    <property name="CopyrightText" value="Etomic Ltd., 2005" />
                    <property name="CopyrightHref" value="" />
                </documenter>
            </documenters>
        </ndoc>
    </target>
```

■**Note** It is worth exploring the NDoc product to determine the switches you would prefer for your own documentation.

---

publish

The final target representing real work is publish. Here we will move required assets to the distribution folder ready for packaging, and then create an identifiable zip file in the publish folder.

The tasks used in this target are not complex. We use the version number we obtained earlier in the script to tag the zip file. The full target is shown here:

```
<target name="publish" description="Place the compiled assets in agreed area.">
    <copy todir="D:\dotNetDelivery\BuildArea\Distribution\">
        <fileset basedir="D:\dotNetDelivery\BuildArea\Output\">
            <include name="TransformerEngine.dll"/>
            <include name="TransformerGui.exe"/>
```

```
        </fileset>
    </copy>

    <zip
      zipfile="D:\dotNetDelivery\BuildArea\Publish\➥
              Transformer-Build-${sys.version}.zip">
        <fileset basedir="D:\dotNetDelivery\BuildArea\Distribution\">
          <include name="**" />
        </fileset>
    </zip>
</target>
```

Remember that the code shown in bold for the `fileset` means "include all files and folders recursively." If you need to refresh your memory on `filesets` (and tasks in general) turn back to Chapter 3 for a moment, or check out the NAnt documentation. Note that I have included only the assets required for the function of the application. I could have chosen to include the help documentation (for example) with the distribution. For the moment, though, this is a satisfactory outcome for this target.

notify

I have broadly ignored this target for the time being. At the moment it consists only of a message. It could use the `<mail>` task to send emails to interested parties if we needed to:

```
<target name="notify" description="Tell everyone of the success or failure.">
    <echo message="Notifying you of the build process success."/>
</target>
```

■**Note** It may be preferable to place the notify step under the `nant.onsuccess` target rather than as a regular dependency since in fact that is the behavior we seek. In the same way the `fail` target may perform a similar but negative action.

---

fail

Similarly, there is no great need for the `<fail>` task itself other than to pass a message upon failure as shown here:

```
<target name="fail">
    <echo message="Notifying you of a failure in the build process."/>
</target>
```

Examining the Output

The work for the build file is complete. To run the build file in its entirety, we use this command:

```
nant -f:Transformer.Build.xml -D:debug=true go
```

To ensure that we have met the requirements of the use case, we can investigate the resulting output by looking at the NAnt log and the actual assets.

```
---------- NAnt ----------
NAnt 0.85
Copyright (C) 2001-2004 Gerry Shaw
http://nant.sourceforge.net

Buildfile: file:///Transformer.Build.xml
Target(s) specified: go
```

Here's some general information about the running build file—no problems so far.

```
  [sysinfo] Setting system information properties under sys.*

clean:

    [delete] Deleting directory 'D:\dotNetDelivery\BuildArea\Source\'.
    [delete] Deleting directory 'D:\dotNetDelivery\BuildArea\Output\'.
    [delete] Deleting directory 'D:\dotNetDelivery\BuildArea\Docs\'.
    [delete] Deleting directory 'D:\dotNetDelivery\BuildArea\Reports\'.
    [delete] Deleting directory 'D:\dotNetDelivery\BuildArea\Distribution\'.
     [mkdir] Creating directory 'D:\dotNetDelivery\BuildArea\Source\'.
     [mkdir] Creating directory 'D:\dotNetDelivery\BuildArea\Output\'.
     [mkdir] Creating directory 'D:\dotNetDelivery\BuildArea\Docs\'.
     [mkdir] Creating directory 'D:\dotNetDelivery\BuildArea\Reports\'.
     [mkdir] Creating directory 'D:\dotNetDelivery\BuildArea\Distribution\'.
```

The <sysinfo> task and the clean target have now run successfully. We should be able to see a clean environment ready for use in the buildarea folder.

```
get:

    [vssget] Getting '$/Solutions/Transformer/' to ➥
'D:\dotNetDelivery\BuildArea\Source\'...
```

Here we have successfully taken the files from VSS and placed them into the source folder, as shown in Figure 4-9.

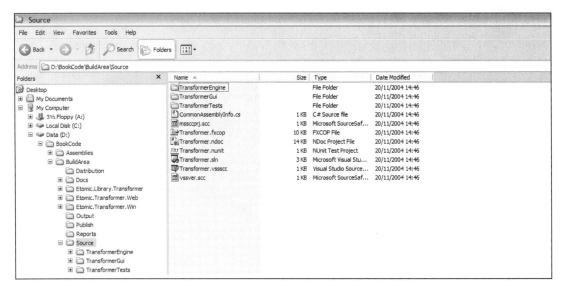

Figure 4-9. *Source code folder*

version1:

```
    [attrib] Setting file attributes for 1 files to Normal.
    [asminfo] Generated file
'D:\dotNetDelivery\BuildArea\Source\CommonAssemblyInfo.cs'.
    [attrib] Setting file attributes for 1 files to ReadOnly.
```

version2:

Versioning is working correctly, but neither the actual version number nor the VSS labeling has been used because we set the debug property to true for the test run of the script. Running with -D:debug=false would produce the following results instead, which show the effects of using the true version number and labeling the VSS database.

version1:

```
    [version] Build number '1.0.1.0'.
    [attrib] Setting file attributes for 1 files to Normal.
    [asminfo] Generated file
'D:\dotNetDelivery\BuildArea\Source\CommonAssemblyInfo.cs'.
    [attrib] Setting file attributes for 1 files to ReadOnly.
```

version2:

```
    [vsslabel] Applied label 'NAnt - 1.0.1.0' to '$/Solutions/Transformer/'.
```

Now the label has been applied in VSS, as shown in Figure 4-10. Following the compilation step, we can check that the version has been applied correctly as well.

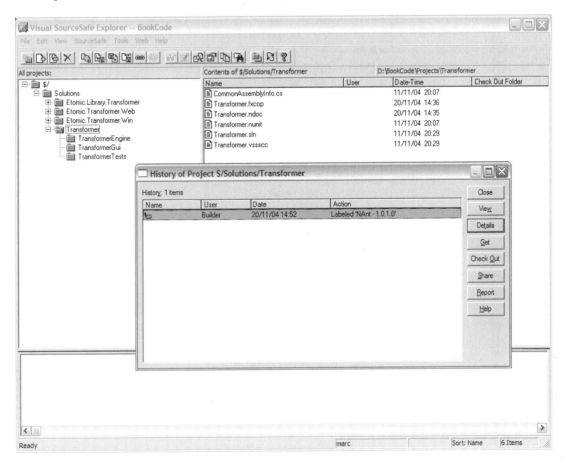

Figure 4-10. *VSS labels*

```
[solution] Starting solution build.
[solution] Building 'TransformerEngine' [Debug] ...
[solution]
d:\dotNetDelivery\BuildArea\Source\TransformerEngine\ApplicationEngine.cs(52,54):
warning CS1574: XML comment on
'TransformerEngine.ApplicationEngine.SaveFileContents(string, string)' has cref
attribute 'contents' that could not be found
[solution]
d:\dotNetDelivery\BuildArea\Source\TransformerEngine\ApplicationEngine.cs(53,47):
warning CS1574: XML comment on
'TransformerEngine.ApplicationEngine.SaveFileContents(string, string)' has cref
attribute 'path' that could not be found
[solution] Building 'TransformerTests' [Debug] ...
[solution] Building 'TransformerGui' [Debug] ...
          [resgen] Read in 83 resources from
'D:\dotNetDelivery\BuildArea\Source\TransformerGui\MainForm.resx'
          [resgen] Writing resource file...  Done.
```

The build step itself produces a few warnings, but on inspection they relate to the XML comments rather than to problems with the compilation itself. We can remedy this by accessing the source code file specified in the message and resolving the path detailed in the XML comments or removing the erroneous comment if it is superfluous. If we take a look in the output directory, we can see the generated assets, as shown in Figure 4-11.

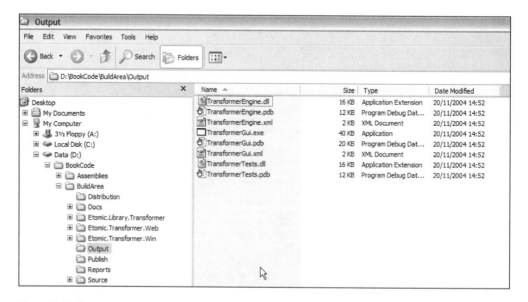

Figure 4-11. *Generated assets*

Also, let us take a look at the assembly version. If we were working with the 1.0.1.0 label, we would see something similar to Figure 4-12.

Figure 4-12. *Viewing the correct assembly version*

test:

```
<?xml version="1.0" encoding="utf-8"?>1
    [exec] Microsoft FxCopCmd v1.30
    [exec] Copyright (C) 1999-2004 Microsoft Corp.  All rights reserved.
    [exec]
    [exec] Loaded ComRules.dll...
    [exec] Loaded DesignRules.dll...
    [exec] Loaded GlobalizationRules.dll...
    [exec] Loaded NamingRules.dll...
    [exec] Loaded PerformanceRules.dll...
    [exec] Loaded SecurityRules.dll...
    [exec] Loaded UsageRules.dll...
    [exec] Loaded TransformerEngine.dll...
    [exec] Loaded TransformerGui.exe...
    [exec] Initializing Introspection engine...
    [exec] <NOTE>
    [exec]   : Data flow analysis is currently disabled. Enabling this
    [exec]   : functionality will increase the number of code correctness
    [exec]   : checks that run but will also slow analysis by at least 2x.
    [exec]   : To enable analysis globally, choose 'Settings' from
    [exec]   : the Tools menu and click 'Analysis Engines'. Select
```

```
    [exec]   : 'Introspection', click 'Settings' and check the box labeled
    [exec]   : 'Enable Control Flow Analysis'. To enable data flow analysis
    [exec]   : for this project only, choose 'Options' from the Project menu.
    [exec]   : Click the 'Spelling & Analysis' tab and set the
    [exec]   : 'Control Flow Analysis' drop-down to 'True'.
    [exec] </NOTE>
    [exec] Analyzing...
    [exec] Could not initialize spell-checker for 'en-us' locale.
Is Office installed? To resolve this exception, install Office
or disable spelling rules for namespaces, members, types, parameters
and resources.
    [exec] Analysis Complete.
    [exec] * Rules gave the following errors:
    [exec] * 'TypeNamesShouldBeSpelledCorrectly' threw 1 exceptions:
    [exec] * -Could not initialize spell-checker for 'en-us' locale.
Is Office installed? To resolve this exception, install Office
or disable spelling rules for namespaces, members, types, parameters
and resources.
    [exec] *    at
Microsoft.Tools.FxCop.Sdk.Introspection.UsageRuleUtilities.GetSpellChecker()
    [exec]    at
Microsoft.Tools.FxCop.Rules.Usage.TypeNamesShouldBeSpelledCorrectly ➡
.Check(TypeNode type)
    [exec]     at Microsoft.Tools.FxCop.Engines.Introspection.AnalysisVisitor ➡
.CheckType(TargetType value, TypeNode type)
    [exec] * 1 total rule exceptions.
    [exec] Writing 8 messages...
    [exec] Writing report to D:\dotNetDelivery\BuildArea\Reports\fxcop.xml...
    [exec] Done.
    [exec] D:\dotNetDelivery\Chapter4\Transformer.Build.xml(95,4):
    [exec] External Program Failed:
D:\dotNetDelivery\FxCop\1.30\FxCopCmd.exe (return code was 2)
    [style] Processing 'D:\dotNetDelivery\BuildArea\Reports\fxcop.xml'
to 'D:\dotNetDelivery\BuildArea\Reports\fxcop.html'.
```

This target offers a lot of commentary. Essentially the NUnit tests have run silently, and the report has been produced in the way we discussed earlier. FxCop has been complaining about various things and generally been quite verbose, though in fact it has produced the required report, despite the complaint that the "External Program Failed."

We will seek to address this in Chapter 6, though for now the outcome is satisfactory. We can view the XML and HTML outputs in the reports folder, as shown in Figure 4-13.

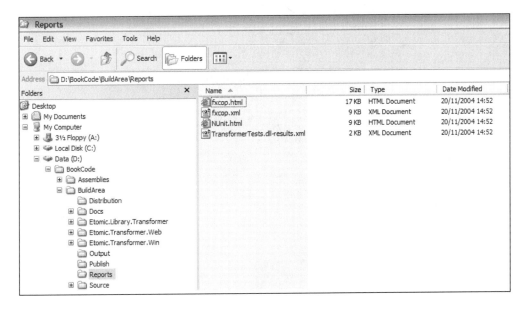

Figure 4-13. *Reporting outputs*

```
document:

    [ndoc] Initializing...
    [ndoc] Merging XML documentation...
    [ndoc] Building file mapping...
    [ndoc] Loading XSLT files...
    [ndoc] Generating HTML pages...
    [ndoc] Generating HTML content file...
    [ndoc] Compiling HTML Help file...
    [ndoc] Done.
```

Documentation has been successfully generated, and it can be viewed in the docs folder, as shown in Figure 4-14. Reviewing the documentation will reveal that there are some missing comments that will need to be addressed by the developer.

```
publish:

    [copy] Copying 2 files to 'D:\dotNetDelivery\BuildArea\Distribution\'.
    [zip] Zipping 2 files to 'D:\
    dotNetDelivery\BuildArea\Publish\Transformer-Build-0.0.0.0.zip'.
```

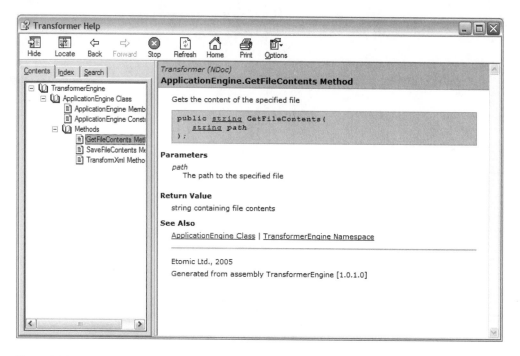

Figure 4-14. *Documentation output*

The publishing step has worked with no problems, and the zipped assets (shown in Figure 4-15) can be viewed in the `publish` folder.

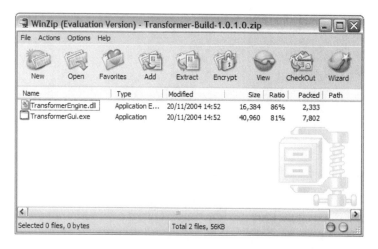

Figure 4-15. *Published assets*

```
notify:

    [echo] Notifying you of the build process success.

go:


BUILD SUCCEEDED - 1 non-fatal error(s), 7 warning(s)
Total time: 106.2 seconds.
Output completed (2 min 0 sec consumed) - Normal Termination
```

Following some final messages, including the stop-gap notify target execution, we can see that the script has succeeded and has in fact met all of the aspects of the use case in its execution. A job well done.

Opportunities for Refactoring

Before we move on to the deploy file, we should consider how the build file can be improved.

In Chapter 5, we will learn how standards impact the efficiency of the generation of build files, and the ease with which a "standard" process can be achieved. But even without these standards, we can improve the script we have written with a few simple changes.

In terms of refactoring, we should consider two factors:

Duplication of settings. By its nature, an XML-based script is going to be heavily laden with settings in the form of nested elements and attributes containing information about the specifics of an operation. Removing these can save significant editing time, reduce the rigidity of the script, and remove the risk of missing settings.

Duplication of script (or code). For the same reasons, reusing functionality is an obvious area to examine as well.

The duplication of script functionality is worth assessing, but it is likely that we will gain the greatest savings in this area when faced with multiple projects. Therefore, we will leave this to one side until the next chapter.

We can make some gains in terms of settings in isolation, however. Again, when faced with more scripts we may see more opportunities, but even now there are some items worth examining.

A quick search over the script reveals 37 occurrences of the partial path D:\dotNetDelivery. This is a little problematic if you are using the source code in a different location. Although an Edit ➤ Replace can tackle the immediate issue, this is not a helpful state of affairs if we are working with multiple systems and hope to reuse the script.

Refactoring Settings

The obvious solution is to extract this information into a set of properties and use those properties throughout the solution. Here is an example:

```
<property name="core.directory" value="D:\dotNetDelivery\BuildArea"/>
<property name="core.source" value="${core.directory}\Source"/>
<property name="core.output" value="${core.directory}Output"/>
<property name="core.docs" value="${core.directory}Docs"/>
<property name="core.reports" value="${core.directory}Reports"/>
<property name="core.distribution" value="${core.directory}Distribution"/>
<property name="core.publish" value="${core.directory}Publish"/>

<property name="vss.dbpath" value="D:\dotNetDelivery\VSS\srcsafe.ini"/>
<property name="vss.path" value="$/Solutions/Transformer/"/>
```

We then use Edit ➤ Replace to swap in the property names where appropriate. In just a few minutes we have made significant strides in ensuring the flexibility of the script. We have not particularly improved the reusability at this point, though.

Although the changes look simple, keep in mind these important points:

The naming conventions for the properties are very specific. `core.*` properties are identified as those related to the process but not necessarily the project. We would expect to be able to make changes to these regardless of the project.

Removing duplication counts here, too. Wherever possible, edits should be isolated to only one property. For example, `core.directory` needs to be altered only once.

Standard conventions are important. All of the directory values end with a trailing slash. It is perhaps smarter to have a convention rather than worry about what the convention is. Typically, I do not use a trailing slash in directory properties and then add extra slashes as required when using other properties.

In addition to the properties listed at the beginning of this section, you'll notice that the word "Transformer" appears 21 times in the script. However, we will not address that right now, because there are some broader considerations for project names (to be discussed in Chapter 5). We will address these considerations later, though.

Note The refactored build file is available in the source code as `Transformer.Build.Refactored.xml` and behaves in the same way as the original.

Creating the Deploy File

We will now leave behind the build file and take a look at the deploy file. Deployment of this particular application should be simple since there is no environment information to consider. In this case we are deliberately taking a simple view of the actual deployment situation and can consider other scenarios at a later stage.

Core Settings

Having refactored the settings in the build file, we can approach this script in a more enlightened way. In the partial script that follows, I have set out the important properties needed for the deployment, including where the assets can be obtained, where they should be deployed, and a location to act as a work area:

```xml
<?xml version="1.0" encoding="utf-8" ?>
<project name="Transformer" default="help">
    <description>Deploy file for the Transformer application</description>

    <property name="nant.onfailure" value="fail"/>

    <property name="core.directory" value="D:\dotNetDelivery\BuildArea"/>
    <property name="core.publish" value="${core.directory}\Publish"/>

    <property name="core.deploy" value="D:\dotNetDelivery\TempDeploy"/>
    <property name="core.environment"
        value="D:\dotNetDelivery\Program Files\Transformer"/>
    <target
        name="go"
        description="The main target for full deploy process execution."
        depends="selectversion, get, selectenvironments, createenvironments, ➥
position, configure, notify"
    />
```

selectversion

We need to be able to tell NAnt which version we want to deploy. The convention we used in the build file was sys.version, and we will stick with that here. We can pass through a sys.version on the command line, which means no work is required in this section. However, for the sake of convention, we will stick to using the debug switch to select version 0.0.0.0. Therefore, this target looks like this:

```xml
<target name="selectversion"
    description="Selects the correct version of the system.">
    <if test="${debug}">
        <property name="sys.version" value="0.0.0.0"/>
    </if>
</target>
```

This target could become much more complex once we begin to take account of different configurations, such as debug or release.

The notes on how to call the deploy script from the command line are in the help target (which we look at a bit later).

get

After the (very simple) selection of version, the first action should be to obtain the assets and unpackage them to a working area. In this case, it is a matter of creating the working area and then grabbing and unzipping the archive into it:

```
<target name="get" description="Grab the correct assets.">
    <delete dir="${core.deploy}" failonerror="false"/>
    <mkdir dir="${core.deploy}\${sys.version}\"/>
    <copy
        file="${core.publish}\Transformer-Build-${sys.version}.zip"
        todir="${core.deploy}"/>
    <unzip
        zipfile="${core.deploy}\Transformer-Build-${sys.version}.zip"
        todir="${core.deploy}\${sys.version}\"/>
</target>
```

selectenvironments

As discussed earlier, we are not considering at this point the differing environment possibilities, and so there is no work in this target:

```
<target name="selectenvironments" description="Select environments">
    <!--Enter tasks for selectenvironments target-->
</target>
```

createenvironments

Creating the environment is as simple as creating the directory as specified at the top of the script. We also append the specific version of the application as in this example we can have multiple side-by-side instances of the software:

```
<target name="createenvironments" description="Create the environments required">
    <delete dir="${core.environment}\${sys.version}\" failonerror="false"/>
    <mkdir dir="${core.environment}\${sys.version}\"/>
</target>
```

position

With the environment created, we can perform a copy of the assets into the environment. In this case there are very few assets of course.

```
<target name="position" description="Place required assets">
    <copy todir="${core.environment}\${sys.version}\">
        <fileset basedir="${core.deploy}\${sys.version}">
            <include name="**"/>
        </fileset>
    </copy>
</target>
```

configure

Under most scenarios we would expect to have to alter configuration in some way, but in this simple application there is nothing to do:

```
<target name="configure" description="Amend configuration settings as necessary">
    <!--Enter tasks for configure target-->
</target>
```

notify

Once again, a straightforward message is sufficient:

```
<target name="notify" description="Tell everyone of the success or failure.">
    <echo message="Notifying you of the deploy process success."/>
</target>
```

fail

This target will also make do with a simple message:

```
<target name="fail">
    <echo message="Notifying you of a failure in the deploy process."/>
</target>
```

help

We have added notes to the help target to assist with the execution of the script:

```
<target name="help">
    <echo message="The skeleton file for the deploy process is designed ➡
to execute the following targets in turn:"/>
    <echo message="-- selectversion"/>
    <echo message="-- get"/>
    <echo message="-- selectenvironments"/>
    <echo message="-- createenvironments"/>
    <echo message="-- position"/>
    <echo message="-- configure"/>
    <echo message="-- notify"/>
    <echo message="This file should be run with a Boolean value for 'debug'."/>
    <echo message="-- True indicates that no versioning be set (0.0.0.0)."/>
    <echo message="-- False indicates that a regular version be set(1.0.x.0)."/>
    <echo message="Example: -D:debug=true"/>
    <echo message="This file should be run with a version number for ➡
'sys.version'."/>
    <echo message="-- If debug=true then the default will be used (0.0.0.0)."/>
    <echo message="Example: -D:sys.version=1.0.7.0"/>
</target>
```

Examining the Output

So the current deployment script is not too complicated, we can execute the script with the following:

nant -f:Transformer.Deploy.xml -D:debug=true go

or with this:

nant -f:Transformer.Deploy.xml -D:debug=false -D:sys.version=1.0.2.0 go

Based on a debug run, we can see the following output:

```
---------- NAnt ----------
NAnt 0.85
Copyright (C) 2001-2004 Gerry Shaw
http://nant.sourceforge.net

Buildfile: file:///Transformer.Deploy.xml
Target(s) specified: go


selectversion:


get:

    [delete] Deleting directory 'D:\dotNetDelivery\TempDeploy\'.
     [mkdir] Creating directory 'D:\dotNetDelivery\TempDeploy\0.0.0.0\'.
      [copy] Copying 1 file to 'D:\dotNetdelivery\TempDeploy\'.
     [unzip] Unzipping ➡
'D:\dotNetDelivery\TempDeploy\Transformer-Build-0.0.0.0.zip' ➡
to 'D:\TempDeploy\0.0.0.0\' (10379 bytes).

selectenvironments:


createenvironments:

    [delete] Deleting directory ➡
'D:\dotNetDelivery\Program Files\Transformer\0.0.0.0\'.
     [mkdir] Creating directory ➡
'D:\dotNetDelivery\Program Files\Transformer\0.0.0.0\'.

position:

      [copy] Copying 2 files to ➡
'D:\dotNetDelivery\Program Files\Transformer\0.0.0.0\'.
```

```
configure:

notify:

     [echo] Notifying you of the deploy process success.

go:


BUILD SUCCEEDED
Total time: 5.6 seconds.
Output completed (30 sec consumed) - Normal Termination
```

Broadly speaking, not much happened. All we have really done here is unzip some assets to a directory. However, even with this limited interaction, you should be able to see that deployment could quickly become a problem once we have moved beyond pure .NET Windows applications. Once interaction with other systems, databases, multiple configurations, and the like are taken into account, we will have a tricky problem to solve.

With that said, bear in mind that for simple utilities or tools, this deployment script might be perfectly adequate.

■**Note** We will look at techniques for handling deployment complexity in the next chapter to some extent, and also in the advanced chapters toward the end of the book.

Summary

We have walked through the creation of a build and deployment script in some depth. Although we have concentrated on a simple application, the same issues that arise for complex applications have appeared here in one form or another.

We have refactored the original script to a small extent and considered where other gains through refactoring may be obtained as we progress.

In addition, we have linked groups of tasks together to achieve our ends, and we discovered some of the limitations that we may need to tackle.

In the next chapter we will complicate the scenario further, which will lead to refactoring of the code itself and a refactoring of the build files to gain further efficiencies.

Further Reading

For a great practical guide to unit testing (and other types of testing), a good read is *Test-Driven Development in Microsoft .NET*, by James Newkirk (Microsoft Press, 2004).

CHAPTER 5

■■■

Process Standards

We have successfully created build and deploy scripts for a simple candidate application. Additionally, we identified a few areas for improvement and made useful changes to improve the flexibility of the resulting scripts.

In accordance with the Design to Deliver initiative, the next challenge is to provide scripts across multiple systems to ensure the viability of the initial work. We can also take advantage of refactoring and standardization to assist the large-scale integration of all systems under our control.

At the end of this chapter we should be broadly satisfied with the delivery process that is in place for a couple of systems, and be aware of outstanding issues that remain to be addressed.

Another Case Study

Those bright sparks at Etomic have done it again. Following the immeasurable success of the Transformer application, someone suggested it might be a great idea to have a web version of the application.

Implementing a web version is quite simple because the interface and application logic for the Transformer application are cleanly separated. Therefore, a new user interface (UI)—in this case a web interface—can easily be coded using the same application logic. It is not as feature-rich as the Windows version, but it utilizes the same engine assembly, so in principle, it could be. Bear in mind that permitting HTML input via the Web could be a security concern—something the Etomic team may have missed!

The web application looks like the screen shown in Figure 5-1.

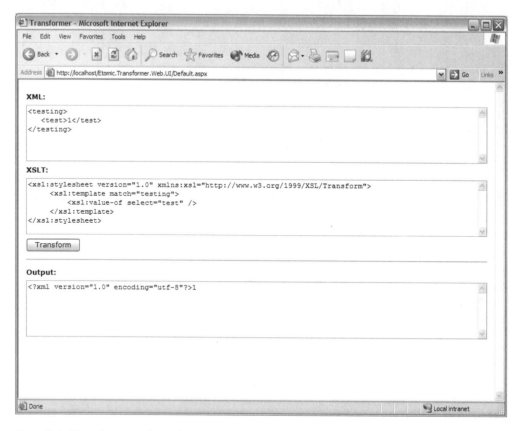

Figure 5-1. *Transformer web application*

Considering the Delivery Scenario

We now have two simple applications with their own interfaces, sharing a common set of application logic. The application logic is controlled through the use of unit tests. Although I have not used it in this instance, the Microsoft User Interface Application Block (available from the MSDN web site at http://msdn.microsoft.com/library/default.asp?url=/library/en-us/dnbda/html/uip.asp) is a useful framework for providing separation of interface and application logic.

It would be quite straightforward to have these four projects (the two UI projects, the engine assembly and the unit tests) held under one solution, but that approach would probably not provide the desired delivery scenario.

Building under one solution means that a new version of each system/UI is created each time a change is made to one or the other, or to the application engine. This may not be what the teams who are developing and maintaining the systems are looking for.

For example, if a new feature is placed in the application logic, then the team handling the web UI implementation may not want to use this feature at this time. They may be happy with the existing engine or not have the time in the project schedule to consider testing. The point is that they should be able to decide when they want to use a new engine. Similarly, changes to one interface impact on the other since both interfaces have to be built at the same time. In this case, the implementations are separate and no real justification exists for coupling the two.

■**Note** Perhaps one justification is that the applications are considered a suite and so coupling the activities is perceived as a good idea. Clearly contexts will differ from system to system.

Seemingly then, the best idea is to have three independent processes for delivery of the subsystems and systems. The independence is only theoretical, of course, since the interfaces ultimately rely on the engine subsystem for delivery, but we can provide more choices.

The Solutions

The solutions can be found in the Visual SourceSafe (VSS) database as follows:

Etomic.Library.Transformer. This solution contains the application logic engine assembly and the corresponding unit-testing assembly.

Etomic.Transformer.Win. This solution references the `Etomic.Library.Transformer.Engine` assembly and contains a project representing the Windows interface.

Etomic.Transformer.Web. This solution references the `Etomic.Library.Transformer.Engine` assembly and contains a project representing the web interface.

We will discuss the naming and organization of the solutions in the next section, where we will also consider other useful standards.

The Build Process

The build process for the three solutions is the same for the most part. The main difference in terms of the defined process is that there are no unit tests in either of the user interface solutions. The only unit testing implemented is in the Etomic.Library.Transformer solution. Therefore, this activity is curtailed in the scripts for the other two solutions, though we can include the FxCop analysis as before.

The Deploy Process

The deployment process is a different story. All three solutions have different specifics, although overall the process matches the use case described in the previous chapter. The differences relate to the delivery of different kinds of system: a web application, a Windows application, and an assembly. There are other possibilities, too, such as Windows services and web services, but these are probably the most common and therefore represent a good starting point. The main differences are as follows:

Etomic.Library.Transformer. Because this is an assembly that is to be used by other systems, it is likely that the deployment itself will be simple. However, the assembly needs to be published in a certain way to ensure that the systems that utilize it can see it and use it during their own builds. We will therefore also need to publish multiple versions of the assembly in a standard way so that the other systems can select the correct version.

Etomic.Transformer.Win. Windows applications are simpler to deploy than web applications since they require no infrastructure such as a web site or virtual directory. There may be need for configuration and so on, but otherwise an XCOPY deployment to a specific folder is probably enough.

Etomic.Transformer.Web. The deployment of the web application is more complex because it will require applying the same configuration settings as the Windows application and also the additional step during environment creation of creating a virtual directory for the site to run in.

Once again, because we are considering applications with no real deployment complexity, we will see only a limited amount of deployment script. That is not to say that our script will not do the job, but we will not have to focus on standardizing and refactoring the deploy scripts in the same way we will the build scripts.

Consideration of Standards

If we were just to move on and produce a build script for these components and systems, we would no doubt be successful since NAnt would easily accommodate our requirements. But at this point we should consider our goal: the implementation of a standard set of scripts and/or processes that are quick and that ease the integration of new systems.

If we imagine for a moment that the Transformer applications are more complex than the code presented here, then the scenario itself is one that is quite common: multiple interfaces/systems utilizing shared common code. This gives us the opportunity to consider broader standards for the way in which the team should organize the environment and the solutions they have in order to successfully and efficiently deliver the resulting products. This sounds a little like Design to Deliver.

The following are some areas worth considering for standardization. We will discuss them here and then see how they impact on the scripts later.

Naming Conventions

The use of sensible naming conventions standardized across solutions can facilitate the creation of build scripts as well as help team members understand the systems they will work with.

One common standard uses the company name, followed by the system name, the subsystem name, and so on—for example, *Etomic.Transformer.Engine*.

In particular, there are specific types of project that, if named the same thing, become a lot easier to handle in the scripts than those with more "individuality." Candidates for naming standards are

The solution file. The solution file is referred to in the `<solution>` task. The file also represents the discrete "unit" that a build script is prepared for. Therefore, the name of the file is important.

The test project. If a solution has an assembly specifically for unit testing, then naming it "Tests" aids with identification during the delivery process.

The UI project. Again, it may be advantageous to provide a standard UI name, particularly when a web application is involved and additional information needs to be provided to the `<solution>` task.

This convention is valuable because it allows for easy matching of assemblies related to the company or the subsystem. If assemblies are named in this way, then it is a great idea to name solution and project files in a way that dovetails with this policy. For instance, for the Transformer engine project, I would name the solution file "Etomic.Library.Transformer" (I added the library name because we intend to share the project contents), and then name the individual projects a single name such as "Engine" or "Tests". I would then set the output assembly names to be "Etomic.Library.Transformer.Engine.dll" and "Etomic.Library.Transformer.Tests.dll" respectively.

If it is possible to standardize on naming of projects and solutions, then you should do so as there will undoubtedly be some efficiency gained through the ability to remove awkward parameters and properties and maintain only standard scripting functions. Consider the following properties that appear in the build files for this chapter:

```
<property name="company.name" value="Etomic"/>
<property name="solution.name" value="${company.name}.Library.Transformer"/>
<property name="project.name.1" value="${solution.name}.Engine" />
```

Here we have ensured that the solution names and content are defined at the top of the build file. As we explained, having standards to allow properties such as this aids the construction of filters and the like for the provision of documentation, distribution packages, and so on.

In a best case, it may be possible to reuse a build script only through changes to these properties.

Source Control Organization

Although organizing VSS is straightforward, it is also very easy to get it wrong, or to let the standards slip since VSS is often perceived as quite static once the source control system is created. Deciding how to organize your source control system and manage it is an important part of a configuration management policy for the development team. It should not be entered into lightly since it is difficult to alter structures later on—at least without losing the history of the systems held under the source control system. You may not agree with the approach presented here, and that is fine. What *is* important is that your own development team reaches an agreement at the outset of introducing these processes.

In the VSS database included with the book code, you'll find a project/folder called `Solutions`; all solutions are then held a level below this, as Figure 5-2 shows.

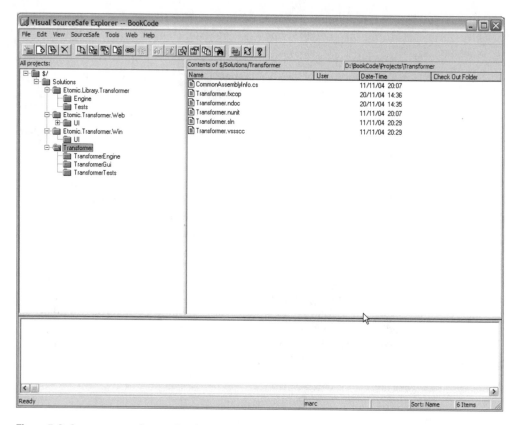

Figure 5-2. *Source control organization*

In a real situation, it is likely—given the limitations of VSS—that there will be multiple VSS databases. Organizing them in the same way, with the same `builder` user account, is efficient because it means that all VSS access becomes the same, with the exception of the solution name. Therefore, by using the naming standards we described earlier, along with this organization, this approach can easily be parameterized to standard targets that could lead to efficiency through refactoring.

VS .NET Settings

We saw several settings in the last chapter that are worth employing. Let us recap those here:

CommonAssemblyInfo.cs. The shared "versioning" file is very useful. All projects should implement this shared information in the same way. Versioning should then become a standard activity; the common file will always contain the same information and will be held in the same place relative to the solution root. This technique can also be used to link to a common SNK file to be used for strong naming (for example).

Documentation. Documentation output should be given the same name as the assembly with the addition of the `.xml` extension, so that we can attempt to use pattern matching to provide the NDoc outputs. The inputs required for NDoc are the assembly name and the XML documentation name, so clearly there is some benefit to using the same name.

Assembly names. Assemblies should be named for the solution and the project name as discussed in the section "Naming Conventions." In fact, in the previous chapter we danced around the issues involved with naming; here we will address them head on.

Note In case you have forgotten already: remember the naming conventions!

A Note on Web Projects

While we are thinking about the organization of VS .NET solutions, it is a good time to consider the problems associated with web projects. Web projects behave differently than Windows projects because they map to virtual directories. Unfortunately, this means they cause several problems:

Build behavior. The build script needs to differ for a web project since additional information regarding web projects has to be supplied to the `<solution>` task. The standard UI naming may come in useful here.

Versioning. It is not possible to "link" files such as `CommonAssemblyInfo.cs` to complete the versioning trick. Therefore, this leads to either using some other method, or at least repeating the versioning for the individual `AssemblyInfo.cs` file for the web projects. Whichever method is chosen is not satisfactory in terms of standardization.

Source control. Web projects tend to play havoc with VSS, because they must be placed at a different level than other projects in the solution, causing problems with standardization and therefore inefficiencies in providing scripts.

These problems are painful, though they can be solved directly if desired. However, after a lot of experimentation, I find I much prefer to use a regular class library to produce a web application than using the web projects option. This avoids the links to IIS and the need to construct virtual directories at the behest of Visual Studio, allowing the code to be held wherever you like instead of where Visual Studio would like it.

Note I will be using this technique for the Etomic.Transformer.Web solution. In Visual Studio .NET 2005 the projects are all the same—about time too!

Swapping Web Projects for Class Libraries

Unfortunately, the best approach is not as simple as just using a class library and adding web pages to the project. You will quickly find that adding a web form (for example) is not an available option.

These configuration options are all held by VS .NET in a few folders, and some of this configuration has to be changed in order to use a class library type project to contain web information. You will find a good set of instructions at

`http://pluralsight.com/wiki/default.aspx/Fritz.AspNetWithoutWebProjects`

These instructions explain how to change the configuration of the solution and how to apply the onetime changes to the VS .NET configuration folders. It is well worth the small amount of effort to set up.

Third-Party Components

Nothing is nicer than discovering that someone has already coded the tool you need (like NAnt, or log4net), but there is nothing nice about discovering that when you open a solution from source control that it contains references to assemblies that you do not have on your machine, or that are not in the same location. Controlling the use of third-party assemblies, and your own shared assemblies, is worthwhile in terms of avoiding frustration time for developers and reducing issues during development of build scripts.

The simplest approach to maintaining libraries of assemblies is to manage them through a shared folder. This folder maintains all shared assemblies, and the developers must use the contents of the folder when developing their solutions. This approach relies on all developers using the same mapped share to access the assemblies, but this is not too onerous.

There are a number of ways in which this could be managed, depending on how aggressive you would prefer to be in terms of progression and version update.

Nonaggressive Library Management

With this method, each assembly has its own folder that contains each named version of the assembly, as shown in Figure 5-3.

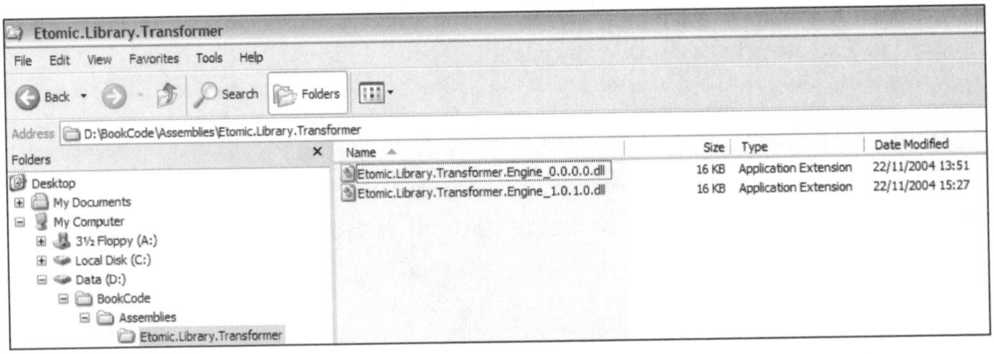

Figure 5-3. *Nonaggressive library management*

This allows the developer to select a specific version of an assembly that does not change. This means the impact from version upgrades is minimal, but of course it could lead to a confused situation in terms of the deployed assemblies. Without some kind of progression, over a significant period of time it may not be possible to integrate newer versions of assemblies into solutions without extensive development and regression work. For this reason, you may prefer to use the next method, which gives the process a few more teeth.

Aggressive Library Management

Under a more aggressive library management, each assembly has its own folder that contains three more folders, as shown in Figure 5-4.

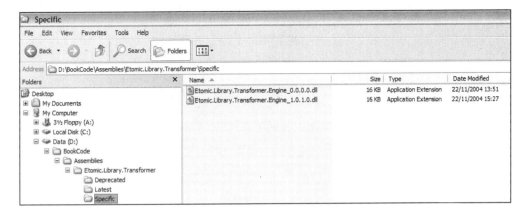

Figure 5-4. *Aggressive library management*

The folders are used as follows:

Latest. This folder contains the latest assembly version with the regular (rather than versioned) assembly name.

Specific. This folder contains the latest named version of an assembly and the historical versions of the assembly, as in the nonaggressive approach.

Deprecated. This folder contains versions that are not to be used in active developments any longer.

The process for using these folders is fairly obvious:

A developer should always refer to the latest version of an assembly.

The latest version is replaced as required.

All versions are available in the Specific folder.

Any build of a system dependent on the shared assembly will pick up the latest version and use it during the build.

In the event of a failure, a developer faces two choices: fix the problem so that the latest version can be utilized, or choose a specific version and stick with that. The advantage is that the developer must consciously choose to limit the version of an assembly used with their system and thus the balance will generally fall in favor of a fix (coders being coders).

Finally, the Deprecated folder can be used to remove specific versions of assemblies that are no longer desired. Moving an assembly from Specific to Deprecated will of course result in a failed build for dependent systems and so again forces a decision to be made.

The important aspect of the process is that at no time are we being especially hawkish about the upgrade policy since the decision to use an older version is always available. The point is that the issues surrounding older versions are always visible to the development team and require intervention and decision making. It can be easy to fail to manage these aspects of the development environment by simply forgetting about them rather than by actively failing at them.

■**Note** Where components are actually more than one assembly, then the folder structure may have to be enhanced to handle these multiple assemblies. The principle is the same, though.

This particular organizational standard offers us several clues for the deployment of our own library component, and we will see this in operation.

Tools and Support Organization

A final useful standard is the management of the tools and supporting information used by the processes and the development team. You can be just as frustrated using tools and utilities that are supposed to aid development activities as you can by lack of success of those tools if they are not managed correctly.

This particular management activity is problematic since developers are likely to adapt their environments as they see fit—they are humans, after all. My preferred approach is to publish a standard that requires adherence by the developers with only occasional enforcement of the standards to prove the point that voluntary adherence is the best way!

In Chapter 1, we discussed tackling this problem if you use a virtual development environment such as VMWare to control the "vanilla" development environment. A virtual environment offers a quick turnaround of development machine rebuilds, and provides the ability to truly declare that development environments can be destroyed and rebuilt at any time. This prevents developers from personalizing the development machines too much and actually encourages discussion about tools and versions to be maintained on the vanilla virtual environment. The integration of new team members also becomes easier since everyone is looking "through the same eyes."

I am only briefly mentioning the use of a virtual environment, but do not underestimate the benefits of doing so. At the same time, be sure to take into account the cost for the licenses and perhaps additional memory, as well as the overhead of managing the software and preparing the virtual sessions.

Note When we implemented this practice for real, most developers—myself included to some extent—were skeptical about the improvements and the central management (although these were usually dressed up as a better excuse such as performance issues). But after only a couple of versions of the desktop, the improvements were there for all to see. In fact, over two years we have released only four live versions of the virtual environment, which is a testament to the success of this policy. I still keep a few personal utilities, though, of course!

Finally, apart from the tools there may be a variety of support assets needed to complete delivery processes. For example, if you provide strong naming for every assembly as a standard, then you may keep a (nonsecret) public-private key pair for use in a shared location. Or perhaps you use several XSLT assets to transform build outputs. These all need to be maintained somewhere. You should also bear in mind that all of the build scripts and similar assets should themselves be maintained under source control. Script files have a tendency to suffer from poor configuration management, particularly those script files that are involved in configuration management!

Creating the Build Files

We have seen a significant set of standards in the previous section. They are not difficult standards to implement and maintain, and are generally common sense. But they are not fail-safe. If we need proof of the advantage they offer when considering delivery, then we can provide that proof through the build and deploy scripts for the three solutions comprising the Transformer suite of applications.

What Has Changed?

We left Chapter 4 with a relatively satisfactory build script for the Transformer solution as it was then. We now have three solutions to contend with, and so there is a build file, deploy file, and a build number file for each solution found in the source code for this chapter. Let us consider a number of changes in turn rather than an exhaustive look through each file.

General Organization

Now that we are working with multiple solutions, the organization of the build area is unsatisfactory since it handles only one solution. The natural progression is to subdivide the build area by solution and then by the conventions we used in Chapter 4 (such as the `build` and `output` folders). Changes to the `core.*` properties reflect the addition of the solution name to the folder paths.

Use of Naming Conventions

The addition of the following code (this is the version in the `Etomic.Library.Transformer.Build.xml` file) has proven beneficial to certain aspects of the script:

```
<property name="company.name" value="Etomic"/>
<property name="solution.name" value="${company.name}.Library.Transformer"/>
<property name="project.name.1" value="${solution.name}.Engine" />
```

We use the properties as follows:

company.name. This property is used to assemble the other properties and is also used in the versioning task and the NDoc task for providing copyright information.

solution.name. This is an extremely useful property used to construct the build area, select the correct VSS path, specify the correct build number file, provide assembly versioning information by way of the product name, supply information for NDoc, provide the name of the distribution package, and finally, of course, provide the name of the solution file for the build task. All of this is possible through the sensible application of naming standards.

project.name.1. This is a more specific property and provides information for the FxCop and NDoc tasks. Until we have some method of supplying filtering information adequately for these tasks, we need to have these specific properties, but we should make a note at this point that it would be nice to remove reliance on these project.name.x properties. If a solution consisted of multiple assemblies—as would probably be the norm—then we would expect to see a set of project.name.x properties.

Additionally, we have used the unit-testing naming convention of "Tests" to pick up the unit-test assembly in the unit-testing target (in Etomic.Library.Transformer.Tests.dll). The same standard information can be seen in the other build scripts as well.

Organizational Standards

We have also implemented the standards as described in the previous section in terms of source control organization, the VS .NET settings, the use of class libraries instead of web projects, and also the shared assembly area at D:\BookCode\Assemblies.

It is difficult to assess the implications of the standards in isolation since they are tied together in terms of usage and therefore in terms of tokenizing of this information within the scripts, but we can see the effects the standards have on the build scripts.

Comparing the Build Files

The application of these particular standards mean that the similarities between the build files are significant. Table 5-1 shows the differences highlighted in the files using the differencing capabilities of VSS.

Table 5-1. *Web build vs. Windows build*

Line	Difference
2, 3	The description of the solution the build file is designed for
8	The solution.name property
99	The use of .dll in the web file compared to the use of .exe in the Windows file for the FxCop analysis

Line	Difference
108	The same in the NDoc task
142–152	The addition of specific copy tasks and filters for the web assets

We can also compare the web build file (or the Windows build file) against the library build file. The differences are shown in Table 5-2.

Table 5-2. *Web build vs. library build*

Line	Difference
2,3	The description of the solution the build file is designed for
8	The `solution.name` property
9	The `project.name.1` property
97–103	The inclusion of the unit-testing information
142–152	The addition of specific copy tasks and filters for the web assets
173+	The inclusion of the NUnit report failure target in the library file

Again, very few differences exist between the two files. While this is encouraging, we should consider why there are differences, whether there would be more with a more complete application, and what we can do to eliminate the differences:

Solution naming. This is always going to be different, of course. This does not constitute a particular issue and presents an opportunity to pass the solution name as a parameter to the script execution.

.exe vs .dll. Although this difference could have been prevented in FxCop and NDoc at the points demonstrated, it would have presented itself in the XML aspect of NDoc, so there is no particularly obvious way to tackle this problem in itself.

NDoc. At first glance, the solution would be to use a `fileset` filter to provide the information necessary for documentation instead of explicitly stating the documentation requirements, but it is more problematic than that. Even if the particular solution assemblies can be differentiated (which may not be as easy as you think), then it is not obvious whether they are supposed to be documented. You could argue that all assemblies should be documented. If so, then there is potentially a solution here.

FxCop. This particular task is challenging since it does not have an especially friendly management method. We are stuck with this awkward task for the time being, but we can tackle it by extending NAnt, and we will.

Unit testing. The unit testing is similar to the NDoc situation, although the identification of testing assemblies is now obvious because we are using the test-naming pattern from the standards. However, the tasks will begin to fail if they find no unit testing to perform or transform. Since we need the tasks to fail, the solution is to perform checks on the existence of files and so on, but this is not necessarily a pleasant experience.

Publish. Web projects certainly have their own patterns for organizing assets because they contain so many different assets, such as images, web forms, and the like. Perhaps with a little more effort we could arrive at a standard pattern for publishing.

So there are some problems in the files. All in all, though, things are generally satisfactory. Across different types of solutions—particularly those with differing features such as unit testing—we need to make structural changes to the script file. However, in solutions of the same type and with the same features, changes are broadly parameter changes. At this point it would be fairly easy to continue to work with the scripts as they are, but we can also make some changes now to improve the scripts.

Refactoring the Build Files

Apart from the differences between the files, the similarities are important too. We can be pleased with the standardization process if we can remove as much of the commonality as possible to reduce duplication and make the edits and changes required for a new solution as obvious as possible.

Interestingly, the majority of the other targets are identical. Dragging out these common areas into a master build file means that we can call into the specific tasks for each solution but reduce code duplication. We can follow some fairly simple steps to complete our first pass at this work.

The first thing we will do is create a new build file called `Build.Core.xml`. This file will act as the starting point for all of our building activities:

```
<?xml version="1.0" encoding="utf-8" ?>
<project name="Build.Core" default="help">
    <description>Build file to perform core common functionality.</description>
```

We will then maintain all of the properties used in the regular build files, but amend the `solution.name` line slightly:

```
<property name="company.name" value="Etomic"/>
<property name="solution.name" value="${company.name}.${solution.stub}"/>
```

The `solution.stub` property is not defined in the `Build.Core.xml` file but is instead expected to be passed at runtime. We will make a tweak to the `help` target to reflect this:

```
<echo message="This file should be run with a value for 'solution.stub'."/>
<echo message="Example: -D:solution.stub=Transformer.Web"/>
```

Now, if we investigate the targets in the build file, we can see that up to and including the target, the targets are identical in all three build files. Thus we can remove this code and place it into the `Build.Core.xml` file. We then need to add a go target to the core file, which will take care of the targets we have extracted from the build files.

```
<target name="go"
    description="The main target for full build process execution."
    depends="clean, get, version1, version2, specific"
    />
```

The go target now handles only the targets we have decided are common across all three solutions. Additionally, I have added a new target called specific. This target will be used to complete the process by calling the specific build file for the specified solution. The specific target looks like this:

```
<target name="specific">
    <nant
        buildfile="${solution.name}.Build.xml"
        target="go"
        inheritall="true"
        />
</target>
```

This code makes use of NAnt's ability to call other build files. This task tells NAnt to call the target go in the specified file. Also, it tells NAnt to pass through all of the current properties to the called build file; in this way the called build file "inherits" all of the properties.

The next step is to make some changes to the specific build files themselves. These changes are in three areas: the required targets, the properties, and the help target.

First of all, we will no longer be calling the specific files independently; they must be called through the core file to be successful. Therefore, the help target should reflect this:

```
<target name="help">
    <echo message="This file should not be executed. Use Build.Core.xml"/>
</target>
```

Next is the elimination of the targets that have now been moved to the core file. This means that targets clean, get, version1, and version2 can all be deleted. The go target must reflect this change too:

```
<target name="go"
    description="The main target for full build process execution."
    depends="build, test, document, publish, notify"
    />
```

Finally, almost all of the properties are set in the core file, so they can all be removed from the specific files. The only exception is the project.name.1 property (and any others in a more complex scenario). So the Etomic.Transformer.Library has only one property:

```
<property name="project.name.1" value="${solution.name}.Engine" />
```

We have performed some very simple refactoring to remove duplication. In fact, the number of lines of code in the new files is 413 while the old files contained 578. Significantly, the specific files now have only about 100 lines of code instead of about 200. Over numerous systems this in itself is a major reduction in duplication and maintenance effort.

Note Do not lose sight of the fact that the refactoring of common functionality is only due to the enforcement of standards across the solutions. As soon as the standards are not followed, it becomes harder to use the same patterns and parameter settings to achieve common results.

Running the new scripts involves a command such as the following:

```
nant -f:Build.Core.xml -D:debug=true -D:solution.stub=Transformer.Win
```

Further Refactoring

We can do more to achieve further decreases in duplication, such as tackling the publish pattern. I have not investigated the commonality of the filtering and organization patterns, but we can suppose for a moment that there is no common ground.

We are only three solutions into the investigation and we may yet find that areas which looked common are not in fact common at all. You should be careful how far you take this in the early part of your investigations. A gold star goes to anyone astute enough to notice that I did not refactor the build target even though it is the same in all three projects. Currently it looks like this in all three projects:

```
<target name="build" description="Compile the application.">
   <solution solutionfile="${core.source}\$solution.name}.sln"
      configuration="Debug" outputdir="${core.output}\"/>
</target>
```

Although it is simple enough at the moment, it will most definitely differ when COM objects, the GAC, and so on are involved; there will be other types of work to do, such as exposing the objects to .NET and the like.

In this instance, some parts of the web project are different from the assembly project and the Windows project, so I could perhaps refactor both of these targets into the core file and use a conditional statement to decide which is needed. We can do this now.

We could also refactor the targets to Build.Core.xml, but I have chosen to make a separate file to contain utility targets and the like since Build.Core can become confusing quickly—at the moment it is linear and therefore understandable.

Also, we need to call back into the target because we have to pass properties to the publish target, and this could become a conceptual challenge.

The beginnings of Build.Common.xml look like this:

```
<?xml version="1.0" encoding="utf-8" ?>
<project name="Build.Common" default="help">
  <description>Build file to perform core common functionality.</description>

  <target name="help">
    <echo message="Build.Common file contains common functionality for builds."/>
    <echo message="This file should not be executed. Use Build.Core.xml instead"/>
  </target>

</project>
```

Next we can extract the publish steps from the web and Windows/assembly build files into two separate targets in the Build.Common file. We will call the targets publish.web and publish.win, respectively:

```xml
<target name="publish.web">
    <copy todir="${core.distribution}\">
        <fileset basedir="${core.source}\UI">
            <include name="**"/>
            <exclude name="obj/**"/>
            <exclude name="**/*.cs"/>
            <exclude name="**/*.resx"/>
            <exclude name="**/*.csproj"/>
            <exclude name="**/*.vspscc"/>
            <exclude name="**/*.scc"/>
        </fileset>
    </copy>

    <copy todir="${core.distribution}\bin\">
        <fileset basedir="${core.output}\">
            <include name="*.dll"/>
            <exclude name="*Tests*"/>
        </fileset>
    </copy>

    <zip zipfile="${core.publish}\${solution.name}-Build-${sys.version}.zip">
        <fileset basedir="${core.distribution}">
            <include name="**"/>
        </fileset>
    </zip>
</target>

<target name="publish.win">
    <copy todir="${core.distribution}\">
        <fileset basedir="${core.output}\">
            <include name="*.dll"/>
            <include name="*.exe"/>
            <exclude name="*Tests*"/>
        </fileset>
    </copy>

    <zip zipfile="${core.publish}\${solution.name}-Build-${sys.version}.zip">
        <fileset basedir="${core.distribution}\">
            <include name="**" />
        </fileset>
    </zip>
</target>
```

Clearly there is a lot of common script here that could be further refactored, but we will concentrate on the former refactoring. We need a step for deciding which target should be invoked. We can do this with a target called `publish` in the `Build.Common` file as follows:

```
<target name="publish">
    <if test="${solution.isweb}">
        <call target="publish.web"/>
    </if>
    <ifnot test="${solution.isweb}">
        <call target="publish.win"/>
    </ifnot>
</target>
```

This means that there needs to be a Boolean property in the specific build files. Therefore we need to add the following line (with the appropriate value) to each of the build files:

```
<property name="solution.isweb" value="false"/>
```

We then need to edit the `publish` target in each to the following:

```
<target name="publish"
        description="Place the compiled assets, reports etc. in agreed location.">
    <nant buildfile="Build.Common.xml" target="publish" inheritall="true"/>
</target>
```

The result is a further reduction in code in the specific files.

■**Note** This could have been implemented by passing the name of the target from the specific build file instead of a Boolean value and a conditional statement. In fact, that method would be preferred if there were more than two options for publishing. The reason I did not specify the target here was also that I wanted to hide the implementation details from the specific scripts in case I decide to change things internally to the common file.

■**Caution** Introducing this further refactoring has had the desired effect, but you should be wary of the dependencies now introduced on the publish step as well as the gains. Changes to the `fileset` pattern could have serious negative as well as positive impact on the build process.

Creating the Deploy Files

We will now leave the build files alone and take a look at the deploy scripts. We discussed the processes for deployment at the beginning of the chapter, and we can indeed see that the deployment processes of the three solutions are different. We will take a brief look at each file and the most relevant aspects for deployment.

Etomic.Library.Transformer.Deploy.xml

The properties to run this file are as follows:

```
<property name="nant.onfailure" value="fail"/>


<property name="company.name" value="Etomic"/>
<property name="solution.name" value="${company.name}.Library.Transformer"/>
<property name="project.name.1" value="${solution.name}.Engine"/>


<property name="core.directory" value="D:\BookCode\BuildArea"/>
<property name="core.projectarea" value="${core.directory}\${solution.name}"/>
<property name="core.publish" value="${core.projectarea}\Publish"/>


<property name="core.deploy" value="D:\TempDeploy"/>
<property name="core.environment" value="D:\BookCode\Assemblies"/>
```

The first few properties are the same as those for the build file. Perhaps there will be some opportunity to join the two files so that they do not have to be maintained separately, with the additional maintenance and risk that is introduced.

The next three properties are duplicates as well.

After that, the final properties are specific to deployment. The first is a random folder to be used for unpackaging the application and any other bits and pieces of work before actually positioning the assets. The second property is more important—it points to the actual location for the assets to be published.

The next interesting steps are the "getting" of the assets and their unpackaging:

```
<target name="get" description="Grab the correct assets.">
    <delete dir="${core.deploy}\" failonerror="false"/>
    <mkdir dir="${core.deploy}\${sys.version}\"/>
    <copy file="${core.publish}\${solution.name}-Build-${sys.version}.zip"
        todir="${core.deploy}\"/>
    <unzip zipfile="${core.deploy}\${solution.name}-Build-${sys.version}.zip"
        todir="${core.deploy}\"/>
</target>
```

The tasks here are simple enough to follow. Then in this instance, we need to ensure that the environment for the assembly exists through the following:

```
<target name="createenvironments" description="Create the environments required">
    <mkdir dir="${core.environment}\${solution.name}\Latest\"
        failonerror="false"/>
    <mkdir dir="${core.environment}\${solution.name}\Specific\"
        failonerror="false"/>
    <mkdir dir="${core.environment}\${solution.name}\Deprecated\"
        failonerror="false"/>
</target>
```

Notice this includes the initial setup of the aggressive library management discussed earlier as part of the standards.

Finally, all that remains is to place the assemblies in the required folders with the relevant names:

```
<target name="position" description="Place required assets">
    <copy
        file="${core.deploy}\${project.name.1}.dll"
        todir="${core.environment}\${solution.name}\Latest\"
        overwrite="true"
        />
    <copy
        file="${core.deploy}\${project.name.1}.dll"
        tofile="${core.environment}\${solution.name}\Specific\ ➡
                            ${project.name.1}_${sys.version}.dll"
        overwrite="true"
        />
</target>
```

Again, these steps are not complicated. The important aspect of this work is the overwriting of the assembly in the Latest folder with whichever published version is being used and then the write of a named version of the assembly to the Specific folder.

Note There is no safeguard on overwriting the Latest version with some older version of the assembly.

Once this file is run, with something like the following line, the assembly is then deployed into the chosen locations, as can be seen in Figure 5-5 and Figure 5-6:

```
nant -f:Etomic.Library.Transformer.Deploy.xml -D:debug=false ➡
-D:sys.version=1.0.1.0
```

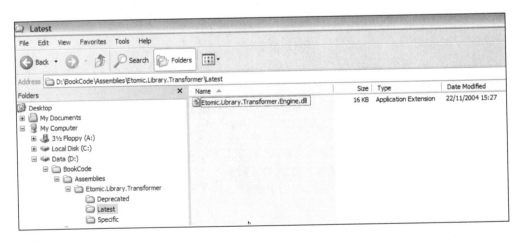

Figure 5-5. *The Latest folder*

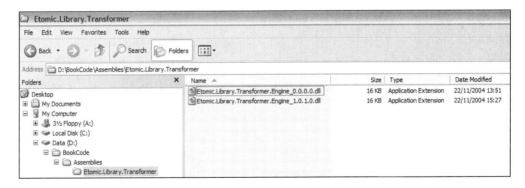

Figure 5-6. *The Specific folder*

Etomic.Transformer.Win.Deploy.xml

The Windows deployment script is similar to the script seen in the previous chapter, with the addition of the newer properties from the enhanced script efficiencies. The key change in the properties is the deployment environment, which is as follows:

```
<property name="core.environment" value="D:\Program Files\${solution.name}"/>
```

Apart from that, the deployment is a straightforward XCOPY.

Following deployment of the 1.0.2.0 version, the structures look as shown in Figure 5-7. Notice the differing versions of the assemblies used in the build of the overall solution.

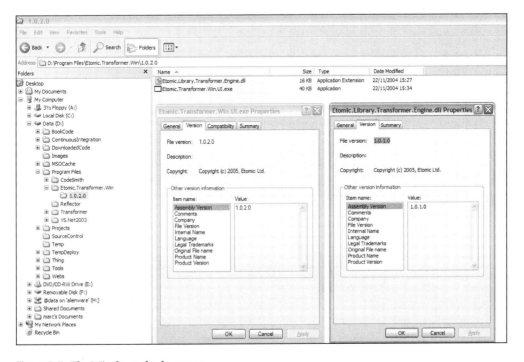

Figure 5-7. *The Windows deployment*

Etomic.Transformer.Web.Deploy.xml

The web deployment script is almost identical to the Windows deployment script. In this instance, the solution name changes (of course), and the `core.environment` property points to a nominated share for web applications—in this case, `D:\Webs`.

Finally, at this point there is one additional line in the `createenvironments` target.

```
<mkiisdir dirpath="${core.environment}\${sys.version}\"
          vdirname="${solution.name}-${sys.version}"/>
```

This is about the simplest use of `<mkiisdir>` there is, but it suffices in this instance.

After this, the deployment becomes another XCOPY scenario. Once it is completed, we can access the web application as shown in Figure 5-8.

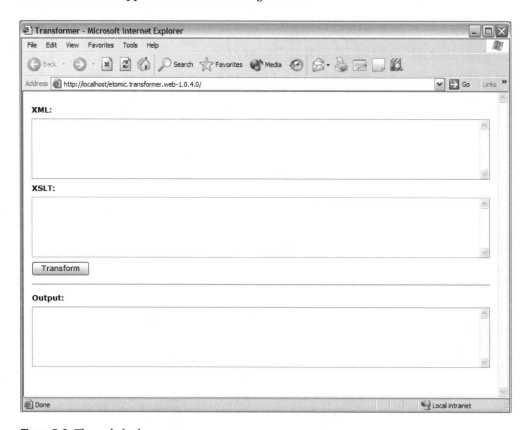

Figure 5-8. *The web deployment*

> **■Note** It may seem that I am paying a lot more attention to the build process than I did to the deployment process. This is true at this point, since the build process is much more feature-rich. The applications at this point are trivial to deploy; they do not contain configuration information or links to databases, for example. We will need to think more about these issues in subsequent chapters.

Observations

We should reflect on what we have seen so far regarding the delivery processes. The following are the key points:

Level of difficulty. It is not especially difficult to create a build and deploy script for an application, particularly a pure .NET application. However, the gains in creating build scripts are in the standardization and efficiency of the overall process for a team of developers, in the same way that a standard architecture helps a developer learn about a system.

Standards and organization. Given that all delivery scenarios will not be the same, we need to make the best use of those aspects that *are* the same, so that it is obvious where the differences lie and the changes that need to be made to deliver a solution. Implementing the standards listed in this chapter is no small task in a preexisting environment, with significant active solutions, but at the same time none of the standards is complicated.

Refactoring. Once a few scripts were completed, refactoring opportunities were immediately obvious and we applied some changes to make obvious gains. However, it also pays to be wary of creating too much commonality between scripts; over the course of the whole implementation program, we may be proved wrong in certain areas. There is also an equal but opposite method of refactoring: that of code generation. Rather than create efficiencies through commonality, we may be able to provide generated build and deploy scripts for an application.

Awkward areas. There are a few holes in the process that are not easily plugged through simple standard scripts. These are areas such as FxCop (a non-NAnt requirement), knowledge of documentation and unit testing requirements, and so on.

Overall, we should be pleased with our efforts so far. The implementation of the Design to Deliver initiative is on track, and it seems to be proven that it can be done for a variety of application types. Although we have not studied areas of complexity yet, we have worked out core standards for issue to the development teams. Further success at this point will require more thought and more complex interactions.

A More Complex Scenario

We have looked at a fairly common scenario and provided a useful delivery process for some differing application types: Windows, web, and a class library. We will continue to develop the processes further for those in the next chapter. Before we move on, though, we can take a look at another application that contains a little more complexity and see how the scripts we have developed perform with this application.

VSSManager

The application we will look at this time is called VSSManager. This is a utility application that allows control of a set of VSS databases from a central control application. This is especially useful for the team at Etomic because it means they can administer their VSS databases through the Web, provide automatic lock-down of databases at release time, and similar activities. The current functionality of VSSManager is described in the use case shown in Figure 5-9.

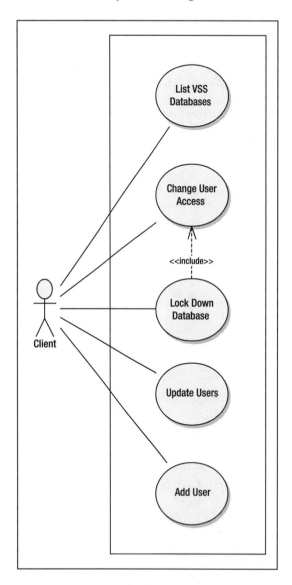

Figure 5-9. *VSSManager functionality*

The important things to consider about the application for us with our "delivery hats" on involve the implementation details for this system:

Automating VSS (a COM application) means that there must be some use of a COM object.

Using the Web to access a database application such as VSS will not work due to permission issues and the requirement to have an interactive process. Therefore, a Windows service has been developed that uses remoting to allow client access to the VSS databases. Apart from the Windows service, there is a console version of the server, which is handy when developing and testing the service. Both perform in the same way.

A separate assembly contains the interfaces for the remote objects that can be referenced by the server application, and will also be required for any client application.

The configuration of the application is handled through the app.config file, which takes lists of databases and users for use by the service. Some custom configuration section handlers have been coded for this task.

Finally, logging is handled using the flexible log4net open source library. This is also configured in the app.config file.

▨**Caution** This little application demonstrates some remoting principles—programming to interface, for example—some use of configuration section handlers, and a little COM interop work, but I would be wary about using it in a production environment. There are some problems with its use, not least of which is the lack of encryption of passwords. On the other hand, it was quite a fun application to develop!

Figure 5-10 shows the packages and dependencies forming the VSSManager application. Given this information, we need to ensure the following in the delivery of this system:

COM interop. We need to ensure that the build correctly exposes the VSS API library to .NET to allow the build to work. We also need to consider how we deploy given the dependency on the VSS API library.

Remoting. We need to ensue that we deploy the remoting interface to the shared assemblies area as well as deploying the main application so that other developers can work with the remoting interfaces to develop the client.

Windows service. We must install and configure the Windows service when we deploy the application.

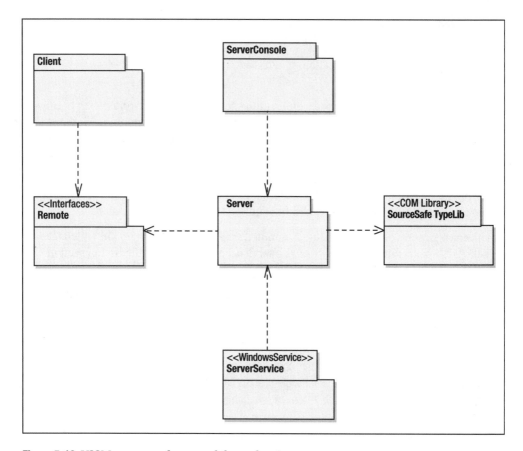

Figure 5-10. *VSSManager packages and dependencies*

So there are a few more things to think about, which will mean a little extra work in the scripts. Before we worry about that, though, we can see how far our regular scripts will take us in the delivery of this application.

In fact, they can take us a considerable distance. To build the application, the Etomic.➥ VSSManager.Build.xml file looks almost the same as the build scripts we have seen for the Transformer suite of applications. Significant changes are, of course, the specifics of the assemblies required:

```
<property name="project.name.1" value="${solution.name}.Remote" />
<property name="project.name.2" value="${solution.name}.Server" />
<property name="project.name.3" value="${solution.name}.Service" />
<property name="project.name.4" value="${solution.name}.ServerConsole" />
<property name="solution.isweb" value="false"/>
```

If you take a look at the rest of the build file, you will be able to see the slight changes to the FxCop and NDoc tasks to include the relevant assemblies from the list above. Finally, there are no unit tests for this application (very naughty!) and so there is no NUnit step.

So we haven't had any problems so far. Running the `Build.Core.xml` script with the following command-line call will successfully build the application:

```
nant -f:Build.Core.xml -D:debug=true -D:solution.stub=VSSManager
```

While this is seemingly straightforward, we should examine the output to think about what has occurred. The output from the build process is shown in Figure 5-11.

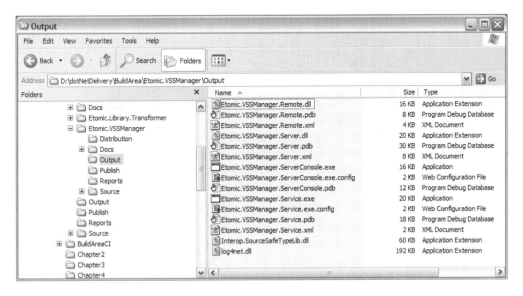

Figure 5-11. *The output from building Etomic.VssManager*

Most of the content found in this folder is to be expected: the compiled assemblies representing the application, the configuration files, and the referenced log4net assembly. Additionally, and importantly, there is a wrapper for the VSS library called `Interop.Source` ⟶ `SafeTypeLib.dll`. This means that the `<solution>` task has handled the generation of this wrapper automatically, which is a very useful feature of the task and of course mirrors the behavior of the VS .NET build process itself.

So in fact, we have had to make no real changes to the build scripts in order to handle this scenario.

The deploy scripts can also handle the deployment of application without much change. Once again, using the Windows application deploy script from Transformer and applying the necessary changes will deploy the application to, for instance, the Program Files folder as usual. Additionally, using the assembly deploy script from the work on Transformer enables us to deploy the remoting interfaces to the shared assembly area. This means that there are two steps to the deployment of the application, but these steps could be chained by including the deployment of the remoting interfaces—the NAnt call to do this—in a `nant.onsuccess` target.

However, despite this successful deployment, we have in fact not handled two of the issues. The first is the dependency on the VSS API and the second is the installation of the Windows service.

The VSS API Dependency

The core issue for this dependency is that it is pointless to deploy the application on a machine unless the VSS API is present. If in fact we can guarantee that it is present, then no changes are needed to the script and the application will work because the interop assembly is included as part of the deployment package.

However, we should actually provide some assurance to the deployment. This can take the form of regenerating the interop assembly on the deployment target at the time of deployment. We can do this with the <tlbimp> task. This task may look like this:

```
<tlbimp typelib="C:\Program Files\Microsoft Visual Studio\VSS\win32\ssapi.dll"
    output="${core.environment}\${sys.version}\Interop.SourceSafeTypeLib.dll"
    namespace="SourceSafeTypeLib" />
```

This code reproduces the interop assembly in a manual way. I have named the output assembly as VS .NET would, and have also included the namespace as VS .NET would. Without this, you may find that the manually generated assembly will not work with your application. We could also have used this technique in the build step if we were using the <csc> task instead of the <solution> task. The code above presumes that VSS is installed in the specified location—which may be true, but it also may not. We can do a better job of this task by accessing the registry to obtain the actual location of the ssapi.dll assembly. The following code retrieves this information:

```
<readregistry property="vss.api"
    key="TypeLib\{783CD4E0-9D54-11CF-B8EE-00608CC9A71F}\5.1\0\win32\"
    hive="ClassesRoot" />
```

This task grabs the value of the specified key and places it in the specified property (in this case vss.api). We can then use the property in the <tlbimp> task instead of the hard-coded location. You can find the key required by searching the registry or by checking the GUID of the required assembly (which is also stored in the relevant .csproj file).

So, using these manual steps means that we have provided some assurance that VSS is present on the deployment target machine. If it were not, these tasks, and therefore the deployment, would fail.

The Windows Service

We have generated a Windows service, so we need to install it, and perhaps set it running as part of the deployment process. We should also uninstall any existing service.

To install a Windows service, we must write an installer class as part of the code for the application. This is a requirement whether NAnt, an MSI, or something else is used as the deployment tool. The code for this can be examined in the solution, but this is not a primary concern for us. Our concern is to actually perform the installation. This can be done using installutil—a utility for this purpose that sits in the .NET Framework folder along with the other .NET utilities, such as ildasm.

Installing the service involves a command-line call such as

```
installutil Etomic.VssManager.Service.exe
```

An uninstall would be performed with the addition of a /u switch. Unfortunately, there is no specific NAnt task wrapping this utility but we can of course use an <exec> task appropriately to call the utility.

This would look as follows:

```
<exec program="${framework::get-framework-directory('net-1.1')}\installutil">
    <arg value="${core.environment}\${sys.version}\${solution.name}.Service.exe"
    />
    <arg value="/LogToConsole=false"/>
</exec>
```

This call finds the framework directory (here presuming we are using the .NET 1.1 Framework in order to call installutil, passing the name of the service and one additional flag to avoid unnecessary output in order to install the service.

Finally, we can start the service with the following task:

```
<servicecontroller action="Start" service="Vss Manager Service" />
```

So with that, we have taken care of the installation of the service.

There is one more interesting detail. The service uses a configuration file in order to operate. Ordinarily, this would need to be placed in the Windows folder since services use this as their working folder. To avoid this, the following line of code appears in the OnStart method for the service, which allows the configuration file to be placed alongside the executable in the same way as, for instance, a Windows application:

```
Directory.SetCurrentDirectory(AppDomain.CurrentDomain.BaseDirectory);
```

In this example, I have not addressed configuration file changes that may be necessary upon deployment. You can find more details of this in Chapter 8, which also includes more complex deployment scenarios.

Changes to the Deployment Script

The above additions for the COM interop and service installer can be added into the deployment script for the service in the configuration target. This target looks like this when completed:

```
<target name="configure" description="Amend configuration settings as necessary">

    <readregistry property="vss.api"
        key="TypeLib\{783CD4E0-9D54-11CF-B8EE-00608CC9A71F}\5.1\0\win32\"
        hive="ClassesRoot" />
    <delete
        file="${core.environment}\${sys.version}\Interop.SourceSafeTypeLib.dll"/>
    <tlbimp typelib="${vss.api}"
        output="${core.environment}\${sys.version}\Interop.SourceSafeTypeLib.dll"
        namespace="SourceSafeTypeLib" />

    <exec program="${framework::get-framework-directory('net-1.1')}\installutil">
        <arg value="/u"/>
```

```
    <arg
      value="${core.environment}\${old.version}\${solution.name}.Service.exe"/>
    <arg value="/LogToConsole=false"/>
  </exec>

  <exec program="${framework::get-framework-directory('net-1.1')}\installutil">
    <arg
      value="${core.environment}\${sys.version}\${solution.name}.Service.exe"/>
    <arg value="/LogToConsole=false"/>
  </exec>

  <servicecontroller action="Start" service="Vss Manager Service" />

</target>
```

So the process is as follows:

Read the registry to obtain the location of the VSS API.

Delete the version of the interop file included with the deployment package.

Create a new version of the interop file.

Uninstall any existing service.

Install the new service.

Start the service.

To uninstall an old version of the service, we need to pass the old version at the command line. The command line to then move from one version to another might look like this:

```
nant -D:debug=false -D:sys.version=1.0.1.0 -D:old.version=1.0.0.0
```

Here is the output of the configuration step:

```
---------- NAnt ----------
NAnt 0.85
Copyright (C) 2001-2005 Gerry Shaw
http://nant.sourceforge.net

Buildfile: file:///Etomic.VSSManager.Deploy.xml
Target framework: Microsoft .NET Framework 1.1
Target(s) specified: configure

configure:

    [delete] Deleting file Interop.SourceSafeTypeLib.dll.

    [exec] Microsoft (R) .NET Framework Installation utility Version 1.1.4322.573
```

```
[exec] Copyright (C) Microsoft Corporation 1998-2002. All rights reserved.
[exec]
[exec] Uninstalling assembly 'etomic.vssmanager.service.exe'.
[exec] Affected parameters are:
[exec]     assemblypath = etomic.vssmanager.service.exe
[exec]     logfile = etomic.vssmanager.service.InstallLog
[exec] Removing EventLog source Vss Manager Service.
[exec] Attempt to stop service Vss Manager Service.
[exec] Service Vss Manager Service is being removed from the system...
[exec] Service Vss Manager Service was successfully removed from the system.

[exec] Microsoft (R) .NET Framework Installation utility Version 1.1.4322.573
[exec] Copyright (C) Microsoft Corporation 1998-2002. All rights reserved.
[exec]
[exec] Installing assembly 'etomic.vssmanager.service.exe'.
[exec] Affected parameters are:
[exec]     assemblypath = etomic.vssmanager.service.exe
[exec]     logfile = etomic.vssmanager.service.InstallLog
[exec] Installing service Vss Manager Service...
[exec] Service Vss Manager Service has been successfully installed.
[exec] Creating EventLog source Vss Manager Service in log Application...
[exec] Committing assembly 'etomic.vssmanager.service.exe'.
[exec] Affected parameters are:
[exec]     assemblypath = etomic.vssmanager.service.exe
[exec]     logfile = etomic.vssmanager.service.InstallLog

BUILD SUCCEEDED
Total time: 5.7 seconds.
Output completed (6 sec consumed) - Normal Termination
```

You should notice that some of the tasks used—<tlbimp>, <readregistry>, and <servicecontroller>—do not actually produce any output.

Once this has been executed, you should be able to see the installed service, as shown in Figure 5-12.

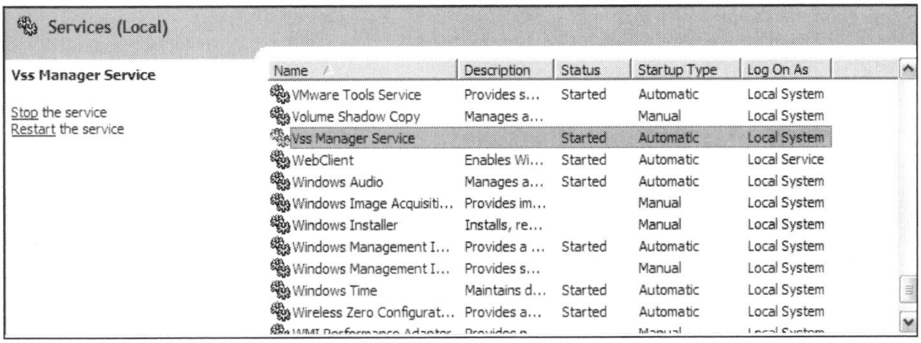

Figure 5-12. *The installed VSS Manager Service*

Finally, with the service installed and the remoting interfaces assembly deployed to the shared assembly folder, a developer is free to create a client to test the service. I have included a simple console client to test connectivity to the service. The build and deploy scripts for the client are included as part of the source code; it follows the same process as a regular Windows application. When this application is executed, you should see a screen similar to that shown in Figure 5-13.

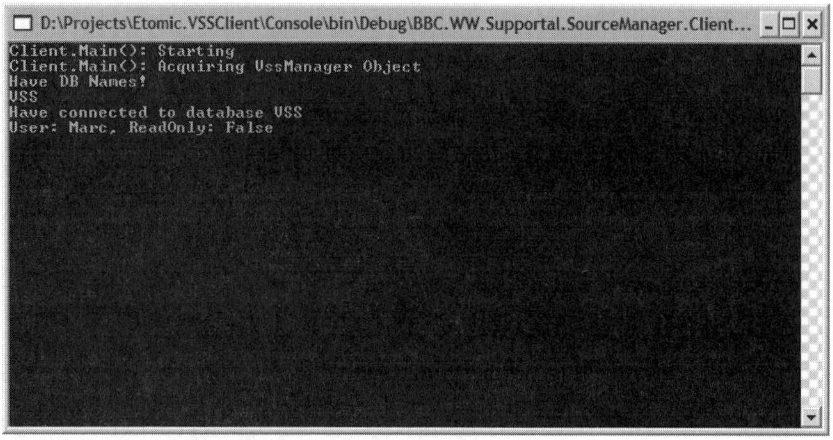

Figure 5-13. *The client console running*

Summary

We now have several applications of different types running from a few build and deploy scripts. We have made the script files more efficient and spotted a few problems that we need to address going forward.

Broadly, we have a functioning process across several applications, and the knowledge to carry us forward into more complex scenarios. We have a list of useful standards for the development teams to work with to ensure that the integration of their projects into the process is as smooth as possible.

In the next chapter we will look at providing improved processes through the use of continuous integration with CruiseControl.NET and explore the effects that this has on the current process.

Subsequent chapters will help us to address some of the remaining issues as we extend NAnt to create new tasks and handle more complex interactions such as configuration and database issues.

Further Reading

For more fun with remoting, check out *Advanced .NET Remoting* by Ingo Rammer (Apress, 2002).

CHAPTER 6

■■■

Continuous Integration

The previous two chapters have seen us construct a satisfactory build process: simple enough to achieve on a large scale—involving scores of projects—but intricate enough to perform the actions required of the process. In addition, standards have been devised to ensure that new solutions will be able to comply easily with the delivery processes, Design to Deliver.

The delivery scripts are loosely organized and are available on demand. Their use relies on the intervention of an operator to ensure that the process is used instead of some other method.

In this chapter we will consider continuous integration (CI) and how it may develop the processes further.

What Is Continuous Integration?

I have mentioned the original article on CI by Martin Fowler at the beginning of the book as we considered the broad processes available for delivery.

Fowler describes several disciplines needed to ensure that automated builds can work, including items such as a "single place where all the source code lives," the automation of building and testing, and the publishing of the built material.

In fact, as we have discovered, it is a little more involved than that, although this summary is accurate enough. Since we have already implemented these aspects in order to provide a general automated build, how much more effort is there to providing CI?

The answer is not all that much, at least on one level: the conceptual one. Under CI, the same processes are occurring as in the build scripts and process that we have already defined, but the trigger to kick off the process changes. Additionally, the management of the source control databases is handed to the CI software (at least in the case of CruiseControl.NET and more than likely others as well) because the source code forms a key part of the trigger process. This is shown in Figure 6-1.

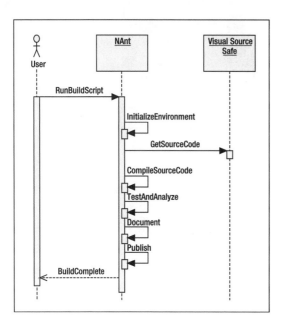

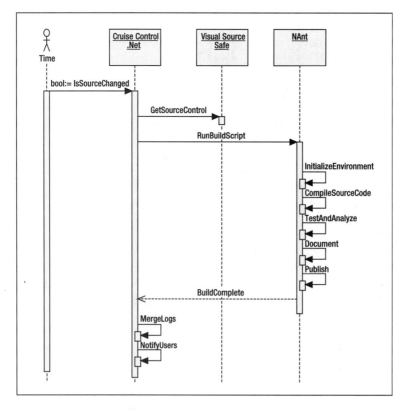

Figure 6-1. *Automated build vs. continuous integration*

Translating the process of continuous integration into a system consists of several core features found in most products designed for CI. The clues for these are in the words *continuous* and *integration*.

Continuous translates to a process that repeats itself constantly against a trigger of some description. With most CI products, this trigger is the monitoring of a source control repository for available changes, though the monitoring may take slightly differing parameters, and the monitored repository may actually be more esoteric than simply source control.

Integration involves providing evidence of success of the process. While the onus is on the user to provide actual integration paths for the solutions under CI, the applications are usually designed to offer feedback such as unit test results. Generally, CI applications will have useful logging and feedback mechanisms to ensure that the team is notified as to the success or failure of a build.

CI then is provided through the use of a suitable trigger. To be truly continuous, that trigger should occur when any source code is freshly committed to the source control database. We will see that other options are available too—less rigid options—but they are not actually continuous in the originally intended sense.

Technically, achieving CI is more of a challenge. The constructs needed to provide a solution consist of a service with something like the following capabilities:

Knowledge of how to trigger the NAnt scripts (or otherwise) to perform the actual build

Knowledge of when to trigger the NAnt scripts: monitoring the source control database for changes

Reporting and feedback methods

Fortunately, CruiseControl.NET (and other CI applications) provide these capabilities more or less out-of-the-box, and so we can use one of these applications rather than creating something from scratch

Now that we have considered the process in a holistic sense, let us examine the opportunities and threats involved with using CI. Broadly, CI provides practical benefits and improvements to the defined processes, and these represent its strengths, whereas the threats lie in the form of cultural issues and perhaps the occasional technical issue.

Opportunities

The CI process is acknowledged as a virtuous one, particularly in an "agile" world where it is almost prescribed. Yet even outside this arena, there are benefits, both direct and indirect, to using CI.

Builds are always up to date. Because the process performs a build cycle as soon as changes are detected to the codebase, there is always a current build. Additionally, reports (e.g., unit test results) are always up to date, demonstrating the features of the system construction. In the event of a failed build, alerts will immediately notify the development team. The net result is a reduction in risk since the chance of failure, particularly failure through lack of use, is limited. CI is providing confidence through continuous repeated attempts at the same process.

A managed process. Although there is formality in the definition of the aims of the build process, there is little structure regarding such issues as when to run the process. CI offers a managed process, or at least the chosen application to run CI offers a managed process.

Formality and structure. Similarly, the application chosen to run CI brings structure and formality to the organization of the assets, scripts, and so on under the umbrella of the CI system. CI gives the build process and its parts a "brand" to operate under. Much as naming the process efforts Design to Deliver helps to raise awareness and understanding through the team, CI (and the CI application) provide a focal point to the visible results of the efforts.

Threats

Keep in mind that implementing CI may be a step too far for your process since there are also some potential threats to the process:

Process not required. If you operate in an environment with a very long-winded approach to system delivery and integration work, then it is possible that CI will not help; its philosophy is simply opposed to the available methodology. Equally, if no one is doing anything with the information, then it may be pointless. In this instance, the threat is that the cultural positioning of the team requires some realignment to use CI effectively.

Lack of discipline. This issue is related to the above point. Agile methods such as CI often require focus to ensure their success. This focus tends to be the kind of focus a development team is happy to apply to a situation and thus the processes succeed—but we must consider that not all development teams, and not all developers, are dedicated to process work in the same way. In this case, the developers may not be disciplined enough to correct failed builds, or to even obtain successful builds in the first place. The appearance of many failed builds—which are supposed to be a "pick-me-up" to dedicated developers—may have the reverse effect on a team not able to dedicate itself to the CI process.

Managing problem areas. As usual, once systems become tricky to build and deploy, then CI may not be so easy to achieve. This could compound the other issues. Of course, the opportunity to ensure a complex delivery presents itself here, but the threat is that there are some particular considerations that simply do not fit well in a CI process. An example of this might be database integration work. We will examine some of the implications for databases in Chapter 8.

Technical Options

We will be using CruiseControl.NET (CCNet) to achieve CI in the sample applications, but it is important to note that other options are available for use. Furthermore, moving between platforms might not present a huge problem, since the features of the systems are generally similar: server and client components, a web presence, XML definition files, and so on. Most importantly, the applications usually provide the build process by wrapping NAnt, and thus the core part of the process will be reusable across different build systems with only minimal changes.

■**Tip** Although this book covers CCNet, you should take a look at other available options and use the one that feels most comfortable. These applications are being actively developed and you may find that one has precisely the feature that you need as a result of its particular implementation. For example, I found the `cctray` application very handy during my initial exploration of CCNet.

CruiseControl.NET

As I write this book, CCNet has reached v0.7, which is a significant shift from the 0.6 version I originally began to use in earnest. I was led to CCNet directly from reading about CI on Fowler's web site. The CCNet site is shown in Figure 6-2.

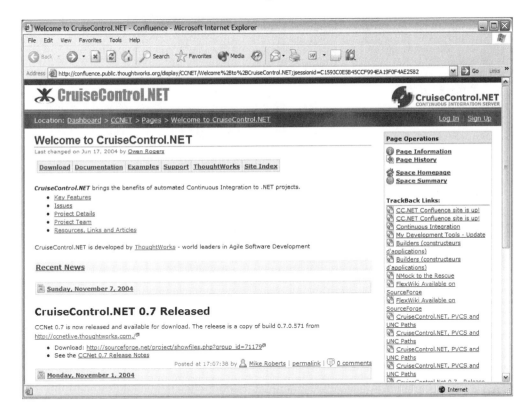

Figure 6-2. *CruiseControl.NET*

CCNet presents a server component that can run as a console or Windows service. The server is accessible through a remoting channel, and there are a number of ways to interact with the server. There is a web site that maintains build information (reports, logs, etc.), which was a major part of the application until v0.7, where it is gradually being deprecated. Instead, it is being replaced with a "web dashboard" that can handle multiple projects and multiple CCNet instances and is proving to be much more useful than individual sites. The dashboard currently lacks some of the reporting functionality, but this is being addressed. There is also an application that sits in the system tray called `cctray` that can access the server remotely in order to trigger builds through a context menu, or you can simply be notified of a build when one occurs through a message in the system tray.

Draco.NET

Draco.NET is described on its site as being inspired by CruiseControl (the Java version of CCNet) and so is an interesting counterpoint to CCNet. It consists of server and client parts, with the emphasis for configuration on the client tools. It is less feature-rich than CCNet but still performs the core functions of the CI process.

Hippo.NET

This application provides a different view of CI, in the form of a Windows GUI. Hippo tends to look friendlier than the other applications because of this, and again provides all of the features you need to operate a CI process.

Note Check out the Further Reading section at the end of this chapter for links to useful resources on other CI applications.

Implementing CI for the Sample Applications

In this section, we will work with the existing sample applications and implement CI for them using CCNet 0.8. We can then assess the applicability of CI and the ease with which the scripts we have so far can be integrated into the process. To begin this work, let us look at CCNet in more detail.

Examining CCNet

CCNet consists of several major parts that all have a role in presenting the full system for CI. We will consider each of these in turn to become familiar with the system before attempting the integration of the existing scripts.

Server

The server component handles all of the actual work of CCNet: the monitoring of the source control repository, the running of the appropriate build scripts, and the management and placement of the resulting information. The executable itself has a configuration file containing, for example, logging information. There is also a specific configuration file—the default is called `ccnet.config`—to hold the information on a solution required by CCNet to operate successfully. The main part of the work will be the recording of the information as required in this XML file.

The server application can be run using a console harness or installed as a Windows service. Ultimately the Windows service is probably the better option so that reboots are easier and so that no open window is required, among other reasons. However, this makes CCNet difficult to work with initially and offers no specific advantage (other than those just mentioned) for doing so. Running as a console application allows rapid feedback and quick restarts with a visible output instead of relying on the log file—even though the log file is very good.

■**Caution** The mailing list for CCNet has various reports of problems with the Windows service that seem to relate to access permissions and environment variables. Encountering these immediately deflects from the core issues—getting the process working—and is another reason to stick to the console application in the meantime.

Web Site

The web site component of CCNet was (before v0.7) the main visible aspect of CCNet. The web site displays server logs, build logs, and other information pertaining to builds, such as the time elapsed since the last build, and other reports such as unit tests, test coverage, and syntactic analysis (FxCop) if included as part of the build process. The web site component can be seen in Figure 6-3.

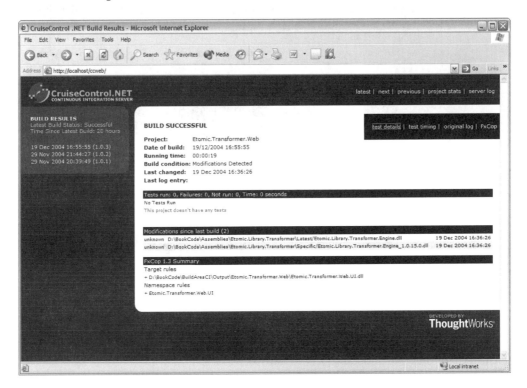

Figure 6-3. *The CCNet web site application*

Unfortunately, the web site only handles one project at a time (a *project* in CCNet terms generally equals a solution in VS .NET terms), or one build script. You can create a web site per build script, but this is prohibitive and painful over many projects.

Note This annoyed me enough to spend some time hacking the web site to support multiple projects. My blog at `http://bitarray.co.uk/marc` contains information on these hacks for v0.6.1, but this has been rendered relatively superfluous thanks to the improved web dashboard in v0.7 and subsequently v0.8.

One useful aspect of the web site is the structure and formality that it provides to the process-at-large, as we discussed when considering the benefits of CI.

As it stands, the web site is being deprecated as of v0.7 as more emphasis is placed on the web dashboard to provide the information required, and this time for multiple projects.

Web Dashboard

Prior to v0.7 of CCNet, the web dashboard was relatively underused, and was implemented as an aggregator of the myriad web sites required for working with multiple projects. As of v0.7, it has become more of the focal point for all projects running under CI. The dashboard is shown in Figure 6-4.

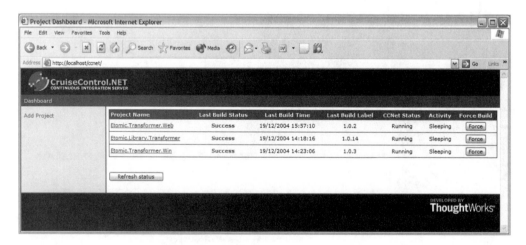

Figure 6-4. *The CCNet web dashboard application*

Configuring the dashboard and the server is much easier now. The dashboard not only aggregates projects, but also aggregates CCNet instances across the same and different machines, utilizing the remoting capabilities of CCNet fully.

As of CCNet 0.8, the dashboard has the same reporting capabilities as the web site had, which means you can view reports such as those for NUnit and FxCop from the dashboard.

The other useful functionality of the dashboard is the ability to trigger a "force build" directly from the dashboard. This is also a feature of cctray but it is handy to have here as well.

The cctray Application

This is a useful application for handling builds and feedback without the use of the web site or dashboard. It sits in the system tray and can be connected to a single project on a CCNet instance at once, though this is easily changed through the application settings. We will see this done later in this chapter.

The main use of cctray is to provide the ability to trigger a force build from a developer's desktop, but additionally it displays the previous build success in a simple way (red or green), and provides notifications when a build is complete. This is useful for teams to stay in touch with the current system status.

Basic Configuration

The first step to configuring CCNet is to obtain the application from the CCNet web site. Once you unzip the contents of the application, you will see the available folders, as shown in Figure 6-5.

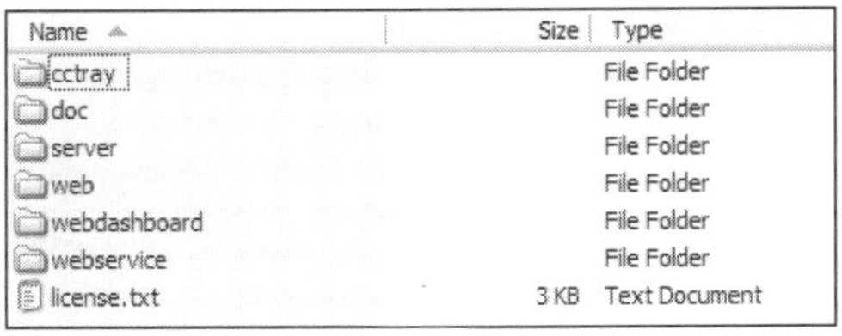

Name ▲	Size	Type
cctray		File Folder
doc		File Folder
server		File Folder
web		File Folder
webdashboard		File Folder
webservice		File Folder
license.txt	3 KB	Text Document

Figure 6-5. *The CCNet applications*

Tip Appendix A gives more information on obtaining the code and source for CCNet and a suggested method for deployment. Additionally, you should always refer to the online documentation to glean the most recent information on the application.

We will be using the web dashboard rather than the web site application, though we will take a quick look at the web application. Both of these should be configured as virtual directories on your machine. In this case, I have configured webdashboard as the ccnet virtual directory, as shown in Figure 6-6.

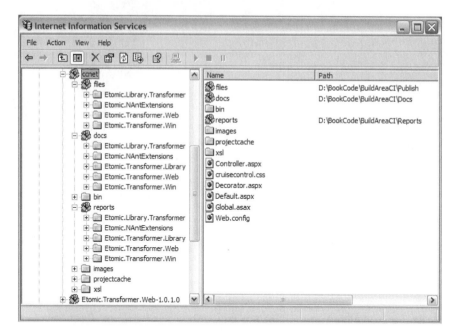

Figure 6-6. *Setting up the dashboard in IIS*

At this point, the dashboard will look as shown in Figure 6-7. It reports an error because it is unable to find the CCNet server application. Addressing that is the next step.

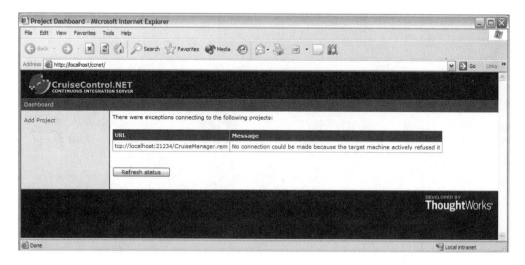

Figure 6-7. *Dashboard error screen*

Configuring the Server

The server is configured with an XML file (by default called ccnet.config), as you might expect. The most up-to-date information on configuration options will always be available on the CCNet documentation web site, but it will look something like the skeleton shown here in terms of the top-level elements for a project. There can be multiple project elements in the ccnet.config file—the root element being <cruisecontrol>. The root element to the ccnet.config file encapsulates one standard child element, the project element, which can appear multiple times. A project element describes all the information necessary to provide CI for a system or subsystem.

```xml
<project>
    <!-- General Settings -->
    <name>Project 1</name>
    <webURL>http://localhost/ccnet/Project1</webURL>
    <workingDirectory>yourWorkingDirectory</workingDirectory>
    <artifactDirectory>yourArtifactDirectory</artifactDirectory>

    <modificationDelaySeconds>2</modificationDelaySeconds>

    <triggers>
        <yourFirstTriggerType ../>
        <yourOtherTriggerType ../>
    </triggers>

    <sourcecontrol type="yourSourceControlType" ../>

    <build type="yourBuildType" ../>

    <labeller type="yourLabellerType" ../>

    <tasks>
        <yourFirstTaskType ../>
        <yourOtherTaskType ../>
    </tasks>

    <publishers>
        <yourFirstPublisherType ../>
        <yourOtherPublisherType ../>
    </publishers>

</project>
```

We will consider the areas marked in bold individually.

General Settings

As we mentioned earlier, the root element to the `ccnet.config` file encapsulates one standard child element, the `project` element, which can appear multiple times. A `project` element describes all of the information necessary to provide CI for a system or subsystem:

```
<project name="Etomic.Library.Transformer">
```

The project name is important since it will appear when you are using the web dashboard, web site, and cctray.

```
<webURL>http://localhost/ccnet/Controller.aspx?_action_ViewProjectReport=true➥
&amp;server=local&amp;project=Etomic.Library.Transformer</webURL>
```

The `webURL` element provides information to be used in the web dashboard for linking to reports and so on. At the time of writing this feature is under development, but works to a certain extent, as we will see later. The URL is always standard, apart from the server location and the project name.

```
<artifactDirectory>
    D:\dotNetDelivery\BuildAreaCI\Publish\Etomic.Library.Transformer\
</artifactDirectory>
```

The `artifactDirectory` element points to an area where artifacts generated during the build can be stored. Here I have pointed the `artifactDirectory` element to the publishing area for the project. There is another element, `workingDirectory`, that should be set in a similar way. The intention seems to be to link to the output or source directory for the project, but this is also linked to in the `sourcecontrol` block for VSS. Omitting the `workingDirectory` element means that a folder will be created as a child relative to the location of the `ccnet.config` file named the same as the project and then with its own child called `WorkingDirectory`.

```
<modificationDelaySeconds>10</modificationDelaySeconds>
```

This element ensures that commits that have occurred less than 10 seconds before the CCNet run are ignored, circumventing any issues with nonatomic commits into source control databases.

Triggers

As we discussed at the beginning of the chapter, the big difference between an automated build and CI is the differing trigger for the build. CI works because it ensures integration as soon as changes are committed to the source control system.

```
<triggers>
    <intervalTrigger />
</triggers>
```

CCNet has a number of different triggers, as shown in Table 6-1.

Table 6-1. *CCNet Trigger Options*

Type	Behavior
intervalTrigger	Polls the source control database every so often (optional) and performs a build if changes are detected. This is the true CI function.
scheduleTrigger	Specifies that an integration cycle should occur at a certain time on a specified day.
filterTrigger	Allows the prevention of an integration cycle by decorating one of the other triggers with a time and day when the integration should not occur.

A project can have multiple triggers assigned to it so that, for example, you can mix the intervalTrigger function with a scheduleTrigger. There are a couple of issues, though: it is hard to tell which trigger performed the latest action and therefore difficult to represent different build behaviors for each in NAnt, such as publishing the nightly build differently. It is not possible to explicitly state a differing build or labeling strategy in the ccnet.config file either, as the elements making up the project are not structured in such a way.

I have chosen to use the true CI method of intervalTrigger but you may find that you prefer to always force a build—particularly if you are just beginning to implement CI into your team.

Source Control

The sourcecontrol element is similar to the VSS tasks we used from NAntContrib to perform the builds outside of CCNet. It is quite straightforward to complete the details:

```
<sourcecontrol type="vss" autoGetSource="true">
    <ssdir>"D:\dotNetDelivery\VSS"</ssdir>
    <project>$/Solutions/Etomic.Library.Transformer/</project>
    <username>builder</username>
    <password>builder</password>
    <workingDirectory>
        D:\dotNetDelivery\BuildAreaCI\Source\Etomic.Library.Transformer
    </workingDirectory>
</sourcecontrol>
```

Notice the workingDirectory (which is not the same as the project workingDirectory): I have swapped the format from <project>\source to source\<project> and will need to reflect this in the NAnt files later on to keep various artifacts together across all projects. We can see why later.

Also, there is an attribute called applyLabel that sits in the sourcecontrol element. Because we did not include it, CCNet does not apply a label itself. For the time being, and perhaps always, I would prefer to control the labeling to VSS from the NAnt scripts as we have done previously. This is because I would like to be able to specify explicitly when labeling should be performed.

CCNet supports a variety of source control databases. Here we are using VSS but we could be using CVS, SourceGear, StarTeam, and so on. Also of interest is the availability of a `filesystem` source control type, which can be used to monitor changes and trigger builds, based on the changes to a folder. The syntax for this element is as follows:

```
<sourcecontrol type="filesystem">
    <repositoryRoot>c:\mycode</repositoryRoot>
</sourcecontrol>
```

This is useful since it means that, for example, shared assemblies can be monitored for change and then a build performed on dependent systems when a change occurs. The most appropriate use of the `filesystem` source control type is for wrapping up the VSS settings and the filesystem settings under a `multi` source control type, as in the following example:

```
<sourcecontrol type="multi">
    <sourceControls>
        <vss autoGetSource="true">
            <ssdir>"D:\dotNetDelivery\VSS"</ssdir>
            <project>$/Solutions/Etomic.Transformer.Win/</project>
            <username>builder</username>
            <password>builder</password>
            <workingDirectory>
                D:\dotNetDelivery\BuildAreaCI\Source\Etomic.Transformer.Win
            </workingDirectory>
        </vss>
        <filesystem>
            <repositoryRoot>
                D:\dotNetDelivery\Assemblies\Etomic.Library.Transformer
            </repositoryRoot>
        </filesystem>
    </sourceControls>
</sourcecontrol>
```

In this example for the Windows application, I have included a VSS database for performing regular builds on source changes, but I have also included a `filesystem` source control type pointing at the `Assemblies` folder where the shared library component is positioned. The result is that when a delivery of the shared component is made (not just a build but a deploy as well), CCNet will detect the change to the folder and trigger a build of the Windows application. This is, once again, in the spirit of true CI, but may not be a desired behavior for your team or environment. We will see how this performs later on.

Build

Once all of the source has been grabbed according to the appropriate triggers and other criteria, the main instruction for CCNet is to perform the build. In the following example, we can see that the nested elements are fairly obvious calls to the NAnt scripts we have previously produced. We can also see that we can pass through command-line parameters into NAnt that enable us to leverage the flexibility of scripts in the way that has proved useful in previous refactoring efforts.

```
<build type="nant">
    <baseDirectory>D:\dotNetDelivery\Chapter6\</baseDirectory>
    <buildArgs>-D:solution.stub=Library.Transformer -D:debug=false</buildArgs>
    <buildFile>Build.Core.xml</buildFile>
    <targetList>
        <target>ci</target>
    </targetList>
    <buildTimeoutSeconds>300</buildTimeoutSeconds>
</build>
```

Here we call a target called `ci` in the `Build.Core.Xml` file. This target does not exist yet, and is another change on the list for that file later on. Additionally, we will always pass through a debug value of `false` while operating under CI. Debug runs will be executed via the regular NAnt command line.

Apart from a nant build type, other types are available. These include the VS .NET builder—using a call to `devenv.exe` to perform the compilation—and a command-line builder that allows the invocation of arbitrary functions—for example, through a `.bat` file—to perform the build.

As time moves on, it is likely that support will be added for other build tools such as MSBuild, Microsoft's own build tool.

labeller

A project can be configured with a specific labeling strategy as is shown in the `labeller` element. CCNet can also be enhanced to handle different labeling techniques. The `defaultlabeller` labeler handles only a prefix and then the incremental build number that CCNet maintains elsewhere. This is different from the NAnt versioning technique that we have used up to this point, and so the build files will need to change to account for this. The script we will use is as follows:

```
<labeller type="defaultlabeller">
    <prefix>1.0.</prefix>
</labeller>
```

Tasks

Next up are a number of tasks that can be run following a successful build. These tasks are run sequentially. One example is a `<nunit>` task, which will perform unit testing as appropriate. This is useful if you are using a builder that is not NAnt but still want to follow the CI process; otherwise, it is probably superfluous.

Caution Mixing up the responsibilities of CCNet and NAnt could cause problems. Moving the unit-test functions into CCNet removes the ability to fully test the process outside the CCNet harness. I think it is probably best to let CCNet handle the triggering and so on, and let NAnt perform the work.

The task that is of interest to us is the <merge> task for attaching the FxCop and NUnit XML outputs to the build log of CCNet. This is easily done with a little matching, as shown here. I probably could have just used a catchall *.xml filter, but it is possible I will use other reports later on.

```
<tasks>
    <merge>
        <files>
            <file>
D:\dotNetDelivery\BuildAreaCI\Reports\Etomic.Library.Transformer\*-results.xml
            </file>
            <file>
D:\dotNetDelivery\BuildAreaCI\Reports\Etomic.Library.Transformer\fxcop.xml
            </file>
        </files>
    </merge>
</tasks>
```

Publishers

Finally, once all work is complete, the build log is published in various ways. The usual method is an xmllogger, which publishes the log to the CCNet web site and dashboards. This is easily implemented in the following way:

```
<publishers>
    <xmllogger />
</publishers>
```

Another useful publisher is the email publisher. It sends an email containing the styled build log to interested parties. There are a few options for this publisher, but in general the script will look something like this:

```
<email from="marc@etomic.co.uk" mailhost="smtp.etomic.co.uk" includeDetails="TRUE">
    <projectUrl>http://localhost/ccnet</projectUrl>
    <users>
        <user name="Marc" group="buildmaster" address=marc@etomic.co.uk"/>
        <user name="Developer" group="developers" ➥
            address="developer@etomic.co.uk"/>
    </users>
    <groups>
        <group name="developers" notification="change"/>
        <group name="buildmaster" notification="always"/>
    </groups>
</email>
```

This task implementation ensures that the buildmaster is always informed when a build is performed regardless of its success or failure. The developers group, however, is only informed when there has been a change in the build status—for example, a shift from success to failed, or vice versa.

■**Note** This publisher has obvious utility but is usually difficult to maintain. If you operate in an environment with many systems and rotating pools of developers (in that agile way), then adding and removing developer interests is a constant game. You may want to consider a blanket policy of "everybody gets everything" and then rely on the developers to filter the unimportant stuff. We see some other options in Chapter 9, too.

This completes the configuration settings we need for our projects. Because we already have a set of functioning automated build scripts and because we have enforced certain standards—naming, organization, and so on—then the script for all three projects is essentially identical. The most obvious differences are in details such as the interested developers for the email publisher, and whether we choose to use a multi source control for the dependent projects.

Amending the Build.Core.Xml File

Before we look at the operation of CCNet, some changes need to be made to the build scripts we have (the integration is not entirely seamless!). The changes are simple, though, and are not needed in the specific build files, but just in the Build.Core.Xml file. The relevant parts of this file are shown here, with the changes in bold:

```xml
<?xml version="1.0" encoding="utf-8" ?>
<project name="Build.Core" default="help">
    <description>Build file to perform core common functionality.</description>

    <property name="nant.onfailure" value="fail"/>

    <property name="company.name" value="Etomic"/>
    <property name="solution.name" value="${company.name}.${solution.stub}"/>

    <property name="core.directory"
            value="D:\dotNetDelivery\BuildAreaCI"/>
    <property name="core.source"
            value="${core.directory}\Source\${solution.name}"/>
    <property name="core.output"
            value="${core.directory}\Output\${solution.name}"/>
    <property name="core.docs"
            value="${core.directory}\Docs\${solution.name}"/>
    <property name="core.reports"
            value="${core.directory}\Reports\${solution.name}"/>
    <property name="core.distribution"
            value="${core.directory}\Distribution\${solution.name}"/>
    <property name="core.publish"
            value="${core.directory}\Publish\${solution.name}"/>

    <property name="vss.dbpath" value="D:\dotNetDelivery\VSS\srcsafe.ini"/>
```

```
<property name="vss.path" value="$/Solutions/${solution.name}/"/>

<sysinfo/>
```

In this section, I have changed around the folder organization so that differing output types are arranged together. I have also arranged a new build area for CI. Because we are using a web site to capture build logs and so on, it makes sense to use the Web to enable the publishing of the assets generated during the build.

This organization allows me to create virtual directories under the CCNet dashboard application mapped to the publish, documentation, and reports folders. When a new project is added to the process, it will appear automatically. The virtual directories should be set to be browsable, and the default document can be set if appropriate (for example, to default.aspx). Figure 6-8 shows this configuration.

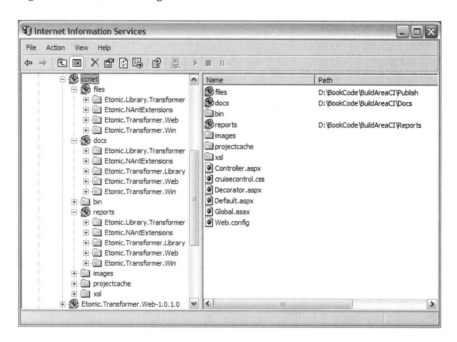

Figure 6-8. *Configuring virtual directories for published assets*

With this configuration, the deploy scripts can be changed to obtain assets via the Web rather than a file share. We will complete the work on the build script first, then look at the deploy scripts.

```
<target name="go" description="Build Target"
        depends="clean, get, version1, version2, specific"/>
<target name="ci" description="CI Target"
        depends="clean, version1, version2, specific"/>
```

The next change is the addition of a target specifically for CI. The differing dependencies are simple: using the CI target, NAnt does not need to get the source code, since CCNet will be handling this work from now on. We maintain the go target so that we can run the script outside of CCNet. As you will have observed in the CCNet configuration, the ci target is called from the nant build element.

```
<target name="clean" description="Clean up the build environment.">
    <!--Do not delete core.source-->
    <delete dir="${core.output}\" failonerror="false"/>
    <delete dir="${core.docs}\" failonerror="false"/>
    <delete dir="${core.reports}\" failonerror="false"/>
    <delete dir="${core.distribution}\" failonerror="false"/>

    <mkdir dir="${core.source}\" failonerror="false"/>
    <mkdir dir="${core.output}\" failonerror="false"/>
    <mkdir dir="${core.docs}\" failonerror="false"/>
    <mkdir dir="${core.reports}\" failonerror="false"/>
    <mkdir dir="${core.distribution}\" failonerror="false"/>
    <mkdir dir="${core.publish}\" failonerror="false"/>
</target>
```

A simple but important change to the clean target is the removal of the deletion of the source directory. As CCNet handles source code differently—it manages the removal of old code automatically—it is unnecessary and can cause CCNet to be confused about changes to the code.

```
<target name="version1" description="Apply versioning to the source code files.">
    <property name="sys.version" value="0.0.0.0"/>
        <ifnot test="${debug}">
            <property name="sys.version" value="${ccnet.label}.0"/>
        </ifnot>

    <!-- Rest of target snipped -->
</target>
```

Since versioning is now handled by CCNet, in terms of the build number, then the versioning statement is changed to remove the reliance on the NAnt <version> task. We can delete the *.Build.Number files as they are no longer required. As the labeler in CCNet only handles prefixes, we need to add a suffix at this point to the ccnet.label property to get the correct number and format. The property ccnet.label is passed through by CCNet as it invokes NAnt. Other useful properties are due to be added too.

■Note A while back there was a useful discussion about these properties on the CCNet mailing list. The addition of certain properties could assist with some of the problems identified earlier—for example, the inability of NAnt to react to different types of incoming CCNet build requests. Keeping an eye on the CCNet JIRA (issue tracking web site) is well worthwhile.

Those are all the changes required for the Build.Core.Xml file, and they are the only changes needed overall to include the scripts generated in Chapter 5 into the CI process.

Amending the Deploy Scripts

As we mentioned earlier, we can adjust the deployment scripts to make use of the virtual directories and web access to the published assets. This is quite straightforward; an example is shown here:

```
<property name="core.publish"
          value="http://localhost/ccnet/files/${solution.name}"/>
```

The core.publish property is now set to the location of the published assets on the web dashboard site. We can then change the get target to obtain the assets via HTTP:

```
<target name="get" description="Grab the correct assets.">
    <delete dir="${core.deploy}\" failonerror="false"/>
    <mkdir dir="${core.deploy}\${sys.version}\"/>
    <get
      src="${core.publish}/${solution.name}-Build-${sys.version}.zip"
      dest="${core.deploy}\${solution.name}-Build-${sys.version}.zip"
      />
    <unzip
      zipfile="${core.deploy}\${solution.name}-Build-${sys.version}.zip"
      todir="${core.deploy}\${sys.version}\"
      />
</target>
```

Creating a Startup Script for the Server

A minor but useful action is to create a startup .bat file for the CCNet server. It should contain something like the following command, and it should be located in the same folder as the ccnet.config file that we have generated. This allows the config file to be maintained somewhere other than where the server executable is located.

```
"D:/dotNetDelivery/Tools/CCNet/0.8/Server/CCnet.exe" -remoting:on ➡
    -config:ccnet.config
```

■**Note** Although the server works with this setting, if it needs to use assets such as the XSL files—for example, when transforming the build log for the email publisher—it will look for the files relative to the ccnet.config file rather than the server application. So there are two options: copy the XSL files to the same relative location as the config file, or run the config file from the default location. I have chosen the former because of the need to maintain the cohesion of the source code for the book.

We are now in a position to run the server. This can be done by executing the batch file we created earlier. If everything is okay, we will see a screen like the one in Figure 6-9.

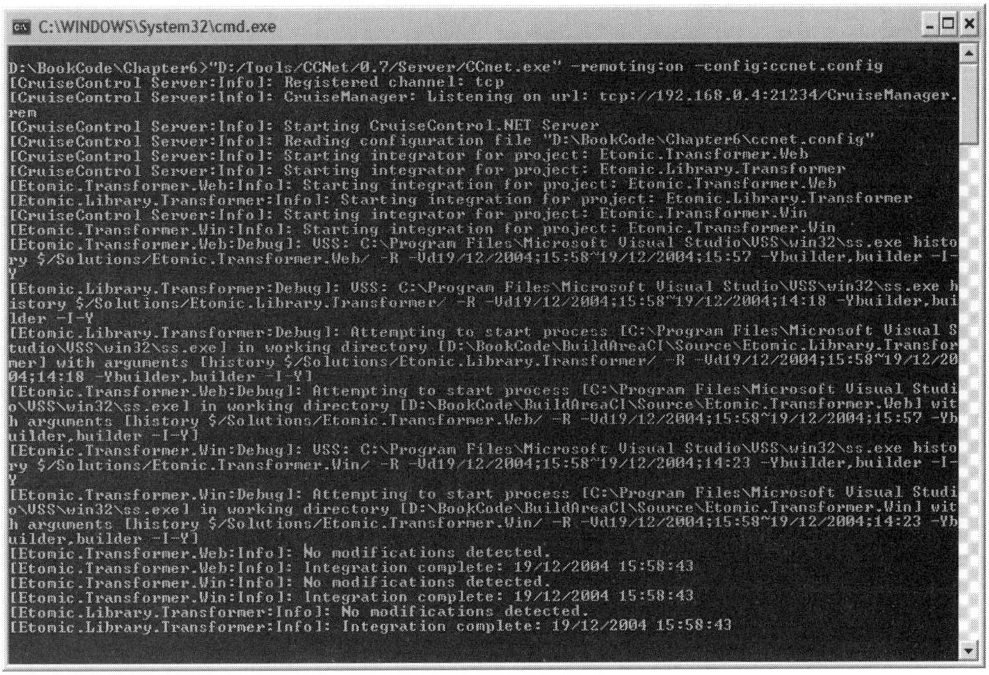

Figure 6-9. *The CCNet server console*

The first time that you run the server it is likely that builds will be attempted for all of the projects since CCNet has no records of the projects. To avoid this, you could change the `trigger` type to a scheduled type at some later point in time. This allows the server to run without building. You can then selectively force-build the projects individually to ensure that the process works.

Examining the Dashboard

Regardless of the method chosen to ensure that the scripts work, the server is now running, which means the dashboard is available for use and examination. After a few builds, the dashboard screen will likely look something like the one shown in Figure 6-10.

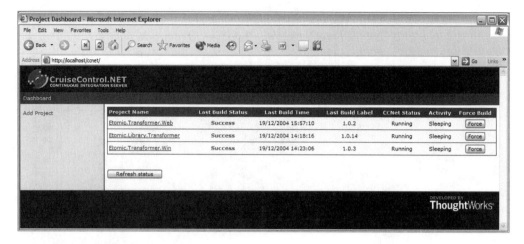

Figure 6-10. *The functional CCNet dashboard*

In Figure 6-10 we can see that our three projects have been successfully built a number of times. We can drill into the individual projects by clicking on the name link. The initial screen, at the time of writing, has no details, but the formatted build log can be viewed by clicking on the link for the desired build. Figure 6-11 demonstrates this output.

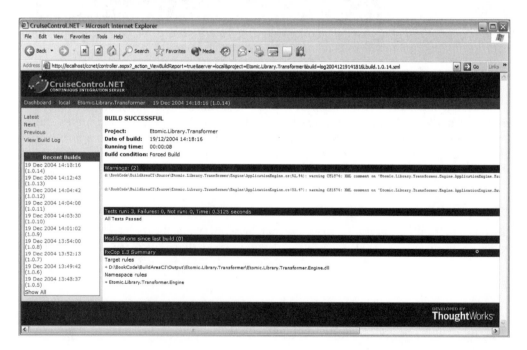

Figure 6-11. *A CCNet build log*

Here the build log shows that the unit tests were successfully run, and lists any modifications (in this case none!) to the source code of the project, along with the reason the build was run: in this case, it was forced.

If we move back to the main screen for the dashboard, then we can force a build using the buttons to the right if desired. There is also another way of doing it, as we see in the next section.

Examining the cctray application

cctray is an application that sits in the system tray of a developer's machine, as shown in Figure 6-12.

Figure 6-12. *The cctray application*

cctray takes advantage of the remoting interface of the CCNet server in the same way as the dashboard and so can also be used to monitor the build status of projects and to force a project build. The cctray icon is green when the build is successful and red when it fails. The settings for the application are simple: connect to the required CCNet server instance and select a project for monitoring, as shown in Figure 6-13.

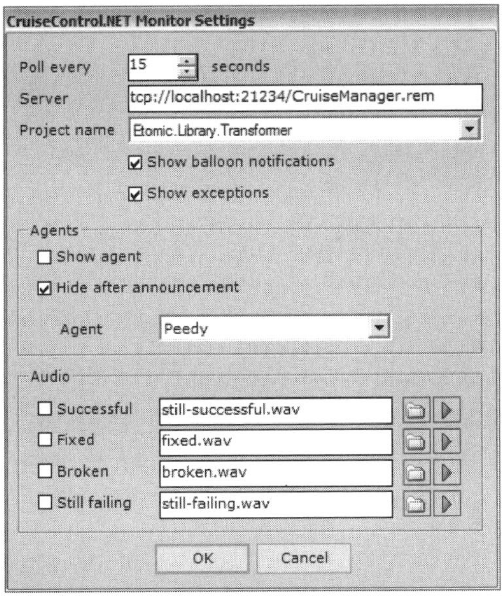

CruiseControl.NET Monitor Settings	
Poll every	15 ⬍ seconds
Server	tcp://localhost:21234/CruiseManager.rem
Project name	Etomic.Library.Transformer ▾
	☑ Show balloon notifications
	☑ Show exceptions

Agents
☐ Show agent
☑ Hide after announcement

Agent Peedy ▾

Audio
☐ Successful still-successful.wav 📁 ▷
☐ Fixed fixed.wav 📁 ▷
☐ Broken broken.wav 📁 ▷
☐ Still failing still-failing.wav 📁 ▷

OK   Cancel

Figure 6-13. *cctray settings*

Right-clicking on the cctray icon and selecting the Force Build option will force the build of the currently selected project for the CCNet server instance. During the interval of the build, no other force build can be performed, and the icon for the build becomes yellow. At the end of the build cycle, a balloon will appear from cctray notifying you of success or failure, as shown in Figure 6-14.

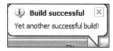

Figure 6-14. *A cctray notification*

Tip This small feature of the CCNet suite is a friendly way to introduce the development team to the principles of CI or automated builds.

Examining the State File

When CCNet begins looking after a project, it maintains the information in a state file. This will be called something on the order of <project>.state and resembles the following:

```
<?xml version="1.0" encoding="utf-16"?>
<IntegrationResult xmlns:xsd=http://www.w3.org/2001/XMLSchema ➥
xmlns:xsi="http://www.w3.org/2001/XMLSchema-instance">
    <Status>Success</Status>
    <LastIntegrationStatus>Success</LastIntegrationStatus>
    <ProjectName>Etomic.Transformer.Web</ProjectName>
    <BuildCondition>IfModificationExists</BuildCondition>
    <Label>1.0.3</Label>
    <StartTime>2004-12-19T16:55:55.4036619-00:00</StartTime>
    <EndTime>2004-12-19T16:56:14.4661619-00:00</EndTime>
    <WorkingDirectory>
        D:\dotNetDelivery\Chapter6\Etomic.Transformer.Web\WorkingDirectory
    </WorkingDirectory>
</IntegrationResult>
```

This file ensures that the server can be restarted without losing any information. Ordinarily there is no need to tamper with this file, but it is useful to know that it can be manipulated to perform testing or to reset or modify a label, for example.

Testing the multi Source Control

During the configuration of the CCNet server, we set up both the Windows and web projects to be triggered on the basis of a deployment of the library assembly using the multi source control type. We can test this out, and the amended deploy files that take advantage of the virtual directories we created, by deploying the library assembly and ensuring that a build of the Windows and web applications occurs. We can check the available assets for the library as shown in Figure 6-15.

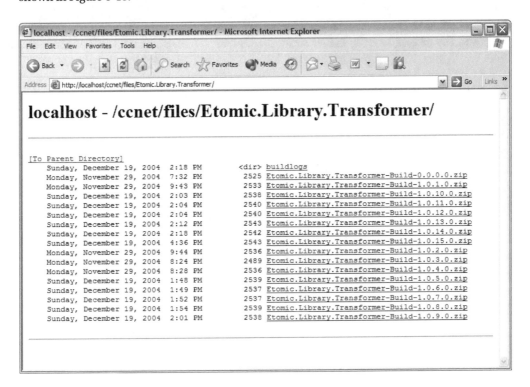

Figure 6-15. *Published assets*

The latest version of the library assembly is 1.0.15.0 (and we should take note of the poor sort order of the folder!). Figure 6-16 also shows the latest versions of the Windows application—1.0.3.0—and the web application—1.0.2.0.

Following the deployment of the library file, we would expect each of these to be updated. The library can be deployed by running the relevant deploy file with the following command line:

```
nant -f:etomic.library.transformer.deploy.xml -D:debug=false ➡
-D:sys.version=1.0.15.0 go
```

We know that the deployment has been successful because of the resulting onscreen messages and because the HTTP calls worked correctly.

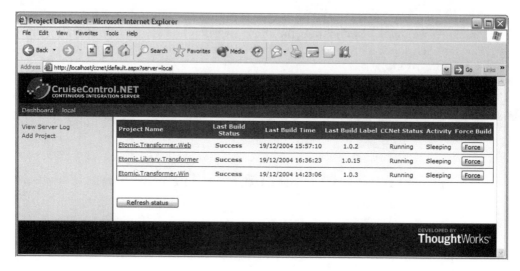

Figure 6-16. *Current version information*

As soon as the deployment has proven a success, the next poll of the source control locations by CCNet results in the output shown in Figure 6-17: a build is being attempted by the server for both the Windows and web applications.

Figure 6-17. *CCNet server attempting a build*

Once the builds have been successfully completed (we hope), the dashboard looks like the one shown in Figure 6-18.

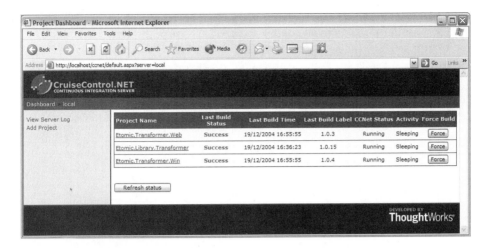

Figre 6-18. *Updated version information*

Both of the build numbers are incremented for the dependent applications, suggesting that all is well with the multi source control configuration. We can prove that this is indeed the case by viewing the build log for one of the applications—in the case of Figure 6-19 we are viewing the web application—and looking at the Modifications Since Last Build section. In this section we can see that the monitor did indeed pick up the changes in this area, performing a build.

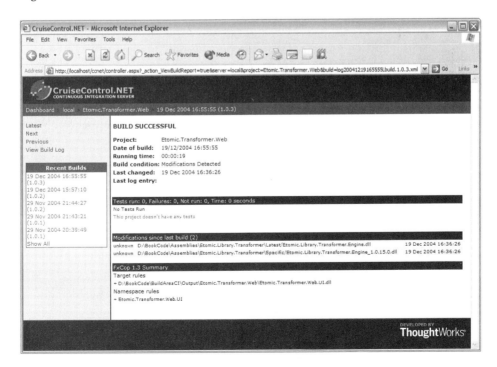

Figure 6-19. *The web application build log*

Since we reference the latest version of the library assembly in the web project, the new published assets (version 1.0.3.0) should contain the latest version of the library assembly (version 1.0.15.0). If you take a look inside the zip file for the project, you will find that this is indeed the case, as Figure 6-20 shows.

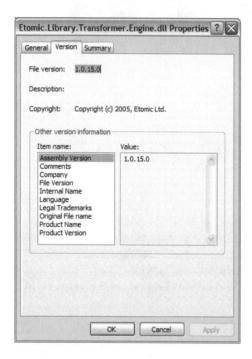

Figure 6-20. *The assembly version proof*

Examining the `multi` source control setting has allowed us to see the power of CI first-hand. Instead of relying on the development team to ensure compatibility of new library assemblies, we provide our own assurance by demanding the integration of the new assembly (and new source code and so on) as soon as these assets become available to the system by their committal to the source control repository.

Enhancing CCNet

Chapter 7 discusses extending NAnt and creating new tasks to plug into the NAnt architecture. This is a very useful feature of NAnt and allows extension of the framework without branching the NAnt source code—although there is always a chance that the code will undergo a significant change of some kind and break the enhancement.

Unfortunately, this is not the case with CCNet. The source code itself is very extensible and is well organized, as can be seen in Figure 6-21.

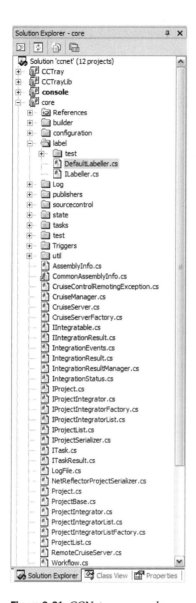

Figure 6-21. *CCNet source code*

Extending most features in CCNet is usually just a case of implementing the relevant interface. In Figure 6-21 the `ILabeller` interface and `DefaultLabeller` concrete implementation of this interface can be seen, but additionally CCNet uses a library called `NetReflector` that requires us to attribute properties in the class to translate the `ccnet.config` file for the feature (if indeed the feature is part of the `ccnet.config` file). The following small code snippet shows this for the `DefaultLabeller`:

```
[ReflectorType("defaultlabeller")]
public class DefaultLabeller : ILabeller
{
    private string _labelPrefix = "";

    public static string INITIAL_LABEL = "1";

    [ReflectorProperty("prefix", Required=false)]
    public string LabelPrefix
    {
        get { return _labelPrefix; }
        set { _labelPrefix = value; }
    }
    ..snip...
}
```

All of this means that the only way to enhance CCNet is through the modification of the actual source code. This is not a problem if you do not intend to upgrade the version of CCNet you are using, but given the nature of the software and its rapid development cycle, this is probably unlikely. Constantly upgrading the changes against a new codebase is also likely to be onerous.

Summary

In this chapter we have come to the end of the basic configuration for automated delivery of .NET solutions. We have built successively upon a set of initially simple scripts, and maintained that simplicity as we have increased the number of applications using the process. This has been possible through the implementation of a set of standards that are not too intrusive, but are effective to provide the necessary hooks for build automation as we have defined them.

Specifically in this chapter we have used CruiseControl.NET to provide a harness to encapsulate the build process we have developed, but also to implement continuous integration for our applications.

In subsequent chapters we will focus on the development of more advanced features to the system we have in place to squeeze some more functionality out of NAnt and CCNet while also using some other tools.

Further Reading

The original CI article can be found at http://martinfowler.com/articles/ continuousIntegration.html.

There is a good comparison of various CI tools in *Open Source .NET Development: Programming with NAnt, NUnit, NDoc, and More* by Brian Nantz (Addison-Wesley, 2004).

CruiseControl.NET and its most up-to-date information can be found at http://ccnet.thoughtworks.com.

Draco.NET can be found at http://draconet.sourceforge.net.

Hippo.NET can be found at http://hipponet.sourceforge.net.

Microsoft will be releasing their own build tool, MSBuild, with Visual Studio 2005. It is certainly worth gaining an appreciation of this tool. We will discuss it further in Chapter 10. A useful source of information can be found at `http://msdn.microsoft.com/longhorn/ toolsamp/default.aspx?pull=/library/en-us/dnlong/html/msbuildpart1.asp`.

Extending NAnt

In this chapter we are going to look at extending NAnt with new tasks to assist the processes we have put in place. We will look at some of the source code for NAnt, focusing on the most important parts from an extender's perspective. Then we will construct a new task to use with the scripts we already have.

NAnt Functionality

Although NAnt performs most of the tasks we would like it to, in Chapter 4 we discovered that it could not handle the required analysis by FxCop since there was no specific task for the utility. NAnt's <exec> task let us perform the required analysis but in an unfriendly way. By *unfriendly* I mean that the appearance of the script to perform the analysis was not satisfactory to enable the standardization of the FxCop analysis through the <exec> task. Consider the code again:

```
<exec
    program="D:\dotNetDelivery\Tools\FxCop\1.30\FxCopCmd.exe"
    commandline="/f:${core.output}\${project.name.1}.dll ➥
    /o:${core.reports}\fxcop.xml /r:D:\dotNetDelivery\Tools\FxCop\1.30\Rules\"
    failonerror="false"
/>
```

The basic problem is the construction of the commandline attribute. As more assemblies are added, the line simply becomes longer and more unwieldy. The <exec> task allows the addition of commandline arguments in a different way—through an embedded set of argument elements—but this still does not provide precisely the flexibility we would like.

At this point then, we should crack open the shell to NAnt and take a look at the parts that are interesting to us.

Note Apart from digging into the source code itself, trusty Reflector is very useful for this task.

We will not spend much time looking at the low-level framework for NAnt—beautiful though it is. We are looking to perform specific work, namely the creation of new tasks, rather than developing the platform itself.

The NAnt source code consists of 14 projects at the time of writing. The most important to us is the NAnt.Core project, which as you will be able to see from Figure 7-1 contains many familiar-sounding class names in terms of their similarity to actual NAnt task names. The other projects are largely related to specific task types, such as Visual Studio .NET.

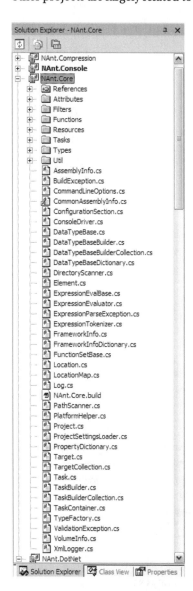

Figure 7-1. *The NAnt.Core project*

Those classes in the root of this project form the framework to NAnt: the project, target, and task classes, for example. These are of course far from the full picture, and there are a whole host of supporting structures. In the subfolders of the project are additional classes to support the framework. The subfolders contain the following:

Attributes. These supporting classes allow a simple and effective way of providing the XML structure and validation to a new task. We will make use of these, and see them in action when we explore the tasks.

Filters. These support the use of `filtersets` for token replacement and so on, a relatively new feature in NAnt.

Functions. Similarly, these classes provide the function capabilities of NAnt, another relatively new feature.

Resources. Currently contains only the `projecthelp.xslt` file.

Tasks. Contains several of the general-purpose tasks for NAnt. We will look at some of these later. They are a great starting point for considering a new task.

Types. Another set of supporting classes for tasks. These are the types we discussed back in Chapter 3—elements with specific functionality such as `FileSet`. We will make use of these too.

Util. Contains some additional supporting classes, particularly command-line parsing support.

A simplified view of the relationships between the classes we are interested in for task creation is shown in Figure 7-2.

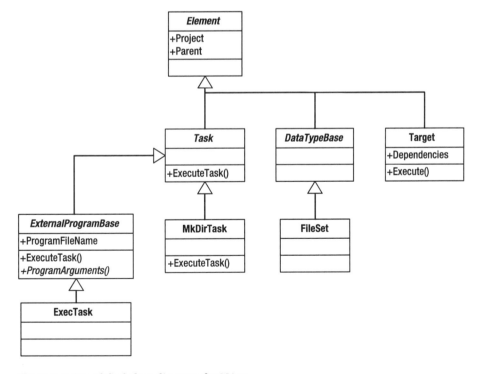

Figure 7-2. *Simplified class diagram for NAnt*

A significant amount of work occurs in the project class related to the loading of the script file and the organization of the elements within the project. The element class itself then handles a lot of common functionality and manages references to parents and the main project. The use of attributes to mark up an individual class with XML structural details also avoids more plumbing code.

Therefore, when creating a NAnt task, the code is generally very efficient. The concentration is on the code to complete the task rather than the integration of the task into the NAnt framework. We can explore this further now.

Investigating NAnt Tasks: <mkdir>

A look through any of the code for NAnt tasks will reveal many similarities. The first thing to notice is the many attributes used throughout the classes. These are the required items of code that ensure the integration of the task into the framework other than the inheritance of the Task class itself.

A Look at <mkdir>

The <mkdir> task is a good place to start in terms of seeing a simple task integrated into the framework. The code for the <mkdir> task is as follows:

```
using System;
using System.Globalization;
using System.IO;

using NAnt.Core.Attributes;
using NAnt.Core.Util;

namespace NAnt.Core.Tasks {
    [TaskName("mkdir")]
    public class MkDirTask : Task {

        private DirectoryInfo _dir;

        [TaskAttribute("dir", Required=true)]
        public DirectoryInfo Dir {
            get { return _dir; }
            set { _dir = value; }
        }

        protected override void ExecuteTask() {
            try {
                if (!Dir.Exists) {
                    Log(Level.Info, "Creating directory '{0}'.", Dir.FullName);
                    Dir.Create();
                    }
                } catch (Exception ex) {
```

```
            throw new BuildException(string.Format(CultureInfo.InvariantCulture, ⮕
                "Directory '{0}' could not be created.", Dir.FullName), ⮕
                Location, ex);
        }
    }
  }
}
```

As you can see, the creation of the task is straightforward. In this instance the task is simple, but despite this, you might expect to have a more complicated method of integration than is demonstrated here. This is one of the core strengths of the NAnt code: it is easily and readily extensible.

The items in bold are worth considering in more detail. The `TaskName` attribute is used at the class level to define the name of the element as it will appear in a build file `<mkdir>`. The class then inherits from the `Task` class, which means that it will need to override the `ExecuteTask` method. In order to complete the function of folder creation (the purpose of `<mkdir>`), the task needs to know the folder it must create. To expose the public property to the build file, another attribute is used. In this case `TaskAttribute` describes the name of the attribute and also includes a simple validation to ensure that the attribute is included when using the task (Required=true).

The `ExecuteTask` method can then be written as needed. The main point to notice in this simple method is the catch and rethrow of an exception as a `BuildException`. This is a convention through all task code. This code allows us to use the `<mkdir>` task in build files as such this:

```
<mkdir dir="${core.source}\" failonerror="false"/>
```

Note that the `failonerror`, `if`, and `unless` attributes are all part of the base `Task` implementation and so behave in the same way across all tasks.

A Look at <copy>

There can be more complex behaviors through the use of attributes with additional attribute types. `<copy>` is a good task to illustrate this. We are not concerned at this point with the actual implementation of the `<copy>` task but with the features of its implementation in a build file. The following code demonstrates the use of the `<copy>` task from our own publish target in the scripts we have. I have added the additional `overwrite` attribute.

```
<copy todir="${core.distribution}\bin\" overwrite="true">
    <fileset basedir="${core.output}\">
        <include name="*.dll"/>
        <exclude name="*Tests*"/>
    </fileset>
</copy>
```

In principle, the `<copy>` task does not perform a much more complex task than the `<mkdir>` task, but in order to provide the requisite level of utility to ensure the `<copy>` task is successful, it includes various features such as pattern-matching of files to copy. There is also a property that will require casting a string to a Boolean during parsing. We can see how both of these features are implemented in the task.

First, the Boolean overwrite property is implemented as follows:

```
[TaskAttribute("overwrite")]
[BooleanValidator()]
public bool Overwrite {
    get { return _overwrite; }
    set { _overwrite = value; }
}
```

So there is no difference in the TaskAttribute implementation itself, but the inclusion of a second attribute, BooleanValidator, ensures that the value used for the overwrite attribute can be converted to a Boolean. Opening the code to the BooleanValidatorAttribute class reveals the following code:

```
public override void Validate(object value) {
    }
```

A failure to convert the attribute value to a Boolean will result in a BuildException being thrown. This is the essential behavior of the other validator attribute classes, though some have additional options, such as the StringValidatorAttribute, which can ensure the passed string is not empty as follows:

```
[StringValidator(AllowEmpty=false)]
```

The Int32ValidatorAttribute can also accept a minimum and maximum value as follows:

```
[Int32Validator(0, 24)]
```

The validators provide the mechanism for ensuring that scripts are well formed at runtime and so should be used extensively during development of your own tasks to avoid a variety of errors and problems.

Note The SDK documentation with NAnt provides useful assistance with the attributes, but exploration and experimentation is probably the easiest road to success.

Next up is the use of the FileSet in the <copy> task. Once again, we are not overly concerned with the implementation of the FileSet class itself, just how to use it in a task that we construct. In this case the inclusion of the BuildElement attribute, followed by the name of the element, allows us to use a FileSet, as the following code shows:

```
[BuildElement("fileset")]
    public virtual FileSet CopyFileSet {
        get { return _fileset; }
        set { _fileset = value; }
    }
```

This attribute allows the instantiation and use of a FileSet within the <copy> task. The Build* attributes allow a lot of flexibility and complexity in the construction and execution of a task. Consider this line from the <nant> task (which we already know is very flexible in any case):

```
[BuildElementCollection("properties", "property", ElementType=typeof(PropertyTask))]
```

This line allows a collection of <property> elements to be nested into the <nant> task in the following form:

```
<nant>
    <properties>
        <property name="foo1" value="bar1"/>
        <property name="foo2" value="bar2"/>
    </properties>
...
</nant>
```

In many ways, it is not a case of wondering whether something can be done, but understanding how best to do it.

Tip When planning a task, consider the XML implementation compared to existing tasks and then look at the implementation of that task. You will not go far wrong.

A Look at <version>

The <version> task is of course a NAntContrib task, but the premise and implementation is precisely the same. If you remember from our work on versioning, this task provides an updated version number to a property upon request. The code is as follows:

```
<version buildtype="increment" revisiontype="increment"
         path="${solution.name}.Build.Number"/>
```

The interesting aspect of this task is that it sets a property (by default sys.version) with the new number. We can see how it does this in the following code (this time from Reflector):

```
protected override void ExecuteTask()
{
    string text1 = this.CalculateVersionNumber();
    this.Project.Properties[this.Prefix + "version"] = text1;
    ...
}
```

Each task has a reference to the master project (among other things) and so can manipulate various aspects of the build file, such as setting properties, reacting to events, and so on.

If we were to expand on the <version> task, we might add a property called sys.version.prior, which would enable us to use the <vssdiff> task to produce a changes report in the following way:

```
<vssdiff
    dbpath="${vss.dbpath}"
    path="${vss.path}"
    label="NAnt - ${sys.version.prior}"
    user="builder"
    password="builder"
    outputfile="ChangeLog.xml"
/>
```

The VSS comparison report needs a label to work from, which would be supplied by the sys.version.prior property and provides the following sort of output:

```
<vssdiff label="NAnt - 1.0.6.0" generated="14/11/2004 15:54:17"
        project="$/Solutions/Transformer/">
<item
    name="EngineTests.cs"
    path="$/Solutions/Transformer/TransformerTests/EngineTests.cs"
    action="Checked in $/Solutions/Transformer/TransformerTests"
    date="14/11/2004 15:51:52"
    version="4"
    user="Marc"
    comment="Fixed the failing XML output test." />
<item ... />
<item ... />
</vssdiff>
```

With a little bit of XSLT, we could be on our way to an automated release notes report. Being able to tweak NAnt in this way can provide a big benefit.

Caution I advise against changing the actual NAnt source code, though. Provide your own version, or a subclass of the original code, since you will need to refresh the codebase at some point, even if you are not using nightly builds. If your idea is useful, then send an email to the NAnt developer list as a suggestion, too.

A Look at <exec>

Finally, we can look at the <exec> task to see the particular behaviors it has. This task is quite complex because it is used to execute and capture many different command-line outputs.

In general, though, the main point to notice is that the <exec> task actually inherits from ExternalProgramBase, which in itself inherits from Task, as shown in Figure 7-3.

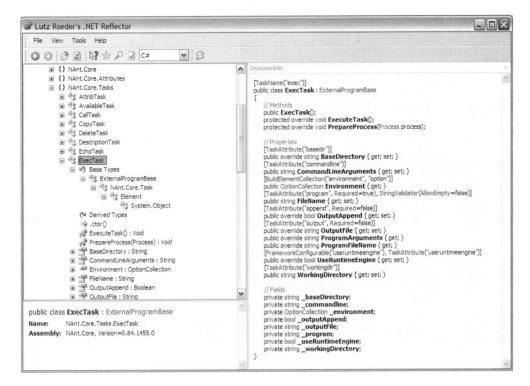

Figure 7-3. *<exec> task hierarchy*

The important features of the implementation of the <exec> task and the override of the <ExternalProgramBase> task are the implementations of the ProgramArguments and ProgramFileName properties.

We can use the ExternalProgramBase class in the same way that the <exec> task does. This base class provides all of the process capture and environmental configuration information that is commensurate with running external programs from within .NET so that we do not have to worry about this implementation. In fact, the ExecuteTask method can generally just execute the base method on ExternalProgramBase, as can be seen in the <exec> task itself:

```
protected override void ExecuteTask() {
    base.ExecuteTask();
    if (ResultProperty != null) {
        Properties[ResultProperty] = base.ExitCode.ToString(
            CultureInfo.InvariantCulture);
    }
}
```

Creating a NAnt Task: <fxcop>

We have looked at the core features that we need to consider when constructing a task by assessing the general structures of the NAnt model, and by looking at examples in existing code, mainly tasks. With this knowledge, we should be able to create a new task to perform the FxCop analysis without using the <exec> task.

FxCop Task Requirements

The task at hand should not be especially complex. In short, we want to be able to provide a level of generic behavior to the task in order to use our standards to implement this task without it requiring specific attention.

Consider again the original call:

```
<exec
    program="D:\dotNetDelivery\Tools\FxCop\1.30\FxCopCmd.exe"
    commandline="/f:${core.output}\${project.name.1}.dll ➥
    /o:${core.reports}\fxcop.xml /r:D:\dotNetDelivery\Tools\FxCop\1.30\Rules\"
    failonerror="false"
/>
```

The task includes these features:

Executable. The path and name of the executable.

Files. The files for analysis can be marked as a single directory where all assemblies are dynamically loaded, or individually with the /f switch.

Rules. The rules can be marked as a single directory where all rules assemblies are dynamically loaded, or individually with the /r switch.

Output. The resulting XML report is output to the file and path specified by the /o switch.

These are the features we have chosen to use, but other command-line options are available. Running the /help switch on the executable produces the output shown in Figure 7-4.

The list of switches contains some potentially useful options, but none of them move us closer to the end result. A good start is then just to use what we already had.

The files (and to a lesser extent rules) options are a little limited, since they accept only a folder and will attempt to analyze every assembly in the folder. This might be useful, but in practice it will mean that referenced assemblies will be included, and assemblies that do not require analysis—perhaps test assemblies—will be included as well. Ideally, it would be better to have a FileSet-type behavior for these options.

Figure 7-4. *FxCopCmd.exe options*

<fxcop> Task Usage

Bearing in mind the brief discussion on requirements, the following might be the way in which we would like to use the <fxcop> task:

```
<fxcop executable="fxcopcmd.exe" report="report.xml">
    <targets basedir="D:\AssembliesFolder">
        <include name="*.dll" />
    </targets>
    <ruleset basedir="D:\RulesFolder">
        <include name="*.dll" />
    </ruleset>
</fxcop>
```

This would in turn translate to the actual implementation of this task in our build file, as in the following:

```
<fxcop executable="D:\dotNetDelivery\Tools\FxCop\1.30\FxCopCmd.exe"
       report="${core.reports}\fxcop.xml"
       failonerror="false">
    <targets basedir="${core.output}">
        <include name="${solution.name}*.dll" />
        <include name="${solution.name}*.exe" />
        <exclude name="*Tests*" />
    </targets>
    <ruleset basedir=" D:\dotNetDelivery\Tools\FxCop\1.30\Rules">
        <include name="*.dll" />
    </ruleset>
</fxcop>
```

This should represent a generic piece of script, which ensures that only the required assemblies for a solution are analyzed. This is a good starting point for creating the `<fxcop>` task. Now let us move on to the coding.

Creating the Visual Studio Project

The Etomic.NAntExtensions solution contains the code for the `<fxcop>` task under the General-Tasks project, as shown in Figure 7-5.

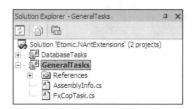

Figure 7-5. *Etomic.NAntExtensions solution*

The project is configured as per the required standards to add easily to the build process. We will do that once we have completed the simple coding work, though in reality you may want to do this immediately to ensure the continuous integration process operates effectively.

There needs to be a reference to the `NAnt.Core` assembly, which can be found in the `\bin` folder of NAnt. If you are using a nightly build and standard folders to hold NAnt across development machines, you may prefer to directly reference that assembly than move the required assemblies into the managed assemblies area.

Once the reference is in place, coding can begin.

Implementing the <fxcop> Task

The `<fxcop>` task is not a heavy-duty coding exercise, since we can rely on much of the framework already in place. We just need to ensure that the XML structure and features of the task are implemented, and that the correct external process arguments are available.

The coding starts with the following lines:

```
using System;
using System.IO;

using NAnt.Core;
using NAnt.Core.Attributes;
using NAnt.Core.Types;
using NAnt.Core.Tasks;
```

These statements ensure we have access to the necessary types in NAnt.Core.dll.
We then declare the class as follows:

```
[TaskName("fxcop")]
public class FxCopTask : ExternalProgramBase
{}
```

Here we state that the task will be known as <fxcop> in a build file. We have also inherited
ExternalProgramBase rather than Task because of the additional functionality. It makes sense
to inherit from ExternalProgramBase when we are attempting to wrap a command-line tool.
Inheriting from Task is better when we are creating a task process from the ground up.

We now add the relevant properties to the class to complete the XML structure. Let us
start by adding a property to represent the path to the executable file:

```
private string _executable;

[TaskAttribute("executable")]
[StringValidator(AllowEmpty=false)]
public string Executable
{
    get{return _executable;}
    set{_executable = value;}
}
```

In this case, the attribute will be known as executable. Additionally we have included a
validator to ensure that the attribute is not empty since this is unacceptable to the task.

Next, we add the output information:

```
private FileInfo _output;

[TaskAttribute("report")]
[StringValidator(AllowEmpty=false)]
public FileInfo Report
{
    get{return _output;}
    set{_output = value;}
}
```

Although we are passing a string, we can hold a FileInfo object since this conversion is
fine. Again, the task must always produce a report, and so we have included a validator to
ensure that this attribute is not empty.

Note If I was considering a public release of such a task, then I would probably have the option of using console output rather than simply an XML file, but this task is to suit my own purposes, of course, and I can afford to be selfish for v1!

We then move on to including the two `FileSet` structures for the task: the targets and the rules.

```
private FileSet _ruleset = new FileSet();
private FileSet _targets = new FileSet();

[BuildElement("ruleset")]
public FileSet RuleSet
{
    get{return _ruleset;}
    set{_ruleset = value;}
}

[BuildElement("targets")]
public FileSet Targets
{
    get{return _targets;}
    set{_targets = value;}
}
```

At this point, the properties are complete and we move on to ensuring the execution of the analysis. The things we need to do are: override and provide the name of the executable (`ProgramFileName`), override and provide the command-line arguments (`ProgramArguments`), and then override the `ExecuteTask` method.

Overriding the `ProgramFileName` is simple:

```
public override string ProgramFileName
{
    get{return this.Executable;}
}
```

Providing an accurate command line is a little more involved; we need to provide three different sets of switches. Fortunately, the switches are all of the same format and so we produce the command line in a common way. First, we create an enumeration of the different switches:

```
private enum FxCopArgument
{
    Target,
    Rule,
    Output
}
```

Then we generate a small method for formatting an argument correctly given the argument value and the type of switch required:

```
private string FormatArgument(string argument, FxCopArgument fxArg)
{
    string argumentPrefix = "";
    if (fxArg == FxCopArgument.Target) argumentPrefix = "f";
    if (fxArg == FxCopArgument.Rule) argumentPrefix = "r";
    if (fxArg == FxCopArgument.Output) argumentPrefix = "o";
    return String.Format(@" /{0}:""{1}""", argumentPrefix, argument);
}
```

Finally, we override the actual property `ProgramArguments` and provide the command line by looping through the available files from the two `filesets`. We also add the output file to the command line. The property then looks like this:

```
public override string ProgramArguments
{
    get
    {
        string progargs = "";

        //Get the targets for the run
        foreach(string file in Targets.FileNames)
            progargs += FormatArgument(file, FxCopArgument.Target);

        //Get the rules for the run
        foreach(string file in RuleSet.FileNames)
            progargs += FormatArgument(file, FxCopArgument.Rule);

        //Get the output for the run
            progargs += FormatArgument(this.Report.FullName, ➥
                                    FxCopArgument.Output);

        return progargs;
    }
}
```

All we need to do now is to override the `ExecuteTask` method. As discussed earlier, in general the only action required is to invoke the base `ExecuteTask` method, but we will also provide a little debugging information and check for some obvious problems that will cause a failure—such as not having any rules and/or not having any targets for analysis. This method looks like the following:

```
protected override void ExecuteTask()
{
    Log(Level.Debug, "CommandLine is: {0}", this.CommandLine.ToString());
    if(this.Targets.FileNames.Count < 1)
    {
        string errorMessage = "Task must contain at least one target assembly";
```

```
            Log(Level.Error, errorMessage);
            throw new BuildException(errorMessage);
        }
        if(this.RuleSet.FileNames.Count < 1)
        {
            string errorMessage = "Task must contain at least one valid rule assembly.";
            Log(Level.Error, errorMessage);
            throw new BuildException(errorMessage);
        }
        base.ExecuteTask();
}
```

That completes the coding aspects of the task. We had to perform a little more integration work than with a regular task because of the reliance on the command line, but we have standardized another aspect of the process and the exercise was simple when you consider the impact on the scripts.

Testing the Task

Testing the task is quite straightforward. We can create a simple build file to test the features we are looking for. Ideally, the task should be unit tested, but this can be hard to achieve where there is a reliance on contextual information. I have constructed a test as follows using the outputs from the original Transformer application in Chapter 4. This is a good test because it outputs three different assemblies with differing stubs. The test assembly should not be analyzed. Here is the script file:

```xml
<?xml version="1.0" encoding="utf-8" ?>
<project name="Etomic.NAntExtenstions.FxCop.Debug" default="go">

<target name="go">

    <loadtasks
assembly="D:\dotNetDelivery\Chapter6\Etomic.NAntExtensions\GeneralTasks\➥
        Bin\Debug\Etomic.NAntExtensions.GeneralTasks.dll"/>

    <fxcop executable="D:\dotNetDelivery\Tools\FxCop\1.30\FxCopCmd.exe"
        report="D:\Temp\fxcop.xml" failonerror="false">
        <targets basedir="D:\dotNetDelivery\BuildArea\Output">
            <include name="Transformer*.dll" />
            <include name="Transformer*.exe" />
            <exclude name="*Tests*" />
        </targets>
        <ruleset basedir=" D:\dotNetDelivery\Tools\FxCop\1.30\Rules">
            <include name="*.dll" />
        </ruleset>
    </fxcop>

</target>
</project>
```

Notice that I have used the <loadtasks> task to load an assembly held somewhere other than the NAnt \bin folder. This approach is useful during debugging and construction of a task, but can also be used in production scripts, as we will consider next. The resulting output of this script is

```
Buildfile: file:///Etomic.NAntExtensions.FxCop.Debug.xml
Target(s) specified: go


go:

[loadtasks] Scanning assembly "Etomic.NAntExtensions.GeneralTasks" for extensions.
   [fxcop] Microsoft FxCopCmd v1.30
   [fxcop] Copyright (C) 1999-2004 Microsoft Corp.  All rights reserved.
   [fxcop]
   [fxcop] Loaded ComRules.dll...
   [fxcop] Loaded DesignRules.dll...
   [fxcop] Loaded GlobalizationRules.dll...
   [fxcop] Loaded NamingRules.dll...
   [fxcop] Loaded PerformanceRules.dll...
   [fxcop] Loaded SecurityRules.dll...
   [fxcop] Loaded UsageRules.dll...
   [fxcop] Loaded TransformerEngine.dll...
   [fxcop] Loaded TransformerGui.exe...
   [fxcop] Initializing Introspection engine...
   [fxcop] <NOTE>
   [fxcop]    : Data flow analysis is currently disabled. Enabling this
   [fxcop]    : functionality will increase the number of code correctness
   [fxcop]    : checks that run but will also slow analysis by at least 2x.
   [fxcop]    : To enable analysis globally, choose 'Settings' from
   [fxcop]    : the Tools menu and click 'Analysis Engines'. Select
   [fxcop]    : 'Introspection', click 'Settings'and check the box labeled
   [fxcop]    : 'Enable Control Flow Analysis'. To enable data flow analysis
   [fxcop]    : for this project only, choose 'Options' from the Project menu.
   [fxcop]    : Click the 'Spelling & Analysis' tab and set the
   [fxcop]    : 'Control Flow Analysis' drop-down to 'True'.
   [fxcop] </NOTE>
   [fxcop] Analyzing...
   [fxcop] Analysis Complete.
   [fxcop] Writing 6 messages...
   [fxcop] Writing report to D:\Temp\fxcop.xml...
   [fxcop] Done.

BUILD SUCCEEDED
Total time: 2.8 seconds.
Output completed (4 sec consumed) - Normal Termination
```

Excellent. The output in the FxCop.xml report is also correct. The console output and report demonstrate that the correct filters are applied from the FileSets and that the correct executable and output report file were also used.

Running the build file in debug mode demonstrates the actual command line used for FxCop. It also shows many other debug statements; the only one we are interested in is reproduced here:

```
[fxcop] CommandLine is:
/f:"D:\dotNetDelivery\BuildArea\Output\TransformerEngine.dll"
/f:"D:\dotNetDelivery\BuildArea\Output\TransformerGui.exe"
/r:"D:\dotNetDelivery\Tools\FxCop\1.30\Rules\ComRules.dll"
/r:"D:\dotNetDelivery\Tools\FxCop\1.30\Rules\DesignRules.dll"
/r:"D:\dotNetDelivery\Tools\FxCop\1.30\Rules\GlobalizationRules.dll"
/r:"D:\dotNetDelivery\Tools\FxCop\1.30\Rules\NamingRules.dll"
/r:"D:\dotNetDelivery\Tools\FxCop\1.30\Rules\PerformanceRules.dll"
/r:"D:\dotNetDelivery\Tools\FxCop\1.30\Rules\SecurityRules.dll"
/r:"D:\dotNetDelivery\Tools\FxCop\1.30\Rules\UsageRules.dll"
/o:"D:\Temp\fxcop.xml"
```

This differs slightly from the original command line, since it expands each rule and file individually instead of using a directory. This is no big deal, though, and so we can consider the implementation of this task a success at this time.

Adding the Solution to the Build Process

We can create build and deploy scripts for the solution we have just generated and add them to CruiseControl.NET without too much difficulty.

I have chosen to deploy the assemblies I generate myself to the Program Files\ ${solution.name} folder, in the same way that we deployed the Windows version of Transformer, and I will use <loadtasks> to dynamically load the assemblies at runtime.

The standard build file changes are highlighted in the script as follows:

```
<?xml version="1.0" encoding="utf-8" ?>
<project name="Etomic.NAntExtensions" default="help">
    <description>
        Build file for the Etomic.NAntExtensions application.
    </description>
    <property name="project.name.1" value="${solution.name}.GeneralTasks" />
    <property name="solution.isweb" value="false"/>
```

First, names are changed as appropriate for the solution, followed by the naming of the individual assemblies—of which there is only one for this solution. Subsequently, the build script follows precisely the same format that we have come to expect, with only minor tweaks for the .dll extension as opposed to an .exe extension.

```
<target
    name="go"
    description="The main target for full build process execution."
    depends="build, test, document, publish, notify"
    />

<target name="build" description="Compile the application.">
    <solution
        solutionfile="${core.source}\${solution.name}.sln"
        configuration="Debug" outputdir="${core.output}\"/>
</target>

<target name="test" description="Apply the unit tests.">

    <exec
        program="D:\dotNetDelivery\Tools\FxCop\1.30\FxCopCmd.exe"
        commandline="/f:${core.output}\${project.name.1}.dll ➡
                /o:${core.reports}\fxcop.xml ➡
                /r:D:\dotNetDelivery\Tools\FxCop\1.30\Rules\"
        failonerror="false"/>

    <style style="D:\dotNetDelivery\Tools\FxCop\1.30\Xml\FxCopReport.xsl"
        in="${core.reports}\fxcop.xml" out="${core.reports}\fxcop.html"/>

</target>

<target name="document" description="Generate documentation and reports.">
    <ndoc>
        <assemblies basedir="${core.output}\">
            <include name="${project.name.1}.dll" />
        </assemblies>
        <summaries basedir="${core.output}\">
            <include name="${project.name.1}.xml" />
        </summaries>
        <documenters>
          <documenter name="MSDN">
            <property name="OutputDirectory" value="${core.docs}\" />
            <property name="HtmlHelpName" value="${solution.name}" />
            <property name="HtmlHelpCompilerFilename" value="hhc.exe" />
            <property name="IncludeFavorites" value="False" />
            <property name="Title" value="${solution.name} (NDoc)" />
            <property name="SplitTOCs" value="False" />
            <property name="DefaulTOC" value="" />
            <property name="ShowVisualBasic" value="False" />
```

```
                    <property name="ShowMissingSummaries" value="True" />
                    <property name="ShowMissingRemarks" value="False" />
                    <property name="ShowMissingParams" value="True" />
                    <property name="ShowMissingReturns" value="True" />
                    <property name="ShowMissingValues" value="True" />
                    <property name="DocumentInternals" value="True" />
                    <property name="DocumentProtected" value="True" />
                    <property name="DocumentPrivates" value="False" />
                    <property name="DocumentEmptyNamespaces" value="False" />
                    <property name="IncludeAssemblyVersion" value="True" />
                    <property name="CopyrightText"
                        value="${company.name} Ltd., 2005" />
                    <property name="CopyrightHref" value="" />
                </documenter>
            </documenters>
        </ndoc>
    </target>

    <target name="publish" description="Place assets in agreed locations.">
        <nant buildfile="Build.Common.xml" target="publish" inheritall="true"/>
    </target>

    <target name="notify" description="Tell everyone of the success or failure.">
        <echo message="Notifying you of the build process success."/>
    </target>

    <target name="fail">
        <echo message="Notifying you of a failure in the build process."/>
    </target>

    <target name="help">
        <echo message="This file should not be executed. Use Build.Core.xml"/>
    </target>
</project>
```

The deploy file changes are also very simple, requiring only names to be changed. The deploy file is based on the deploy file for the Transformer Windows application, since this is how the NAntExtensions assembly will also be deployed. The small changes required are a testament to the scripts being suitable for reuse.

```
<?xml version="1.0" encoding="utf-8" ?>
<project name="Etomic.NAntExtensions" default="help">
  <description>Deploy file for the Etomic.NAntExtensions application</description>

    <property name="nant.onfailure" value="fail"/>

    <property name="company.name" value="Etomic"/>
    <property name="solution.name" value="${company.name}.NAntExtensions"/>
```

```
<property name="core.publish"
        value="http://localhost/ccnet/files/${solution.name}"/>

<property name="core.deploy" value="D:\TempDeploy"/>
<property name="core.environment"
        value="D:\Program Files\${solution.name}"/>

<target name="go"
    description="The main target for full deploy process execution."
    depends="selectversion, get, selectenvironments, ➡
            createenvironments, position, configure, notify"
    />

<target name="selectversion" description="Selects the correct version">
    <if test="${debug}">
        <property name="sys.version" value="0.0.0.0"/>
    </if>
</target>

<target name="get" description="Grab the correct assets.">
    <delete dir="${core.deploy}\" failonerror="false"/>
    <mkdir dir="${core.deploy}\${sys.version}\"/>
    <get
        src="${core.publish}/${solution.name}-Build-${sys.version}.zip"
        dest="${core.deploy}\${solution.name}-Build-${sys.version}.zip"
        />
    <unzip
        zipfile="${core.deploy}\${solution.name}-Build-${sys.version}.zip"
        todir="${core.deploy}\${sys.version}\"
        />
</target>

<target name="selectenvironments" description="Select environments">
    <!--Enter tasks for selectenvironments target-->
</target>

<target name="createenvironments" description="Create the environments">
    <mkdir dir="${core.environment}\${sys.version}\" failonerror="false"/>
</target>

<target name="position" description="Place required assets">
    <copy todir="${core.environment}\${sys.version}\">
        <fileset basedir="${core.deploy}\${sys.version}">
            <include name="Etomic.*"/>
        </fileset>
    </copy>
</target>
```

```
    <target name="configure" description="Amend config settings as necessary">
        <!--Enter tasks for configure target-->
    </target>

    <!-- REMAINDER SNIPPED -->

</project>
```

To add this solution to CruiseControl.NET, we need to add a new `project` element to the `ccnet.config` file, as shown next. Once again, the changes required are based on name changes—in several places because we cannot use properties in the `ccnet.config` file—rather than any significant logic changes.

```
<project name="Etomic.NAntExtensions">

<webURL>
        http://localhost/ccnet/Controller.aspx?_action_ViewProjectReport=true➡
            &amp;server=local&amp;project=Etomic.NAntExtensions
</webURL>

    <artifactDirectory>
        D:\dotNetDelivery\BuildAreaCI\Publish\Etomic.NAntExtensions\
    </artifactDirectory>

    <labeller type="defaultlabeller">
        <prefix>1.0.</prefix>
    </labeller>

    <triggers>
        <intervalTrigger />
    </triggers>

    <modificationDelaySeconds>10</modificationDelaySeconds>

    <sourcecontrol type="vss" autoGetSource="true">
        <ssdir>"D:\dotNetDelivery\VSS"</ssdir>
        <project>$/Solutions/Etomic.NAntExtensions/</project>
        <username>builder</username>
        <password>builder</password>
        <workingDirectory>
            D:\dotNetDelivery\BuildAreaCI\Source\Etomic.NAntExtensions
        </workingDirectory>
    </sourcecontrol>

    <build type="nant">
        <baseDirectory>D:\dotNetDelivery\Chapter7\</baseDirectory>
        <buildArgs>-D:solution.stub=NAntExtensions -D:debug=false</buildArgs>
        <buildFile>Build.Core.xml</buildFile>
        <targetList>
```

```
                <target>ci</target>
            </targetList>
            <buildTimeoutSeconds>300</buildTimeoutSeconds>
        </build>

        <tasks>
            <merge>
                <files>
                    <file>
    D:\dotNetDelivery\BuildAreaCI\Reports\Etomic.NAntExtensions\*-results.xml
                    </file>
                    <file>
    D:\dotNetDelivery\BuildAreaCI\Reports\Etomic.NAntExtensions\fxcop.xml
                    </file>
                </files>
            </merge>
        </tasks>

        <publishers>
            <xmllogger />
        </publishers>

</project>
```

Using the Task

Once a successful delivery of a version of the Etomic.NAntExtensions solution has been made and it is deployed, we can use the task.

Removing the current calls to the <exec> task and replacing with the all new <fxcop> task is not a difficult problem, and can be accomplished in a short amount of time, particularly since the standard pattern for matching assemblies for analysis works across all projects, as is highlighted in the following code. This should be added to Build.Common.xml:

```
<target name="report.fxcop">
    <fxcop
        executable="D:\dotNetDelivery\Tools\FxCop\1.30\FxCopCmd.exe"
        report="${core.reports}\fxcop.xml"
        failonerror="false">
        <targets basedir="${core.output}">
            <include name="${solution.name}*.dll" />
            <include name="${solution.name}*.exe" />
            <exclude name="*Tests*" />
        </targets>
        <ruleset basedir=" D:\dotNetDelivery\Tools\FxCop\1.30\Rules">
            <include name="*.dll" />
        </ruleset>
    </fxcop>
</target>
```

Because this target has been added to the common file, the call to the <exec> task can be removed by adding the following call in its place in each of the build files:

```
<nant buildfile="Build.Common.xml" target="report.fxcop" inheritall="true"/>
```

On its own, this call will generate an error because the assembly containing the <fxcop> task extension has not been loaded into the runtime. In order to do this, we can add a <loadtasks> task to the Build.Core.xml file. In this case, I am loading the assembly included under the Tools, folder but you could of course use another version and place the <loadtasks> task under the <sysinfo> task in the file:

```
<sysinfo/>
<loadtasks
path="D:\dotNetDelivery\Tools\Etomic.NAntExtensions\➥
    Etomic.NAntExtensions.GeneralTasks.dll"/>
```

With this done, we can use the regular script calls, or the CruiseControl server to build any of the solutions. When we run the script, we will see the following additional results, which demonstrate that the assembly is being loaded:

```
 [loadtasks] Scanning assembly "Etomic.NAntExtensions.GeneralTasks" ➥
for extensions.
```

Also, the <fxcop> task will run and the results (as previously observed) will be seen. The reports are being generated as required, and we have standardized and generalized even more of the build files.

We now have the four solutions operating within the CruiseControl.NET environment, as shown in Figure 7-6.

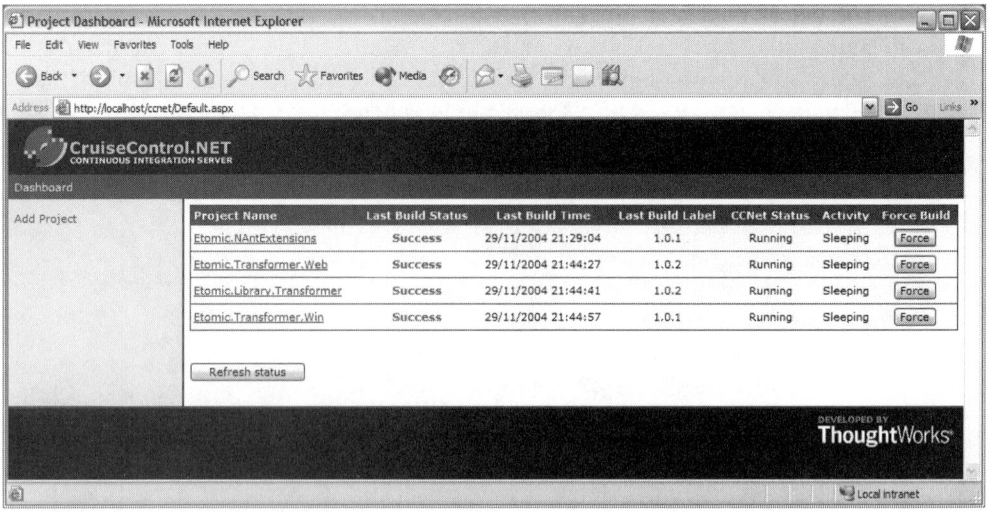

Figure 7-6. *CruiseControl.NET web dashboard*

Summary

We have taken a closer look at the behavior and structure of NAnt. As we have discovered, it is easy to extend, and a variety of features are available to assist in the construction of tasks with minimum integration effort, including specific support of command-line type tasks and specific tasks to aid the use of any custom assemblies.

Extending NAnt is a pleasure rather than a pain. The framework for the application provides utility rather than forces increased thought on the part of the developer.

We will make further extensions to NAnt in the next chapter, where things start to get a little complex as we look at the integration of databases into the build process.

CHAPTER 8

■■■

Database Integration

In this chapter we look at two problems that we have ignored until now. The first is the integration of the database, which can cause problems unless managed carefully. The second problem is a related one: the deployment of environments using multiple servers.

We are going to take a look at likely scenarios and requirements for database integration and solutions for the automated and continuous integration of the database environments. We will then look at how this impacts our current framework for delivery and apply some changes to handle these more complex scenarios. Finally, we will tackle issues with automating the deployment of Data Transformation Services (DTS) packages, an area that is easy to overlook.

The Problems with the Database

So what is the problem with the database? Well, there are a number of issues that by themselves are not so severe, but when combined and then considered against the process we are attempting to install, they demand our attention:

Lack of source control. Generally, source control for databases is quite poor, or at least is full of risk. Generally no real automated links exist between databases and source control systems, so it is easy to lose control of database assets that are stored in the source control database. Once confidence in those assets is lost, we are in trouble. VS .NET has made some strides toward improving source control support for SQL Server, and I hope that this improvement continues over time, but it still does not easily provide the required level of automated control.

Attention to detail. Because of the lack of automated source control facilities, managing database assets requires diligence and attention to detail. This usually means the handling of many migration scripts and administration scripts. Once again, if this area is not managed correctly and diligently at all times, then the development and migration picture will not be complete. Worse, this may not be obvious for some time until the script is needed.

Standing data. The final big issue with the database is the need for development and migration to occur against standing user data. Whereas the code for an application is simply the logical model and should be replaced entirely on each release, the database is both the logical model and the data itself. Management of development and migration scripts for the database needs to take account of this at all times.

We can take several steps to solve these problems within the delivery framework we currently have:

Provide automated management of source control. If the scripts are available, then it is quite easy to provide tasks that add the scripts to source control when required. To best accomplish this, the next measure is important.

Outline a standard for managing DDL and SQL scripts. As usual, to best manage automated processes on a larger scale, a standard mechanism for storing database scripts aids the implementation of standard techniques.

Provide automated integration mechanisms. In the same way that the scripts can be added automatically to source control, as long as they are available we can automate the running of the scripts to provide the migration to the required database.

These measures do not offer a panacea to database integration issues but do provide a framework and standards—and therefore a set of measures/safeguards—to database integration. The developer is still responsible for diligently preparing the scripts for database development, though.

We need to consider how best to apply these potential solutions in our given scenario.

Database Scenarios

Most code development these days involves using a "local development" model. In other words, the code is created on the developers' local machines, and the shared source control database is the integration point and provides the mechanism for sharing new code. The automated delivery processes then provide the isolated continuous integration process as already specified. Database development is not necessarily handled in the same way, but it can be. The actual model used affects the requirements for handling database integration. Figure 8-1 shows the local database development model.

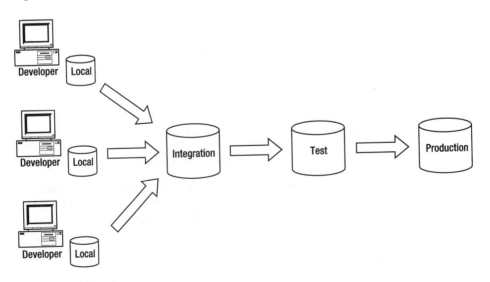

Figure 8-1. *Local database development*

This model demonstrates the use of local SQL Server instances on developers' machines. In this model, we need to provide database integration at the software system's build time since the integration will have to occur on a separate instance of the database for testing.

The next model, shown in Figure 8-2, is a shared development database instance.

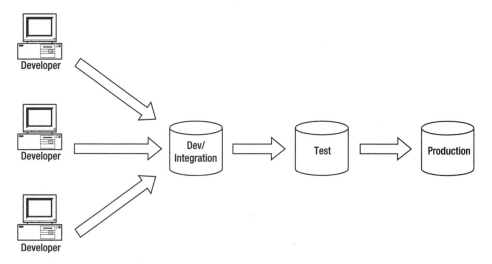

Figure 8-2. *Shared database development*

In this model, one database is shared between all developers. This means that regular integration occurs as a matter of course. Therefore, we do not necessarily need to run a database integration at build time since we have the complete database for testing already available. This may be risky, though, and it may be preferable to run an integration on a separate database instance in any case. Otherwise, we may just want to perform an integration when we choose to deploy the system to another environment.

Another factor is the number of database instances that require integration. We may want to perform integration to a database containing only artificial test data specifically designed for unit or system testing and then perform another integration to a database containing a copy, or agreed representative copy, of the production database.

With this in mind, it seems to make sense to ensure that the process we have in place allows for integration and testing at build time since this seems to be the most likely scenario we will come across one way or another.

Planning the Database Tasks

Based on the above discussion, there are a few tasks we can provide as building blocks for database integration. Table 8-1 lists these tasks.

Table 8-1. *Required Database Tasks*

Name	Purpose
Control	Adding new migration scripts to the source control database
Analyze	Assessing the database for changes and providing automated migration scripts
Integrate	Running migration scripts on a particular database instance
Configure	Ensuring that the tested/deployed code runs on the required database instance

With those tasks (or suites of tasks), we should be able to handle our requirements for database integration. The Analyze step is a special case and goes further than in our original discussion. We had planned to work with scripts provided by developers and integrate using these scripts, but there are also possibilities for the automation of the migration itself. This will be the icing on the cake for database integration. Let us consider this list in a little more detail, and then examine the impact on the delivery process.

Control Task

This task should provide the facilities to add new migration scripts to source control in an ordered manner to ensure that the database development and migration path is complete and auditable. In fact, this task does not need to actually use source control, as long as it manages the assets in a way acceptable for configuration management, although this may well be under source control. We manage code assets in VSS, but manage the compiled code in zip files stored (and backed up!) on the CCNet server. We could do the same thing with the database assets, bypassing the source control database, though it is preferable to maintain the assets under source control because they cannot be regenerated in the same way that compiled assemblies can.

We need to decide what scripts are required, and what to do with these scripts during an integration cycle. This is not as easy as it might first sound. Do we want to simply maintain ALTER scripts? Perhaps we want to take a full CREATE script following a successful set of tests. We may want to do the same with the test data as well. Do we remove the migration scripts following a successful build (so that they cannot be changed)? If the build fails, do we want to leave them so that they can be changed?

Analyze Task

Providing automated database integration in terms of the actual migration scripts would be a huge boon; it significantly reduces the risk of developers failing to manage the scripts accurately and thus introducing build problems. Doing this is a complex business, though. There are two potential areas to analyze: the scripts defining the database structure, and the scripts defining the data. The database structure scripts are a good target initially since there are no semantic issues to deal with. Handling data migration and updates automatically could be a real headache and may ultimately be handled best manually. For this task we will utilize a third-party tool.

Integrate Task

Integration itself should be quite straightforward as long as the scripts are available. This step will involve looking at the scripts available and applying them in the correct order to the correct environment. Ultimately, though, this should just be a case of running multiple script processing tasks.

Configure Task

This task ensures that unit tests are carried out against the correct database instance and that when the system is deployed, the correct application instance points at the correct database instance. There are a few ways that this kind of work can be achieved that are also applicable to other configuration settings: the generation of configuration files on the fly, replacing individual configuration elements, or pointing the master configuration file to child configuration files from instance to instance and environment to environment.

The Impact on Continuous Integration

We need to thread the database migration tasks into the regular process. Figure 8-3 demonstrates how the process looks with the new task inserted.

The diagram demonstrates the opportunity for us to include database integration after the compile and testing steps of the regular process. As we will see, the database integration step will consist of some substeps itself, but for now we should recognize that post-testing of the code is the preferred time for the database work. The reasons for this relate to the nature of database integration: it is to a certain extent a one-way process—rollback is at least painful—because of the lack of natural support for this sort of operation on a database platform. We will see this demonstrated later.

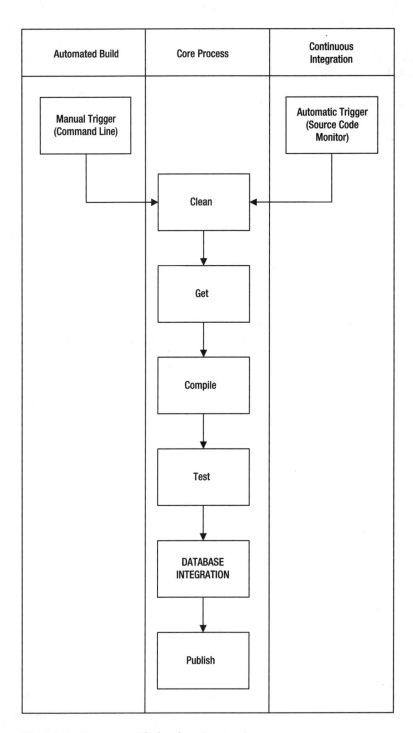

Figure 8-3. *CI process with database integration*

Implementing the Database Tasks

In order to implement the database tasks, we must use a combination of existing NAnt tasks, new custom tasks (or some clever <exec> tasks) and the aforementioned third-party tool to handle automated database integration.

We will tackle the Analyze and Integrate tasks initially, then concern ourselves with source control and configuration issues after we have handled the guts of the work. In looking at the Analyze and Integrate tasks, we will effectively be looking at two differing solutions: one for manual scripts and one for automated scripts for the database integration. We will consider the task for processing manually generated SQL scripts first.

Manual SQL Script Processing Task

So, as discussed earlier, the manual integration task needs to be able to look at a series of migration scripts and execute them in the correct order on a designated target database.

Therefore, in order to use this task, we need something like the following information: the folder where the database scripts are, the correct ordering of the scripts, and the database details (server, database name, user and password credentials).

This means that the following NAnt script could do the job quite nicely:

```
<dbIntegrate
        folder="D:\BookCode\Chapter8\DBTest1\"
        compare="CreationTime"
        server="localhost"
        database="TestDB-Integration"
        uid="sa"
        pwd="w1bbl3"
/>
```

Of course, this task does not currently exist. We need to generate the code for this task, but we are used to this now from our work on the <fxcop> task in Chapter 7.

■**Note** As usual, the code for this task can be found in the VSS database.

The code for the integration is actually quite simple. The project for this particular task looks like the one shown in Figure 8-4.

Figure 8-4. *ManualDBTasks project*

Note The code for this chapter could be included as part of the previous NAntExtensions solution, but I have separated the projects for clarity.

The code for all six XML attributes is broadly the same and is quite simple. I could have used a fileset for the script folder(s), but this would confuse the ordering of the scripts and is probably not the desired scenario.

```
private DirectoryInfo _folder;
private string _compareOption;

//Database Info
private string _server;
private string _database;
private string _username;
private string _password;

[TaskAttribute("folder", Required=true)]
public DirectoryInfo Folder
{
    get{return _folder;}
    set{_folder = value;}
}


/// <summary>
/// Available options "Name", "LastWriteTime", "CreationTime"
/// </summary>
[TaskAttribute("compare", Required=true)]
public string CompareOption
```

```
{
    get{return _compareOption;}
    set{_compareOption = value;}
}

[TaskAttribute("server", Required=true)]
public string Server
{
    get{return _server;}
    set{_server = value;}
}

[TaskAttribute("database", Required=true)]
public string Database
{
    get{return _database;}
    set{_database = value;}
}

[TaskAttribute("uid", Required=true)]
public string Username
{
    get{return _username;}
    set{_username = value;}
}

[TaskAttribute("pwd", Required=true)]
public string Password
{
    get{return _password;}
    set{_password = value;}
}
```

The key points to notice about the previous code is the use of a `DirectoryInfo` type for the folder, which NAnt can handle automatically, and the available options for the Compare➡ Option. These are not particularly friendly ways of describing the sorting options for the folder, but are in fact the way that the .NET Framework describes the options. Since we will be using a reflective comparer, it is easier to use the default names. The three options mentioned (`Name`, `LastWriteTime`, `CreationTime`) are not exhaustive but are the most likely ordering to be needed for our purposes (more complete code should limit these options, of course).

■Note The code for the comparer is held in the `ObjectComparer.cs` file. This is a useful general-purpose comparer and is ideal for the task at hand.

The <execute> method then looks like this:

```
protected override void ExecuteTask()
{
    //Get and sort the files
    FileInfo[] files = _folder.GetFiles();
    Array.Sort(files, new ObjectComparer(new String[]{_compareOption}));

    //Execute the SQL into the database
    foreach(FileInfo fi in files)
    {
        Log(Level.Info, fi.Name);
        ExecTask e = new ExecTask();
        e.Project = this.Project;
        e.FileName = @"osql.exe";
        e.CommandLineArguments = String.Format(@"-U {0} -P {1} -S {2} -d {3} -i {4}", ➥
                            this._username, this._password, ➥
                            this._server, this._database, fi.FullName);

            e.Execute();
    }
}
```

This method is deceptively simple and makes use of the aforementioned comparer to provide a set of ordered files followed by the internal use of the NAnt <exec> task to complete its work. Once the files are ordered, the task loops through the list and creates a new <exec> task, attaching it to the current project, setting the arguments as required, and then executing the task. The effect is to dynamically generate as many tasks as required to complete the execution of all the database scripts. If written as a regular NAnt task, the <exec> task would look like the following (as an example):

```
<exec
    program="osql.exe"
    commandline="-U sa -P w1bbl3 -S localhost -d TestDB-Integration -i ➥
C:\BookCode\Chapter8\DBTest1\Users.sql"
/>
```

Using the <exec> task facilities saves us from having to handle all of the SQL-DMO bits and pieces that would otherwise be needed through this automation and therefore provides us with a simple and elegant solution that will suffice for our current needs.

We can test this custom task in the usual way: using a NAnt script. We will create a simple database TestDB-Development by using scripts. These scripts can then be used to update the integration database TestDB-Integration. The database scripts are as follows. The first, Users.sql, contains the initial CREATE script for a table Users:

```
CREATE TABLE [dbo].[Users] (
        [ID] [uniqueidentifier] NOT NULL ,
        [Name] [char] (50) COLLATE SQL_Latin1_General_CP1_CI_AS NOT NULL ,
        [Email] [char] (255) COLLATE SQL_Latin1_General_CP1_CI_AS NULL
```

```
)
GO

ALTER TABLE [dbo].[Users] ADD CONSTRAINT [PK_Users] PRIMARY KEY CLUSTERED  ([ID])
GO
```

The next script, `Users-AddPostcode.sql`, alters the Users table and adds a new column, PostCode, to the existing table:

```
ALTER TABLE [dbo].[Users] ADD [Postcode] [char] (10) COLLATE
SQL_Latin1_General_CP1_CI_AS NULL
GO
```

The NAnt script to test out the new task is as follows, and can sit in the debug/bin folder for the extensions project:

```
<?xml version="1.0"?>
<project>
    <loadtasks assembly="Etomic.ManualDBTasks.dll"/>
    <dbIntegrate
        folder="D:\BookCode\Chapter8\DBTest1\"
        compare="CreationTime"
        server="localhost"
        database="TestDB-Integration"
        uid="sa"
        pwd="w1bbl3"
    />
</project>
```

Prior to the execution of the NAnt script, the database contains no user tables, as can be seen in Figure 8-5.

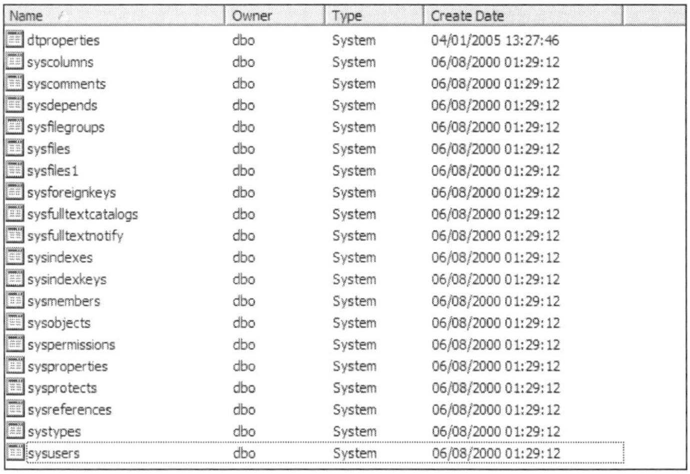

Name	Owner	Type	Create Date	
dtproperties	dbo	System	04/01/2005 13:27:46	
syscolumns	dbo	System	06/08/2000 01:29:12	
syscomments	dbo	System	06/08/2000 01:29:12	
sysdepends	dbo	System	06/08/2000 01:29:12	
sysfilegroups	dbo	System	06/08/2000 01:29:12	
sysfiles	dbo	System	06/08/2000 01:29:12	
sysfiles1	dbo	System	06/08/2000 01:29:12	
sysforeignkeys	dbo	System	06/08/2000 01:29:12	
sysfulltextcatalogs	dbo	System	06/08/2000 01:29:12	
sysfulltextnotify	dbo	System	06/08/2000 01:29:12	
sysindexes	dbo	System	06/08/2000 01:29:12	
sysindexkeys	dbo	System	06/08/2000 01:29:12	
sysmembers	dbo	System	06/08/2000 01:29:12	
sysobjects	dbo	System	06/08/2000 01:29:12	
syspermissions	dbo	System	06/08/2000 01:29:12	
sysproperties	dbo	System	06/08/2000 01:29:12	
sysprotects	dbo	System	06/08/2000 01:29:12	
sysreferences	dbo	System	06/08/2000 01:29:12	
systypes	dbo	System	06/08/2000 01:29:12	
sysusers	dbo	System	06/08/2000 01:29:12	

Figure 8-5. *Empty TestDB-Integration*

Executing the test NAnt script produces the following results:

```
---------- NAnt ----------
NAnt 0.85
Copyright (C) 2001-2004 Gerry Shaw
http://nant.sourceforge.net

Buildfile: file:///NAntExtenstions.ManualDBTasks.Debug.xml

[loadtasks] Scanning assembly "Etomic.ManualDBTasks" for extensions.
[dbIntegrate] Users.sql
     [exec] 1> 2> 3> 4> 5> 6> 1> 2> 3> 1>
[dbIntegrate] Users-AddPostcode.sql
     [exec] 1> 2> 1>


BUILD SUCCEEDED
Total time: 0.9 seconds.
Output completed (2 sec consumed) - Normal Termination
```

The results demonstrate that the custom task assembly is loaded, and that the <dbIntegrate> task executes the Users.sql and Users-AddPostcode.sql scripts in the correct order (that is, by CreationTime). We can also see the nested <exec> tasks being executed for each script. Following this execution, the Users table is included in the database TestDB-Integration, as shown in Figure 8-6.

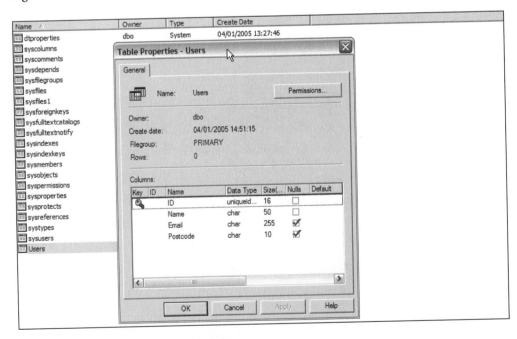

Figure 8-6. *Table Users in database TestDB-Integration*

We could tidy up and bulletproof the code for the integration task, but essentially this task now does what we need it to do as part of the delivery process.

■**Note** The same script can also be used to run SQL scripts rather than DDL scripts. We will see this later on.

Automated Integration Task

Next we turn our attention to the automation of the migration scripts themselves. Generating migration scripts is no small task; it is not a simple matter of exporting the database schema. Something like that will perhaps suffice for the generation of a CREATE script for a database, which is useful in itself, but automated migration scripts require the use of ALTER scripts, the removal and addition of constraints, and other tricks and techniques to modify a schema while the database itself contains data. This is something best left to those who specialize in that, and I certainly do not.

Instead, the following tools are a huge boon to the task at hand. Better still, they have fully exposed .NET APIs for programming against, and that can mean only one thing: even more custom NAnt tasks!

The Red Gate Tools

Red Gate Software Ltd. (www.red-gate.com) produces a suite of tools known as the Red Gate SQL Bundle, which contains various tools for SQL Server, as shown in Table 8-2.

Table 8-2. *Red Gate SQL Bundle*

Tool	Description
SQL Compare	Provides comparison and synchronization scripts of schemas of SQL Server databases
SQL Data Compare	Provides comparison and synchronization scripts of data held on SQL Server databases
DTS Compare	Provides comparisons of server and DTS configurations for SQL Server
SQL Packager	Packages a SQL Server (data and schema) into either a C# project or an executable for deployment elsewhere
SQL Toolkit	Provides access to the API for extension and use of the SQL Compare, SQL Data Compare, and SQL Packager tools

---

■**Tip** You can download a trial 14-day version from the web site that should allow you to test the concepts and code in this chapter.

Using the Tools

Let us take a quick look at the use of the tools as they come out of the box, though the majority of the work we will do uses the APIs in order to work within NAnt.

There are two flavors of tools in the current version: the regular GUI tools and also a set of command-line tools, which are just as feature-rich and probably more accessible for rapid comparisons and synchronization.

We will concentrate on the SQL Compare tool, which is used to compare and synchronize database schemas. However, the SQL Data Compare and DTS Compare are very similar in terms of operation. The Packager application is a little different—its core responsibility is not comparison and synchronization, but instead it handles the packaging of a database into an executable program or C# project.

Firing up the GUI produces a "nag" screen if you are using an unlicensed copy of the software. After this, a screen asking for connection information will appear. This can be used directly as shown in Figure 8-7, or it can be canceled and a preexisting project can be loaded.

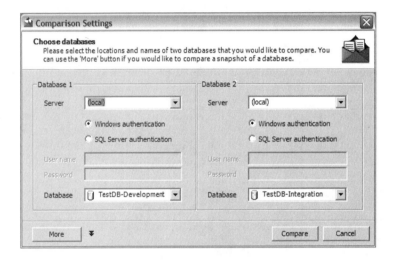

Figure 8-7. *The SQL Comparison Settings screen*

■Tip The help files that come with the product are more comprehensive than those found with many products, although the tool is relatively straightforward to use.

After we enter the information and click OK, SQL Compare does its magic and compares the two databases. We are dealing with very simple databases and so the information provided is minimal. In this instance, I have removed the PostCode column from the TestDB-Integration database; the effects of this can be seen in Figure 8-8.

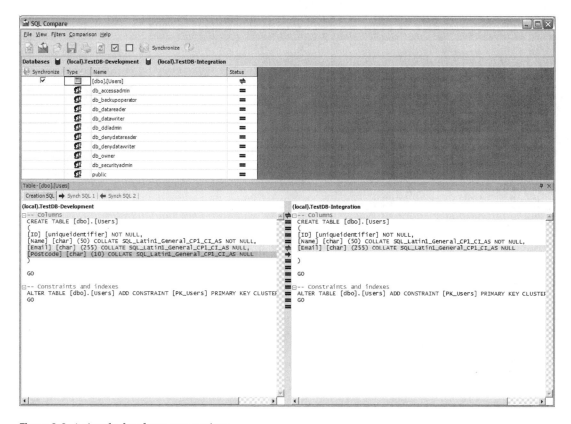

Figure 8-8. *A simple database comparison*

Figure 8-8 shows that SQL Compare detected the differences between the two databases and produced the CREATE scripts (with highlighted differences) for the two databases. Additionally, the synchronization, or ALTER, scripts can be viewed by clicking the relevant tabs.

Clicking the Synchronize button then walks the user through a series of screens and results in the execution of the relevant script to provide the database synchronization. Figure 8-9 shows the screen after TestDB-Integration has been updated to the latest development version.

So that is a simple example of the use of the SQL Compare tool. Its real power and utility comes in its continuous use to provide migration capabilities without developers having to think too hard about it, and in its use with more complex databases. Here, for instance, it is not possible to see how SQL Compare handles the addition and removal of constraints in the correct order to ensure error-free schema changes.

Tip If you make wholesale changes to database design—such as the change of a primary key data type—then you may well run into some problems. SQL Compare cannot do everything, but it can do quite a lot. (I would spend more time worrying about the decision to change the data type . . .) The point is that SQL Compare is more likely to be successful when used in small steps in a continuous way—in precisely the same way as unit testing and continuous integration is more successful with small steps.

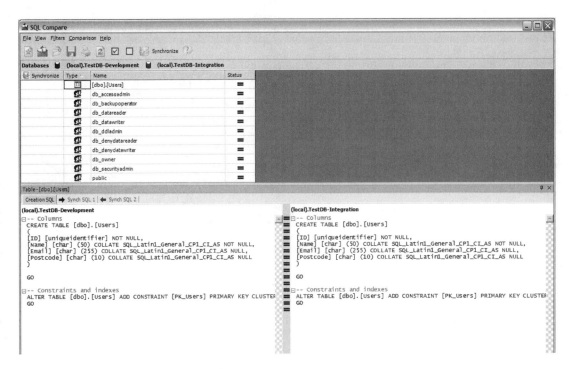

Figure 8-9. *SQL Compare following synchronization*

We can also use the command line to perform the same operations. The command-line tool comes with an enormous amount of switches and parameter possibilities and so is easiest to use when performing regular activities such as quick comparisons.

We can use the command shown in Figure 8-10 to perform a comparison between the two databases.

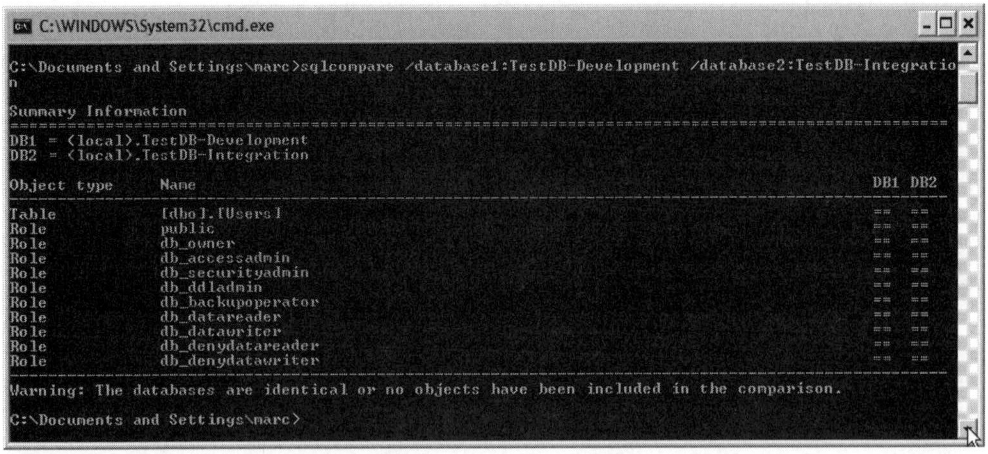

Figure 8-10. *SQL Compare command line*

As can be seen, the databases are fully synchronized, as we would expect from the efforts using the SQL Compare GUI.

Automating the Red Gate Bundle

The APIs for SQL Compare and the other tools in the bundle are well documented, and there are also useful code samples that demonstrate how to synchronize databases.

While the previous task is useful, effectively it is simply ordering and executing a series of SQL scripts. It is flexible and can be used as needed in whatever database scenario we have.

This time, since we are expecting SQL Compare to do all of the work in terms of script production as well as synchronization, we need to think a little about what the deliverables from the process should be. In terms of sensible assets to maintain for a build, we should probably maintain a full CREATE script for the database in the current build and then also maintain the migration necessary for a move from the prior build to the current one. With these two assets, we can then synchronize the integration environments or create a new integration environment as desired.

We should also consider that, as discussed previously, we may wish to synchronize multiple database instances, though we may only want to maintain synchronization assets for one of the instances; after all, the databases should be the same.

With these points in mind, the following task would be useful:

```
<dbAutoIntegrate
    folder="D:\BookCode\Chapter8\DBTest2\"
    server="localhost"
    database="TestDB-Development"
    uid="sa"
    pwd="w1bbl3"
    write="true"
    caption="0"
    >
    <databases>
        <database server="localhost" database="TestDB-Integration" ➥
                uid="sa" pwd="w1bbl3" write="true"/>
        <database server="localhost" database="TestDB-System" ➥
                uid="sa" pwd="w1bbl3" write="true"/>
    </databases>
</dbAutoIntegrate>
```

The task will have a few features. The attributes in the main element contain the standard four pieces of database information (server, database, username, and password) as well as three other pieces of information: folder is the folder in which the scripts should be stored when produced, write tells the task whether to produce a script for that particular step (in the case of the main element, whether to produce the CREATE script), and caption allows us to pass through information to assist in the naming of the produced scripts (we would ordinarily pass through the build number).

The task is a little more complicated by the inclusion of child elements describing multiple target databases for synchronization. In the previous example I have included the regular integration database and also a System Test database server. I have marked both to have the scripts produced, but in fact I would probably only maintain the migration scripts for the integration database. We will make a new type to represent these child elements in the main task. We will call this new type DBInfo. It will be a custom NAnt element that we will create to hold the information for each target database.

Implementing the DBInfo type is straightforward (in fact, thinking of a name for the type was harder since the SQL Compare APIs use Database):

```
[ElementName("database")]
public class DBInfo : Element
{
    private string _server;
    private string _database;
    private string _username;
    private string _password;

    private bool _write;

    [TaskAttribute("server", Required=true)]
    public string Server
    {
        get{return _server;}
        set{_server = value;}
    }

    [TaskAttribute("database", Required=true)]
    public string Database
    {
        get{return _database;}
        set{_database = value;}
    }

    [TaskAttribute("uid", Required=true)]
    public string Username
    {
        get{return _username;}
        set{_username = value;}
    }

    [TaskAttribute("pwd", Required=true)]
    public string Password
    {
        get{return _password;}
        set{_password = value;}
    }

    [TaskAttribute("write", Required=true), BooleanValidator()]
    public bool Write
    {
```

```
        get{return _write;}
        set{_write = value;}
    }
}
```

Therefore, the DBInfo type is just a property bag with no logic of its own. We will see how this is used in the task implementation that follows.

The task is going to behave as shown in Figure 8-11.

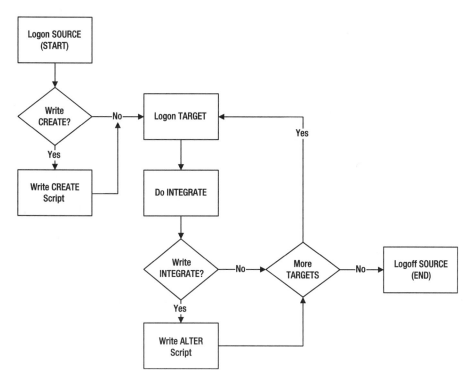

Figure 8-11. *<dbAutoIntegrate> task process*

As usual, the first part of the code for this task involves setting up the attributes and elements of the task, as follows:

```
private DirectoryInfo _folder;

//Database Info
private string _server;
private string _database;
private string _username;
private string _password;

private DBInfo[] _dbInfos;
```

```csharp
private bool _write;
private string _caption;

private Database _source;

[TaskAttribute("folder", Required=true)]
public DirectoryInfo Folder
{
    get{return _folder;}
    set{_folder = value;}
}

[TaskAttribute("server", Required=true)]
public string Server
{
    get{return _server;}
    set{_server = value;}
}

[TaskAttribute("database", Required=true)]
public string Database
{
    get{return _database;}
    set{_database = value;}
}

[TaskAttribute("uid", Required=true)]
public string Username
{
    get{return _username;}
    set{_username = value;}
}

[TaskAttribute("pwd", Required=true)]
public string Password
{
    get{return _password;}
    set{_password = value;}
}

[BuildElementCollection("databases", "database")]
public DBInfo[] DBInfos
{
    get{return _dbInfos;}
    set{_dbInfos = value;}
}
```

```
[TaskAttribute("write", Required=true), BooleanValidator()]
public bool Write
{
    get{return _write;}
    set{_write = value;}
}

[TaskAttribute("caption", Required=true)]
public string Caption
{
    get{return _caption;}
    set{_caption = value;}
}
```

There are two things to notice in this code. The first is the inclusion of a class-level Database type. The source database is used throughout the task and is declared here. The Database type is from the SQL Compare APIs. The second is the inclusion of an array of DBInfo types, as we described earlier. I could have used this for the source database, too, but seeing as there will never be more than one source database, I have not done so. Here I am using an array since it is all that is needed for the operations the task will perform, but this could equally have been a strongly typed collection.

■**Tip** Digging around in the NAnt source code will provide many examples of the use of nested elements, too.

To use the collection, a different attribute is required for the property: BuildElement➡ Collection. This attribute accepts the names of the element and child elements (notice that it does not have to be named the same as the type) and allows the task to be built as the sample script earlier showed.

The next step is to override the ExecuteTask method on the task itself as usual:

```
protected override void ExecuteTask()
{
    _source = new Database();
    _source.Register(new ConnectionProperties(this._server, ➡
                                               this._database, ➡
                                               this._username, ➡
                                               this._password), ➡
                                               Options.Default);

    if(this._write)DoCreateScript();
    DoAlterScripts();

    _source.Dispose();
}
```

This task instantiates and prepares the source database. It then hands off responsibility to other internal methods for the actual work before disposing of the database as per the standards described in the API documentation.

■**Note** As usual, my code does not contain supporting code such as error handling. For production code, I consider it to be imperative to trap and handle errors, particularly with items such as the database registration in the above code.

We can take a look at the DoCreateScript and DoAlterScripts methods next.

```
private void DoCreateScript()
{
    Log(Level.Info, "Handling CREATE Script");
    ExecutionBlock createScript = CalculateScript(null);
    WriteScript(String.Format("CREATE-{0}.sql", _caption), ➥
                              createScript.ToString());
    createScript.Dispose();
}

private void DoAlterScripts()
{
    foreach(DBInfo db in _dbInfos)
    {
    Log(Level.Info, String.Format("Handling migration for {0}", db.Database));

    Database target = new Database();
    target.Register(new ConnectionProperties(db.Server, db.Database, ➥
                                         db.Username, db.Password),➥
                                         Options.Default);

    ExecutionBlock alterScript = CalculateScript(target);
    ExecuteScript(alterScript, target);

    if(db.Write) WriteScript(String.Format("ALTER-{0}-{1}.sql", db.Database, ➥
                             _caption), alterScript.ToString());

        alterScript.Dispose();
        target.Dispose();
    }
}
```

DoCreateScript is quite simple, performing a logging action and then handing responsibility to another method for the actual script calculation, and then to another method for the writing of the script. You can see that the script will be named "CREATE-", followed by the required caption as specified in the NAnt script, for example, the project name and/or build number.

DoAlterScripts is a little more involved. It loops through the target databases, creating new Database types for each and then again calculating the scripts and writing them (with the name format ALTER-<database>-<caption>) if necessary. Additionally, once the script is calculated it is executed on the target database, providing the required synchronization.

Both of these methods use the common methods described next for script calculation, execution, and writing. Where DoAlterScripts passes a target database to the CalculateScript method, DoCreateScript passes a null to the method. This feature of the APIs forces a full migration script—effectively a CREATE script—to be produced and so is ideal for scripting the full database schema. Both scripts also dispose of the blocks generated, as per the API standards. If you look at the examples provided with the bundle, you will see that the code is similar in terms of the actual work being done.

The three remaining methods look like this:

```
private ExecutionBlock CalculateScript(Database target)
{
   Differences differences = _source.CompareWith(target, Options.Default);
   foreach (Difference difference in differences)
   {
      difference.Selected=true;
   }

   Work work=new Work();
   work.BuildFromDifferences(differences, Options.Default, true);
   return work.ExecutionBlock;
}

private void ExecuteScript(ExecutionBlock script, Database target)
{
   Utils utils = new Utils(); //This is a RedGate Utils Class
   utils.ExecuteBlock(script, ➥
                      target.ConnectionProperties.ServerName, ➥
                      target.ConnectionProperties.DatabaseName, ➥
                      target.ConnectionProperties.IntegratedSecurity, ➥
                      target.ConnectionProperties.UserName, ➥
                      target.ConnectionProperties.Password);
}

private void WriteScript(string caption, string content)
{
   Log(Level.Info, String.Format("Writing script {0}", caption));
   FileStream script = new FileStream(Path.Combine(this._folder.FullName, ➥
                                      caption), FileMode.Create);
   StreamWriter sw = new StreamWriter(script);
   sw.Write(content);
   sw.Close();
   script.Close();
}
```

Note Ah, the pleasure of third-party APIs. With my nitpicking hat on, I would say that it would be very useful if there were a few changes such as a method `differences.SelectAll` to save looping through the collection, and it would be nice if `ExecuteBlock` could accept a `Database` type instead of the individual connection information. Grumble, grumble.

I have not included much in the way of feedback in the task. It would probably be sensible to include some suitable debugging logging statements, such as writing out the SQL to the NAnt logger and so on.

With that, the job is done. In order to test the task we can create a simple scenario with multiple databases to run the automatic integration. Let us use the same trivial example as before—the useless Users table—and set up the databases as shown in Table 8-3.

Table 8-3. *Test Databases*

Database	Settings
TestDB-Development	The full Users table, with the PostCode column
TestDB-Integration	The Users table without the PostCode column
TestDB-System	The Users table without the PostCode column

We can verify that the databases are not equal by using SQL Compare.

We will use the NAnt task to generate the full script for TestDB-Development, and then to script and synchronize the two testing databases. This looks as follows:

```xml
<?xml version="1.0"?>
<project>
    <loadtasks assembly="Etomic.NAntExtensions.RedGateDBTasks.dll"/>
    <dbAutoIntegrate
        folder="D:\BookCode\Chapter8\DBTest2\"
        server="localhost"
        database="TestDB-Development"
        uid="sa"
        pwd="w1bbl3"
        write="true"
        caption="0"
        >
        <databases>
            <database server="localhost" database="TestDB-Integration"
                        uid="sa" pwd="w1bbl3" write="true"/>
            <database server="localhost" database="TestDB-System"
                        uid="sa" pwd="w1bbl3" write="true"/>
        </databases>
    </dbAutoIntegrate>
</project>
```

Because this is a debug script, I am passing 0 as the caption. Running the script produces the results shown here.

Note Bear in mind that if you are using the unlicensed version of SQL Compare, then a nag screen will be shown. This precludes the use of the task in an automated environment because of the interactive nagging.

```
---------- NAnt (RedGate) ----------
NAnt 0.85
Copyright (C) 2001-2005 Gerry Shaw
http://nant.sourceforge.net

Buildfile: file:/// AntExtensions.RedGateDBTasks.Debug.xml
Target framework: Microsoft .NET Framework 1.1

[loadtasks]
    Scanning assembly "Etomic.NAntExtensions.RedGateDBTasks" for extensions.
[dbAutoIntegrate] Handling CREATE Script
[dbAutoIntegrate] Writing script CREATE-0.sql
[dbAutoIntegrate] Handling migration for TestDB-Integration
[dbAutoIntegrate] Writing script ALTER-TestDB-Integration-0.sql
[dbAutoIntegrate] Handling migration for TestDB-System
[dbAutoIntegrate] Writing script ALTER-TestDB-System-0.sql

BUILD SUCCEEDED
Total time: 6.5 seconds.
Output completed (7 sec consumed) - Normal Termination
```

The output is as we would expect. If we look into the output folder, we will find the scripts shown in Figure 8-12.

Name ▲	Size	Type	Date Modified
ALTER-TestDB-Integration-0.sql	1 KB	SQL Script File	07/01/2005 11:21
ALTER-TestDB-System-0.sql	1 KB	SQL Script File	07/01/2005 11:21
CREATE-0.sql	2 KB	SQL Script File	07/01/2005 11:21

Figure 8-12. *Output from the <dbAutoIntegrate> task*

These scripts contain the output we would expect from running SQL Compare manually to perform the same actions. Performing a diff on the two synchronization scripts demonstrates that they are the same. Running the CREATE script in a new database and then performing a SQL Compare on the databases will demonstrate that they are the same too.

With that, our database schema synchronization woes are banished on a practical level. We can consider some process implications a little later.

Thinking about Data Synchronization

The tasks we have created were done so with database schema migration and synchronization in mind, although as stated, the manual task will handle any arbitrary SQL.

We do need to consider how to handle data synchronization. In the scenario earlier, the task synchronizes the schema for an integration database that may be used for unit-testing purposes, and a database used for system testing, which may contain a different set of data—for example, a representation of the production system data. Therefore, the data migration requirements could well be different for each database:

Integration database. The integration database may need to be fully refreshed with data for unit testing, or just some standing data such as ISO country codes. Good unit tests should create their own data and then destroy it, but we all know that unit tests come in all varieties.

System database. If the system database does contain a representation of the live data, then migration scripts are needed rather than refresh scripts. This is the ideal time to test those scripts for eventual use in the production environment.

So how to do this? The options are certainly the same—the processing of scripts that are manually generated or the use of SQL Data Compare (for instance) to automatically synchronize the data—but the decision may be different. Whereas synchronization is what we were trying to achieve with the database schemas, it is not our goal with data migration. Data migration also tends to be a more semantic affair than schema migration, and thus developer decision-making skills could be called for.

My feeling is that it is probably best to manually create scripts for data migration and manipulation, using the manual task to run these scripts as part of the delivery process. Tools such as SQL Data Compare could then be used to verify these scripts if desired. Martin Fowler's article on agile databases and Scott Ambler's book *Agile Database Techniques* (see "Further Reading") describe toolkits of scripts for data migration to speed up and standardize this work. This works by taking an approach to database manipulation similar to one a developer might take to code refactoring: creating specific mechanics for performing specific tasks under specific contexts. So, for example, in code refactoring we may choose to "Extract Method" and follow a mechanism to perform this refactoring; in database manipulation we may choose to "Introduce Trigger" following a mechanism to perform this work. The database examples are not quite so rounded as the original work on code refactoring, but there are a lot of ideas and examples in both of these sources. This is a useful practice for a development team. Additionally, in order to make the automation easy given the context of the task we have created, it is a good idea to organize the output of these activities. Table 8-4 shows how this might be done.

Table 8-4. *Organizing Database Scripts*

Name	Content
Schema	Contains the scripts produced by the automated SQL Compare task
Reference	Contains the scripts for the insertion and refresh of standing data such as lookup
Test	Contains scripts for the insertion and refresh of test data if required
Migrate	Contains scripts for the migration (updates, inserts, deletes) of existing production (or production representation) data

With the scripts organized in this way, the task we have created can be used to run the sets of scripts required given the particular database instance. Additionally, we can leverage reusability in the build scripts on a large scale.

A Process for Database Integration

Having worked out the practical details for the actual work to be done, let us consider how we can implement database integration into the CI process. First, we return to the Control and Configure versioning tasks we identified at the outset of this chapter.

Control and Configure Tasks

Neither task requires us to build new code for NAnt, but they do require some thought as to how the database assets should be controlled.

Control

As previously mentioned, the core decision for control is whether to use the source control database. If source control is used, then the files will need to be GETted from the source control database prior to any execution, and any generated files will need to be added to source control when they are produced. In itself, this is not such a problem, but the management of the files may be more awkward than simply adding the files to source control. The issue stems from the coupling of code changes and database changes in the CI process: when should the files be stored in source control? Consider the following scenarios and the possibilities they present:

If no separate database server is used for handling unit testing, the database integration work can wait until the code has been successfully compiled and tested. Only then are the migration scripts generated and used on the integration server. At the end of the cycle, these scripts are then a specific version and migration step on the database life cycle, and so the existing scripts should be removed and stored safely (both the automatic and the manual scripts) because they have already been applied.

If a separate database server is used for unit testing, then the integration (or at least some of it) needs to occur before testing of the code is complete. If a code-based error occurs, it may not be desirable to have the database integrated, but at that point it is too late. This is not necessarily a big deal here, but it might be in your own scenario.

If no separate database server is used for integration of any kind (perhaps migration scripts are generated during comparison to the production server but not actually executed), then the scripts need to be removed and stored since they are still a specific version at that point in the build. Although this sounds like a poor scenario, consider the next scenario.

If there is always integration to the integration server, then the migration scripts *must* be applied incrementally and sequentially to the production server when the system is finally deployed. If a system undergoes 20 build cycles before an actual release, all 20 database integrations must be applied since the changes are made only once to the static database server. In the previous scenario, the migration scripts are formed against the currently released platform and are not incremental. The advantage is that only one set of migration scripts is required. The disadvantage is that the increments become larger, and therefore carry more risk since they are not in the spirit of CI.

If you are going to implement database integration in a CI way, the final scenario is preferable in terms of the best process, although clearly there is some overhead to the actual deployment. With some cunning file manipulation, this could be made fairly seamless: if the deployment to the production server triggered the removal of the migration scripts rather than the build process, the correct scripts could be maintained together from release to release rather than build to build, though this will result in duplication of scripts in the code zip files (in the context of the current process). We could deal with this in a couple of ways, as we will see in a moment.

With that in mind, publishing of database assets can be handled in the same way as the web assets: through the use of zip files and an HTTP-accessible folder for GETting prior to deployment.

Configuration

With regard to configuration, if unit tests are to be carried out on one of the integrated databases, then the configuration file for the unit tests needs to be changed, or just made available prior to the tests being run. Fortunately, there is an attribute on the <nunit2> task that allows us to include an application configuration file. This can easily be parameterized to ensure that the correct configuration file is used by the automated build process:

```
<nunit2>
    <formatter type="Xml" usefile="true" extension=".xml"
            outputdir="${core.reports}\" />
    <test appconfig="myconfig.config">
        <assemblies basedir="${core.output}\">
            <include name="*Tests.dll"/>
        </assemblies>
    </test>
</nunit2>
```

Therefore, this is a relatively straightforward configuration issue, though it does add another parameter to the build file, which could be standardized to the form <solution.name>.➥ Tests.Config or something similar. In the next section, we address some additional configuration concerns.

Deployment Considerations

Both of the deployment issues we examine here may seem relatively minor at first glance, but they can cause a headache if not handled effectively. Let us consider three deployment scenarios; they may be applicable in any combination:

Automatic deploy following build. When the build is complete, we could deploy the latest version automatically. Perhaps the latest version would point at the integration database instance. In this scenario, the integration version is "just for show" and serves no purpose in the delivery pipeline (e.g., quality assurance, or QA). On the other hand, the system test database might be used for deployment, so that part of the QA pipeline is automated too. The problem here is that the build action under the CI process can occur at any time, which might not be ideal if system testing is already taking place.

Deploy new instance. If the deployment process is separate from the CI process, this is the first of two possibilities. In this scenario, we deploy a clean build of a specific version of the system. This is the simpler of the two scenarios.

Integrate existing instance. In this deployment scenario, we deploy against an existing version of the system. This is no problem in terms of code—we simply replace all code assets—though in fact we may have to consider the management of noncode assets (e.g., uploads from users) during deployment. For the database, that means applying the incremental migration scripts.

We will build scripts allowing both the deployment of a new system/database instance, and the integration of an existing instance.

Using the Correct Database Instance

Once the site is deployed, we need to ensure that the application points to the correct database instance. This configuration issue is actually a subset of the overall configuration issues for deployment. It can be easily handled when we do not have many configuration settings to change, but the process can become unwieldy when many changes are involved. Possible strategies include the following:

`<xmlpoke>`. Because configuration files are XML-based, the `<xmlpoke>` task can be used to change values, add keys, and so on. On a small scale, this is a very useful task, but making several changes to files can become unwieldy and a maintenance headache.

Configuration file linking. General configuration settings for a system can be held in companion config files and referred to from the main config file. For example, `web.config` might refer to settings held in `dev.config`, `test.config`, and so on. Using a single `<xmlpoke>` and a few cleanup tasks could handle a bulk configuration change. The benefit of this scenario is that the data for change is held outside the actual process.

Configuration service. Similarly, using the Microsoft Configuration Management Block (or some other configuration service, perhaps Nini, which you can find at `http://nini.`➥ `sourceforge.net/`) typically means that the configuration change can be handled in the same minimal way. The benefit is the same, and in addition all configuration data across all applications is maintained in one location.

We will use the simplest scenario, the `<xmlpoke>` task, to handle the configuration changes we need. In fact, with the use of the other two scenarios, the impact to the delivery scripts is minimal: there will still need to be some kind of `<xmlpoke>` to point the configuration file to the appropriate companion or service.

Asset Management

As mentioned earlier, the deployment scenario could entail multiple migrations to move the database version on by several builds. The deployment script should take account of this. This issue could be handled simply by passing the current and desired build numbers of the database and then looping through the database deployment routines. Or it may be worthwhile to build a custom task to handle these issues separately. We will see an implementation of this in our deployment scripts.

Implementing Database Integration

Once again, the wizards at Etomic have produced another work of software art. This time they have extended the web-based Transformer application so that it can use a database to store the XML and XSLT snippets. These can then be viewed and used by other users of the application.

Note In fact, this would be a natural extension of the previous application from Chapters 4, 5, and 6 but for clarity, and purposes of the previous examples, I have created a new application called Etomic.Share➥ Transformer. The code is in the "usual" place in the VSS database. Additionally, it does not rely on the separate engine assembly for the same reason, though I imagine it would if this was a real application.

Figure 8-13 shows the new screen for the application that has generated all the excitement at Etomic.

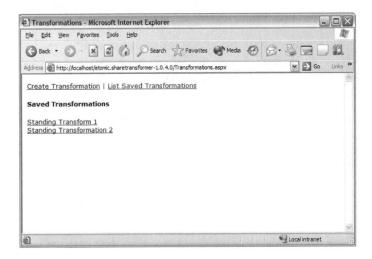

Figure 8-13. *Etomic.ShareTransformer application*

To implement an automated build, and then continuous integration, for this application we will follow the standard steps from the previous Design to Deliver work. Once this is satisfactory, we will add in the database integration tasks, at which point we will finally decide which process to use and then add the CI scripts for CCNet. Finally, we will need to carry out some fairly significant work on our simple deployment scripts to handle the various deployment scenarios satisfactorily.

The Build Script

In this version of our build scripts, I have amended the `Build.Core.Xml` file to load all noncore assemblies separately, which we discussed earlier as a possible best practice. It looks like this:

```
<loadtasks
    assembly="D:\dotNetDelivery\Tools\NAntContrib\0.85rc2\bin\➥
            NAnt.Contrib.Tasks.dll"/>
<loadtasks
    assembly="D:\dotNetDelivery\Tools\NUnit2Report\1.2.2\bin\➥
            NAnt.NUnit2ReportTasks.dll"/>
<loadtasks
    assembly="D:\dotNetDelivery\Tools\Etomic.NAntExtensions\ ➥
            Etomic.NAntExtensions.GeneralTasks.dll"/>
```

I have loaded the Red Gate task assembly from the debug directory, but of course this should form part of the Etomic.NAntExtensions project we have already constructed.

The build script for the application (without considering database issues) is quite simple:

```
<?xml version="1.0" encoding="utf-8" ?>
<project name="Etomic.ShareTransformer" default="help">
    <description>
        Build file for the Etomic.ShareTransformer application.
    </description>

    <property name="project.name.1" value="${solution.name}.UI" />
    <property name="project.name.2" value="${solution.name}.Engine" />
    <property name="solution.isweb" value="true"/>

    <target name="go" depends="build, test, document, publish, notify"/>

    <target name="build" description="Compile the application.">
        <solution solutionfile="${core.source}\${solution.name}.sln"
            configuration="Debug" outputdir="${core.output}\"/>
    </target>

    <target name="test" description="Apply the unit tests.">
        <property name="nant.onfailure" value="fail.test"/>
        <nunit2>
            <formatter type="Xml" usefile="true" extension=".xml"
                    outputdir="${core.reports}\" />
            <test>
                <assemblies basedir="${core.output}\">
                    <include name="*Tests.dll"/>
```

```xml
            </assemblies>
        </test>
    </nunit2>

    <nunit2report out="${core.reports}\NUnit.html">
        <fileset>
            <include name="${core.reports}\*.Tests.dll-results.xml" />
        </fileset>
    </nunit2report>

    <nant buildfile="Build.Common.xml" target="report.fxcop"
        inheritall="true"/>

    <style
        style="D:\Tools\FxCop\1.30\Xml\FxCopReport.xsl"
        in="${core.reports}\fxcop.xml" out="${core.reports}\fxcop.html"/>

    <property name="nant.onfailure" value="fail"/>
</target>

<target name="document" description="Generate documentation and reports.">
    <ndoc>
        <assemblies basedir="${core.output}\">
            <include name="${project.name.1}.dll" />
            <include name="${project.name.2}.dll" />
        </assemblies>
        <summaries basedir="${core.output}\">
            <include name="${project.name.1}.xml" />
            <include name="${project.name.2}.xml" />
        </summaries>
        <documenters>
            <documenter name="MSDN">
              <property name="OutputDirectory" value="${core.docs}\" />
              <property name="HtmlHelpName" value="${solution.name}" />
              <property name="HtmlHelpCompilerFilename" value="hhc.exe" />
              <property name="IncludeFavorites" value="False" />
              <property name="Title" value="${solution.name} (NDoc)" />
              <property name="SplitTOCs" value="False" />
              <property name="DefaulTOC" value="" />
              <property name="ShowVisualBasic" value="False" />
              <property name="ShowMissingSummaries" value="True" />
              <property name="ShowMissingRemarks" value="False" />
              <property name="ShowMissingParams" value="True" />
              <property name="ShowMissingReturns" value="True" />
              <property name="ShowMissingValues" value="True" />
```

```xml
                    <property name="DocumentInternals" value="True" />
                    <property name="DocumentProtected" value="True" />
                    <property name="DocumentPrivates" value="False" />
                    <property name="DocumentEmptyNamespaces" value="False" />
                    <property name="IncludeAssemblyVersion" value="True" />
                    <property name="CopyrightText"
                                value="${company.name} Ltd., 2005" />
                    <property name="CopyrightHref" value="" />
                </documenter>
            </documenters>
        </ndoc>
    </target>

    <target name="publish"
      description="Place the compiled assets, reports etc. in agreed location.">
        <nant buildfile="Build.Common.xml" target="publish" inheritall="true"/>
    </target>

    <target name="notify"
       description="Tell everyone of the success or failure.">
        <echo message="Notifying you of the build process success."/>
    </target>

    <target name="fail">
        <echo message="Notifying you of a failure in the build process."/>
    </target>

    <target name="fail.test">
        <nunit2report out="${core.reports}\NUnit.html">
            <fileset>
                <include name="${core.reports}\Etomic.*.Tests.dll-results.xml" />
            </fileset>
        </nunit2report>
    </target>

    <target name="help">
        <echo message="This file should not be executed. Use Build.Core.xml"/>
    </target>

</project>
```

There is nothing that we have not seen before in this script. One of the more interesting areas is the test target. If you look at the source code, the developer has included a config file that is used by NUnit when the unit-testing task is called. This can be seen in the source code shown in Figure 8-14 and then in the output directory shown in Figure 8-15.

Figure 8-14. *App.config in Etomic.ShareTransformer.Tests assembly*

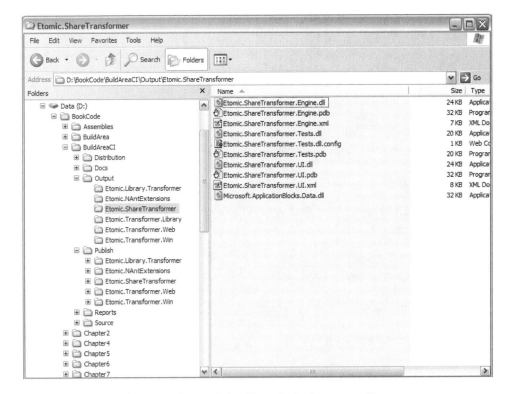

Figure 8-15. *Etomic.ShareTransformer.Tests.dll.config in the output directory*

The developer of this application does not require a specific data load in the database for the unit tests since they generate the required data for testing in the unit tests themselves and then remove it. This can be seen in the following code from TransformationTests.cs:

```
[TearDown]
public void TearDown()
{
    DeleteAllTransformations();
}
```

```
[Test]
public void TestGetAll()
{
    DeleteAllTransformations();

    Transformation t = new Transformation();
    t.Output = "aaa";
    t.Title  = "aaa";
    t.Xml    = "aaa";
    t.Xslt   = "aaa";
    t.Save();
    t.Save();
    t.Save();

    ApplicationEngine engine = new ApplicationEngine();
    IList transforms = engine.GetAllTransformations();

    Assert.IsTrue(transforms.Count == 3);
}

private void DeleteAllTransformations()
{
    using(SqlCommand cmd = new SqlCommand("delete transformations", ➥
                                    new SqlConnection(_dbConn)))
    {
        cmd.Connection.Open();
        cmd.ExecuteNonQuery();
        cmd.Connection.Close();
    }
}
```

Given this, we can choose to leave the unit tests to run against the development database and then integrate the database following successful unit testing. Or we can integrate the database prior to the unit testing and then run the unit tests against the integration database instance. Alternatively, we can run the tests against the development database instance, then perform the database integration and run the unit tests against the integration database instance as a "gold-plated" solution. In fact, this is what we will do in our own integration.

To implement the database integration step, we need to add a new target called database and then add this to the dependencies in the build file as follows:

```
<target name="go" description="The main target"
        depends="build, test, database, document, publish, notify"/>

<target name="database" description="Handle database integration">
</target>
```

That was the easy part. We can now fill it up with the required steps for integration. To recap, we will do the following:

Compile and run unit tests across the code of the application to ensure a certain level of build success.

Produce a CREATE script for the current development database.

Run an integration cycle on the integration database instance and write these migration files, too.

Point the configuration file for the unit tests to the integration database instance and then run the unit tests again.

Publish the database assets in the same way as the code assets and then remove the "one-off" artifacts, such as the schema script.

We can accomplish this with the following set of scripts in the database target. First up is the integration step for the CREATE and migration scripts:

```
<dbAutoIntegrate
    folder="D:\BookCode\Chapter8\${solution.name}.dbscripts\schema"
    server="localhost"
    database="${solution.name}-dev"
    uid="sa"
    pwd="w1bbl3"
    write="true"
    caption="${sys.version}"
    >
    <databases>
      <database server="localhost" database="etomic.sharetransformer-integrate"
              uid="sa" pwd="w1bbl3" write="true"/>
    </databases>
</dbAutoIntegrate>
```

The integration scripts are written to a specific working area with folders arranged as described earlier.

We then flag the CREATE script to be written, and specify the database instance for migration.

■**Note** The migration instance must exist to begin with, though it does not need to contain any information.

Once this work is done, we can point the unit test configuration to the integration test instance as follows:

```
<attrib file="${core.output}\${solution.name}.Tests.dll.config" readonly="false" />
<xmlpoke
    file="${core.output}\${solution.name}.Tests.dll.config"
    xpath="/configuration/appSettings/add[@key = 'DbConnectionString']/@value"
    value="server=localhost;database=etomic.sharetransformer-integrate; ➥
                        uid=transformer;pwd=transform3r" />
<attrib file="${core.output}\${solution.name}.Tests.dll.config" readonly="true" />
```

This code is similar to the versioning code in terms of ensuring the relevant file can be written to. The `<xmlpoke>` task accepts an XPath query to change the configuration file.

▪ Note I have included the data for the poke directly in the build file (along with other information). This should of course be factored out at the earliest opportunity. If all of your database integration scenarios are the same, then this task can be moved into the `Build.Common.xml` file since it can be completely parameterized.

Finally, we can re-call the `test` target and rerun the unit tests (and the analysis that is a part of the `test` target) before publishing the assets to the publish folder, thereby making them accessible for deployment.

▪ Note The original test files will be overwritten by the new test call. Whether this matters is up to you. This can easily be handled through the parameterization of the test filenames and a few changes to the `test` target.

```
<call target="test"/>

<zip zipfile="${core.publish}\${solution.name}-DB-${sys.version}.zip">
    <fileset basedir="D:\BookCode\Chapter8\${solution.name}.dbscripts\">
        <include name="**"/>
    </fileset>
</zip>

<delete includeemptydirs="false">
    <fileset basedir="D:\BookCode\Chapter8\${solution.name}.dbscripts\schema\">
        <include name="*" />
    </fileset>
</delete>
```

The delete step in this example only includes the generated files in the schema folder since I am not using any others. In fact, you would probably want to include the removal of scripts in the migrate folder too, because it is likely that these scripts refer to a specific database migration. The scripts in test and reference are more likely to be generally applicable, or constantly maintained across versions. For this build, so that we can test it in deployment, I have included a script in reference called transformations.xml. This file consists of three entries to be inserted into a new database instance and will be included in the published package.

That is that. Running the build script produces the following significant output for the database target:

```
database:

[dbAutoIntegrate] Handling CREATE Script
[dbAutoIntegrate] Writing script CREATE-0.0.0.0.sql
[dbAutoIntegrate] Handling migration for etomic.sharetransformer-integrate
[dbAutoIntegrate]
    Writing script ALTER-etomic.sharetransformer-integrate-0.0.0.0.sql

[attrib] Setting file attributes for 1 files to Normal.
[xmlpoke] Found '1' nodes matching XPath expression
    '/configuration/appSettings/add[@key = 'DbConnectionString']/@value'.
[attrib] Setting file attributes for 1 files to ReadOnly.

test:
    <testing output snipped>

[zip] Zipping 3 files to
    'D:\BookCode\BuildAreaCI\Publish\Etomic.ShareTransformer\ ➥
    Etomic.ShareTransformer-DB-0.0.0.0.zip'.
[delete] Deleting 2 files
```

You can use the SQL Bundle tools to confirm that the development and integration instances are identical if you like.

With the background work completed and the build scenario determined, the actual implementation in the build task was not so onerous. Of course, your own scenario may be different.

The next step is to deploy the assets generated. To test out the agreed steps, we should place the system under CI and run a few iterations so that we have some assets to work with. The ccnet.config file for this is included with the source code, and contains nothing of any consequence to the database integration—it is the same ccnet.config script we always use.

If you like, you could make some changes to the database before each iteration, just for fun. Running a few iterations will result in the some assets being available in the publish location for Etomic.ShareTransformer, as shown in Figure 8-16.

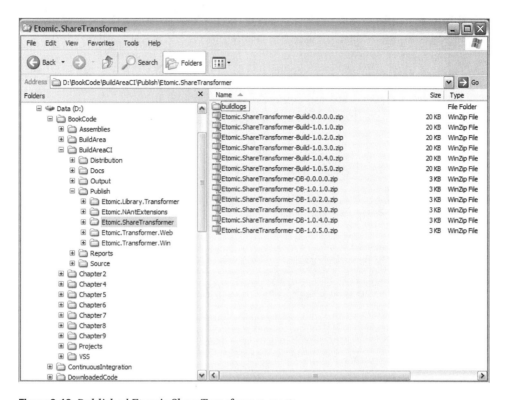

Figure 8-16. *Published Etomic.ShareTransformer assets*

At this point, we can move on to construct the database deploy scripts.

The Deploy Script with Database Deployment

We will construct a deployment script for a fresh database deployment and also a script to handle incremental deployment. First, let us quickly review the standard web deployment script we have previously used:

```xml
<?xml version="1.0" encoding="utf-8" ?>
<project name="Etomic.ShareTransformer" default="help">
    <description>
        Deploy file for the Etomic.Transformer.Web application
    </description>

    <property name="nant.onfailure" value="fail"/>
    <property name="company.name" value="Etomic"/>
    <property name="solution.name" value="${company.name}.ShareTransformer"/>
    <property name="core.publish"
```

```
                    value="http://localhost/ccnet/files/${solution.name}"/>
    <property name="core.deploy" value="D:\dotNetDelivery\TempDeploy"/>
    <property name="core.environment"
              value="D:\dotNetDeliveryWebs\${solution.name}"/>


    <loadtasks
        assembly="D:\dotNetDelivery\Tools\NAntContrib\0.85rc2\➥
                                        bin\NAnt.Contrib.Tasks.dll"
    />

    <target name="go"
      depends="selectversion, get, createenvironments, position, database, ➥
                 configure, notify"/>

    <target name="selectversion"
            description="Selects the version of the system.">
        <if test="${debug}">
            <property name="sys.version" value="0.0.0.0"/>
        </if>
    </target>

    <target name="get" description="Grab the correct assets.">
      <delete dir="${core.deploy}\" failonerror="false"/>
      <mkdir dir="${core.deploy}\${sys.version}\"/>
        <get
          src="${core.publish}/${solution.name}-Build-${sys.version}.zip"
          dest="${core.deploy}\${solution.name}-Build-${sys.version}.zip"
          />
        <unzip
          zipfile="${core.deploy}\${solution.name}-Build-${sys.version}.zip"
          todir="${core.deploy}\${sys.version}\"/>
    </target>

    <target name="createenvironments"
            description="Create the environments required">
      <mkdir dir="${core.environment}\${sys.version}\" failonerror="false"/>
      <mkiisdir dirpath="${core.environment}\${sys.version}\"
                vdirname="${solution.name}-${sys.version}"/>
    </target>

    <target name="position" description="Place required assets">
        <copy todir="${core.environment}\${sys.version}\">
            <fileset basedir="${core.deploy}\${sys.version}">
                <include name="**"/>
            </fileset>
        </copy>
    </target>
```

```
<target name="database" description="Deploy the database changes">
</target>

<target name="configure"
        description="Amend configuration settings as necessary">
</target>

<target name="notify"
        description="Tell everyone of the success or failure.">
    <echo message="Notifying you of the deploy process success."/>
</target>

<target name="fail">
    <echo message="Notifying you of a failure in the deploy process."/>
</target>

</project>
```

I have amended the dependencies to include the database target—the configure target has always been there. Both of these targets are empty currently. This deploy script will operate as expected and deploy the web assets as we have previously seen. This is not a lot of help, though, since they will be pointing to the incorrect database: the development instance. The details of the database step can be implemented as follows:

```
<target name="database" description="Deploy the database changes">
    <get
        src="${core.publish}/${solution.name}-DB-${sys.version}.zip"
        dest="${core.deploy}\${solution.name}-DB-${sys.version}.zip"
        />

    <unzip zipfile="${core.deploy}\${solution.name}-DB-${sys.version}.zip"
        todir="${core.deploy}\DB-${sys.version}\"/>

    <delete>
        <fileset basedir="${core.deploy}\DB-${sys.version}\schema">
            <include name="ALTER*" />
        </fileset>
    </delete>

    <dbIntegrate
        folder="${core.deploy}\DB-${sys.version}\schema"
        compare="CreationTime"
        server="localhost"
        database="${solution.name}-Test"
        uid="sa"
        pwd="w1bbl3"
        />
```

```
    <dbIntegrate
            folder="${core.deploy}\DB-${sys.version}\reference"
            compare="CreationTime"
            server="localhost"
            database="${solution.name}-Test"
            uid="sa"
            pwd="w1bbl3"
        />
</target>
```

The use of the `<dbIntegrate>` task requires the inclusion of the `ManualDBTasks` assembly and so the following `<loadtasks>` is required (again, referencing the debug assembly):

```
<loadtasks
    assembly="D:\dotNetDelivery\Tools\Etomic.NAntExtensions\ ➡
                Etomic.NAntExtensions.GeneralTasks.dll"/>
```

The `database` target gets and unzips the assets in the same way as the regular code deployment target. After this, it removes the ALTER script from the `schema` folder as we are interested only in the CREATE script, before executing the CREATE script using the `<dbIntegrate>` custom task, and then executing the input of the reference data with another task.

■Note This works entirely satisfactorily, though the manual database task is now looking a little long in the tooth. I should add to my notebook that this task could be refactored to include multiple script types to be executed and perhaps revisit the `fileset` issue to save on duplication of information and effort. But that is for another time.

The configuration step is identical to the build script, and therefore suffers from the same data/process mix issue:

```
<target name="configure" description="Amend configuration settings as necessary">
    <attrib file="${core.environment}\${sys.version}\web.config"
            readonly="false" />
    <xmlpoke
        file="${core.environment}\${sys.version}\web.config"
        xpath="/configuration/appSettings/add[@key = ➡
                                    'DbConnectionString']/@value"
        value="server=localhost;database=etomic.sharetransformer-test; ➡
                            uid=transformer;pwd=transform3r" />
    <attrib file="${core.environment}\${sys.version}\web.config"
            readonly="true" />
</target>
```

Once again, that is that. Running this deployment script in the usual way will result in a fresh deployment of the chosen application version. Here is the output from the execution of the script against version 1.0.4.0 of the application:

```
---------- NAnt ----------
NAnt 0.85
Copyright (C) 2001-2004 Gerry Shaw
http://nant.sourceforge.net

Buildfile: file:///Etomic.ShareTransformer.Deploy-CREATE.xml
Target(s) specified: go

[loadtasks] Scanning assembly "NAnt.Contrib.Tasks" for extensions.
[loadtasks] Scanning assembly "Etomic.NAntExtensions.ManualDBTasks" for extensions.

selectversion:

get:

    [delete] Deleting directory 'D:\TempDeploy\'.
     [mkdir] Creating directory 'D:\TempDeploy\1.0.4.0\'.
       [get] Retrieving
'http://localhost/ccnet/files/Etomic.ShareTransformer/Etomic.ShareTransformer-
Build-1.0.4.0.zip' to 'D:\TempDeploy\Etomic.ShareTransformer-Build-1.0.4.0.zip'.
     [unzip] Unzipping 'D:\TempDeploy\Etomic.ShareTransformer-Build-1.0.4.0.zip'
to 'D:\TempDeploy\1.0.4.0\' (19571 bytes).

createenvironments:

 [mkiisdir]
Creating/modifying virtual directory 'Etomic.ShareTransformer-1.0.4.0' on
'localhost:80'.

position:

      [copy] Copying 2 files to 'D:\Webs\Etomic.ShareTransformer\1.0.4.0\'.

database:

       [get] Retrieving
'http://localhost/ccnet/files/Etomic.ShareTransformer/Etomic.ShareTransformer-DB-
1.0.4.0.zip' to 'D:\TempDeploy\Etomic.ShareTransformer-DB-1.0.4.0.zip'.
     [unzip] Unzipping 'D:\TempDeploy\Etomic.ShareTransformer-DB-1.0.4.0.zip' to
'D:\TempDeploy\DB-1.0.4.0\' (2229 bytes).
    [delete] Deleting 1 files.

[dbIntegrate] CREATE-1.0.4.0.sql
      [exec] 1> 2> 1> 2> 1> 2> 1> 2> 1> 2> 1> 2> 1> 2> 3> 1> 2> Msg 15023, Level
16, State 1, Server ALIENVM, Procedure sp_grantdbaccess, Line 126
      [exec] User or role 'Transformer' already exists in the current database.
      [exec] 1> 2> Creating role db_owner
```

```
    [exec] 1> 2> 'Transformer' added to role 'db_owner'.
    [exec] 1> 2> 1> 2> Creating [dbo].[Transformations]
    [exec] 1> 2> 3> 4> 5> 6> 7> 8> 9> 10> Msg 2714, Level 16, State 6, Server
ALIENVM, Line 1
    [exec] There is already an object named 'Transformations' in the database.
    [exec] Warning: The table 'Transformations' has been created but its maximum
row size
    [exec] (24533) exceeds the maximum number of bytes per row (8060). INSERT or
UPDATE
    [exec] of a row in this table will fail if the resulting row length exceeds
8060
    [exec] bytes.
    [exec] 1> 2> 1> 2> (1 row affected)
    [exec] 1> 2> Creating primary key [PK_Transformations] on
[dbo].[Transformations]
    [exec] 1> 2> Msg 1779, Level 16, State 1, Server ALIENVM, Line 1
    [exec] Table 'Transformations' already has a primary key defined on it.
    [exec] Msg 1750, Level 16, State 1, Server ALIENVM, Line 1
    [exec] Could not create constraint. See previous errors.
    [exec] Warning: The table 'Transformations' has been created but its maximum
row size
    [exec] (24533) exceeds the maximum number of bytes per row (8060). INSERT or
UPDATE
    [exec] of a row in this table will fail if the resulting row length exceeds
8060
    [exec] bytes.
    [exec] 1> 2> 1> 2> (1 row affected)
    [exec] 1> 2> 1> 2> 3> 4> 5> 6> The database update failed
    [exec] 1> 2> 1>

[dbIntegrate] Transformations.sql
    [exec] 1> 2> 1> 2> 1> 2> 3> 4> 5> 6> 7> 8> 9> 10> 11> 12> 13> 14> 15> 16>
17> 18> Msg 2627, Level 14, State 1, Server ALIENVM, Line 1
    [exec] Violation of PRIMARY KEY constraint 'PK_Transformations'. Cannot
insert
    [exec] duplicate key in object 'Transformations'.

configure:

    [attrib] Setting file attributes for 1 files to Normal.
   [xmlpoke] Found '1' nodes matching XPath expression
'/configuration/appSettings/add[@key = 'DbConnectionString']/@value'.
    [attrib] Setting file attributes for 1 files to ReadOnly.
```

```
notify:

    [echo] Notifying you of the deploy process success.

go:

BUILD SUCCEEDED
Total time: 3.7 seconds.
Output completed (5 sec consumed) - Normal Termination
```

The output clearly shows the execution of the relevant database scripts (and some warnings), and indeed the application has been correctly deployed and configured, as can be seen in Figure 8-17.

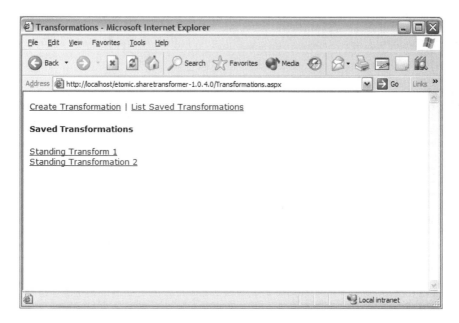

Figure 8-17. *Etomic.ShareTransformer v1.0.4.0*

Checking the web.config and other files will also demonstrate that all is well.

So that is fine for a clean build, but what about a migrated build? This is slightly more involved than the clean build for the reasons discussed before. To recap, because the database has its migration scripts produced during each code build but not every code build is deployed, when the deployment finally occurs, the application of the migration scripts from the previously deployed version must be applied sequentially to move the database to the current version.

In practice this means that we need to provide some looping functionality for the database step in a way that assesses the database versions.

To actually implement this, we leave the previous deployment script generally unaltered, but we move the content of the database target into a new target called databaseincrement. This target is not part of the master dependencies, but will be called as needed by the database target. The databaseincrement target looks like this:

```
<target name="databaseincrement">
    <get
        src="${core.publish}/${solution.name}-DB-${db.version}.zip"
        dest="${core.deploy}\${solution.name}-DB-${db.version}.zip"
     />
    <unzip zipfile="${core.deploy}\${solution.name}-DB-${db.version}.zip"
        todir="${core.deploy}\DB-${db.version}\"/>

    <delete>
        <fileset basedir="${core.deploy}\DB-${db.version}\schema">
                <include name="CREATE*" />
        </fileset>
    </delete>

    <dbIntegrate
        folder="${core.deploy}\DB-${db.version}\schema"
        compare="CreationTime"
        server="localhost"
        database="${solution.name}-Test"
        uid="sa"
        pwd="w1bbl3"
    />
</target>
```

Note that we are now deleting the CREATE script since we are interested in the ALTER scripts. Additionally, we have removed the step that adds the reference data so that we concentrate on the schema.

■**Note** In a real-life scenario, you would likely want to apply each set of migration scripts, too, and then load in the final set of reference data. This final step could be handled in the regular database target.

The database step therefore contains the looping function:

```
<target name="database" description="Deploy the database changes">
    <foreach item="String"
            in="${etomic::get-db-version-list(old.db.version , sys.version)}"
            delim=" ,"
            property="db.version">
        <call target="databaseincrement"/>
    </foreach>
</target>
```

Complexity alert! I have stayed away from introducing scripted functions into the delivery scripts where possible to avoid a move into even more "options" (read: confusion). In this instance, though, I need an adequate way of providing a list to loop through, from the old database version to the desired deployment version. This means that the execution of this script relies on a new command-line input: the old.db.version property.

The list I am looking for is something like the following:

1.0.2.0, 1.0.3.0, 1.0.4.0

This assumes I am migrating from version 1.0.2.0 to 1.0.4.0. To provide this list, the following script function will do the trick:

```
<script language="C#" prefix="etomic" >
  <code><![CDATA[
  [Function("get-db-version-list")]
  public static string GetDBVersionList(string firstVersion, string lastVersion)
  {
    int start, end, major, minor;
    Match match;

    Regex versionRegEx = ➥
        new Regex (@"(?<major>\d*)\.(?<minor>\d*)\.(?<build>\d*)\.\d*", ➥
                  RegexOptions.Compiled);

    match = versionRegEx.Match(firstVersion);
    major = Int32.Parse(match.Groups["major"].Value);
    minor = Int32.Parse(match.Groups["minor"].Value);
    start = Int32.Parse(match.Groups["build"].Value);

    match = versionRegEx.Match(lastVersion);
    end = Int32.Parse(match.Groups["build"].Value);

    StringBuilder dbList = new StringBuilder();
    for(int i=start+1; i<end+1; i++)
    {
       dbList.Append(String.Format("{0}.{1}.{2}.0,", major.ToString(), ➥
                                      minor.ToString(), i.ToString()));
    }

    if (dbList.ToString().Length > 0)
       return dbList.ToString().Substring(0, dbList.ToString().Length-1);
    else
       return "";
    }
  ]]></code>
</script>
```

The code is another straightforward piece of C#, using a regular expression to pull apart the version number, create a list, and then put the version numbers back together again. Once again, thanks to the flexibility of NAnt, we can tackle a problem quickly and effectively.

■Note Sadly, we cannot tackle my own oversight so effectively. Because I have wrapped the version number logic in the process, I am stuck with working with the full version number here without some significant refactoring of the scripts. (Actually, it is not that big a deal, but I like to moan at myself now and then to keep myself in check.) The bigger problem here is that the previous function does not handle a move, for example, from 1.0.0.0 to 1.1.0.0, since we are dealing with only the third digit. Oh well—another entry in the notebook.

With the addition of the function, this deploy script is complete. It can be run on an existing database version with the following command line (assuming you are moving from version 1.0.2.0 to 1.0.4.0):

```
nant -f:Etomic.ShareTransformer.Deploy.ALTER.xml go -D:sys.version=1.0.4.0 ➥
    -D:old.db.version=1.0.2.0 -D:debug=false
```

The most relevant output here is as follows:

```
database:

databaseincrement:

    [get] Retrieving
'http://localhost/ccnet/files/Etomic.ShareTransformer/Etomic.ShareTransformer-DB-
1.0.3.0.zip' to 'D:\TempDeploy\Etomic.ShareTransformer-DB-1.0.3.0.zip'.
    [unzip] Unzipping 'D:\TempDeploy\Etomic.ShareTransformer-DB-1.0.3.0.zip' to
'D:\TempDeploy\DB-1.0.3.0\' (2228 bytes).
    [delete] Deleting 1 files.
[dbIntegrate] ALTER-etomic.sharetransformer-integrate-1.0.3.0.sql
    [exec] 1> 2> 3> 4> 5> 6> 7> 1> 2> 1> 2> 1> 2> 1> 2> 1> 2> 1> 2> 1> 2> 1> 2>
3> 4> 5> 6> The database update succeeded
    [exec] 1> 2> 1>

databaseincrement:

[get] Retrieving
    'http://localhost/ccnet/files/Etomic.ShareTransformer/
    <remainder>
    <etc>
1.0.4.0.zip' to 'D:\TempDeploy\Etomic.ShareTransformer-DB-1.0.4.0.zip'.
    [unzip] Unzipping 'D:\TempDeploy\Etomic.ShareTransformer-DB-1.0.4.0.zip' to
'D:\TempDeploy\DB-1.0.4.0\' (2229 bytes).
```

```
    [delete] Deleting 1 files.
[dbIntegrate] ALTER-etomic.sharetransformer-integrate-1.0.4.0.sql
     [exec] 1> 2> 3> 4> 5> 6> 7> 1> 2> 1> 2> 1> 2> 1> 2> 1> 2> 1> 2> 1> 2>
3> 4> 5> 6> The database update succeeded
     [exec] 1> 2> 1>

configure:

    [attrib] Setting file attributes for 1 files to Normal.
    [xmlpoke] Found '1' nodes matching XPath expression
'/configuration/appSettings/add[@key = 'DbConnectionString']/@value'.
    [attrib] Setting file attributes for 1 files to ReadOnly.
```

We can see that two executions of the databaseincrement target occur, moving the old version (1.0.2.0) through 1.0.3.0 to version 1.0.4.0. Superb.

Note You have probably already realized that this script can be used to perform a "clean" build by simply applying all migration scripts from the very first build.

Adding the old version of the database at the command line is effective but might be seen as a bit kludgy. My suggestion for alternative solutions is to use <xmlpoke> and <xmlpeek> to maintain a state or version file, or try to use the <version> task to do the same. I spent a little time messing around with this idea, and found it satisfactory.

At this point, we are now able to analyze, integrate, and deploy a system with a database as we wish. Now for something completely different...

Considering DTS Packages

DTS (Data Transformation Services) packages are a very useful feature of SQL Server, and I have seen heavy use of DTS features for handling a variety of scheduled tasks. Unfortunately, they can be a pain to deploy effectively because they are prone to poor standards for configuration and also because it can be awkward to ensure quality.

The DTS Compare tool from the SQL Bundle does an excellent job of analyzing differences between server instances, which means the physical porting of a DTS package from server to server is less painful than manual inspections. However, there is another problem. Usually a DTS package will need to be configured differently from server to server—different FTP server information, for example. The only real option is to access the package on the production server and make changes to variables throughout the tasks within the package. This is possible, but in my experience leads to heated debates between developers and operations personnel as to who forgot to set the variables or who set them incorrectly. This reduces the confidence in DTS package deployment and can affect the success of a project.

The effort and risk can be reduced to some extent through the introduction of some standard tasks in DTS packages and, as usual, a bit of organization.

■**Note** DTS is of course a little bit obscure and archaic. The code that follows works with a minimum of effort but could be accomplished, probably to a higher quality, with a specific custom task implemented in VB 6.0, or C# if you are daring. I hope that the next version of SQL Server has improved configuration and deployment capabilities for DTS packages.

Figure 8-18 shows a package with two steps at the beginning: Load XML File and Set Variables. The first is a VBScript task, and the second is a Dynamic Properties task. We will use these to simplify package configuration.

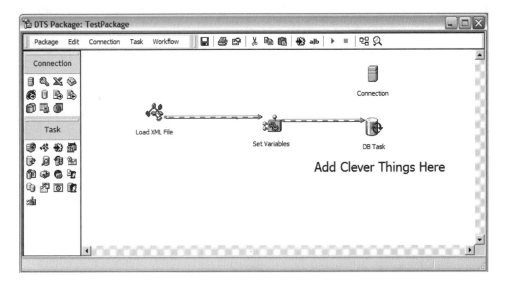

Figure 8-18. *Standard DTS package configuration*

Organization

Generally speaking, DTS packages have a tendency to generate artifacts since they are used to push around data feeds in various formats. These artifacts can be organized sensibly, server to server, by maintaining standard shares in the same way on each server in the form \\<server name>\<dts share name>\<project name>. The artifacts for DTS packages can then be maintained neatly and cleaned up from this area.

Additionally, we will use this space to maintain an XML file containing the configuration for the DTS package.

Load XML File Task

The XML files to be stored in the project folder have the following trivial format:

```
<?xml version="1.0" encoding="UTF-8"?>
<parameters>
    <parameter name="ConnectionString">My connection string</parameter>
    <parameter name="Another Name">Another Value</parameter>
</parameters>
```

The Load XML File task should then contain the following (VBScript) code:

```
Function Main()
    Dim oXML
    Set oXML = CreateObject("Microsoft.XMLDOM")
    oXML.Async = False
    oXML.ValidateOnParse = False
    oXML.Load(DTSGlobalVariables("xmlPath").value)
    If oXML.XML = "" Then
        Main = DTSTaskExecResult_Failure
    Else
        Set oRootElement = oXML.documentElement
        for i = 0 to oRootElement.childNodes.length -1
            strName = oRootElement.childNodes.item(i).getAttribute("name")
            strValue = oRootElement.childNodes.item(i).text
            DTSGlobalVariables(CStr(strName)).value = strValue
        next
        Main = DTSTaskExecResult_Success
    End If
End Function
```

■**Note** Ugh! At least you only have to type it once; you can copy and paste from that point forward.

Love VBScript or hate it, this task loads up the simple XML file and sets global variables for the package according to all of the entries in the XML file. In order for the task to work, there needs to be one preexisting global variable, which should be called xmlPath and which should point to the XML configuration file, as shown in Figure 8-19.

Figure 8-19. *Initial global variables settings*

After this step is executed successfully, the new global variables will also be present, as can be seen in Figure 8-20.

Figure 8-20. *Global variables after Load XML File task*

Set Variables Task

With all of the settings available as global variables, the Dynamic Properties task Set Variables can be used to push the variables into the settings of the other tasks for the package, as shown in Figure 8-21.

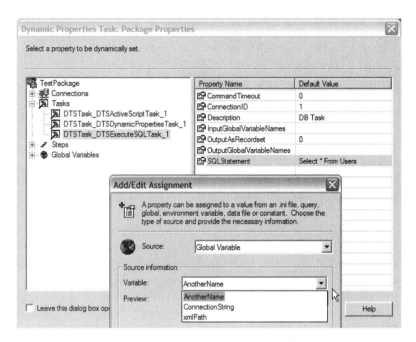

Figure 8-21. *Configuring a Dynamic Properties task*

Generally speaking, global variables can be used to set just about any aspect of a DTS package, including properties that are exposed on custom tasks that you may use. You may find that these standards work well as they are.

The result of this work for each DTS package is that when a package is deployed to another environment, the only configuration change that needs to occur is the correct setting of the xmlPath global variable—a minimum of manual effort and risk.

■Note There are other options as well. You could use a SOAP call or similar approach to dynamically load the settings instead.

Summary

There has been a lot to learn in this chapter, but I hope you will agree that the results in terms of describing the beginnings of a database integration framework are satisfactory. The work highlights the fragility and lack of utility for such processes at this time, but with a toolset like SQL Bundle and NAnt and a little thought and creativity, these processes can work. Discipline is required to actually carry through these concepts to a production scenario, and if you review the processes, you will identify risks that cannot easily be covered—such as "How do I roll back in the event of a failure?" The scripts provide an easy means to handle such issues, but they do not avoid the original problem. On the other hand, we suffer these problems daily in any case.

In the next chapter, we will look at generating further efficiency to the delivery process and the scripts through the use of code-generation techniques.

Further Reading

There are several Internet papers on the subject of agile database management and development (as opposed to straightforward integration). These two are very worthwhile:

Evolutionary Database Design (http://martinfowler.com/articles/evodb.html)

XP and Databases (www.extremeprogramming.org/stories/testdb.html)

This book contains a great deal of techniques and suggestions on the same subject: *Agile Database Techniques: Effective Strategies for the Agile Software Developer* by Scott Ambler (Wiley, 2003).

■■■

CHAPTER 9

Code Generation

The end of our exploration of automated builds and continuous integration (CI) approaches rapidly. In the last couple of chapters we have looked at complicated techniques that could be examined in even further detail. All of the configuration and script files we have used consist of XML, and so the opportunities for the transformation of this information naturally present themselves. This chapter explores these transformation and generation techniques, identifying some suitable areas for consideration. Then, we wrap up by considering what has been achieved through the Design to Deliver work.

■**Note** "Code generation" may be too grandiose a term for the transformation and production work in this chapter, as of course the generation is of XML configuration and script files rather than code for compilation. However, the term is a common and obvious one to use.

Why Use Code Generation?

When we began tackling automated builds and CI, we found that we could apply simple, but strict, standards to ensure the compliance of relevant applications to remove the overhead in maintaining differing build solutions for every system—the risk being that in fact we would end up with a myriad of differing processes, too, which would not necessarily improve confidence in the delivery phase of a project. Of course, the trivial examples of a book can only touch upon the actual complexity inherent in the delivery of a software system, though we have seen examples of additional complexity. In particular, our exploration of database integration has added significant additional infrastructure, process possibilities, and configuration requirements to the mix. We are left with three core issues at this juncture:

Separation of concerns. Increasingly, the configuration information is becoming entwined with the process descriptions: in NAnt-speak, more and more properties are required for the build scripts. Although I have not paid as much attention to ensuring this is minimized in the previous chapter, it would still be the case that information would be repeated and/or included inappropriately as first-class information for a build script.

"Specific" system steps. We have spent some time factoring out the common aspects of build scripts and moving these to common locations. Some areas have not been addressed adequately, such as the very specific documentation steps. Annoyingly, the documentation step only differs according to the inputs rather than the process: the settings for the `<ndoc>` task are the same in every case but the assemblies to be documented differ. Additionally, some steps may differ because the process will vary slightly from system to system. For instance, database integration could be handled in a few different ways, as we discussed. These steps might differ from system to system.

Administration overhead. The two previous issues currently mean that there is a potential administration overhead to the maintenance of the delivery process. This comes from a couple of directions. First, changes to process may mean multiple changes across multiple systems where steps have been approximately the same. This means greater effort and risk of change, and could therefore mean additional rigidity. Second, storing data such as environmental information inside the build scripts means that it is likely this is repeated information. Managing the knowledge of the development environment/network also means managing the build scripts. So while we have gained efficiencies by using NAnt in the first place, to protect this advantage we also need to take care of the effort involved in using NAnt, too.

To alleviate these problems, we can put more significant effort into common scripts and common processes. As we have seen in previous chapters, this is an effective and recommended practice, and it will work particularly well against a set of similar systems such as web/database systems. We should remember that this is one of the core problems we originally set out to solve.

We could also put some effort into more advanced NAnt techniques—additional scripting tasks and functions can perform more detailed analysis of source code and enhance the build scripts. Again, a stated aim was to attempt to avoid too much "clever" decision making by encapsulating logic in the build scripts, but some areas could be considered. One such potential solution is to perform more analysis of the solution file to glean further build information.

However, this approach is not effective in obtaining information such as deployment environments, since such information is simply not held within the source code.

A final problem is that some information is held in the CCNet configuration file and other related (or even identical) information is held in the companion NAnt scripts. We could perhaps use the `<xmlpeek>` task to read from the CCNet configuration file for some of the information, but again, CCNet does not hold *all* of the required information.

The generation of the files through some automated mechanism is a possibility, because it can solve all three of the issues rather than just one or two. In principle, we could take a master file of data and process information and generate the CCNet, build, and deploy files from this master. The drawback is that we need to provide an additional framework for the process once more, but the advantages are that we tackle the issues in the following way:

Separation of concerns. Data will be held outside of the CCNet, build, and deploy scripts in one common location. This data could therefore be fed by another system. All data is held in the same location and so the impact of environmental changes on the delivery process can be assessed and performed in the same location, using specific analytical transforms of the same information.

"Specific" system steps. We can address specific system steps by having a catalog of available differing steps to be generated according to flags in the master file. As already mentioned, we cannot get away from the need to have specific steps, but with good refactoring efforts combined with generation techniques we can build up an options library to cover many of the possibilities.

Administration overhead. Having the files for delivery automatically generated clearly removes administration overhead from the scripts themselves. Administration is then targeted solely at the master settings file. This minimizes the need to understand the entire build process for the administration user and opens the door for automatic production of this master file from some "systems catalog" or control center, which in turn could mean a friendly UI for the management of delivery scripts.

So there is some virtue in investigating code generation techniques to further aid the delivery effort. At this point, we will move on from the argument itself, and investigate the use of code generation to provide build scripts.

Tools for the Task

There are a couple of major options for code generation in this instance: the use of XSLT, or the use of some other code-generation harness.

Basic File Manipulation

By *basic file manipulation* I mean the use of file manipulation techniques such as AWK or even NAnt's own `filterchain` functionality (see Chapter 3) to perform token replacement of varying degrees of sophistication. For example, regular expressions can perform some clever token replacement beyond that of "Search and Replace."

XSLT

XSLT is the natural choice for the transformation of XML into some other XML (or indeed another file type). However, in this instance we will be taking a single XML source file and producing multiple new XML files. This means that the process is not simply a case of producing the XSLT required for transformation. There needs to be other constructs and a framework to ensure the production of the required files.

This in itself is not such a serious problem. It is something of a cop-out because I am not very good at XSLT. If, like me, you find using XSLT a bit confusing, you might want to consider the next option.

CodeSmith

Actually, CodeSmith is not the only option—several tools of the same ilk are available. CodeSmith (www.ericjsmith.net/codesmith) is a code-generation application. It allows the production of template files, which are compiled and executed against supplied parameters allowing the generation of all manner of code files. Generally, these tools are seen as a useful way to provide such services as data access layers for applications (though if you are interested in this, I might suggest LLBLGen Pro [www.llblgen.com] or other similar tools built specifically for that task), but in fact code generation can be used in many places to enhance productivity.

CodeSmith comes in two flavors: the first is the free download that can be used to compile and run the template files (.cst); the second is the CodeSmith Studio application that offers an environment for the production of the template files, and improved feedback on template generation. It costs a little, but if you become "code generation infected," then it is well worth the cost. I imagine that you will save the expense in no time at all once you put the tool to use.

■**Tip** On the CodeSmith web site, many people contribute templates and the like for anything from data access to design pattern implementations. It is a very useful resource.

What are the advantages and disadvantages of each approach? Table 9-1 shows the differences.

Table 9-1. *Comparing Code-Generation Techniques*

Feature	Token Replacement	XSLT	CodeSmith
Easy to use	✓	✗	✗
Platform portability	✓	✓	✗
Harness/scaffolding present	✗	✗	✓
Handles decision-making logic	✗	✓	✓

Both XSLT and CodeSmith are likely to be the most useful for the process, thanks to the power and flexibility they deliver. We will use both of these technologies to deliver code generation to our processes. We will look at the scaffolding to harness XSLT to deliver the files we need and also see how CodeSmith can deliver the same. It is worth investigating a text on XSLT (see "Further Reading") since it is too large a subject to consider in depth here. There is no other reference on CodeSmith, apart from the help files, so let us begin with it.

Investigating CodeSmith

Before we begin the actual work of providing code-generation capabilities for the delivery process, we can investigate some features of CodeSmith to ensure that it can provide what we need. Figure 9-1 shows the CodeSmith IDE. If you do not wish to purchase CodeSmith, you can download a simple version that allows the execution of templates but does not offer the added help of the IDE. Take a look at Appendix A for further information.

The IDE consists of three areas. To the left is the editing window, which lets you construct, compile, and execute templates. To the right at the top is the available linked folders providing rapid access to template files. To the right at the bottom are the properties relating to the currently open template file.

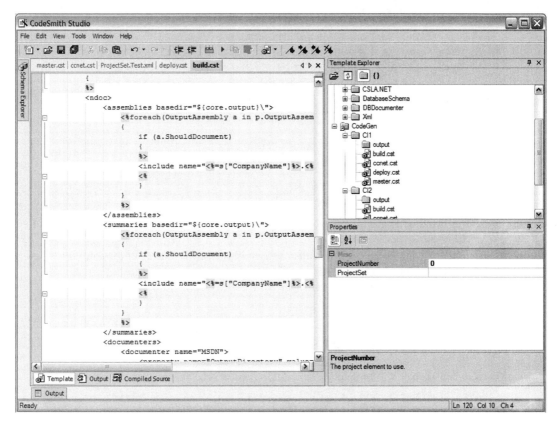

Figure 9-1. *The CodeSmith IDE*

Tip Our use of CodeSmith is not designed as a full tour of the product. We recommend you gain some familiarity with the IDE before continuing.

You can hook up the navigator to the CodeGen folder in the source code for this chapter to begin working with the following examples.

Using Properties

Using CodeSmith, we can very easily produce a template that accepts a parameter and produces some arbitrary output. Consider the following template:

```
<%--
Name:        test.single.cst
Author:      Marc Holmes
Description: Generates a file with a single variable.
%>
```

```
<%@ CodeTemplate Language="C#" TargetLanguage="Text" Src="" Inherits=""
    Debug="False" Description="Generates a file with a single variable." %>
<%@ Property Name="SolutionName" Type="System.String" Default="Etomic.Test" ➥
    Optional="False" Category="Project" Description="The project name " %>


This file generated by CodeSmith on <%= DateTime.Now.ToLongDateString() %>
Name: <%=SolutionName%>
```

When executed using `Etomic.Test.1` as the `SolutionName` property (the type is set to `System.String`), the following output is observed:

```
This file generated by CodeSmith on 17 January 2005
Name: Etomic.Test.1
```

So this is perfectly acceptable where we need only enter single property values to handle the transformation, but in fact we have multiple values for the same property (as we have multiple solutions). We cannot run CodeSmith multiple times since all of the solutions need to be in the same file for the `ccnet.config` file.

The following template file demonstrates the use of a collection as a property:

```
<%--
Name:        test.multiple.cst
Author:       Marc Holmes
Description:  Generates a file with multiple variables.
%>
<%@ CodeTemplate Language="C#" TargetLanguage="Text" Src="" Inherits=""
    Debug="False" Description="Generates a file with multiple variables." %>
<%@ Property Name="SolutionNames" Type="System.String[]" Default="Etomic.Test" ➥
Optional="False" Category="Project" Description="The project name" %>


This file generated by CodeSmith on <%= DateTime.Now.ToLongDateString() %>
<%
foreach(string SolutionName in SolutionNames)
{
%>
Name: <%=SolutionName%>
<%
}
%>
```

In this instance I have used a string array—CodeSmith can handle most framework types automatically—to maintain the list of solution names. I can then use some C# to loop through the array and produce output for each value in the array. When we try to input the array for this template, the property editor identifies the need for a collection editor and produces the screen shown in Figure 9-2.

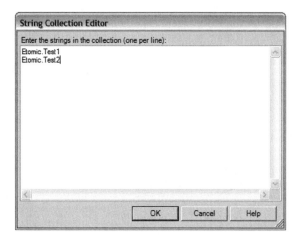

Figure 9-2. *Collection editing in CodeSmith*

The resulting output looks like this:

```
This file generated by CodeSmith on 17 January 2005
Name: Etomic.Test.1
Name: Etomic.Test.2
```

This is much closer to our desired use of CodeSmith. There are more complicated requirements, however: the need to use XML as the input to CodeSmith, and the need to output multiple files.

Fortunately, both of these issues are handled neatly by CodeSmith with a little work on our part. The code used in the following solutions is lifted from the samples that come with CodeSmith and is repurposed for my specific needs here.

First, we must use an XML file for input. Consider the following very basic XML file that we might want to use to maintain the master information:

```
<?xml version="1.0"?>
<ProjectSet xmlns="http://www.etomic.co.uk">
    <Projects>
        <Project Name="Etomic.Test.1"/>
        <Project Name="Etomic.Test.2"/>
    </Projects>
</ProjectSet>
```

At the moment, this is no more complicated than the string array from the earlier example, but of course this schema can be extended. CodeSmith can handle the input of such a file through the creation of two things: an XML-serializable type and a suitable property editor. Fortunately, CodeSmith comes with the appropriate `XmlSerializedFilePicker` control and so we just need to reference and utilize the control.

The following code could be used to handle the above XML file:

```
using System;
using System.Xml.Serialization;
using System.ComponentModel;

using CodeSmith.CustomProperties;

namespace Etomic.CodeSmithExtensions.BuildAutomation
{
    [TypeConverter(typeof(XmlSerializedTypeConverter))]
    [Editor(typeof(CodeSmith.CustomProperties.XmlSerializedFilePicker),
    typeof(System.Drawing.Design.UITypeEditor))]
    [XmlRoot("ProjectSet", Namespace="http://www.etomic.co.uk", IsNullable = false)]
    public class ProjectSet
    {
        [XmlArray("Projects")]
        public Project[] Projects;
    }

    public class Project
    {
    [XmlAttribute]
    public string Name;
    }
}
```

The boldfaced code here references the aforementioned control and a converter for the XML file. In order to use these, the following assemblies must be referenced in the project: CodeSmith.CustomProperties.dll and CodeSmith.Engine.dll.

The other attributes in this example configure the XML-serializable types needed for the XML (or vice versa!). This is a trivial example: ProjectSet contains a collection of projects. A project has a single attribute: name.

If you compile this assembly and place it in the CodeSmith folder along with the other CodeSmith assemblies, then the following template can be assembled.

Tip It seems to be easier to place the additional CodeSmith assemblies in the main CodeSmith folder. I obtained several access errors when attempting to use the extensions from other areas—even those "approved" by CodeSmith.

```
<%--
Name:        test.xml.cst
Author:      Marc Holmes
Description: Generates a file with an XML file input.
%>
```

```
<%@ CodeTemplate Language="C#" TargetLanguage="Text"
    Description="Generates a file with an XML file input." %>
<%@ Assembly Name="Etomic.CodeSmithExtensions.BuildAutomation" %>

<%@ Property Name="ProjectSet"
      Type="Etomic.CodeSmithExtensions.BuildAutomation.ProjectSet"
      Description="The XML file containing the project definitions." %>

This file generated by CodeSmith on <%= DateTime.Now.ToLongDateString() %>
Name: <%=ProjectSet.Projects[0].Name%>
```

In this template an additional directive is needed: the assembly directive. This instructs CodeSmith to load the extension assembly, which would not occur by default, so that it can be used in the template. Subsequently, the property ProjectSet can be typed to the ProjectSet type within the extension assembly. Finally, we can use the type as we might expect to in C# code.

When we use the properties window to select the XML file, the correct property editor is chosen thanks to the declarative code attributes in the ProjectSet type. The CodeSmith window appears as shown in Figure 9-3 at this point.

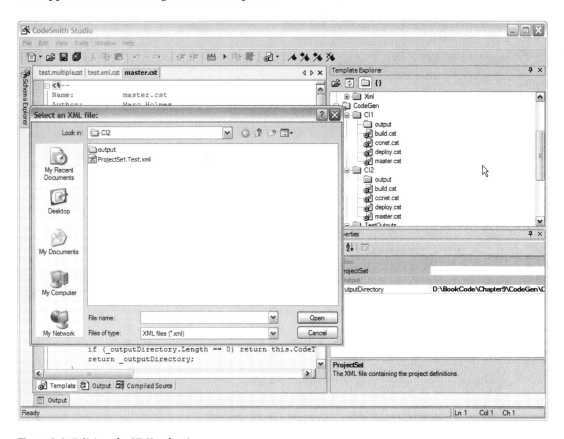

Figure 9-3. *Editing the XML selection*

Once the desired XML input file is selected and the template is executed, the output is as expected:

```
This file generated by CodeSmith on 17 January 2005
Name: Etomic.Test.1
```

At the moment, the `ProjectSet` type is very simple, but we can extend it as required. We will explore this further as we begin the real work in earnest. There is still one more issue, however.

Generating Multiple Files

The examples so far have generated only one file. Once again, there is a fairly simple code-based method for generating multiple output files. Bear in mind that we will also need to tackle this issue using XSLT in a little while.

The `TestOutputs` folder in the source code for Chapter 9 contains four templates. The first three—`ccnet.cst`, `build.cst`, and `deploy.cst`—are simply placeholders for what will be the delivery scripts, but they are needed to test the example. The fourth—`master.cst`—contains the code that handles the multiple outputs.

The CodeSmith API can be used to perform the actions we need. First, the declarative code is as follows:

```
<%--
Name:       master.cst
Author:     Marc Holmes
Description:  Creates all required outputs for the build automation.
%>
<%@ CodeTemplate Language="C#" TargetLanguage="Text" Src="" Inherits="" ➥
Debug="False" Description="Creates required outputs for the build automation." %>
<%@ Assembly Name="Etomic.CodeSmithExtensions.BuildAutomation" %>
<%@ Assembly Name="System.Design" %>
<%@ Import NameSpace="System.IO" %>

<%@ Property Name="ProjectSet"
            Type="Etomic.CodeSmithExtensions.BuildAutomation.ProjectSet"
Description="The XML file containing the project definitions." %>
```

We are loading in the extension assembly as before since this is the master template, and therefore the template will supply variables too. Additionally, because we will be producing file-based output, we import the `System.IO` namespace. We are also going to use a "folder picker" dialog box, which requires the loading of the `System.Design` assembly. The output➥ Directory property is provided as follows:

```
private string _outputDirectory = String.Empty;

[Editor(typeof(System.Windows.Forms.Design.FolderNameEditor), ➥
typeof(System.Drawing.Design.UITypeEditor))]
[CodeTemplateProperty(CodeTemplatePropertyOption.Optional)]
```

```
[Category("Output")]
[Description("The directory to output the results to.")]
public string OutputDirectory
{
    get
    {
    if (_outputDirectory.Length == 0) return ➥
        this.CodeTemplateInfo.DirectoryName + "output";
        return _outputDirectory;
    }
    set
    {
    if (value.EndsWith("\\")) value = value.Substring(0, value.Length - 1);
        _outputDirectory = value;
    }
}
```

This property ensures that a folder picker dialog box is used in the property editor to select the output folder, though in fact the property is a string. A little tidying is performed in the getter and setter for the property.

The next two methods required for the template are lifted from the CodeSmith documentation and massaged to our needs:

```
public CodeTemplate CompileTemplate(string templateName)
{
    CodeTemplateCompiler compiler = new CodeTemplateCompiler(templateName);
    compiler.Compile();

    if (compiler.Errors.Count == 0)
    {
        return compiler.CreateInstance();
    }
    else
    {
        for (int i = 0; i < compiler.Errors.Count; i++)
        {
            Response.WriteLine(compiler.Errors[i].ToString());
        }
        return null;
    }
}

public CodeTemplate GetTemplate(string templateName)
{
    return this.CompileTemplate(this.CodeTemplateInfo.DirectoryName + ➥
templateName);
}
```

Essentially, these two methods allow the loading of template files, followed by the compilation of the template. The template file then exists as a CodeTemplate type with its own set of methods and properties.

Next is the code required to perform the actions we will be looking for: we want to produce a single ccnet.config file containing all project information, and a single build file and deploy file per project in order to replicate the standards already in place. We need the other three code template files to do this. They will be held in the following code:

```
private CodeTemplate _ccnetTemplate;
private CodeTemplate _buildTemplate;
private CodeTemplate _deployTemplate;
```

The main method for the template is as follows:

```
public void Go()
{
    DateTime startTime = DateTime.Now;

    Response.WriteLine("Beginning generation...");

    _ccnetTemplate = this.GetTemplate("CCNet.cst");
    _buildTemplate = this.GetTemplate("Build.cst");
    _deployTemplate = this.GetTemplate("Deploy.cst");

    _buildTemplate.SetProperty("ProjectSet", ProjectSet);
    _deployTemplate.SetProperty("ProjectSet", ProjectSet);
    for(int i = 0; i < ProjectSet.Projects.Length; i++)
    {
        Response.WriteLine("Preparing Build for " + ➥
ProjectSet.Projects[i].Name);
        _buildTemplate.SetProperty("ProjectNumber", i);
        _buildTemplate.RenderToFile(OutputDirectory + "\\" + ➥
ProjectSet.Settings["CompanyName"] +"." +ProjectSet.Projects[i].Name ➥
+".Build.xml", true);
        Response.WriteLine("Preparing Deploy for " + ➥
ProjectSet.Projects[i].Name);
        _deployTemplate.SetProperty("ProjectNumber", i);
        _deployTemplate.RenderToFile(OutputDirectory + "\\" + ➥
ProjectSet.Settings["CompanyName"] +"." +ProjectSet.Projects[i].Name ➥
+".Deploy.xml", true);
    }

Response.WriteLine("Preparing CCNet...");

_ccnetTemplate.SetProperty("ProjectSet", ProjectSet);
_ccnetTemplate.RenderToFile(OutputDirectory + "\\ccnet.config", true);
```

```
Response.WriteLine("Generation complete. Execution time: " + ➥
    (DateTime.Now - startTime).ToString());
Response.WriteLine("To view the output go here: " + OutputDirectory);
}
```

This code handles everything necessary to produce the output files we require. The most interesting points are as follows:

The template members are loaded and compiled using the helper functions (for example, ccnet.cst).

The relevant properties on the child templates are set as required. In the case of these templates, the ProjectSet property is passed through to each child template. Additionally for the build and deploy templates, the index of the relevant project is passed through.

With the parameters set, the RenderToFile method can be called to save the output to the appropriate location, with the appropriate name.

In the case of the build and deploy files, the project collection is looped through so that an output file is rendered separately for each project.

Finally, in order to kick off the execution of this template, the following (very ASP-like) code is added at the bottom of the master template as the entry point:

```
<%
this.Go();
%>
```

This template can then be executed by selecting a relevant output directory (or leaving it blank to accept the default) and the relevant XML input file. The output from the master template (to the screen) looks like this:

```
Beginning generation...
Preparing CCNet...
Preparing Build for Etomic.Test.1
Preparing Deploy for Etomic.Test.1
Preparing Build for Etomic.Test.2
Preparing Deploy for Etomic.Test.2
Generation complete. Execution time: 00:00:00.6093750
To view the output go here: D:\dotNetDelivery\Chapter9\CodeGen\TestOutputs\Output
```

Reviewing the output folder reveals the files shown in Figure 9-4.

Name △	Size	Type	Date Modified
ccnet.config	1 KB	Web Configuration …	17/01/2005 22
Etomic.Test.1.Build.xml	1 KB	XML Document	17/01/2005 22
Etomic.Test.1.Deploy.xml	1 KB	XML Document	17/01/2005 22
Etomic.Test.2.Build.xml	1 KB	XML Document	17/01/2005 22
Etomic.Test.2.Deploy.xml	1 KB	XML Document	17/01/2005 22

Figure 9-4. *The output folder*

These files look very familiar! They do not contain any interesting information yet, but the scaffolding needed to begin the real work is complete.

Investigating XSLT

Of course, with XSLT then there is no IDE to investigate, but there is a complex toolset to understand. Have a look at "Further Reading" for some suggested material.

We took some time to look at the capabilities of the CodeSmith IDE, before we began to look at some coding to support the delivery processes. In a moment we are going to look at specific CodeSmith templates to provide the code generation, and also XSLT templates to do the same. There is one area where we also need to provide some framework code to aid the use of XSLT: a processor to output multiple files.

Again, the aim is to produce one ccnet.config file and then one build file and one deploy file per project. Ordinarily, XSLT will transform one XML file. With a little coding we can generate the same output as we have seen with CodeSmith.

Ultimately, this code will be used by NAnt to regenerate its own files (we can see this later on) so we will use a `<script>` task for this framework code. Let us take a look.

Generating Multiple Output Files with XSLT

To start this work, we will create a separate NAnt file, in this case called Builder.XSLT.xml. The build file is quite simple, with a single target called XsltBuilder and a call to this target. The XsltBuilder target will contain a script task to perform the generation. We saw an example of this in Chapter 3.

So the skeleton for Builder.XSLT.xml looks like this:

```
<?xml version="1.0"?>
<project>
    <target name="XsltBuilder">
        <script language="C#">
            <imports>
                <import namespace="System.Xml"/>
                <import namespace="System.Xml.Xsl"/>
                <import namespace="System.Xml.XPath"/>
            </imports>
            <code><![CDATA[

public static void ScriptMain(Project project)
{}
            ]]></code>
        </script>
    </target>

    <call target="XsltBuilder"/>

</project>
```

I have extended the `<script>` task to include the various XML namespaces that will be required for the scaffolding code. All that we need to do now is fill in the blanks, beginning with the `ScriptMain` method:

```
public static void ScriptMain(Project project)
{
   string projectSetFile = project.Properties["xslt.projectset"];
   string outputDir = project.Properties["xslt.output"];
   string xsltDir = project.Properties["xslt.directory"];

   XmlDocument dom = new XmlDocument();
   dom.Load(projectSetFile);

   ProduceCcnetConfigFile(xsltDir, outputDir, dom);
   ProduceBuildAndDeployFiles(xsltDir, outputDir, dom);
}
```

As you know, we need to pass through the NAnt project as a requirement of the `Script➥ Main` method. We can then use the properties (for instance) in the project within the script. Here I have assumed that the three properties in bold are available in the NAnt script. We will implement those later. The other action of the entry point is to load the `ProjectSet` XML file that we saw in the CodeSmith examples into memory as an XML document. We then move to produce the relevant files. The `ProduceCcnetConfigFile` method looks like this:

```
static void ProduceCcnetConfigFile(string xsltDirectory, ➥
                              string outputDirectory, ➥
                              XmlDocument dom)
{
   string outputPath = Path.Combine(outputDirectory, "ccnet.config");
   string xsltFile = Path.Combine(xsltDirectory, "Ccnet.xsl");
   TransformXml(dom, xsltFile, outputPath, null);
   Console.WriteLine("Produced file: " + outputPath);
}
```

This is quite a straightforward method, performing a simple transformation to provide the `ccnet.config` file. The `TransformXml` utility method is shown here:

```
static void TransformXml(XmlDocument document, string xsltFile, ➥
                      string outputPath, XsltArgumentList arguments)
{
   string output = "";
   XmlUrlResolver resolver = new XmlUrlResolver();
   XslTransform stylesheet = new XslTransform();
   stylesheet.Load(xsltFile);

   using(MemoryStream stream = new MemoryStream())
   {
```

```
        stylesheet.Transform(document.DocumentElement.CreateNavigator(), ➦
                             arguments, stream, resolver);
        stream.Position = 0;

        using(StreamReader sr = new StreamReader(stream))
        {output = sr.ReadToEnd();}
    }

    using(StreamWriter sw = new StreamWriter(outputPath))
    {sw.WriteLine(output);}
}
```

This method performs a transformation accepting further arguments for the transformation (this is important for the build and deploy files as we will see a bit later) and then writes out the resulting transformed output to the requested location.

Producing multiple outputs based on the single input file is a little more complicated. The opening method, `ProduceBuildAndDeployFiles`, is shown here:

```
static void ProduceBuildAndDeployFiles(string xsltDirectory, ➦
                                       string outputDirectory, ➦
                                       XmlDocument dom)
{
    string companyName = dom.DocumentElement.SelectSingleNode("Settings")➦
                         .Attributes["CompanyName"].InnerText;

    int index = 1;
    foreach(XmlNode projectNode in ➦
            dom.DocumentElement.SelectNodes("Projects/Project"))
    {
        string projectName = projectNode.Attributes["Name"].InnerText;
        string solutionName = string.Join(".", new string[] { companyName, ➦
                                                              projectName });
        ProduceBuildAndDeployFile("Build", xsltDirectory, outputDirectory,➦
                                  solutionName, projectNode, dom, index);
        ProduceBuildAndDeployFile("Deploy", xsltDirectory, outputDirectory,➦
                                  solutionName, projectNode, dom, index);
        index++;
    }
}
```

As you might expect, this method loops over the XML file containing the `ProjectSet`, picking out the required solution name information in order to name the files appropriately, and then calls the `ProduceBuildAndDeployFile` method for the build and deploy transformation for each node (or project). This is very similar to the code we created for CodeSmith. The `ProduceBuildAndDeployFile` method is as follows:

```
static void ProduceBuildAndDeployFile(string type, string xsltDirectory,➥
                                      string outputDirectory,➥
                                      string solutionName, ➥
                                      XmlNode projectNode,➥
                                      XmlDocument dom, int index)
{
    string xslt = Path.Combine(xsltDirectory, type + ".xsl");
    string outputFile = GetOutputFileName(outputDirectory, solutionName, type);

    XPathNodeIterator iterator = ➥
        projectNode.ParentNode.CreateNavigator().Select("Project[" + index + "]");
    XsltArgumentList arguments = new XsltArgumentList();
    arguments.AddParam("ProjectData", "", iterator);

    TransformXml(dom, xslt, outputFile, arguments);
    Console.WriteLine("Produced file: " + outputFile);
}
```

This method performs the "clever bit" by selecting the relevant project and ensuring that the transformation call uses the correct project information. It uses a single helper method, GetOutputFileName:

```
static string GetOutputFileName(string outputDirectory, ➥
                                string solutionName, string type)
{
    return Path.Combine(outputDirectory, string.Join(".", ➥
                        new string[] {solutionName, type, "xml" }));
}
```

So we have now provided a set of code to ensure that we can use XSLT to perform the same process, in terms of generating the multiple files required, as CodeSmith. We can include the required properties to this script as follows:

```
<property name="xslt.projectset" ➥
          value="d:\dotnetdelivery\chapter9\data\projectset.xslt.xml"/>
<property name="xslt.directory" value="d:\dotnetdelivery\chapter9\xslt"/>
<property name="xslt.output" value="d:\dotnetdelivery\chapter9"/>
```

Now we can run the NAnt script. When this script is run, we see the following results:

```
---------- NAnt ----------
NAnt 0.85
Copyright (C) 2001-2005 Gerry Shaw
http://nant.sourceforge.net

Buildfile: file:///Builder.XSLT.xml
Target framework: Microsoft .NET Framework 1.1
```

```
XsltBuilder:

   [script] Scanning assembly "ocwe9toj" for extensions.
Loading projectset...
Producing ccnet.config file...
Producing build and deploy files...

BUILD SUCCEEDED
Total time: 0.7 seconds.

Output completed (2 sec consumed) - Normal Termination
```

The relevant points are the usual dynamic assembly compilation message and then the subsequent outputs as the files are generated. Clearly, we need to produce the actual templates for transformations, but we now have the appropriate framework in place for the process.

■**Tip** I think that I would probably create a custom NAnt task for this purpose if I were to pursue XSLT as my transformation tool of choice. Also, consider that it is much easier to create the script for this task inside the VS .NET IDE for debugging purposes and then make tweaks and changes to make it NAnt-friendly at later stages.

With much of the framework in place now, we should consider the purpose of our work: the actual code generation.

Targets for Generation

There are three main targets for generation: the ccnet.config file, the build file, and the deploy file. These files may end up being a series of subtemplates, but for now they fall under those general categories.

CruiseControl.NET Configuration Files

The easiest target is the ccnet.config file. As we have already seen in previous chapters, thanks to the imposed standards, the project settings for this file are almost identical. Consider the following project from ccnet.config:

```
<project name="Etomic.Library.Transformer">
    <webURL>
       http://localhost/ccnet/Controller.aspx?_action_ViewProjectReport=true&amp;➥
       server=local&amp;project=Etomic.Library.Transformer
    </webURL>
    <artifactDirectory>
       D:\dotNetDelivery\BuildAreaCI\Publish\Etomic.Library.Transformer\
    </artifactDirectory>
```

```
        <modificationDelaySeconds>10</modificationDelaySeconds>

        <triggers>
            <intervalTrigger />
        </triggers>

        <sourcecontrol type="vss" autoGetSource="true">
            <ssdir>"D:\dotNetDelivery\VSS"</ssdir>
            <project>$/Solutions/Etomic.Library.Transformer/</project>
            <username>builder</username>
            <password>builder</password>
            <workingDirectory>
              D:\dotNetDelivery\BuildAreaCI\Source\Etomic.Library.Transformer
            </workingDirectory>
        </sourcecontrol>

        <build type="nant">
            <baseDirectory>D:\dotNetDelivery\Chapter6\</baseDirectory>
            <buildArgs>-D:solution.stub=Library.Transformer ➥
                       -D:debug=false</buildArgs>
            <buildFile>Build.Core.xml</buildFile>
            <targetList>
                <target>ci</target>
            </targetList>
            <buildTimeoutSeconds>300</buildTimeoutSeconds>
        </build>

        <labeller type="defaultlabeller">
            <prefix>1.0.</prefix>
        </labeller>

        <tasks>
            <merge>
                <files>
                    <file>
D:\dotNetDelivery\BuildAreaCI\Reports\Etomic.Library.Transformer\*-results.xml
                    </file>
                    <file>
D:\dotNetDelivery\BuildAreaCI\Reports\Etomic.Library.Transformer\fxcop.xml
                    </file>
                </files>
            </merge>
        </tasks>

        <publishers>
            <xmllogger />
        </publishers>
</project>
```

The most obvious candidate for simple code generation is the capture of the solution name information. This is what we will do for our first pass at the generation of the ccnet.➥ config file. Other pieces of candidate information, however, are repeated throughout the ccnet.config file and should ideally be separated from the config file itself as the information is either environmental or project-based:

CI server URL. This could be subject to change, or perhaps multiple master files with differing CCNet servers exist using the same templates.

General VSS information. The location and access information of the VSS database could change, or there could be multiple VSS and server instances.

Project version prefix. This will change from project to project, and would probably be the first candidate I would account for.

File locations. This is also environment information and liable to change.

We will address a few of these for this demonstration of code generation.

Tip Working through code-generation targets is generally easier to do than observe. The trick is to identify candidates and work on that basis until they are proved worthwhile. It may seem tricky to start with, but this passes with time. The potential benefits are worth the investment in time.

The CodeSmith Template

To provide the variables required for the output of an automated ccnet.config file, we need to amend the simple serializable type we used earlier, and we will need to alter it further for the build and deploy scripts. The input file may look like this:

```xml
<?xml version="1.0"?>
<ProjectSet xmlns="http://www.etomic.co.uk">
    <Settings
        CompanyName="Etomic"
        CcnetUrl="http://localhost/ccnet"
        VssFolder="D:\dotNetDelivery\VSS"
        VssUsername="builder"
        VssPassword="builder"
        EnvironmentMain="D:\dotNetDelivery\BuildAreaCI"
        EnvironmentTempDeploy="D:\dotNetDelivery\TempDeploy"
    />
    <Projects>
        <Project Name="Library.Transformer"/>
    </Projects>
</ProjectSet>
```

The crucial difference here is the addition of a Settings element and a number of name/value pairs. This slightly odd implementation of the Settings element allows the easy use of name/value pairs since XML serialization does not allow the serialization of hashtables (or other structures implementing IDictionary).

This input file needs to be translated into the serializable type as shown before and the assembly deployed to the CodeSmith assemblies directory. The changes are as follows:

```
public class ProjectSet
{
    [XmlElement]
    public SettingCollection Settings = new SettingCollection();

    [XmlArrayAttribute("Projects")]
    public Project[] Projects;
}
```

Here I have added a new XmlElement called Settings. This is a new type, SettingCollection, that looks like this:

```
public class SettingCollection : NameValueCollection, IXmlSerializable
{
    #region IXmlSerializable Members

    public void WriteXml(System.Xml.XmlWriter writer)
    {
        //Not Required
    }

    public System.Xml.Schema.XmlSchema GetSchema()
    {
        //Not Required
        return null;
    }

    public void ReadXml(System.Xml.XmlReader reader)
    {
        while (reader.MoveToNextAttribute())
        {
            this.Add(reader.Name, reader.Value);
        }
    reader.Read();
    }

    #endregion
}
```

The SettingCollection type is the implementation of my quick fix for the IDictionary problems. I want to be able to refer to the values of individual settings by name, which means a key/value pair construct is most appropriate. The NameValueCollection type is a good choice; it implements ICollection but not IDictionary (which is not serializable). To ensure I get the desired effect from reading the Settings element, I have implemented the IXmlSerializable interface. Microsoft currently does not give this interface much attention, although that is likely to change in .NET 2.0. The interface allows the implementer to control the behavior of XML serialization. In our previous example, I have only implemented the ReadXml method since I will not need to write the type for at least the time being. The GetSchema method is only used when working with ADO and DataSet paraphernalia.

This code is part of the BuildAutomation.2 project.

■**Note** We do not have the space to discuss the subject of XML serialization at any great length. For our purposes, there is not too much to know, though!

Following this, the ccnet.cst template should look like the following; the areas replaced by information from the data file are in bold:

```
<%--
Name:          ccnet.xml.cst
Author:        Marc Holmes
Description:   Providing the ccnet.config file using an XML file.
%>
<%@ CodeTemplate Language="C#" TargetLanguage="Text" ➡
        Description="Providing the ccnet.config file using an XML file." %>
<%@ Assembly Name="Etomic.CodeSmithExtensions.BuildAutomation.2" %>
<%@ Import Namespace="Etomic.CodeSmithExtensions.BuildAutomation" %>

<%@ Property Name="ProjectSet" ➡
            Type="Etomic.CodeSmithExtensions.BuildAutomation.ProjectSet" ➡
            Description="The XML file containing the project definitions." %>

<?xml version="1.0" encoding="utf-8" ?>
<cruisecontrol>
<%
SettingCollection s = ProjectSet.Settings;
foreach(Project p in ProjectSet.Projects)
{
%>
<project name="<%=s["CompanyName"]%>.<%=p.Name%>">
    <webURL>
        <%=s["CcnetUrl"]%>Controller.aspx?_action_ViewProjectReport=true&amp;➡
server=local&amp;project=<%=s["CompanyName"]%>.<%=p.Name%>
    </webURL>
    <artifactDirectory>
```

```
        <%=s["EnvironmentMain"]%>\Publish\<%=s["CompanyName"]%>.<%=p.Name%>\
    </artifactDirectory>
    <modificationDelaySeconds>10</modificationDelaySeconds>

    <triggers>
        <intervalTrigger />
    </triggers>

    <sourcecontrol type="vss" autoGetSource="true">
        <ssdir>"<%=s["VssFolder"]%>"</ssdir>
        <project>$/Solutions/<%=s["CompanyName"]%>.<%=p.Name%>/</project>
        <username><%=s["VssUsername"]%></username>
        <password><%=s["VssPassword"]%></password>
        <workingDirectory>
            <%=s["EnvironmentMain"]%>\Source\<%=s["CompanyName"]%>.<%=p.Name%>
        </workingDirectory>
    </sourcecontrol>

    <build type="nant">
        <baseDirectory>D:\dotNetDelivery\Chapter9\</baseDirectory>
        <buildArgs>-D:debug=false</buildArgs>
        <buildFile><%=s["CompanyName"]%>.<%=p.Name%>.Build.xml</buildFile>
        <targetList>
            <target>ci</target>
        </targetList>
        <buildTimeoutSeconds>300</buildTimeoutSeconds>
    </build>

    <labeller type="defaultlabeller">
        <prefix>1.0.</prefix>
    </labeller>

    <tasks>
        <merge>
            <files>
                <file>
<%=s["EnvironmentMain"]%>\Reports\<%=s["CompanyName"]%>.<%=p.Name%>\*-results.xml
                </file>
                <file>
<%=s["EnvironmentMain"]%>\Reports\<%=s["CompanyName"]%>.<%=p.Name%>\fxcop.xml
                </file>
            </files>
        </merge>
    </tasks>

    <publishers>
        <xmllogger />
```

```
      </publishers>
</project>
<%
}
%>
</cruisecontrol>
```

Based on our previous experience with the template files, it should be fairly obvious what this template file is doing. Reviewing the outputs will reveal a `ccnet.config` file, which is close to one of our previous hand-coded `ccnet.config` files. The main thing missing from this template is the ability to use multisource control, as we did with the web and Windows applications. Accounting for this should be quite straightforward, though, and we will move on to the build files. Other differences include the call to the build file itself; previously we called a file called `Build.Core.xml` and passed through a solution name in order to call the specific file. As we will see in just a moment, code generation brings a different dynamic to code, and here we have adjusted to call a build file for a project specifically from the outset.

The XSLT Template

The XSLT template looks very similar, and it is easy to see the differences between the Code-Smith syntax and the XSLT syntax. Depending on your familiarity with either syntax, you may find one easier to understand than the other:

```
<?xml version="1.0" ?>
<xsl:stylesheet version="1.0" xmlns:xsl="http://www.w3.org/1999/XSL/Transform">
<xsl:output method="xml" indent="yes" encoding="utf-8" />

   <xsl:template match="ProjectSet">
   <cruisecontrol>
      <xsl:for-each select="Projects/Project">
         <xsl:variable name="ProjectName">
            <xsl:value-of select="../../Settings/@CompanyName" />.➡
            <xsl:value-of select="@Name" />
         </xsl:variable>
         <project name="{$ProjectName}">
         <webURL><xsl:value-of select="../../Settings/@CcnetUrl" />➡
/Controller.aspx?_action_ViewProjectReport=true&amp;server=local&amp;project=➡
                <xsl:value-of select="$ProjectName" /></webURL>
         <artifactDirectory>
            <xsl:value-of select="../../Settings/@EnvironmentMain" />➡
            \Publish\<xsl:value-of select="$ProjectName" />\
         </artifactDirectory>
         <modificationDelaySeconds>10</modificationDelaySeconds>

         <triggers>
            <intervalTrigger />
         </triggers>
```

```xml
<sourcecontrol type="vss" autoGetSource="true">
   <ssdir>"<xsl:value-of select="../../Settings/@VssFolder" />"</ssdir>
   <project>$/Solutions/<xsl:value-of select="$ProjectName" />/
   </project>
   <username>
      <xsl:value-of select="S../../Settings/@VssUsername" />
   </username>
   <password>
      <xsl:value-of select="../../Settings/@VssPassword" />
   </password>
   <workingDirectory>
      <xsl:value-of select="../../Settings/@EnvironmentMain" />➥
         \Source\<xsl:value-of select="$ProjectName" />
   </workingDirectory>
</sourcecontrol>

<build type="nant">
   <baseDirectory>D:\dotNetDelivery\Chapter9\</baseDirectory>
   <buildArgs>-D:debug=false</buildArgs>
   <buildFile>
      <xsl:value-of select="$ProjectName" />.Build.xml
   </buildFile>
   <targetList>
      <target>ci</target>
   </targetList>
   <buildTimeoutSeconds>300</buildTimeoutSeconds>
</build>

<labeller type="defaultlabeller">
   <prefix>1.0.</prefix>
</labeller>

<tasks>
  <merge>
    <files>
      <file>
   <xsl:value-of select="../../Settings/@EnvironmentMain" />\Reports\➥
   <xsl:value-of select="$ProjectName" />\*-results.xml
      </file>
      <file>
   <xsl:value-of select="../../Settings/@EnvironmentMain" />\Reports\➥
   <xsl:value-of select="$ProjectName" />\fxcop.xml
      </file>
    </files>
  </merge>
</tasks>
```

```
        <publishers>
            <xmllogger />
        </publishers>

    </project>
        </xsl:for-each>
    </cruisecontrol>
</xsl:template>
</xsl:stylesheet>
```

Some areas where XSLT-specific directives are made appear in bold. Personally, I find the mix between XSLT and XML tags very confusing, though IDEs such as Altova's XMLSpy (`www.altova.com/products_ide.html`) can make life easier. Having said that, I think you will agree that there is not too much difference otherwise.

Build Files

The last time we visited the build files, we paid considerable attention to ensuring they were efficient, with as much commonality factored out as possible. Since then, we have looked at adding in database steps and so on; the focus of that work was not on efficiency, however. Code generation offers efficiency in a different way. That is to say, it does not matter how much code there is because it does not require a developer to produce it.

■**Note** This is not to say that code generators can happily be inefficient in terms of "tight code," though—reams and reams of code will eventually hinder performance, or the ability to trace defects, and so on!

With that in mind, let us consider the three artifacts we have to perform a current build:

Build.Core.xml. This file contains several common tasks but also handles all of the variables (or properties) for the overall process. Since we will need to pass the variables from our data file, this file is impacted by the code-generation work.

Build.Common.xml. This file contains some useful common tasks but no real variables. We could leave it unchanged if we desired.

<project.x>.Build.xml. This is the very file we have targeted in order to remove the project-specific implementations of the build process.

So what is the point of revisiting the other artifacts? Well, as we explained, we have to generate some of `Build.Core.xml` in order to gain the benefits of sharing a single set of primary data. Alternatively, we could split this file into two: one containing variables and the other the functions. Perhaps the functions could all be moved into the `Build.Common.xml` file; we considered some of these possibilities earlier in the book.

With code generation, however, a new alternative emerges. We could in fact collapse all three scripts into single build scripts for each project. The common code is then repeated across all projects, but in this case that is the point—all of the code becomes common.

Another rationale is that using code generation to handle the structure of build scripts is reinforced by not having any nongenerated code. The temptation could be to tweak the core or common files without considering that they are responsible for all projects in the same way as the generated files are: we will end up with two artifacts handled in different ways but in fact with the same responsibilities.

Therefore, I have chosen to join the build scripts together once more. An individual build script will be self-contained and fully generated. This will aid independent debugging of the templates on a project-to-project basis, and marks the strategy for the build scripts clearly. Also, because NAnt offers no real strategy to handle these kinds of references, some of the complexity of handling these references is removed from the delivery scenario.

Finally, before we take a look at the logic needed in the build script we should consider the additional flexibility that code generation is introducing. Because we can perform loops, conditionals, and other more complex functions within the generation routines, we can add more explicit settings to the NAnt scripts themselves. This may manifest itself as less pattern matching for files because we can name them explicitly and remove generality from them. In this sense, an overall design should be considered. For example, I could use the functions of code generation to provide the decision making for the script (Is a database target necessary? Am I publishing a web or Windows application?) and leave the scripts themselves to follow a linear process, effectively reducing the complexity of the build scripts at the expense of a more complex data file and generation process. This is because the build scripts must perform consistently many times over the course of a project without resorting to debugging and tracking of decision paths. I am happier to spend time tracking defects while developing the generation templates than in the middle of an actual development. Removing decision making from the scripts themselves removes risk from the process, which is always a good thing. Additionally, the scripts are likely to be easier to debug.

So let us move on to the practical implementation of the build file. As you may recall, the main issue with the specific build file was the identification of assemblies within the solution for testing and documentation purposes.

■**Tip** Another way to handle this instead of code generation is to write some functionality to parse the solution and `.csproj` files for a system to extract the names of the assemblies and inject this information into the build script. This is perfectly possible, but the parser may lack the semantical knowledge to actually get the decision correct. How do you know if an assembly is supposed to be documented? Perhaps if documentation settings are in place? Maybe they were missed/included by mistake?

Assuming that we are receiving a feed of primary information, the knowledge required about assemblies can be held in this feed. Our feed may look like the following:

```
<?xml version="1.0"?>
<ProjectSet xmlns="http://www.etomic.co.uk">
    <Settings
        CompanyName="Etomic"
        CcnetUrl="http://localhost/ccnet"
        VssFolder="D:\dotNetDelivery\VSS"
```

```
            VssUsername="builder"
            VssPassword="builder"
            EnvironmentMain="D:\dotNetDelivery\BuildAreaCI"
    />
    <Projects>
            <Project Name="Library.Transformer" ProjectType="Library" ➥
                    HasDatabase="false">
            <OutputAssemblies>
            <OutputAssembly Name="Engine" AssemblyType="dll" ShouldTest="false" ➥
                    ShouldDocument="true"/>
            <OutputAssembly Name="Tests" AssemblyType="dll" ShouldTest="true" ➥
                    ShouldDocument="false"/>
            </OutputAssemblies>
            </Project>
    </Projects>
</ProjectSet>
```

Here we have included a collection of OutputAssemblies. An OutputAssembly type captures the name of the assembly (the full name can be derived from the company, project, and assembly name as per the agreed standards). Also captured is the assembly type, whether it should be unit tested, and whether it should be documented.

The project has been extended to include information on the type of project (a library assembly, a Windows Form application, or a web application) and whether a database is involved.

The CodeSmith Template

This additional information is easily implemented in the serializable type with the following changes:

```
public class OutputAssembly
{
    [XmlAttribute]
    public string AssemblyType;

    [XmlAttribute]
    public string Name;

    [XmlAttribute]
    public bool ShouldDocument;

    [XmlAttribute]
    public bool ShouldTest;
}
```

The OutputAssembly is a very straightforward type. It is included in the project definition as you might expect:

```
public class Project
{
    [XmlAttribute]
    public string Name;

    [XmlAttribute]
    public bool HasDatabase;

    [XmlAttribute]
    public string ProjectType;

    [XmlArray]
    public OutputAssembly[] OutputAssemblies;
}
```

With the inclusion of this information, amending the necessary parts of the build script is relatively easy. We have now merged the files together, so the template contains a lot of code, but the template constructs that are relevant are covered here.

First, the injection of the data into the top-level variables looks like this:

```
<%
Project p = ProjectSet.Projects[ProjectNumber];
SettingCollection s = ProjectSet.Settings;
%>

<project name="<%=s["CompanyName"]%>.<%=p.Name%>" default="help">
    <description>
        Build file for the <%=s["CompanyName"]%>.<%=p.Name%> system.
    </description>

    <property name="nant.onfailure" value="fail"/>

    <property name="company.name" value="<%=s["CompanyName"]%>"/>
    <property name="solution.name" value="${company.name}.<%=p.Name%>"/>

    <property name="core.directory" value="<%=s["EnvironmentMain"]%>"/>
    <property name="core.source"
            value="${core.directory}\Source\${solution.name}"/>
    <property name="core.output"
            value="${core.directory}\Output\${solution.name}"/>
    <property name="core.docs" value="${core.directory}\Docs\${solution.name}"/>
    <property name="core.reports"
            value="${core.directory}\Reports\${solution.name}"/>
    <property name="core.distribution"
            value="${core.directory}\Distribution\${solution.name}"/>
    <property name="core.publish"
            value="${core.directory}\Publish\${solution.name}"/>
```

```
<property name="vss.dbpath" value="<%=s["VssFolder"]%>\srcsafe.ini"/>
<property name="vss.path" value="$/Solutions/${solution.name}/"/>
```

So the ccnet.config and the build script files are now genuinely sharing a common source
of data. One point to notice here (and you may have noted the same thing in the ccnet.config
template file) is that I have not parameterized the individual folder names for the source code,
for publishing and so on. This is because the data file is designed to allow relatively arbitrary
changes to account for environment and similar changes. In fact, changing the name of publishing locations is not straightforward because these locations maintain historical artifacts
and therefore a migration process of some sort is likely needed if these variables are changed.
For the time being then, I do not allow arbitrary changes in this area. (The CCNet server URL
itself can change to allow multiple server instances from the same set of templates; otherwise
the same applies here.)

Further down the script we come to the points where identification of assets is needed.
For instance, the unit-testing task looks like this:

```
<nunit2>
    <formatter type="Xml" usefile="true" extension=".xml"
                outputdir="${core.reports}\" />
    <test>
    <assemblies basedir="${core.output}\">
    <%
    foreach(OutputAssembly a in p.OutputAssemblies)
    {
        if (a.ShouldTest)
        {
    %>
    <include
      name="<%=s["CompanyName"]%>.<%=p.Name%>.<%=a.Name%>.<%=a.AssemblyType%>" />
    <%
        }
    }
    %>
    </assemblies>
    </test>
</nunit2>
```

So here is an example of explicitly stating the assemblies to be unit tested. There is now
no need to use NAnt's pattern-matching for decision making in this area, though it might not
be a good idea to tell the developers that in the interest of keeping those standards up!

Several constructs of this type appear throughout the file, all doing the same thing. This
code repetition could undoubtedly be factored into a method in the template to return the
relevant array of assemblies.

Finally in this script is an example of the larger decision making being used in the template-
generation step. Previously, a property in the specific build file described whether or not an
application was a web application:

```
<property name="solution.isweb" value="true"/>
```

This has now been removed, and this information is held in the data file as the `ProjectType`. The build file template checks this information and includes the relevant target, removing the conditional from the build file and therefore the runtime execution of the build file:

```
<%
if(p.ProjectType == "WebForm")
{
%>
    <target name="publish">
    ...snipped...
    </target>
<%
}
else
{
%>
    <target name="publish">
    ...snipped...
    </target>
<%
}
%>
```

That is about it for the build file with CodeSmith. Next up is the XSLT file.

The XSLT Template

Once again, most areas of the template are the same as CodeSmith, though with differing syntax. For this reason, we will not reproduce the entire template here, though it is included with the source code for the book. We should address one significant issue, though: the use of {} (curly brackets). These are used by XSLT and NAnt for different purposes, and using the curly brackets within an XSLT style sheet will cause XSLT to attempt to process the brackets and their contents as a directive when in fact the intent was to mark a NAnt property. So this code will not work correctly:

```
<property name="core.source" value="${core.directory}\Source\${solution.name}"/>
```

To get around this, the following XSLT syntax is required:

```
<property name="core.source">
  <xsl:attribute name="value">${core.directory}\Source\${solution.name}
  </xsl:attribute>
</property>
```

This means that the appearance of the generated file is a bit different under XSLT with the inclusion of the closing tag, although in fact it is perfectly acceptable to NAnt. The use of this syntax is a little more annoying in XSLT than CodeSmith, and certainly the curly brackets issue is very confusing during debugging.

Some argue that properties can be avoided altogether since the build file is generated on demand and so can be fully hard-coded. You may like to pursue this as an option if you are using XSLT.

Deployment Files

The deployment files we have generated have been less sophisticated than the build files, although they became a little more involved with the inclusion of more complex scenarios such as database integration. This is because NAnt is primarily a build tool, but we should acknowledge once more that deployment quickly becomes more involved once there are GACs to access, registry settings to change, and the like.

Another feature of the deployment files is that they are generally quite specific depending on the project type. Even at this simple example level, the deployment of a library component differs from the deployment of a Windows application, which in turn differs from the deployment of a web application. In this case, it may be worth having different templates for these various scenarios; code generation best practice would probably suggest maintaining a collection of templates rather than jamming a whole bunch of complexity into one or two monolithic templates, which also sounds like what we are doing with the build scripts themselves!

To use a different deployment template depending on the project, we could alter the master template:

```
public void Go()
{
    DateTime startTime = DateTime.Now;

    Response.WriteLine("Beginning generation...");

    _ccnetTemplate = this.GetTemplate("CCNet.cst");
    _buildTemplate = this.GetTemplate("Build.cst");
    _deployTemplate = this.GetTemplate("Deploy.cst");

    _buildTemplate.SetProperty("ProjectSet", ProjectSet);
    _deployTemplate.SetProperty("ProjectSet", ProjectSet);
    for(int i = 0; i < ProjectSet.Projects.Length; i++)
    {
        Response.WriteLine("Preparing Build for " + ProjectSet.Projects[i].Name);
        _buildTemplate.SetProperty("ProjectNumber", i);
        _buildTemplate.RenderToFile(OutputDirectory + "\\" +
                        ProjectSet.Settings["CompanyName"] +"." +
                        ProjectSet.Projects[i].Name +".Build.xml", true);
        Response.WriteLine("Preparing Deploy for " +
                        ProjectSet.Projects[i].Name);
        _deployTemplate.SetProperty("ProjectNumber", i);
        _deployTemplate.RenderToFile(OutputDirectory + "\\" +
                        ProjectSet.Settings["CompanyName"] +"." +
                        ProjectSet.Projects[i].Name +".Deploy.xml", true);
    }

    Response.WriteLine("Preparing CCNet...");

    _ccnetTemplate.SetProperty("ProjectSet", ProjectSet);
    _ccnetTemplate.RenderToFile(OutputDirectory + "\\ccnet.config", true);
```

```
Response.WriteLine("Generation complete. Execution time: " + ➥
                    (DateTime.Now - startTime).ToString());
Response.WriteLine("To view the output go here: " + OutputDirectory);
}
```

The deploy template is selected at the start of the process. Instead, it could be selected on each iteration of the loop in the following way:

```
_deployTemplate = this.GetTemplate(String.Format("{0}.cst", ➥
                    ProjectSet.Projects[i].ProjectType));
```

I have not made this change in the source code since I am implementing only one scenario, but the method is clear.

The deployment file requires only one additional setting to facilitate the deployment of the library assembly we have used as an example. This requires no change to the `ProjectSet` type. The final version of the `ProjectSet` data file is as follows:

```
<?xml version="1.0"?>
<ProjectSet xmlns="http://www.etomic.co.uk">
    <Settings
        CompanyName="Etomic"
        CcnetUrl="http://localhost/ccnet"
        VssFolder="D:\dotNetDelivery\VSS"
        VssUsername="builder"
        VssPassword="builder"
        EnvironmentMain="D:\dotNetDelivery\BuildAreaCI"
        EnvironmentTempDeploy="D:\dotNetDelivery\TempDeploy"
    />
    <Projects>
    <Project Name="Library.Transformer" ProjectType="Library" ➥
            HasDatabase="false">
      <OutputAssemblies>
        <OutputAssembly Name="Engine" AssemblyType="dll" ShouldTest="false" ➥
                    ShouldDocument="true"/>
        <OutputAssembly Name="Tests" AssemblyType="dll" ShouldTest="true" ➥
                    ShouldDocument="false"/>
      </OutputAssemblies>
    </Project>
    </Projects>
</ProjectSet>
```

So only the addition of the temporary deployment area (`EnvironmentTempDeploy`) has been necessary. The remainder of the deployment file is a matter of straightforward token replacement.

As I was working, I discovered that there is no semantic information in the `OutputAssembly` information to indicate whether or not an assembly should be deployed. In this instance I have added a temporary fix to the template to ignore test assemblies. Also note that I should remove the pattern-matching from the build `publish` target, which is part of this issue. Sometimes, this template tweaking takes a little time.

Caution When you are generating code, make sure you check that parameters have been introduced into the resulting script correctly rather than running the script to find errors. Do I speak from experience? You betcha. When constructing this chapter I left the `TempDeploy` variable empty and ran the deploy script. The script deleted half my D: drive by the time I had the wherewithal to stop the NAnt process. I will leave it to you to figure out whether good configuration management saved the day, or whether I spent half a day repairing VS .NET, downloading lost code and realizing I had not checked in the code for the chapter for a couple of days . . .

With the three templates constructed (and debugged), the master template can be invoked to generate the concrete build files for the defined projects.

Tip When you are working with the templates and need to run them independently of the master template, you can invoke them individually by passing the XML data file and a project number (default 0) to work with.

When you run the master template in CodeSmith, you should see something like the following output, which is also reminiscent of the XLST NAnt script we have created:

```
Beginning generation...
Preparing Build for Library.Transformer
Preparing Deploy for Library.Transformer
Preparing CCNet...
Generation complete. Execution time: 00:00:01.4531529
To view the output go here: D:\dotNetDelivery\Chapter9
```

Investigating the content as suggested by the output reveals a screen similar to the one shown in Figure 9-5.

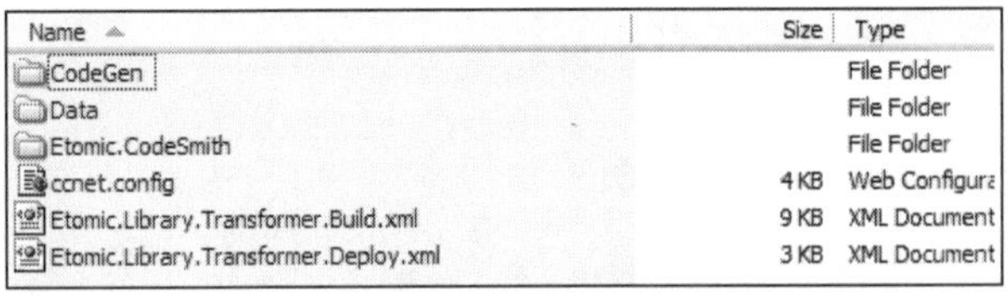

Name ▲	Size	Type
CodeGen		File Folder
Data		File Folder
Etomic.CodeSmith		File Folder
ccnet.config	4 KB	Web Configura
Etomic.Library.Transformer.Build.xml	9 KB	XML Document
Etomic.Library.Transformer.Deploy.xml	3 KB	XML Document

Figure 9-5. *Results of code generation*

All that is missing is the batch file to start up the CCNet server. Once the server is started, the CCNet dashboard will include the project, as shown in Figure 9-6. This of course means we can perform builds and deployments with the generated files.

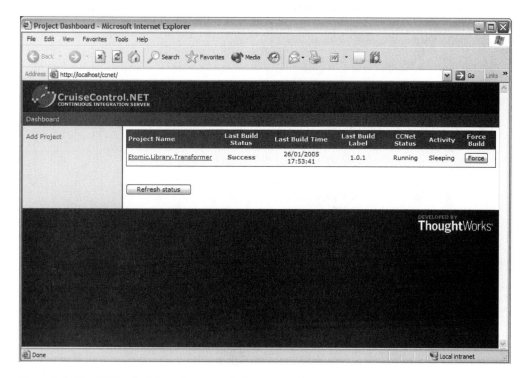

Figure 9-6. *The CCNet dashboard now includes our project.*

Setting up the templates required some time to put the initial constructs in place, but making changes from this point on is easy. Subsequent regeneration is not so time consuming—it takes about one second.

We have one final trick to consider.

Managing Generation Automatically

CodeSmith can be executed from the command line. As it happens, this means we can automate CodeSmith through NAnt or CCNet, or even both. Running CodeSmith from the command line requires the following call:

```
"D:\Program Files\CodeSmith\v2.6\CodeSmithConsole" ➥
    /template:"D:\dotNetDelivery\Chapter9\CodeGen\CI2\master.cst" ➥
    /properties:"D:\dotNetDelivery\Chapter9\ProjectSet.xml"
```

The CodeSmith console utility applies the specified properties file against the specified template file, which seems like an obvious action. The properties file differs from the test data we were using in that we need to embed the serializable `ProjectSet` type inside the regular XML definition for a collection of properties for CodeSmith. You can see that in the following code, where I have highlighted in bold the additional `OutputDirectory` property and the other wrapping elements:

```xml
<?xml version="1.0" encoding="utf-8"?>
<codeSmith>
  <propertySet>
  <property name="OutputDirectory">D:\dotNetDelivery\Chapter9</property>
  <property name="ProjectSet">
     <ProjectSet xmlns:xsd="http://www.w3.org/2001/XMLSchema"
       xmlns:xsi="http://www.w3.org/2001/XMLSchema-instance"
       xmlns="http://www.etomic.co.uk">
       <Settings
          CompanyName="Etomic"
          CcnetUrl="http://localhost/ccnet"
          VssFolder="D:\dotNetDelivery\VSS"
          VssUsername="builder"
          VssPassword="builder"
          EnvironmentMain="D:\dotNetDelivery\BuildAreaCI"
          EnvironmentTempDeploy="D:\dotNetDelivery\TempDeploy"
       />
       <Projects>
       <Project Name="Library.Transformer" HasDatabase="false" ➡
               ProjectType="Library">
          <OutputAssemblies>
             <OutputAssembly AssemblyType="dll" Name="Engine" ➡
                            ShouldDocument="true" ShouldTest="false" />
             <OutputAssembly AssemblyType="dll" Name="Tests" ➡
                            ShouldDocument="false" ShouldTest="true" />
          </OutputAssemblies>
       </Project>
       </Projects>
     </ProjectSet>
  </property>
  </propertySet>
</codeSmith>
```

Running the command with this input file produces the output shown in Figure 9-7.

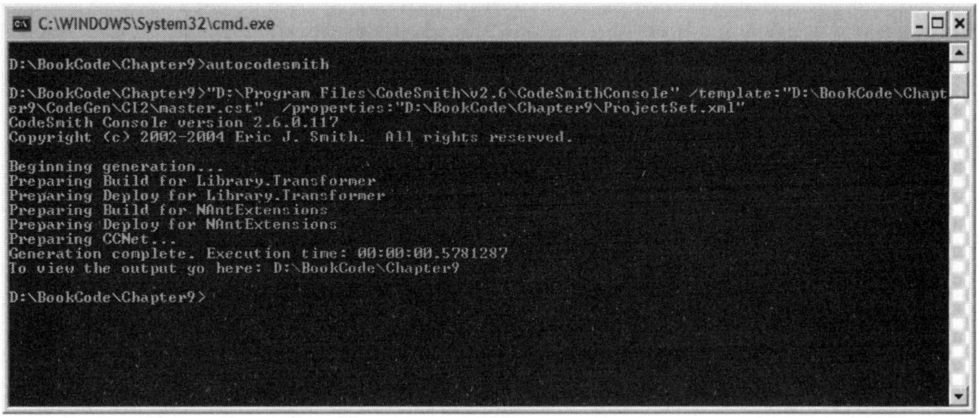

Figure 9-7. *Running CodeSmith at the command line*

This now opens the door to using CCNet to provide the generation on demand.

A New CruiseControl Instance

We can set up a new CCNet instance by passing through a different set of parameters on start-up. We will call this the CodeSmith instance:

```
"D:/dotNetDelivery/Tools/CCNet/0.8/Server/CCnet.exe" -remoting:off ➡
-config:ccnet.codesmith.config
```

As the command suggests, we will not implement remoting on this instance—it is not needed. We will point the instance to a separate configuration file called ccnetadmin.config, which looks like this:

```
<?xml version="1.0" encoding="utf-8" ?>
<cruisecontrol>
<project name="CodeGeneration">
    <modificationDelaySeconds>10</modificationDelaySeconds>

    <triggers>
        <intervalTrigger />
    </triggers>

    <sourcecontrol type="filesystem">
        <repositoryRoot>D:\dotNetDelivery\Chapter9\Data</repositoryRoot>
    </sourcecontrol>

    <build type="nant">
      <baseDirectory>D:\dotNetDelivery\Chapter9\</baseDirectory>
      <buildFile>Builder.CodeSmith.xml</buildFile>
      <buildTimeoutSeconds>300</buildTimeoutSeconds>
    </build>
```

```
<publishers>
      <xmllogger />
 </publishers>

</project>
</cruisecontrol>
```

This is a very minimalist implementation for CCNet, but that is all we need to ensure that the delivery scripts are generated whenever a change is made to the `ProjectSets.xml` data file. The main change here is that we drop the `ProjectSet.xml` file into its own folder so that it can be monitored by CCNet's filesystem source control provider in isolation.

`Builder.CodeSmith.xml` is a simple NAnt script that runs the command-line version of CodeSmith:

```xml
<?xml version="1.0"?>
<project>
<exec program="D:\Program Files\CodeSmith\v2.6\CodeSmithConsole">

<arg value="/template:D:\dotNetDelivery\Chapter9\CodeSmith\CI2\master.cst"/>
<arg
  value="/properties:D:\dotNetDelivery\Chapter9\Data\ProjectSet.CodeSmith.xml" />

</exec>
</project>
```

When the `CCNetServer-CodeSmith.bat` file is run, the output shown in Figure 9-8 is generated as this new CCNet instance begins monitoring and generating the files for the regular instance of CCNet.

Figure 9-8. *The CCNet admin instance*

Now the CCNet server is responsive almost immediately to any changes to the `ProjectSet` file—changes such as environment settings, or the addition of new projects.

We can do the same thing with the XSLT framework we created earlier. Because we already have the XSLT-based transformation framework running under NAnt, we can reuse that code to form `Builder.XSLT.xml`, the equivalent of `Builder.CodeSmith.xml`.

We can create a batch file specifically to create a different CCNet server instance (though this will actually perform the same job as the CodeSmith version). We have to make only one change to the `ccnet.CodeSmith.config` file (which is now called `ccnet.xslt.config`) to make it work with the XSLT framework:

```
<build type="nant">
    <baseDirectory>D:\dotNetDelivery\Chapter9\</baseDirectory>
    <buildFile>Builder.XSLT.xml</buildFile>
    <buildTimeoutSeconds>300</buildTimeoutSeconds>
</build>
```

The result of either version is the same. The advantage of the XSLT version is that only .NET, NAnt, and CCNet are involved, whereas the CodeSmith harness is required otherwise. On the other hand, the XSLT version is a custom piece of work without any control to the harness.

With our efforts successful at this point, we can add a new project (such as NAntExtensions) to the project set so that it too is included in the code-generation process:

```
<?xml version="1.0" encoding="utf-8"?>
<codeSmith>
    <propertySet>
    <property name="OutputDirectory">D:\dotNetDelivery\Chapter9</property>
    <property name="ProjectSet">
        <ProjectSet xmlns:xsd="http://www.w3.org/2001/XMLSchema" ➥
                    xmlns:xsi="http://www.w3.org/2001/XMLSchema-instance" ➥
                    xmlns="http://www.etomic.co.uk">
            <Settings
                CompanyName="Etomic"
                CcnetUrl="http://localhost/ccnet"
                VssFolder="D:\dotNetDelivery\VSS"
                VssUsername="builder"
                VssPassword="builder"
                EnvironmentMain="D:\dotNetDelivery\BuildAreaCI"
                EnvironmentTempDeploy="D:\dotNetDelivery\TempDeploy"
            />
            <Projects>
            <Project Name="Library.Transformer" HasDatabase="false" ➥
                    ProjectType="Library">
                <OutputAssemblies>
                    <OutputAssembly AssemblyType="dll" Name="Engine" ➥
                                    ShouldDocument="true" ShouldTest="false" />
                    <OutputAssembly AssemblyType="dll" Name="Tests" ➥
                                    ShouldDocument="false" ShouldTest="true" />
                </OutputAssemblies>
            </Project>
```

```
            <Project Name="NAntExtensions" HasDatabase="false" ➡
                    ProjectType="Library">
                <OutputAssemblies>
                    <OutputAssembly AssemblyType="dll" Name="GeneralTasks" ➡
                                    ShouldDocument="false" ShouldTest="false" />
                </OutputAssemblies>
            </Project>
            </Projects>
        </ProjectSet>
    </property>
    </propertySet>
</codeSmith>
```

As soon as the admin instance of CCNet detects these changes, it performs the code generation. As we saw in Figure 9-8, the files for the new project are duly generated and utilized by the regular CCNet server, which loads the new `ccnet.config` file.

Summary

We have investigated what code generation or transformation can offer to the overall process. We have seen that there are a couple of possibilities for generation, and we have implemented a solution using CodeSmith and XSLT as the code-generation tools. We followed the same little-by-little process to complete a simple scenario to provide a basis for more extensive and involved work. Finally, we automated the code generation itself using a new instance of CruiseControl.NET.

I hope you agree that code generation is a technique that offers several benefits to the standardization and operational processes of delivery. We have only started to scratch the surface of the flexibility of a tool like CodeSmith and a framework like XSLT, and once again we have come close to an overwhelming set of options for decision making and script preparation and execution.

In the final chapter, we recap the efforts made throughout this book, and I offer a few final thoughts on the delivery processes that we have defined.

Further Reading

More and more resources on code generation are appearing these days. For a holistic view of the topic, see *Code Generation in Microsoft .NET* by Kathleen Dollard (Apress, 2004).

Kathleen's book contains a fantastic, concise tutorial on XML, XPath, XSLT, and similar topics, but if you need further information, a good book is *XSLT* by Doug Tidwell (O'Reilly, 2001).

CHAPTER 10

■ ■ ■

Closing Thoughts

We have now covered a significant amount of material and seen how solid delivery processes can be introduced across multiple systems in .NET. When situations become more complex, or more open to interpretation and specific circumstances, our ability to provide efficient processes diminishes.

In this final chapter, I would like to summarize the content thus far, considering the questions we raised once again. In addition to identifying our original goals and thinking about the future of delivery processes, I will examine some new issues as well.

What Have We Done?

First, let us look at what we have accomplished. We will begin with the problem that we defined as the reason for the introduction of delivery processes.

The Problem

Way back in Chapter 1 we spent a considerable amount of time thinking about why we need sound delivery processes.

In a nutshell, we must provide consistent, measurable delivery processes across dozens of systems to accomplish these goals:

- To reduce the number of routine tasks for the development team

- To assign responsibility for specific processes to members of the development team

- To remove the reliance on individuals so there are no single points of failure in the delivery processes

We need to do this to improve our service to customers at a time when the software development life cycle is most obvious to them (and therefore failure is more obvious) and to reduce cost, risk, and effort in providing this service.

We discussed these issues in depth, and it is worth reviewing the objectives with your development team from time to time.

The Solution Proposal: Design to Deliver

To tackle the problem, we defined a pattern-based solution we dubbed *Design to Deliver*. This proposal describes an approach to solving the problem and explains the significance of success to the various stakeholders: the developers, customers, and management. Let us take another look at Design to Deliver.

Context

Improving the delivery of a software system by ensuring successful build and deployment features is a focus from the beginning of the coding phase, as is automating these features throughout the system life cycle.

Motivation

For any successful development team involved in medium-sized projects of several months' development, the number of systems to manage will eventually become cumbersome.

Failing to address delivery as a specific, controlled activity leads to a degradation in the delivery processes (whatever form they take) and also increases the risk of failure for a system at a crucial point in its implementation.

Through the implementation of a framework for delivery and the automation of that framework, enabling an efficient, consistent delivery process has the potential to

- Improve software quality through increased value to supporting activities such as unit testing

- Improve customer satisfaction through increased levels of delivery success

- Reduce overhead in administration of delivery

Mechanics

The steps involved in implementing Design to Deliver include the following:

Decide on the desired delivery process for build and deployment. Many things can be included as part of an automated delivery solution. Listing the initial priorities provides a focus for the first attempt. At this point, the automation does not necessarily have to produce a richly developed process. Aiming too high initially does not aid the exploration activities.

Identify the tools to achieve the processes. Providing a list of initial tools ensures that, in a world of limitless possibilities, a constrained approach is followed to ensure the continued focus and simplicity of the delivery process.

Identify an initial candidate for automation. An ideal candidate is a system that is standalone and that does not have too many areas of complexity, such as a database. A good candidate is a console utility or a shared assembly.

Prototype the process with the candidate. The candidate system should then be automated following the steps defined in the initial process. At this point, as more steps are identified, they can be added to the overall process or held over for verification.

Identify more candidates for automation. Following a successful implementation, more candidates can be included in the process. Once more, it is useful to group similar systems to better achieve automation.

Utilize and refactor the initial automation to provide standard scripts. The new candidates should reuse the scripts from the first prototype, but the emphasis should be on refactoring, the reduction of duplicated effort, and the identification of complexity where each project has specific needs not present in the others. Refactoring should also occur in the systems themselves to provide a standard environment and system structure to facilitate the automation; that is, not only should the scripts adapt to the system, but also the system should fall into line with the stated requirements.

Publish standards for the up-front implementation of automation. Scripted solutions for problems should be maintained in a library of solutions. Where systems have been amended to facilitate the automation, these amendments and standard requirements should be published and enforced by the development team at large.

All systems need to be brought into line with delivery standards. Now outside the realm of research and development, the published standards should be introduced as a requirement of all new systems, and incorporated into existing systems when maintenance cycles allow. It is critical to assign responsibility for implementation of standards to the development team at a finely balanced point in time, since implementing any new refactorings and standards across multiple systems will slow progress. At this point, an assessment is needed to determine whether a full-time role is called for to handle the ongoing maintenance of this and other configuration management (CM) activities. In my opinion, this role will be necessary.

New systems should adhere to delivery standards. All new developments must adhere to set delivery processes. Development teams should begin viewing the constructs for delivery as something that must be treated as a project in itself, to be maintained and developed accordingly.

Consequences

Design to Deliver has several consequences:

(+) **Speed of delivery is improved.** Naturally, if the task is automated it will undoubtedly be a lot faster. Significantly, the measurement of time taken could represent a useful metric for success of the initiative: delivery measured in terms of seconds and minutes rather than hours.

(+) **Confidence in delivery is improved.** The ability to repeat efficient delivery constantly and on demand is a significant boon to the development and operations teams. New doors are opened in terms of team capability, such as daily system releases to customers or project teams.

(+) **Scope of manual delivery activities is reduced.** This is another obvious consequence of automating the process. It becomes more likely that some of the supporting processes that do not form a critical path but that are still important—such as the distribution of documentation or the notification of support teams—are guaranteed to occur. The process cannot degrade, and must occur in the same way every time.

(+) **Mundane tasks are automated.** Similarly, these kinds of tasks may be considered mundane in the first place, and thus the effort required in this area is not valued. Here it is removed.

(+) **Quality of the software improves.** A system must conform to the process, forcing the developer to consider and implement delivery features up front, forcing delivery higher up the quality agenda.

(+) **Understanding of delivery improves.** Because there is a framework and stated benefits to the automation of delivery, the reasons for implementing successful delivery on a conceptual basis become clear to the development team. On a practical basis, the actual implementation requirements for a system are detailed.

(+/–) **Options are limited.** It may not be appropriate to use a solution that would ordinarily be appropriate because of difficulty in implementing the standard process. For example, a useful third-party component may not be easy to deploy and thus hampers automation efforts. We need to decide what is a more critical system feature: a useful user interface (UI) widget or successful delivery. On the other hand, limiting these options may be a good idea with more "innovative" developers.

(–) **100% success is not guaranteed.** Despite every effort, it is doubtful that all systems and system features can be fully automated for delivery. Therefore, Design to Deliver does not represent a panacea for delivery, but a road map for improvements to the delivery process with some significant successes expected along the way.

Resulting Context

We are able to confidently deliver software using a standard process. The length of time and the planning required for delivery are known and can be predicted. There is no need for rigid development environments to host our software because we are able to quickly build and deploy a required solution. The complexity and risk of delivery is reduced.
The advantages to the implementation of Design to Deliver are as follows:

Developers. The developers have a clear strategy for the delivery of products and a set of defined standards to work within. They understand what is expected of them and how the process operates. They can consider the delivery of a product—how and when it will be done—at the outset of the project rather than toward the point of delivery. Product delivery can, and does, occur at any point in the project, which is a boon to project managers as well. They are freed up to handle true development, which is what they want to do rather than handle mundane tasks. Removing responsibility for routine tasks from reluctant developers improves morale.

Management. To management, the delivery processes are transparent. Risk is reduced since all systems follow the same overall processes. Standards, and therefore monitoring, are available for the management team. The delivery process encompasses part of an overall configuration management strategy for information technology (IT) and can work within the confines of an existing process quite easily; it is a practical solution without its own paperwork overhead. Development effort for delivery can be calculated beyond just headcount, which means cost benefits can be described to senior management in simple terms: ordinarily a team can only speculate on the effort required to deliver a product, and this usually becomes a simple headcount issue ("We need another Ops member because we have more systems"). With automated processes, the effort to align a system to the process can be fully estimated and the delivery measured. The net effect should be a leveling of headcount required for these processes. The bonus is the additional quality and reduced risk in the same activities *but with fewer people*. Customer service (see the next item) is improved.

Customers. The customer can see their product almost as soon as they request it. The risk of system problems is reduced during user acceptance testing since defects arising from deployment are less common and thus scheduled testing time is more likely to be unaffected by such things (development teams sometimes forget that testing software disrupts the business as much as customers not turning up to testing disrupts the development). The support cycle should be reduced; it becomes easier for small support teams to deliver small changes once complete. If deployment is tricky, support teams tend to "roll up" several bugs into scheduled releases. If deployment is easy, then change can be effected quickly and with confidence. This virtuous circle then increases the time available for actual development and/or support from the team. Finally, incurred costs from delivery are now transparent; they can be accurately specified and estimated at the project outset. They will also be cheaper as ongoing delivery costs are met through the automated system.

The Solution Definition

We spent the remainder of this book defining and implementing the actual solution. We had a great many things to consider during this stage. We also defined a set of use cases to meet the needs of our build and deploy processes.

Build Use Case

Use Case ID: UC1

Use Case Name: Build System

Description: The user triggers a system build through an application interaction. The application requires no further interaction. The application follows a series of steps to build, test, and publish a system. Once complete, a message is displayed to the user and the built assets are available for use.

Preconditions:

The software is in a state that will compile.

The software is available to the build application.

Postconditions:

The system software is compiled and available in a state that will deploy.

Normal Course:

1. The user triggers the build application to perform a build.

2. The application prepares an environment for performing the build process and publishing results and outputs.

3. The application supplies versioning information applicable to the system for use during compilation, management, and publishing. (See Alternative Course 3.1.)

4. The application compiles the system software.

5. The application performs unit testing and compiles other reports on the status of the software.

6. The application creates documentation based on the output of the software compilation.

7. The application publishes the software system assets in an identifiable package and sends a message to the user.

Alternative Courses:

3.1 Where no versioning is required, then a default version number is used that does not impact the regular versioning system.

Exceptions:

E1. All failures. Process stops immediately and sends message to user. (See Exception E2.)

E2. Unit testing. Process produces report on failing unit tests and then stops and sends message to user.

Deploy

Use Case ID: UC2

Use Case Name: Deploy System

Description: The user triggers a system deploy through an application interaction. The application requires no further interaction. The application follows a series of steps to perform a deployment of a system based on the assets delivered from UC1. Once complete, a message is displayed to the user and the system is available for use.

Preconditions:

The software system assets are available in an identifiable package resulting from UC1.

Postconditions:

The system is deployed and available for use.

Normal Course:

1. The user triggers the deploy application to perform a deploy.

2. The application selects the correct deployment package. (See Alternative Course 2.1.)

3. The application gets the correct deployment package and unpackages it.

4. The application selects the correct environment information for deployment.

5. The application prepares the environment based on the information in step 4.

6. The application positions the software system assets in the prepared environment.

7. The application performs any additional configuration steps required by the assets and/or the selected environment.

8. The application sends a message to the user.

Alternative Courses:

2.1 Where no versioning is required, a default version number is used that does not impact the regular versioning system.

Exceptions:

E1. All failures. Process stops immediately and sends message to user.

The use cases held for most of the work in the book, though in fact the implementation detail changed over time as we included new tools (NAnt and CCNet) and new facets to the implementation (database integration and code generation).

Once again, though, these use cases, much like the Design to Deliver initiative, form a good foundation to remind those involved of the core principles behind the introduction of the delivery processes.

The Solution Implementation

In order to implement the defined solution, in this book we used NAnt and CruiseControl.NET to perform the required functions. We identified other options as well, though we also considered the maturity of NAnt and CCNet as products. When applied to the solution, the interactions of these applications appear as shown in Figure 10-1, though there are simpler versions (without CCNet) and more complex versions (once Red Gate tools and code generation are included in the process).

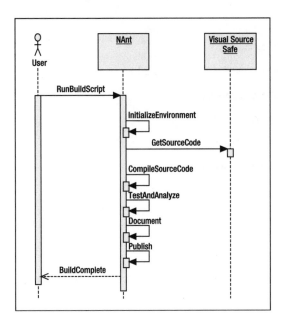

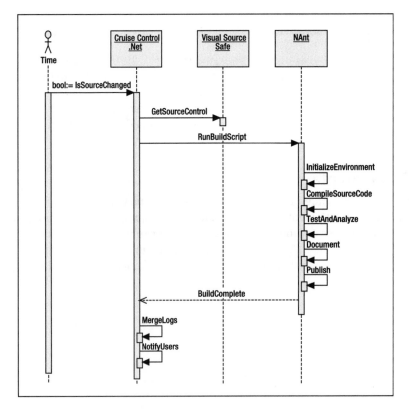

Figure 10-1. *The automated process interactions*

Throughout the book, we have assumed that our software resides on a single host machine. This is unlikely, and probably ill advised in a production environment. Once CCNet and NAnt are implemented for the processes, the deployment may span several servers:

CCNet server. This server would have NAnt, CCNet, and VSS installed and would be responsible for running the build processes. Additionally, the CCNet web dashboard would run on this server.

Repository server. This server would actually hold the VSS databases far away from any running processes (such as the CCNet server). The source control server should not be running any other process. The repository server could also maintain the actual build and deploy scripts, although they would be accessible from the CCNet server.

Deployment servers. Deployment scripts can be used to deploy systems remotely when a deployment scenario is simple, but when component registration (for example) is required, then the deployment can only take place on the target machine. In this case, NAnt should be present on the deployment server, with the scripts and assets accessible from this (or some proxy) location.

We have expanded on NAnt to provide additional functionality and have discovered that NAnt is in fact well placed to provide such functionality. We have also incorporated tools such as Red Gate SQL Bundle into the process to tackle some of the more complex aspects of delivery: in this case, database integration.

Finally, we have looked at removing effort from the delivery process implementation through the use of code-generation techniques.

Best Practices

We have examined many useful practices throughout the book. Here is a quick overview if you are considering your own implementation.

Process

Devising the process is a crucial step to implementing a delivery process. It is easy to get lost in the maze of possibilities and lose sight of the actual objective.

Sell the initiative. As we explained, it is difficult to describe the benefits in a way that management will accept. Additionally, it may be difficult to keep the notion of good delivery processes at the forefront of a development team's collective mind when, after all, there is the business of development to be getting on with. Design to Deliver, which describes both the mechanics of the process and its consequences, will go a long way to solving both management and developer buy-in issues.

Quantify the effects. A crucial part of the delivery of any practice is the ability to quantify the consequences. In the case of delivery processes, an automated build is unlikely to increase the speed of delivery (though it is possible), but it will produce an increase in quality of delivery and less risk through a fixed process. The deploy process automates some manual tasks and checks in a way that is obvious to the development team.

Steer clear of implementation detail. There are numerous ways to implement many of the details of the processes we have defined. There can also be a variety of issues and barriers to implementation. Trying to swallow all of these whole can be too much. Create the notion of the process and its aims, and then move to complete implementation of each part separately.

Start small. In Chapters 4 through 6 we started small, with a simple application, to prove the concept and illustrate the implementation, and to draw out any issues. We then moved on to more complicated scenarios, proving that they too could be delivered in the same way. As these successes flourished, we also became more aware of the overall problems and context.

Continuous integration is for all. Although CI is part of the toolkit employed and advocated by agile teams, it provides the same benefits for teams working in a more structured way. In a waterfall, or similar, approach, CI may not be used or contextualized in the same way as in an agile process, but the gains are similar, if not the same, in both quality and speed. Keep in mind that CCNet can run on a scheduled basis if you really do not want continuous integration processes.

Standards

We implemented some standards in Chapter 5 to ease the integration effort for a solution into the delivery processes:

Small steps. The problem with creating standards is that development teams can quickly become tired of "standard edicts," and you have to be quite sure that the standards will hold. Even with the best of intentions, the credibility of the whole effort could be jeopardized by poor or misguided standards.

Consider the impact. Bear in mind the impact of a standard on any legacy applications. How much work will be involved to ensure compliance throughout all applications? What consequences would a change in the standard have?

Consider supporting standards. Standards are not just about those directly involved in the delivery processes. In Chapter 1 we considered such factors as configuration management and source control management. These standards are worthwhile without delivery processes, but they certainly underpin the delivery processes and will form a large part of the success of the processes.

NAnt

NAnt has been a real workhorse for us, taking the strain of almost all of the processes we have put in place. Here are some things to consider:

Know the tool. This practically goes without saying, but it is crucial to understand what the tool offers as well as what it does not offer. Understanding where it will be in a few months is also very important. It can be easy to sink a lot of effort into solving one problem that can be solved very simply another way. With an open source tool such as NAnt, sometimes the best way to understand its behavior is to crack open the code and figure it out.

Decide on your approach. NAnt is extremely flexible and has many different features, from structural tasks, to functions, to dynamically loaded assemblies. Decide which of these features you will employ under a given context and try to stick to it. If you do not, then you may gain a lot of initial flexibility, but the downside may be that the structure and integrity of the scripts is harmed.

Extend cautiously. Once you understand how to create your own tasks, you may want to see how far you can extend NAnt's functionality. While the framework is very easy to "hook in to," my advice is to do this slowly. Perhaps implement a new task as a `<script>` task first, and then once its utility is proven, implement it as a full task. Perhaps use `<exec>` tasks for command-line tools until the full task is truly warranted. Remember: start small.

CruiseControl.NET

We have used CCNet to provide us with continuous integration (CI) capabilities. A couple of points to keep in mind follow:

Know the tool. As with NAnt, you should fully understand the CCNet tool. Know what it is, what it was built for, and how it works. Understand where CCNet is going.

Separate concerns. CCNet can provide some of the functionality of the delivery processes on its own. My advice is to decide whether NAnt or CCNet will handle the processes before you begin working with the tools. I think that it is preferable to have NAnt handle the process work and to maintain CCNet as the CI provider, service agent, and notification tool. This approach may provide better flexibility if you choose to move away from either tool for some reason.

Other Factors

It also pays to consider these other factors:

Be prepared for change. NAnt or CCNet could change. They are open source tools and as such there is no guarantee of their continuation or compatibility. Utilize their power and flexibility, but be aware that change may occur—and embrace it when it does.

Consider further steps. In Chapter 9 we looked at gaining further efficiency through the use of code generation. You can take other useful steps to support delivery processes. The implementation of the processes is the core aim, but take the time to consider how the processes themselves may be best supported (meta-processes!).

Consider supporting tools. In Chapter 8 we used Red Gate SQL Bundle and found it simple to automate in NAnt. Bear in mind that there is no need to reinvent the wheel. Many tools and APIs are out there, just waiting to be harnessed in a structure such as NAnt. Use them to your advantage and concentrate on the success of the process. Take a look at Brian Nantz's compendium of .NET tools at `http://nantz.org/SushiWiki/wiki.aspx` for some great pointers.

Closing Comments

Apart from the points described above, I would like to share my thoughts on some aspects that have driven the approach taken throughout the book.

Tool Selection

Initially we considered that several tools are available for the provision of automated builds.

We settled on the use of NAnt and CruiseControl.NET because of the history of their respective families: Ant and CruiseControl. If you are going to back an open source project (always a risky proposition), then these two are a good bet. Additionally, the feature set of these products is good: they have many capabilities built in, they can be readily extended (in fact, they are built for extension), and they are actively being developed. Finally, they are free and you cannot beat that price.

These are not the only tools involved in the delivery processes, though. As we quickly discovered, there is no single way to handle the requirements of the process; in fact, there is no single process. Some of the tools we presented are the "natural" choice given the nature of the work and the nature of the core tools. For example, NUnit is clearly integrated into NAnt and is the de facto choice for unit testing in any case. But you should bear in mind that other tools such as MbUnit could be used. They would require the construction of a NAnt task, or perhaps you could make do with the <exec> task. Take into account that any tool with a command line can be automated in this way through NAnt.

Apart from the obvious (and free) productivity tools such as NUnit and FxCop, we also made use of the Red Gate SQL Bundle and CodeSmith. Neither is free: the SQL Bundle product is actually quite expensive. These tools were chosen because they provide specific functionality that cannot be achieved easily, or well, from other sources. In these cases, it would involve a significant ongoing effort to develop solutions without introducing some risk to the delivery process—which is supposed to be all about reducing risk. When it comes down to it, you may need to consider some expenditure to cover specific issues such as database integration.

It Is All About the Standards

We introduced scripts standards to ensure that hooks were available in solutions for versioning and similar services, and for ease of organization and manipulation of solutions. These standards are easy to introduce, so there is not too much effort on the part of the developer, though in fact such standards may be significantly harder to apply in retrospect—and we all have to deal with legacy systems.

The application of these kinds of standards is crucial to the success of your delivery activities. This should be clear from the simple example solutions in this book, and certainly once you have dozens of applications, it will become very clear that standards are a good thing.

It is interesting to note that what seems like an unimportant choice—something like the solution name—can become pivotal to the success of larger-scale reuse of delivery scripts. The solution name is used in various steps: to identify the solution and project files; to identify the produced assemblies; to generate and maintain the delivery scripts and related assets; to generate and maintain the databases, web sites, Windows applications, and related asset storage; to identify the source control solution (and possibly database); and so on. It is probably not a bad thing to spend a little time considering the best name for a solution. It is also smart to utilize such information in this way, since it conforms to the idea of a "common vocabulary"—which matters as much in the physical world as it does in the logical world of application design.

Moving on, organization is the other important standard. Maintaining sensible, standard, predictable folders and locations aids the process in the same way as naming standards. Naming and organization are dependent on each other to some extent. Once again, with dozens of systems operating in the same way, the purpose of good organization (if it is not already a guiding tenet) will become much clearer.

The framework we have pursued focused on the advantage of strength through flexibility and simplicity on a large scale. On the other hand, we have also seen the inherent fragility and immaturity of such processes given the current state of the art (as far as we are concerned, anyway). The thought that the entire process could fail owing to a spelling mistake is a concern but one we live with day in and day out as developers.

If you look after only one or two systems, standards become less important and you focus on providing a custom solution rather than a generic framework for delivery. The organizational standards still hold, and possibly demand more focus if the single system is complex. Despite this, though, following standards such as naming does nothing to harm the creativity of the developer and should be seen as a good thing: new developers moving on to a project will find order and organization, and so on. If nothing else, you will be pleased when you do not have to deal with an assembly called `Bobs.Crazy.Magic.dll` any longer.

Start Small and Work Under a Banner

I think it is fair to say that if you tackle a significant process all in one go in an ever-changing environment, it will go wrong at some point. Developers, being developers, have a tendency to push forward in a beach-head style rather than as a slower-moving solid line of troops, and as such, certain areas of work are more advanced than others at any particular point in time. If the overall picture begins to degrade, then risk and lack of confidence set in. Conversely, moving slowly across the whole picture may result in "analysis paralysis," where no results are achieved because there is so much to think about.

We used a sample application and worked to a standard pattern or initiative to achieve a simply defined process. It was not difficult to obtain some fairly immediate results. The physical deliverables of this work, and the thought involved in this activity, allowed the expansion and creation of standards necessary for the subsequent steps. When continuous integration was implemented, we found that it was not difficult to introduce this process over an already well-constructed foundation. Do not underestimate the importance of the visibility of these small successes to a team that may not understand the purpose of the initiative, or even be skeptical about its use.

As we move on and begin discovering the variations in project delivery specifics, the proven groundwork will provide us with the confidence to move ahead with exploration and the evolution of the simple process into something not so simple. Some of the decisions you make during the latter stages of implementation are much more likely to be contentious and contrary to your own opinion during the earlier stages. This is natural; the more complicated activities are open to greater interpretation from team to team. The important point here is to start small to avoid these issues in the fledgling implementation and cross the bridges of, for example, database integration once things are more comfortable.

Refactoring to Efficiency

There are not many scenarios that NAnt cannot handle as long as we pay attention to the need to deliver the system at some point. Some of these scenarios have been demonstrated throughout the book, but we could write another whole book considering all likely scenarios. NAnt is also good at presenting numerous options for handling any given specific build scenario, and it has several features—such as the built-in functions, a plug-in architecture, and various structural tasks—for achieving these ends. It is a great product, and these are the reasons it is used.

The risk is that all of these means may be employed to achieve an end without planning and without a clear direction. This would be akin to simply attacking a development project without any planning. Even dedicated XP-ers would perform some planning, or have some other supporting framework to ensure structure. The end result of such activities could be that the delivery framework is automated, but is no less convoluted and risk-free than the original nonautomated framework. This sort of risk is similar to those found in other scripted solutions: collections of scripts loosely assembled into a program are prone to be disorganized. Just ask any ASP developer!

I have attempted to eschew the more complicated aspects of NAnt in order to ensure that it remained a scripted process, with minimal decision-making logic. It is unavoidable at times, but using this strategy maintains cohesion in terms of the application of the available feature set.

Alongside this, constant refactoring and time spent looking for opportunities to refactor, simplify, and provide common implementations are worthwhile goals to keep the framework in a maintainable condition. In the initial chapters on the introduction of automation, this is part of the work seen there, but later chapters focused more attention on techniques such as database integration. If you look at the examples, you should be able to see where the efficiency and cohesion of the scripts begins to weaken. In the real world, it is a good idea to stop and revisit these working prototypes and work to retrieve this cohesion and integrate the data to provide further efficiencies.

Complex Scenarios

It is not possible to handle all possible scenarios—there can be so many. We looked in some depth at handling a database web application, but as you can imagine, there are many similar scenarios requiring the same kind of thought. Examples of these are dependencies between multiple solutions, differing languages in the same system, the use of COM objects, the deployment of web services or other types of systems spread across several servers, or the building of other project types, such as Windows services.

We examined only a subset of the available NAnt tasks. NAnt is capable of handling several areas, such as Visual Basic 6.0 compilation. In particular, I made it the purpose of the book to attack the most common scenarios rather than more specific ones. I think that I would relish a "cookbook" of techniques relating to these other areas. Any takers?

Complex scenarios sometimes are what they are; it is not always possible to work with a brand-new application. However, it is always worth considering measures that can ease the delivery of a system. In particular, working with Design to Deliver in mind may mean that complex scenarios do not appear in brand-new projects—which is a good aim.

Views on the Future

Finally, here are a few thoughts on the near future.

Regarding MSBuild

We have mentioned MSBuild on one or two occasions throughout the book. This tool, as you have probably gathered, is designed by Microsoft to enable build scripting in Visual Studio 2005 under .NET 2.0.

It is a huge compliment to the developers of NAnt that Microsoft has effectively taken NAnt and implemented its own version for VS .NET 2005. Looking at some sample code for MSBuild (from the MSDN site), you may be able to spot the similarity:

```
<Project>
    <Item
        Type="FilesToCompile"
        Include="HelloWorld.cs"
    />

    <Target Name="BuildHelloWorldExecutable">
        <Task
            Name="csc"
            Sources="@(FilesToCompile)"
            OutputAssembly="HelloWorld.exe"
            TargetType="exe"
        />
    </Target>
</Project>
```

Hmm. Could you see any similarity? I thought so.

MSBuild will undoubtedly have some impact on the NAnt community. There are a variety of possibilities for this impact:

Until MSBuild is released, we will not know its actual capabilities. That it is tightly integrated into VS .NET 2005 is certain, but its breadth of functionality is much less clear. It seems unlikely that it will support C++, and it is very unlikely to support builds of (for example) Visual Basic 6.0 since this is a tool for .NET 2.0 rather than general use. This tight integration may be a negative to those that do not like to be tied into a particular platform.

MSBuild takes advantage of new solution and project formats under VS .NET 2005. This is an issue that NAnt has been struggling with for a long time under .NET 1.0 and 1.1. While the new formats clearly aid MSBuild, they will also aid NAnt significantly.

MSBuild is extensible in a strikingly familiar way to NAnt. NAnt relies on the community and regular contributors for extension. MSBuild does not need this community—Microsoft has enough of its own community to extend its tool—but there may be a greater sense of community for NAnt for all the usual noncorporate, open source reasons.

NAnt has a big advantage in its adoption. Currently it owns its market and will likely maintain significant loyalty in a genuinely loyal sense, but also in the sense that it may not be easy to remove from development teams' processes even given the similarity of the syntax!

Regardless of the outcome, the effect of NAnt on the delivery phase of the software development life cycle is profound and the good work is for all to see. Delivery tools are about to hit the mainstream (if they have not already) and the development community will wonder how they managed without them.

Other Directions

When my mind is allowed to wander, I think about how things should really be. Random thoughts I have had on the things I would like to see are as follows:

Visualization and IDE integration. Given that NAnt is an XML-based system and operates in a workflow, it would make a lot of sense to a have a visual editor for the delivery process. I am not talking about an application such as NAntPad, but something like the DTS designer. The ability to select a palette of tasks and hang them together with workflow icons, add environment information, and so on would be great for architects of these processes. I am not sure it would add to your productivity with NAnt, but it would clarify a lot of the more complex build scenarios when you are developing them and help you explain them to the development team. Similarly, integrating this pipeline into the IDE (such as VS .NET) is also worthwhile. I think that the solution build functionality of the IDE should be tied to a defined pipeline (if desired). Perhaps MSBuild will bring this to the table when it arrives.

Macro-containers. The joys of "XCOPY deployment" are a lingering memory. .NET has delivered much of what it promised in this area, but I cannot help feeling that something is missing. Since .NET, I am sure that you cannot have failed to notice the sheer number of assemblies that are used from application to application, perhaps simply because it is so easy to do so. One assembly per architectural layer? No problem. Reference loads of third-party assemblies and copy them locally? No problem. The issue is that when dealing with an application, the unpackaged and installed form has no real "identity" other than the folder structures it occupies. My feeling is that delivery of an application, and the handling of applications through the delivery chain, would be better managed through some kind of macro-container, representing the application as a whole. This differs from an installation package (such as an MSI); it would be able to maintain data about an application that could be used by the system or by a developer to pull out information about an application. For example, the application should "know" which are its test assemblies.

This is not just about databases; it is about assets that are not controlled as part of the system solution: DTS packages, media assets, and so forth. Perhaps my vague ideas on macro-containers tie into this area as well.

Conclusion

Working with NAnt and CruiseControl.NET is a great pleasure. The flexibility and power of these frameworks and the possibilities they introduce for defining the process in a formal way should not be underestimated. Their ability to remove the tedium of certain processes from the developer and to ensure compliance is also excellent.

At the same time, these tools highlight flaws and immaturity in the delivery phase of a software solution. This makes me a little sad but hopeful for the future.

Things will improve, particularly as Microsoft gets its act together and begins to deliver tools in this area, which has the tendency to push the world in a specific direction.

Delivery processes are a huge consideration. You can achieve efficient, consistent processes now with planning, effort, and the correct tools by your side.

A Fistful of Tools

Throughout the book, we have used (or will use, depending on whether you have jumped to the end of the book to reveal whodunit) a variety of tools for a variety of purposes. Some of these are stand-alone pieces of software such as a text editor or Visual Studio .NET, but others such as NAnt have a number of dependencies. Some of these are introduced as a matter of choice, but others are selected to address versioning issues among the various software packages.

In this appendix, we discuss the tools we have used directly (and indirectly) to implement the delivery processes.

Software Dependencies

As just mentioned, constructing an environment for automated delivery introduces several dependencies and interactions among software packages. Figure A-1 demonstrates a simplified view of the build server.

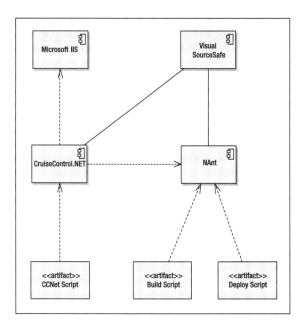

Figure A-1. *Simplified view of software dependencies*

In the diagram, I have shown only the most relevant, specific features of software used for the delivery process. The implication is that the .NET Framework is also a dependency.

Figure A-2 shows a fuller view of the dependencies on all the software used to deliver the specific processes we introduce throughout the book. In particular, you can see the dependencies on, for example, NUnit, the Red Gate SQL Bundle and FxCop; some of these dependencies are introduced through our own extension of NAnt, and others through NAnt itself (such as the NUnit version dependency). I have not marked other dependencies in Figure A-2 if NAnt comes with the relevant assembly, but you should also be aware that your own version may not be the same as the embedded NAnt-based version. For example, I did not show NAnt using NDoc since NAnt comes with the relevant NDoc assembly, but keep in mind that your version of NDoc may not be the same.

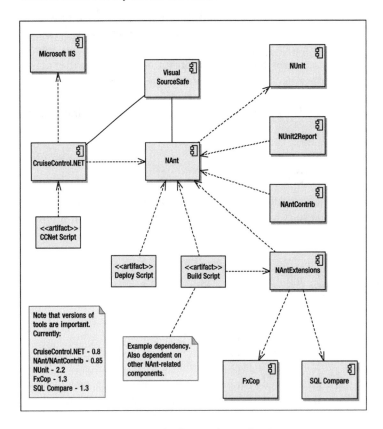

Figure A-2. *Expanded view of software dependencies*

Tool Organization

Given the software dependencies, and the number of tools that we could reasonably apply in the delivery process (we did not touch upon the use of tools for test coverage, or software metrics that could be applied in the analysis stages), it makes sense to follow some kind of organizational strategy for tools.

My general strategy is to organize my tools under a single folder, using the name of the software as the next folder, and then the version of the software as the next folder. This arrangement allows me to add multiple versions of software and change configuration in an obvious way so that, for example, I can test my existing scripts with a new version of NAnt very easily—particularly when configuring EditPlus to handle this (as you will see in a moment). Figure A-3 shows an example of this configuration from my current desktop.

Figure A-3. *Organizing tools effectively*

Automating the Organization

Bearing in mind the effective organization of tools you are using and the scripts and assets of the delivery processes themselves, and taking into account our newfound expertise with a tool such as NAnt, it may not take long to see the possibilities for the automation of the creation of the entire delivery environment using NAnt.

In his book, *Open Source .NET Development: Programming with NAnt, NUnit, NDoc, and More*, Brian Nantz introduces a series of scripts used to obtain his array of open source tools on a regular basis. You could use his approach as a basis for obtaining your own downloads, and then expand it to the creation or update of an environment automatically. I could have done something similar as part of this book, but instead I have outlined in the following script the steps for configuring a desktop to operate the code examples in this book automatically. Organizing the contents of the package involves a zip file called BuildServer.zip, which contains a batch file for triggering the build script, a folder containing the minimum NAnt assemblies for the script to run, and another zip file called Environment.zip. This second zip file contains the scripts for the build server and the tools that allow the server to function. Figure A-4 shows the BuildServer.zip file contents after unzipping, and Figure A-5 shows the basic layout of the Environment.zip file.

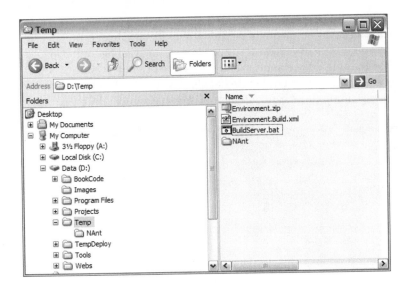

Figure A-4. *BuildServer.zip contents*

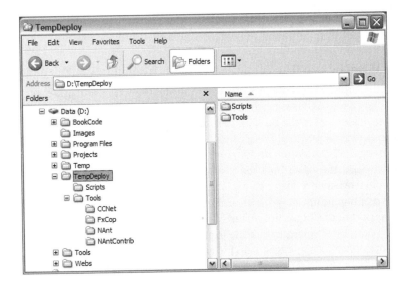

Figure A-5. *Environment.zip contents*

With these assets, the script to prepare the build server looks like the following. Comments inside the script describe the actions I included as well as some that are missing but possibly needed. The script is a useful starting point for completing your own build server setup.

```xml
<?xml version="1.0" encoding="utf-8"?>
<project name="CCNet Server Build" default="help">

<property name="build.drive" value="E"/>
<property name="build.area" value="${build.drive}:\BuildArea"/>
<property name="build.tools" value="${build.drive}:\BuildTools"/>
<property name="build.deploy" value="${build.drive}:\BuildDeploy"/>
<property name="build.scripts" value="${build.drive}:\BuildScripts"/>
<property name="build.server" value="localhost:80"/>

<target name="go" depends="CleanUp, Initialize, RemoveOld, PositionNew, Configure,
CleanUp"/>

<target name="Initialize">
    <!--Make the temporary deployment folder-->
    <mkdir dir="${build.deploy}"/>

    <!--Unzip the environment contents-->
    <unzip zipfile="Environment.zip" todir="${build.deploy}"/>

    <!--There may be a need to preserve the existing assets?-->
</target>

<target name="RemoveOld">
    <!-- Remove IIS Virtual Directories -->
    <deliisdir iisserver="${build.server}" vdirname="ccnet/files"
               failonerror="false"/>
    <deliisdir iisserver="${build.server}" vdirname="ccnet"
               failonerror="false"/>

    <!-- Remove the Tools -->
    <delete dir="${build.tools}" failonerror="false"/>

    <!-- Remove the Scripts -->
    <delete dir="${build.scripts}" failonerror="false"/>
</target>

<target name="PositionNew">
    <!-- Create the process folders -->
    <mkdir dir="${build.area}\source" failonerror="false"/>
    <mkdir dir="${build.area}\output" failonerror="false"/>
    <mkdir dir="${build.area}\reports" failonerror="false"/>
    <mkdir dir="${build.area}\docs" failonerror="false"/>
    <mkdir dir="${build.area}\distribution" failonerror="false"/>
    <mkdir dir="${build.area}\publish" failonerror="false"/>
```

```xml
    <!-- Create the tools folder-->
    <mkdir dir="${build.tools}" failonerror="false"/>

    <!-- Create the script folder-->
    <mkdir dir="${build.scripts}" failonerror="false"/>

    <!-- Move the tools into position-->
    <move todir="${build.tools}">
        <fileset basedir="${build.deploy}\Tools">
            <include name="**/*" />
        </fileset>
    </move>

    <!-- Move the scripts into position-->
<!-- COULD INCLUDE A FILTERSET TO ACCOUNT FOR DIFFERING LOCATIONS OF TOOLS -->
    <move todir="${build.scripts}">
        <fileset basedir="${build.deploy}\Scripts">
            <include name="**/*" />
        </fileset>
    </move>

    <!-- Replace the existing publishing information if necessary-->
</target>

<target name="Configure">
    <!-- Set up the IIS Virtual Directories-->
    <mkiisdir
        iisserver="${build.server}"
        dirpath="${build.tools}\ccnet\0.7\webdashboard"
        vdirname="ccnet" defaultdoc="default.aspx" enabledefaultdoc="true"/>
    <mkiisdir
        iisserver="${build.server}"
        dirpath="${build.area}\Publish"
        vdirname="ccnet/files" enabledirbrowsing="true"/>

    <!-- Set up Environment Variables ?-->
</target>

<target name="CleanUp">
    <!-- Remove the temporary deployment folder-->
    <delete dir="${build.deploy}" failonerror="false" />
</target>

<target name="help">
    <echo message="This script creates a new Build Server environment."/>
</target>
</project>
```

You might find, as I certainly have, that this is in fact one of the first scripts you should get working for the introduction of the automated delivery processes into a production environment. If you are feeling especially clever, you could configure CC.Net to perform this procedure automatically on a periodic basis.

Core Tools

We will now discuss the core tools needed to follow all of the examples in the book and to implement the suggested processes.

NAnt

NAnt can be obtained from `http://nant.sourceforge.net`. Also at that URL you will find links to a knowledgebase wiki, developer and user mailing lists, and current documentation. NAnt is a very active project, and if you are working seriously with the tool you should at least be reading about current issues and upcoming directions from the mailing lists, if not getting involved in them. The authors of NAnt are extremely responsive and helpful.

NAntContrib

The same is true of NAntContrib. Produced for the most part by the same team, NAntContrib contains tasks that are useful but generally applicable for a specific implementation of, for example, a source control system: if you contribute to the NAnt code, this is likely where it will end up. There is some blurring of the lines between the differences of NAnt and NAntContrib task criteria, but regardless, you will need both sets of tools. NAntContrib can be obtained from `http://nantcontrib.sourceforge.net`.

CruiseControl.NET

Our continuous integration provider of choice can be obtained from `http://ccnet.➥ thoughtworks.com`. Also at this URL you will find current documentation, links to user and developer mailing lists, and so on. Everything that can be said of NAnt can be said of CCNet in terms of activity and responsiveness of the development team.

Red Gate SQL Bundle

Unlike NAnt and CCNet, SQL Bundle is a commercial package produced by Red Gate Software. You can download a 14-day trial version from the web site—`www.red-gate.com`—for using the custom database tasks described in Chapter 8. The enormous utility in these tools will probably convince you to purchase a license or two. Red Gate is also the producer of the Ants profiling and load-testing software. Red Gate has a good community atmosphere, and with a small development team, the company is genuinely interested in feedback on its products.

CodeSmith

Finally, CodeSmith, the work of Eric Smith, is available at www.ericjsmith.net. It comes in two flavors: a commercial studio offering with an IDE and some helpful utilities—a must if you are using it seriously—and a free template runner. You can work with all of the examples in the book with the free edition, but once again, you may find that you become hooked on the tool very quickly. I know I did.

Script Editing

Running NAnt from the command line is fun for a while, as is trying to remember all of the task names and their attributes. Eventually, though, it is a good idea to select a favorite text editor to help out. An obvious choice is Visual Studio .NET to build and run the scripts. It is possible to perform NAnt editing using VS .NET, but I have found it generally unsatisfactory and cumbersome. NAnt feels unwieldy when the VS .NET editor is used on it; it may just be a personal thing, though. On the other hand, since a NAnt schema is available you can gain IntelliSense inside VS .NET (which can be a big plus) by placing the XML Schema in the relevant folders in the VS .NET installation. You can find full details on this at http://nant.sourceforge.net/wiki/index.php/FAQ.

As you can tell, I prefer something more lightweight than VS .NET for script work. I am a big fan of EditPlus. I have owned a copy ever since I used to hang around on the Microsoft VBScript newsgroups and learned that Michael Harris, VBScript guru, recommended it. I think it is one of my favorite tools, and all I really do with it is use the edit window. You can download a trial or purchase a license at www.editplus.com.

So, having eschewed the power of VS .NET in favor of the lightweight EditPlus, I also configure EditPlus to run NAnt inside the editor. This is a fairly simple thing to do.

Firstly, select Configure Tools, as shown in Figure A-6, which also shows the EditPlus window.

Next, set the tool settings, as shown in Figure A-7. Note that I have set NAnt to run the version of NAnt that I have placed in my PATH environment variable, but as discussed earlier, if you are using multiple versions of NAnt side by side, you need various tool configurations, not just one. Also, note that the name of the file to run is automatically supplied to the NAnt executable. Finally, note that I have set the hotkey to prompt for additional arguments, and to capture the output in the output window.

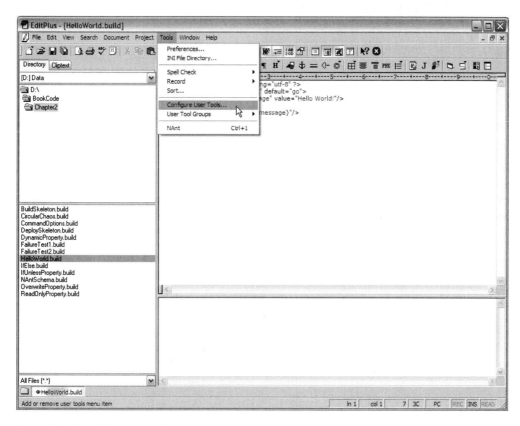

Figure A-6. *The EditPlus application*

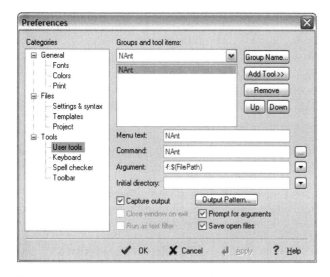

Figure A-7. *Configuring NAnt in EditPlus*

When I press Ctrl+1, I am prompted for arguments. Once I enter those arguments and click OK, the output appears in the output window, as can be seen in the bottom right of Figure A-8.

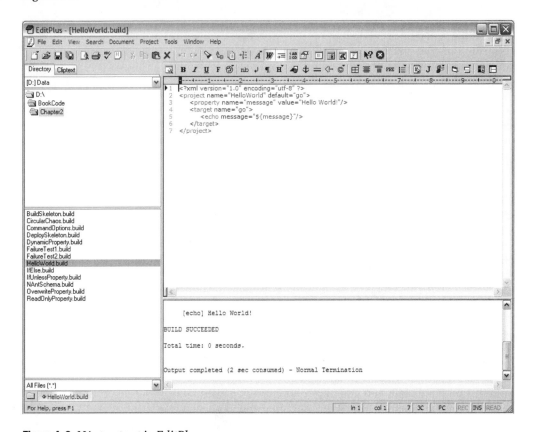

Figure A-8. *NAnt output in EditPlus*

With these steps complete, working with NAnt becomes even more fun. You can do almost everything in the EditPlus environment rather than having to fire up command lines.

Other Tools

These are a selection of other tools that you may need to run the full examples in the book, or that we used to produce analysis and artifacts in the production of the book.

FxCop. This is the Microsoft code analyzer with an extensible rules framework for verifying that your code complies with Microsoft's own internal standards. It is available at www.gotdotnet.com.

NUnit. This is the de facto framework for unit testing in .NET. It is available at http://nunit.org.

NUnit2Report. This is a helpful NAnt task for producing better reports on NUnit logs than the ones that accompany NAnt. It is available at http://nunit2report.sourceforge.net.

NDoc. This is a great utility for the production of documentation files in an MSDN style (among other styles). You can download the full tool from http://ndoc.sourceforge.net, but keep in mind that the relevant libraries are packaged with NAnt already. I recommend that you obtain the full tool, though.

Reflector. This is a must-have for any .NET developer; you can disassemble and review .NET libraries in a snap in a way that ILDASM could only dream of. It has a raft of available add-ins and is constantly being refined. Reflector is available from www.aisto.com/roeder along with some other great tools—particularly the "Boulderdash"-clone game!

Enterprise Architect. You have to use this fantastically feature-rich UML modeling IDE to experience its depth. It costs a bit but nothing in comparison to its rivals, such as Rational XDE. It is available as a 30-day trial from www.sparxsystems.com.au.

Together .NET. While I use Enterprise Architect for serious modeling, Together .NET is great for more agile programming. It is effectively a visualizer for the code models, but it allows superb code production through drag-and-drop class modeling and the like, and it includes automated refactoring features and lets you generate sequence diagrams. It is available from www.borland.com.

Refactory. Another great refactoring tool, Refactory also has metrics information and is useful for rapid identification of code complexity. The metrics can be called from the command line, which means they can be automated in NAnt. Refactory is available from www.xtreme-simplicity.net

Resharper. This is like IntelliSense, except it is so much better—and it keeps your code tidy. Resharper is available from JetBrains at www.jetbrains.com.

APPENDIX B

■ ■ ■

NAnt Sweeper

To round off the book, it seemed like a good idea to consider a task that NAnt really is not suited for. After many chapters of emphatic praise for the tool, what task should be considered a "bridge too far"?

This was a tough challenge indeed, but my erstwhile colleague, Alex Hildyard, came up with an answer. Over the period of a few months, Alex struggled to translate my vague ideas into a workable process and sharpened our existing applications into deliverable products, so it was always likely that he would go "over the edge" at some point.

Alex writes:

Having played around with NAnt for a while, I had the impulse to do something eccentric with it. This was partly to test its limits, and also to show that Build Controllers can be geeks too. I settled on Minesweeper for several reasons. Firstly, it's a small, self-contained puzzle, and therefore even a prolix language like NAnt should be able to express it in a couple of hundred lines. Secondly, the algorithm at the heart of Minesweeper—the logic that uncovers a jagged block of mine-free squares—is easy to formulate as either an iterative or a recursive rule, and therefore it should be well suited to a declarative language like NAnt. Finally, Minesweeper is a game with which most of us are familiar, so a NAnt port would be likely to require minimal explanation.

However, the undertaking did present a number of challenges. An obvious hurdle was that NAnt knows nothing natively about graphics or user interaction. That said, in theory there's nothing to stop you coding a WinForms application and persuading NAnt to run it as a "script" task. But this didn't strike me as very sporting, so I tried to find a way of implementing Minesweeper without recourse to script. Since NAnt allows you to manipulate XML, albeit in a primitive fashion, I decided to delegate the GUI to whatever browser was installed, using XSLT to mark up the game grid and handle basic game logic (for example, displaying a smiley-with-sunglasses when you win the game). The biggest problem here was to find a way to concatenate and process the list of squares that needed to be uncovered, while working with global variables. My solution was to use a string of coordinate pairs, and then to uncover all the squares in the string successively. The method in question (revealSquares) calls itself recursively until it determines that no further changes are required. Ultimately though, I had to admit defeat when it came to the comparatively simple task of soliciting user input and getting the resultant row and column into NAnt variables. Accordingly NAnt Sweeper does include a single script block, although it does little more than read a couple of integers from the command line. I did consider one other possible way of doing things which would have made this unnecessary. This would have involved modifying the XML file so that the board was embedded in a form, and clicking on a square caused the form to repost itself to the server with the row and column and a request for a ".build" file in the query string. You could then open IIS and configure ".build" as a custom MIME type which simply passed the row and column to the NAnt script for execution, and then piped back the "minefield.xml" file when the script had finished executing. But not everyone runs IIS, and I thought the command line version was sufficient to make the point. Anything further, as they say, is left as an exercise for the reader.

Ladies and gentlemen, we give you NAnt Sweeper. NAnt Sweeper is a port of the Minesweeper game that comes with Microsoft Windows. The main points of this application are as follows:

The game relies on a NAnt script and some script tasks to handle the input of coordinates into the Minesweeper map.

It uses an XML file to maintain the map information and uses an XLST style sheet to transform the map into an HTML version of the Minesweeper interface.

The `<xmlpoke>` task is used judiciously to alter the status of the map.

The `minefield.bat` file is called during each turn to reload and re-style the XML-based map file.

You can have some fun investigating Alex's work on your own, but it's even more fun to play the game itself!

Playing NAnt Sweeper

To begin a new game, simply double-click on the `NAntSweeper.bat` file. The NAnt Sweeper screen, shown in Figure B-1, will appear with no squares uncovered.

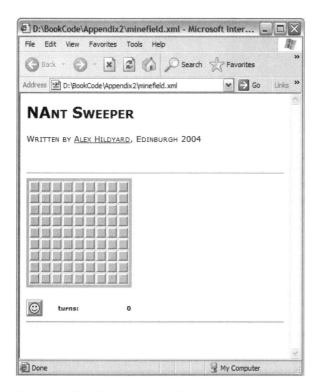

Figure B-1. *The NAnt Sweeper GUI*

A console window will appear and prompt you to enter a row and then a column number. In this instance, I will choose Row 1, Column 4, as shown in Figure B-2.

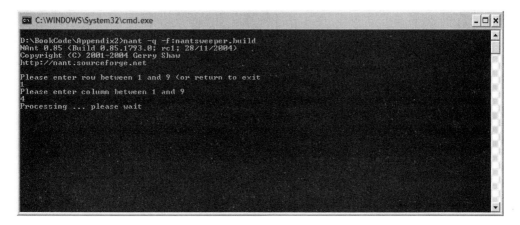

Figure B-2. *Inputting map coordinates into the NAnt Sweeper console UI*

NAnt may take a little time to process the changes because of the number of recursive calls that may be required to perform the reveal (remember, we did mention that this may not be the best use of NAnt). Once the processing is complete, the GUI will be updated, as shown in Figure B-3.

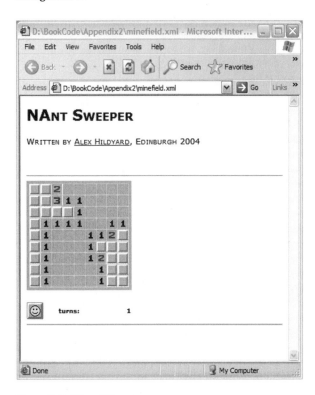

Figure B-3. *Phew! No mine.*

This time, I will choose Row 1, Column 2. As you can see in Figure B-4, I have failed to clear this map. Ah well, I was never very good at such games.

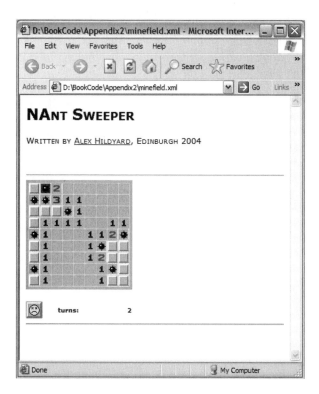

Figure B-4. *Oh dear! Game over.*

As you can imagine, we have had endless fun with NAnt Sweeper. I hope it will be included as part of the regular NAnt package sometime soon. Great job, Alex!

Index

Numbers and Symbols

- (dash)
  for preventing execution of individual
    targets, 41
{} (curly brackets)
  use of in XSLT vs. use in NAnt, 309

A

*A Guide to Software Configuration
    Management* (Artech House, 2000)
  by Alexis Leon, 24
Advanced .NET Remoting (Apress, 2002)
  by Ingo Rammer, 166
aggressive library management
  folders used in, 143
*Agile Database Techniques: Effective
    Strategies for the Agile Software
    Developer* (Wiley, 2003)
  by Scott Ambler, 250, 277
analyze task
  planning for database integration, 229
app.config file
  for configuration of VSSManager
    application, 159
  in Etomic.ShareTransformer.Tests
    assembly, 258
applyLabel attribute
  in the sourcecontrol element, 179–180
artifactDirectory element
  in ccnet.config file, 178
<asminfo> [NAnt] task
  generating an assemblyinfo.cs style file
    with, 74–75
  for updating CommonAssemblyInfo.cs
    file, 107–108
assemblies
  versioning for Transformer application,
    106–108
assembly names
  importance of naming for the solution
    and project name, 141
asset management
  for database integration, 254
assets and source control
  in configuration management, 13–14
<attrib> [NAnt] task
  for allowing a build file to change file
    attributes, 71
  for making CommonAssemblyInfo.cs
    read-write, 108
attributes
  using for tasks, 61–62
automated build
  vs. continuous integration (CI), 168
automated delivery, 6, 8–9
  environment as core aspect for successful,
    9–12
  as part of Design to Deliver, 18
  standardization as crucial aspect of, 9–11
automated integration task, 237–249
automated x process
  defined, 23

B

basedir attribute
  of Project node, 42
best practices
  overview, 327–329
*Beyond Software Architecture: Creating and
    Sustaining Winning Solutions*
    (Addison-Wesley, 2003)
  by Luke Hohmann, 24
"Bob Leaves!" scenario, 3, 5
BooleanValidator attribute, 62
BooleanValidatorAttribute class
  code revealed by opening the code to, 204
Brian Nantz
  *Open Source .NET Development:
    Programming with NAnt, NUnit,
    NDoc, and More* (Addison-Wesley,
    2004) by, 58
build files
  comparing, 146–148
  creating, 145–152
  creating for Transformer application,
    100–101
  differences between, 146–148
  feed file for identification of assemblies,
    305–306
  general organization of, 145
  naming convention properties, 146
  project node as root node of, 42
  refactoring, 148–152
  structures and elements in construction
    of, 41–46
  various properties defined and used in,
    46–52

Build folders
    structures used in Transformer
        application, 99
build process
    defined, 23
    for delivery scenario solutions, 137
    for Etomic delivery process, 21–22
build scripts
    combining into one self-contained, fully-
        generated script, 304–305
    for the Etomic.ShareTransformer
        application, 255–257
    for loading all noncore assemblies
        separately, 255
    Web projects vs. Windows projects, 141
build server
    script to prepare, 341–342
build skeleton
    for Etomic, 53–56
build system use case, 97
Build target
    example of, 110–111
build tasks
    function of, 74–81
build use case, 323–324
Build.Common.xml file
    the beginnings of, 150
    for code generation, 304
Build.Core.xml file
    amending, 183–185
    calling a target called ci in, 181
    code for amending the solution.name line,
        148
    for code generation, 304
    creating, 148
Builder account
    importance of standardizing for VSS
        databases, 99
Builder.CodeSmith.xml script
    forming Builder.XSLT.xml from, 317
    that runs command-line version of
        CodeSmith, 316
Builder.XSLT.xml file
    code for including in code-generation
        process, 317–318
    forming from Builder.CodeSmith.xml
        code, 317
-buildfile, -f option, 32
BuildServer.zip file
    contents of, 340

C
CalculateScript() method
    in <dbAutoIntegrate> task, 247
<call> [NAnt] task
    calling a target within a build file with,
        65–67

case study
    examining the application, 91–96
    introduction, 91
    simple Transformer sample application,
        91–133
    source code for Transformer application, 91
CCNet. *See also* CruiseControl.NET (CCNet)
    basic configuration, 175–176
    build file, 180–181
    enhancing, 194–196
    examining, 172–175
    examining the cctray application, 189–190
    examining the dashboard, 187–189
    examining the state file, 190
    function of cctray application in, 175
    function of server component in, 172–173
    function of web dashboard application in,
        174–175
    obtaining the application from the web
        site, 175
    source code, 195
    source control databases supported by,
        180
    using to provide continuous integration
        capabilities, 329
    web application build log, 194
    web site component of, 173–174
CCNet build log
    example of, 188
CCNet dashboard
    examining, 187–189
    example of, 188
    showing the code generation project, 313
CCNet instance
    setting up CodeSmith instance as new,
        315–318
CCNet server
    attempting a build, 192
    configuring, 177–183
CCNet server console, 187
ccnetadmin.config
    pointing the CodeSmith instance to,
        315–316
ccnet.config file, 172
    for configuring the CCNet server, 177–183
    general settings, 178
    producing a single containing all project
        information, 290–291
    target for code generation, 296–298
    trigger options, 178–179
ccnet.cst template
    after changes, 300–302
CCNetServer-CodeSmith.bat file
    CCNet admin instance, 316
ccnet.xslt.config file
    making it work with the XSLT framework,
        317

cctray application
  continuous integration (CI), 170–172
  examining, 189–190
  function of in CCNet, 175
  settings, 189
cctray icon
  explanation of colors of, 189–190
Checkout/Get target
  function of, 104–105
CI. *See* continuous integration (CI)
ci target
  calling from the nant build element, 185
class libraries
  swapping Web projects for, 142
"Clean As You Go" mantra, 11
Clean target
  for cleaning out existing content, 103–104
  core aspects of, 104
closing thoughts, 319–335
CM. *See* configuration management (CM)
*Code Complete: A Practical Handbook of
    Software Construction* (Microsoft
    Press, 1993)
  by Steve McConnell, 24
code example
  of <csc> [NAnt] task from NAnt
      documentation, 80
  for adding a debug property setting, 105
  for adding a go target to the core file, 148
  for adding a new project element to
      ccnet.config file, 220–221
  for adding a new target called database,
      259
  adding FileSet structures to <fxcop> task,
      212
  adding output information to <fxcop>
      task, 211
  adding sys.version.prior property to
      <version> task, 206
  adding the CREATE and migration scripts
      to database target, 260
  for altering configuration in some way, 131
  amending the Build.Core.xml file, 183–185
  for amending the Build.Core.xml
      solution.name line, 148
  for applying the required style sheet to the
      XML report, 115
  for attaching outputs to the CCNet build
      log, 182
  for automatic production of FxCop reports
      for assemblies, 76
  of the beginnings of Build.Common.xml,
      150
  for Build file Checkout/Get target, 104–105
  for Build file Clean target, 103–104

build script for Etomic.ShareTransformer.
    Test assembly, 255–257
build script for loading all noncore
    assemblies separately, 255
of Build target using <solution> task, 110
CalculateScript() method in
    <dbAutoIntegrate> task, 247
for calling installutil, 163
for calling the ci target from the nant build
    element, 185
for calling the specific build file for the
    specific solution, 149
changes for making the ccnet.xslt.config
    file work, 317
for changing the get target to obtain assets
    via HTTP, 186
of CodeSmith input file, 314–315
of CodeSmith input file for build and
    deploy scripts, 298–302
of CodeSmith templates, 283–285
command line for running deploy script,
    272
of the configuration step for database
    deployment, 266
for configuring a project with a specific
    labeling strategy, 181
for copying assets into the environment,
    130
for creating an actual target, 87–88
for creating a new folder tree, 73
for creating Build.Core.xml file, 148
for creating manual SQL script processing
    task, 232–233
for creating Transformer Build file,
    100–101
for <dbAutoIntegrate> task, 241
of debug run from the deployment script,
    132–133
of declarative code in CodeSmith API, 288
defining a function that returns a string,
    86–87
for defining a property, 46
demonstrating the use of a collection as a
    property, 284
of the deploy file changes for the <fxcop>
    task, 218–220
for deploy file for the Transformer
    application, 129
of the deploy script with database
    deployment, 263–273
for deploying database changes, 265–266
of the DoCreateScript and DoAlterScripts
    methods, 245–246
for ensuring that a log file is defined, 38
for ensuring that the assembly
    environment exists, 153

for error handling, 102–103

for the Etomic build skeleton, 53–56

for the Etomic deploy skeleton, 53–56

ExecuteScript() method in <dbAutoIntegrate> task, 247

extracting the publish steps from web and Windows/assembly build files, 150–152

for fail.test target, 113

for a fileset type, 63

of a filterchain construct, 64

for fixing help target to pass solution.stub property at runtime, 148

of format for storing Load XML File task in project folder, 274

full script for the version1 target, 109–110

for full test target, 115–116

of <fxcop> task implementation in our build file, 210

of <fxcop> task usage, 209–210

general information from running build file, 119

for general settings in ccnet.config file, 177–178

for generating a file with an XML file input, 286–287

for generation of the Transformer application documentation, 116–117

for getting the assets of Etomic.Library.Transformer.Deploy.xml and their repackaging, 153

for go target that accounts for new dependency, 110

for handling XML file for input, 286

of <ifnot> [NAnt] task for calling a function, 85

implementation of serializable type in CodeSmith template, 306

for implementing the Boolean overwrite property, 204

for implementing the <fxcop> task, 211–214

for including a Boolean debug property, 105

for including XSLT version in code-generation process, 317–318

for incrementing build number of the version number, 105

injection of data into top-level variables in CodeSmith template, 307–308

for loading a set of assemblies, 69

for loading NAntContrib Tasks, 105

for loading template files and compilation of template, 289–290

for looping function to deploy database changes, 270

for the main method for the CodeSmith code template files, 290–291

for making CommonAssemblyInfo.cs read-write, 108

for manual SQL script processing task, 231

for mapping the URL of a web project, 79

for migrating from version 1.0.2.0 to 1.0.4.0, 271

of more complex "Hello World" script, 30–31

moving database target content into databaseincrement target, 269–272

nant build type in CCNet, 181

of NAnt command-line usage form, 30

for NAnt "database" element, 242–243

for nesting <property> elements into the <nant> task, 205

for obtaining and unpackaging assets to the work area, 130

output from <fxcop> task testing script, 215

of output from using with -quiet, 34

to output the XSD to a file of your choosing, 41–42

OutputAssembly type in the CodeSmith template, 307

for overriding ProgramArguments for <fxcop> task, 213

for overriding the ExecuteTask method for <fxcop> task, 213–214

overriding the ExecuteTask method on <dbAutoIntegrate> task, 245

for overriding the ProgramFileName for <fxcop> task, 212

for overwriting the AssemblyVersion attribute, 106–107

for placing assemblies in folders with relevant names, 154

for pointing the CodeSmith instance to ccnetadmin.config, 315–316

pointing the unit test configuration to the integration test instance, 261

of properties script with partial output example, 47–48

for properties to run the Etomic.Library.Transformer.Deploy.xml file, 153

for providing default debugging value of sys.version property, 105

providing switches for <fxcop> task, 212–213

for providing updated version number to a property, 205

for publish target, 117–118

for publishing the log to CCNet web site and dashboards, 182–183

for recalling the test target and rerunning the unit tests, 261–262
for refactoring settings, 128
for regenerating the VSSManager interop assembly, 162
for removing properties from specific file, 149
for removing targets from core file, 149
for running the Transformer application build file, 119
of script for generating multiple files in XSLT, 295
script for running NUnit tests, 111
of script for NUnit report property change, 112
of ScriptMain method for XSLT output files, 293
for setting DefaultLogger to be a listener, 37
setting up attributes and elements of <dbAutoIntegrate> task, 243–245
for setting up the <dbAutoIntegrate> task test databases, 248–249
showing a straightforward get of some source code, 84
showing typical use of <style> [NAnt] task, 81
of a simple NAnt "Hello World" script, 28–29
skeleton for Builder.XSLT.xml, 292
for source control element, 179
for SQL script processing task <execute> method, 234
of standard build file script changes for <fxcop> task, 216–218
of a standard library, console, or Windows solution build, 79
for starting VSSManager Windows service, 163
for state file, 190
for telling NAnt which version to deploy, 129
for testing the <fxcop> task, 214
for testing the TestDB-Integration script, 235
from TransformationTests.cs, 258–259
for Transformer application unit test, 93
for updating and linking the CommonAssemblyInfo.cs file, 107–108
for Users-AddPostcode.sql script, 235
Users.sql CREATE script for a table Users, 234–235
using <attrib> [NAnt] task to change file attributes, 71
using <call> [NAnt] to call a target within a build file, 65–67

using <copy> [NAnt] task, 72
using <delete> [NAnt] task, 72
using <exec> [NAnt] task, 76
using <move> [NAnt] task, 72
using a FileSet, 204–205
using <asminfo> [NAnt] task, 74–75
using -buildfile, -f command-line option, 32
using build file to maintain common properties across projects, 67–68
using -D (property override) option, 35–36
using -debug command-line option, 33–34
using -defaultframework, -k command-line option, 32
for using -find in NAnt, 34–35
using FxCop, 111
using <get> [NAnt], 74
using if and unless properties, 49
using ifelse property, 45
using <ndoc> [NAnt] task, 77
using <nunit2> [NAnt] task, 78
using <nunit2> attribute to include an application configuration file, 252
using -quiet command-line option, 34
using the <copy> task with the overwrite attribute, 203
using the <fail> [NAnt] task, 118
for using the <fxcop> task, 221–222
using the <mkdir> task, 202–203
using the <mkiisdir> [NAntContrib] task, 76
using the notify target, 118
using the onfailure property, 51–52
using the <vsslabel> [NAntContrib] task, 84–85
using -verbose, -v command-line option, 32
using <vsscheckin> [NAntContrib] task, 84
for using XmlLogger, 37
using <xmlpeek> [NAnt] and <xmlpoke> [NAnt] tasks, 82–83
using <zip> [NAnt] and<unzip> [NAnt] tasks, 82
of VBScript code for Load XML File task, 274–275
version2 for updating the VSS database, 109
for viewing the Transformer application assembly version, 123–124
for the VSSManager configuration target, 163–166
for walking a directory tree preserving all other assets, 64
for wrapping up the VSS and filesystem settings, 180

WriteScript() method in
<dbAutoIntegrate> task, 247
of XML file for input to maintain master
information, 285
for XSLT ProduceBuildAndDeployFile
method, 294–295
for XSLT ProduceBuildAndDeployFiles
method, 294
for the XSLT ProduceCcnetConfigFile
method, 293
for XSLT TransformXml utility method,
293–294
code generation
build files, 304–309
managing automatically, 313–318
problems associated with and possible
resolutions, 279–281
targets for, 296–313
techniques comparison chart, 282
tools for the task, 281–282
using CodeSmith for, 281–282
using XSLT for, 281
why to use it, 279–281
Code Generation in Microsoft .NET
(Apress, 2004)
by Kathleen Dollard, 318
*Coder to Developer: Tools and Strategies
for Delivering Your Software*
(Sybex, 2004)
by Mike Gunderloy, 24, 58
CodeSmith
call code for running from the command
line, 313
collection editing in, 285
editing the XML selection, 287–288
generating multiple files, 288–292
investigating features of, 282–292
main method for code template files,
290–291
methods for loading template files and
compilation of template, 289–290
results of running input file from the
command line, 315
using an XML file for input, 285
using for code generation, 281–282
using properties to produce a template,
283–288
web site address, 344
CodeSmith IDE, 282–283
CodeSmith instance
setting up as a new CCNet instance,
315–318
CodeSmith template
implementation of in the serializable type,
306
injection of the data into top-level
variables, 307–308

input file for the build and deploy scripts,
298
OutputAssembly type code, 307
XSLT template syntax vs. CodeSmith
syntax in, 302–304
CodeSmith.CustomProperties.dll assembly
referencing in the XML file, 286
CodeSmith.Engine.dll assembly
referencing in the XML file, 286
command-line options
for NAnt, 30
CommonAssemblyInfo.cs
for overwriting the AssemblyVersion
attribute, 106–107
VS .NET setting, 140
company.name property
in build files, 146
complex scenarios
working with, 332
conditional statements
use of in NAnt, 44–46
conditional tasks
defined, 59
function of, 69–71
configuration
basic for CCNet, 175–176
configuration auditing
as part of configuration management, 13
configuration control
as part of configuration management, 13
configuration files
using Microsoft Configuration
Management Block to change, 253
using <xmlpoke> task for changing, 253
configuration identification
as part of configuration management, 12
configuration management (CM)
Alexis Leon's definition of, 12
assets and source control, 13–14
defined, 23
importance of a strong policy for, 12–15
configuration status control
as part of configuration management, 13
configuration step
example for database deployment, 266
configure target
for altering configuration in some way, 131
configure task
planning for database integration, 229
context
as part of Design to Deliver, 17
continuous integration (CI), 167–197
activities described in Martin Fowler
article on, 21–22
vs. automated build, 168–169
calling target from nant build element, 185
defined, 23, 167–170

direct and indirect advantages to using, 169–170

impact on database integration, 229–230

implementing for the sample applications, 172–194

managed process and formality and structure offered by, 170

as a potential process, 8–9

potential threats from implementing, 170

technical options, 170–172

trigger options for ccnet.config file, 178–179

using CruiseControl.NET (CCNet) for, 169

web site address for article by Martin Fowler, 24

control task
planning for database integration, 228

control tasks
for database integration, 251–252

<copy> [NAnt] task
function of, 71–73
looking at, 203–205
vs. <style> task, 63
use of fileset as the name for its fileset element, 63
use of the FileSet in, 204–205

core tools
needed to follow all examples in the book, 343–346

core.publish property
setting in deploy scripts, 186

createenvironments target
<makeiisdir> line in, 156

<cruisecontrol>
as root element in ccnet.config file, 177

CruiseControl.NET (CCNet)
using for continuous integration, 169
using to achieve CI in sample application, 170–172
view of web site, 171
web site address, 196, 343

CruiseControl.NET dashboard
four solutions operating within, 222

<csc> [NAnt] task
function of, 80–81

curly brackets ({})
use of in XSLT vs. use in NAnt, 309

D

-D (property override) option
importance of in NAnt, 30
using, 35–36

dash (-)
using to prevent execution of individual targets, 41

dashboard. *See* CCNet dashboard; web dashboard

data migration
requirements for different databases, 250

data synchronization
handling, 250–251

Data Transformation Services packages. *See* DTS (Data Transformation Services) packages

database deployment
deploy script with, 263–273

database integration, 225–277
adding a new target called database to build file, 259
asset management, 254
continuous integration process with, 230
control and configure tasks, 251–252
deployment considerations, 252–254
implementing, 254–273
output from running deploy script, 272–273
possible script for, 231
the problems with the database, 225–226
a process for, 251–254
required tasks, 228
scenarios, 226–227
solving problems within the delivery framework, 226
using the correct database instance for site deployment, 253

database scripts
organizing, 250

database target
adding CREATE and migration scripts to, 260
adding for database integration, 259
moving content of into the databaseincrement target, 269–272
output from for database integration, 262

database tasks
implementing, 231–251
planning, 228–230
required, 228

databaseincrement target
moving the content of the database target into, 269–272
output showing two executions of, 272–273

databases
local development model, 226
shared development model, 227

<dbAutoIntegrate> task
CalculateScript() method in, 247
code example for, 241
ExecuteScript() method in, 247
output from, 249
process diagram, 243
setting up the attributes and elements of, 243–245

WriteScript() method in, 247

<dbIntegrate> task
execution of the Users.sql and Users-Postcode.sql scripts by, 236

-debug option, 33–34

default attribute
of Project node, 42

-defaultframework, -k option
code example, 32

DefaultLogger option
for IBuilderLogger, 36–39

<delete> [NAnt] task
function of, 71–73

delivery process
defined, 23
for Etomic, 21–23

delivery processes
automated delivery, 6, 8–9
automation, 16–17
continuous integration as a potential process, 8–9
Design to Deliver, 17–20
effect of fear on, 15
environment rigidity problems with, 11
Etomic Build process, 21–22
Etomic deployment process, 22–23
a glossary for, 23
implementation of, 15
importance of consideration of delivery, 15
importance of management of environments, 11
importance of planning in, 14–15
vs. individual delivery, 2
issues of, 319–323
observation key points, 157
other considerations for, 329
segregated delivery, 6–7
simple delivery, 4–5
a solution for, 16–20
standards implemented, 328
summary of, 327–328
thoughts on, 9–15
tools used to implement, 337–347
why they are needed, 1–2

delivery standards
importance of bringing all systems into line with, 18–19

delivery tasks
defined, 60

depends attribute
of target node, 43–44

deploy file
core settings for in the Transformer application, 129–131
creating for the Transformer application, 128–131
examining the output, 132–133

deploy files
creating, 152–156

deploy process
defined, 23
for the delivery scenario solutions, 137
main differences in the three solutions, 137–138

deploy scripts
amending, 186
with database deployment, 263–273

deploy skeleton
for Etomic, 56–58

deploy system use case, 98, 324–325

deploy template
altering the master, 310–311

deployment files
function of, 310–313

deployment process
executing script and examining output, 132–133

deployment scenarios
for database integration, 252–253

description attribute
of target node, 43

Design to Deliver
advantages to implementation of, 20, 322–323
consequences of, 19, 321–322
context, 17
defined, 23
mechanics for implementation of, 18–19
motivation for, 17
process of automation, 17–20
publishing standards for implementation of, 18
the solution proposal, 320–323
steps involved in implementing, 320–321

DoAlterScripts method
function of in <dbAutoIntegrate> task, 245–246

DoCreateScript method
function of in <dbAutoIntegrate> task, 245–246

document target
handled through <ndoc> task, 116–117

documentation
VS .NET setting, 141

Dollard, Kathleen
Code Generation in Microsoft .NET (Apress, 2004) by, 318

Domain-Driven Design: Tackling Complexity in the Heart of Software (Addison-Wesley, 2003)
by Eric Evans, 24

Draco.NET
inspired by CruiseControl (Java version of CCNet), 172

web site address for, 196

DTS Compare tool
from Red Gate Software, Ltd., 237

DTS (Data Transformation Services) packages
considering for database integration, 273–277
organization, 274
standard configuration, 274
TestPackage initial global variables settings, 275

dynamic attribute
of properties, 46
script example, 47–48

Dynamic Properties
configuring, 275–276

E

<echo> [NAnt] task
function of, 81

Edit—>Replace
using to swap in property names, 128

EditPlus application
script editing tool, 344–345

element class
handling of common functionality by, 202

email publisher
for sending styled build log to interested parties, 182

Enterprise Architect
web site address, 347

environment
defined, 23

Environment.zip file
contents of, 340

error handling
in NAnt, 101–103

Essential SourceSafe (Hentzenwerke Publishing, 2001)
by Ted Roche, 24

Etomic
build process, 21–22, 52–58
the build skeleton, 53–56
a delivery process for, 21–23
deploy skeleton, 56–58
deployment process, 22–23
potential processes, 4–9
risks and complexity in, 2–4

Etomic.Library.Transformer
deploy process, 137–138

Etomic.Library.Transformer.Deploy.xml
ensuring that the environment for the assembly exists, 153
getting of assets and their repackaging, 153
properties to run, 153

Etomic.NAntEntensions solution
for creating the Visual Studio project, 210

Etomic.ShareTransformer application
assets, 263
the build script, 255–263
for implementing database integration, 254–273

Etomic.ShareTransformer v1.0.4.0
correctly deployed and configured, 269

Etomic.ShareTransformer.Deploy-CREATE.xml application
output from for database integration, 267–269

Etomic.ShareTransformer.Test assembly
app.config file in, 258

Etomic.ShareTransformer.Tests.dll.config
in the Etomic.ShareTransformer output directory, 258

Etomic.Transformer.Web
deploy process, 137–138

Etomic.Transformer.Web.Deploy.xml file
web deployment, 156

Etomic.Transformer.Win
deploy process, 137–138

Etomic.Transformer.Win.Deploy.xml file
Windows deployment, 155

Etomic.VSSManager
output from building, 161

Etomic.VSSManager.Build.xml file
assemblies required, 160
changes to the deployment script for, 163–166
creating, 160–166

Evans, Eric
Domain-Driven Design: Tackling Complexity in the Heart of Software (Addison-Wesley, 2003) by, 24

excludes and includes nodes
use of in filesets, 63

.exe vs. .dll
differences between build files, 147

<exec> [NAnt] task
function of, 76
hierarchy, 207
looking at particular behaviors of, 206–207
using to call the installutil utility, 163
using to execute FxCop at the command line, 111–112

ExecuteScript() method
in <dbAutoIntegrate> task, 247

ExecuteTask method
overriding, 213–214, 245

<ExternalProgramBase> task
using in the same way as the <exec> class, 207

F

-f (file) option
  importance of in NAnt, 30
fail target
  for notifying of failure in deploy process,
    131
<fail> [NAnt] task
  for passing a message upon failure, 118
  using as debugging task, 70
failonerror attribute
  as core aspect of Clean target code, 104
  of properties, 47
FailOnError property
  translation to the failonerror attribute, 61
fail.test target
  code for, 113
file functions
  NAnt, 85
file tasks
  defined, 59
  function of, 71–74
files
  generating multiple in CodeSmith,
    288–292
fileset
  used by <copy> as name for its fileset
    element, 63
FileSet class
  use of in the <copy> task, 204–205
fileset type
  pattern matching, 63
  used as a nested element by NAnt tasks,
    63–64
filesystem source control type
  for monitoring changes and triggering
    builds, 180
filterchain
  types and function of, 64
filterTrigger
  for CCNet configuration, 179
-find option, 34–35
folders
  used in aggressive library management,
    143
Force Build option
  in cctray application, 190
<foreach> [NAnt] task
  function of, 70
Fowler, Martin
  article on continuous integration (CI),
    21–22
FxCop
  differences between build files, 147
  web site address, 346
FxCop analysis
  running, 111–112

FxCop compliancy, 96
FxCop reports
  automatic production of for assemblies,
    76
  formatting, 115–116
<fxcop> task
  adding a new project element to the
    ccnet.config file, 220–221
  adding the solution to the build process,
    216–221
  creating, 208–222
  deploying file changes for, 218–220
  features included in, 208–209
  implementing, 210–214
  requirements, 208–209
  standard build file script changes for,
    216–218
  testing, 214–216
  using, 209–210, 221–222
FxCopCmd.exe options, 209

G

get target
  for obtaining and unpackaging assets to
    the work area, 130
<get> [NAnt] task
  function of, 74
go target
  adding to the Build.Core.xml file, 148
  code that accounts for the new
    dependency, 110
goals of this book, 319–323
Gunderloy, Mike
  Coder to Developer: Tools and Strategies
    for Delivering Your Software
    (Sybex, 2004) by, 24

H

"Hello World" example
  of a more complex script, 30–31
  of a simple NAnt script, 28–29
help target
  for adding notes to help to assist with
    script execution, 131
Hildyard, Alex
  NAnt Sweeper by, 349–353
Hippo.NET
  for operating a CI process, 172
  web site address for, 196
Hohmann, Luke
  Beyond Software Architecture: Creating
    and Sustaining Winning Solutions
    (Addison-Wesley, 2003) by, 24

I

-I option
  using, 36–39
IBuilderListener interface
  function of, 36–39
IBuilderLogger interface
  function of, 36–39
if attribute
  example of use of, 49
  of properties, 47
  of target node, 43–46
<if> [NAnt] task
  function of, 70–71
ifelse property
  using with target node, 45–46
<ifnot> [NAnt] task
  for calling a function, 85
  function of, 70–71
includes and excludes nodes
  using in filesets, 63
-indent option
  for tabbing output, 35
infiles
  used by <style> as name for its fileset
    element, 63
inheritall
  using to pass properties from first script to
    the second, 68
installutil
  using to install the Etomic.VSSManager
    Windows service, 162–163
Int32ValidatorAttribute class
  acceptance of a minimum and maximum
    value by, 204
integrate task
  planning for database integration, 229
integration databases
  data migration requirements for, 250
internalTrigger
  for CCNet configuration, 179
Interop.SourceSafeTypeLib.dll
  wrapper for the VSS library, 161

L

labeling
  VSS database, 109–110
labeller element
  for configuring a project with a specific
    labeling strategy, 181
Latest folder
  example of, 154
Leon, Alexis
  *A Guide to Software Configuration
    Management* (Artech House, 2000)
    by, 24

library build files
  vs. Web build files, 147
library management
  aggressive, 143–144
  fixing problems in the event of failure, 144
  nonaggressive method, 142–143
-listener option
  using, 36–39
LLBLGen Pro
  using for code generation, 281
Load XML File task
  format for storing in project folder, 274
  VBScript code for, 274–275
<loadtasks> [NAnt] task
  function of, 68–69
  using to load NAntContrib tasks, 104–105
local development database
  use of local SQL instances on developers'
    machines, 226–227
-logfile option
  using, 36–39
-logger option
  using, 36–39

M

management
  importance of for environments, 11–12
ManualDBTasks project
  example of, 232
master template
  sample output from running in
    CodeSmith, 312
McConnell, Steve
  *Code Complete: A Practical Handbook of
    Software Construction* (Microsoft
    Press, 1993) by, 24
mechanics
  for implementation of Design to Deliver,
    18–19
<merge> task
  for attaching outputs to the CCNet build
    log, 182
Microsoft Configuration Management Block
  using to change configuration files, 253
migration scripts
  automation of, 237–249
<mkdir> [NAnt] task
  for creating a new folder tree, 73
  investigating, 202–203
<mkiisdir> [NAntContrib] task
  function of, 76
motivation
  as part of Design to Deliver, 17
<move> [NAnt] task
  function of, 71–73

MSBuild
    being launched by Microsoft, 79
    Microsoft's implementation for VS .NET
        2005, 333–334
    web site address for information about,
        197
multi source control type
    testing, 190–194
    for wrapping up the VSS and filesystem
        settings, 180
mylog.xml file
    contents of, 39

N

name attribute
    of Project node, 42
    of properties, 46
    of target node, 43
NameValueCollection type
    adding to CodeSmith build and deploy
        scripts, 300
naming conventions
    importance of standardization of across
        solutions, 138–139
    use of in build files, 145–146
NAnt
    as .NET port of Ant, 25
    all about, 25–27
    choosing for automation of build
        processes, 26–27
    configuration tasks for database
        integration, 252
    configuring in EditPlus, 345–346
    considerations, 328–329
    control tasks for database integration,
        251–252
    core tool used in book, 343
    defined, 27
    dissecting, 25–58
    error handling in, 101–103
    extending with new tasks, 199–223
    file functions table, 85
    functionality, 199–202
    important tasks, 59–89
    introduction, 25
    list of command-line options, 30
    simplified class diagram for, 201
    a simplified view of loggers and listeners
        in, 36
    web site address for homepage, 58
    what it does, 26
NAnt build file
    defined, 27
    a simple "Hello World" script, 28–29
NAnt build script
    defined, 27

NAnt "database" element
    code example for, 242–243
NAnt default framework
    switch options, 32
NAnt developer mailing lists
    signing up for, 25
NAnt executable, 29–41
    command-line options, 29–30
    default behavior, 29
NAnt functions, 85–86
nant -help command
    results showing the NAnt executable
        screen, 29
NAnt log
    reviewing for Transformer.Build.xml, 119
NAnt nomenclature, 27
NAnt properties
    list of built-in, 50
NAnt script
    defined, 27
NAnt Sweeper, 349–353
NAnt tasks
    build, 74–81
    conditional, 69–71
    creating <fxcop>, 208–222
    file, 71–74
    general features of, 60–68
    introduction, 59–60
    investigating <mkdir>, 202–203
    source control, 83–85
    special for performing actions inside build
        scripts, 85–88
    structural, 64–69
    using attributes, 61–62
    utility, 81–83
NAnt user mailing lists
    signing up for, 25
Nant XML Schema (XSD) file
    investigating the allowed structure of a
        build file through, 41–42
<nant> [NAnt] task
    function of, 67–68
NantContrib
    homepage web site address, 26
NAntContrib tasks
    used in the book, 343
    using the <loadtasks> task to load,
        104–105
NAnt.Core project
    subfolders to support the framework,
        200–201
Nant.Core.DLL
    using Reflector to investigate, 40
NAnt.Core.Type namespace
    reflecting over, 62

nant.onfailure property
  setting, 101–103
Nantz, Brian
  *Open Source .NET Development:
    Programming with NAnt, NUnit,
    NDoc, and More* (Addison-Wesley,
    2004) by, 196
NDoc
  differences between build files, 147
  web site address, 347
NDoc output, 95
<ndoc> [NAnt] task
  function of, 76–77
nested elements
  using for NAnt tasks, 62–64
.NET delivery
  a context for, 1–24
  individual delivery vs. delivery process, 2
  potential processes, 4–9
  why delivery processes are needed, 1–2
NetReflector library
  implementing the DefaultLabeller with,
    195–196
Newkirk, James
  *Test-Driven Development in Microsoft
    .NET* by, 94, 133
Nini configuration service
  web site address for, 253
-nologo option, 34
nonaggressive library management, 142–143
notify target
  function of, 118
  for telling everyone of success or failure,
    131
NUnit report
  formatting, 112–114
NUnit task
  example of, 112
  formatting the report, 112–114
  test results, 94
  web site address, 346
NUnit tests
  running on the NUnit framework, 111
<nunit2> [NAnt] task
  attribute for including an application
    configuration file, 252
  function of, 78
NUnit2Report
  output, 113
  web site address, 346

O

ObjectComparer.cs file
  general-purpose comparer code held in,
    233

onfailure property
  using, 51–52
*Open Source .NET Development:
  Programming with NAnt, NUnit,
  NDoc, and More* (Addison-Wesley,
  2004)
  by Brian Nantz, 58, 196
open source tools
  reference book about, 58
organizational standards
  for build files, 146
output files
  generating multiple with XSLT, 292–296
OutputAssembly type
  function of in build files, 305–306
outputDirectory property
  use of in CodeSmith API, 288–289
overwrite attribute
  code for implementing, 204

P

pattern matching
  for fileset type, 63
planning
  importance of in delivery processes, 14–15
position target
  for copying assets into the environment,
    130
  for placing assemblies in folders with
    relevant names, 154
process standards, 135–166
  considerations of, 138–145
  naming conventions, 138–139
  source control organization, 139–140
ProduceBuildAndDeployFile method
  code for, 294–295
ProduceBuildAndDeployFiles method
  code for, 294
ProduceCcnetConfigFile method
  code for, 293
production environment
  needs for good management of, 12
  simulation of in development and other
    progression environments, 11
project
  NAnt definition, 27
project element
  in ccnet.config file, 177
project node
  attributes of, 42
  basedir attribute, 42
  as root node of a build file, 42
-projecthelp switch
  for figuring out available build file targets,
    39–40

ProjectHelp.xslt
  reflecting over, 40
project.name.1 property
  in build files, 146
ProjectSet data file
  final version of, 311
<project.x>.Build.xml file
  for code generation, 304
properties
  defined and used in build files, 46–52
property
  NAnt definition, 27
property names
  swapping into properties set, 128
property task attributes
  list of, 46–47
prototyping
  for implementation of Design to Deliver,
    18
publish target
  assets in the publish folder, 126
  as core aspect of Clean target code, 104
  differences between build files, 148
  documentation output for Transformer
    application, 125–127
  extracting from the web and
    Windows/assembly build files,
    150–152
  function of for Tranformer application,
    117–118
published assets
  configuring virtual directories for, 184
  labeling, 109–110

Q
-quiet option, 34

R
Rammer, Ingo
  Advanced .NET Remoting (Apress, 2002)
    by, 166
readonly attribute
  of properties, 46
  using for properties, 48
Red Gate Software, Ltd.
  tools for SQL Server, 237–249
Red Gate SQL Bundle
  automating, 241–249
  core tool used in the book, 343
  tools for SQL Server, 237
refactoring
  to achieve decreases in duplication,
    150–152
  for efficiency, 332
  opportunities for improving the build file,
    127–128

using for implementation of Design to
    Deliver, 18
Refactory
  web site address, 347
Reflector
  examining NAnt functionality with,
    199–202
  using to investigate Nant.Core.DLL, 40
  web site address, 347
Resharper
  web site address, 347
Roche, Ted
  Essential SourceSafe (Hentzenwerke
    Publishing, 2001) by, 24

S
scheduleTrigger
  for CCNet configuration, 179
script editing tools, 344
script tasks
  for creating an actual target, 87–88
  function of, 86–88
segregated delivery
  function of and problems with, 6–7
selectenvironments target
  for creating the environment, 130
selectversion target
  for telling NAnt which version to deploy,
    129
server component
  function of in CCNet, 172–173
Set Variables task
  configuring, 275–276
SettingCollection type
  adding to CodeSmith build and deploy
    scripts, 299–300
shared development model
  sharing of database between all
    developers, 227
simple delivery
  example of process, 5
  problems with, 4–5
simulation
  of production environment in other
    environments, 11
software dependencies
  expanded view of, 338
  simplified view of, 337
software tools
  available with source code for book, 93
solution definition
  defining and implementing the solution,
    323–325
solution implementation
  automated process interactions, 325–327

solution naming
  differences between build files, 147
<solution> [NAnt] task
  function of and issues associated with,
    78–80
solution.name property
  in build files, 146
solution.stub property
  tweaking the help target to pass at
    runtime, 148
source code
  for CCNet, 195
source code folder
  BuildArea files placed in, 120
source control
  defined, 23
  organization of, 139–140
  problems with for databases, 225
  problems with in Web projects, 141
  some useful management activities for, 14
source control tasks
  defined, 60
  function of, 83–85
sourcecontrol element
  for CCNet configuration, 179–180
Specific folder
  example of, 155
specific target
  for calling the specific build file for the
    specific solution, 149
SQL Compare tool
  command line, 240
  for comparing and synchronizing
    database schemas, 238–241
  example following synchronization, 240
  from Red Gate Software, Ltd., 237
  a simple database comparison, 239
SQL Comparison Settings screen, 238
SQL Data Compare tool
  from Red Gate Software, Ltd., 237
SQL Packager tool
  from Red Gate Software, Ltd., 237
SQL script processing task
  code for <execute> method, 234
  manual, 231–237
SQL Server
  Red Gate SQL Bundle tools for, 237
SQL Toolkit tool
  from Red Gate Software, Ltd., 237
standardization
  as crucial aspect of automated delivery
    process, 9–11
standards
  importance of to success of delivery
    activities, 330–331

startup .bat file
  creating for the CCNet server, 186
startup script
  creating for the CCNet server, 186–187
structural tasks
  for adding flexibility and power to
    structure of build files, 64–69
  defined, 59
<style> [NAnt] task
  for applying required style sheet to XML
    report, 115
  vs. <copy> task, 63
  function of, 81
  using infile as the name for its fileset
    element, 63
system databases
  data migration requirements for, 250

T
target
  NAnt definition, 27
target node
  attributes of, 43
  using to modularize a build file, 42–46
target test
  recalling and rerunning the unit test,
    261–262
[target] option
  importance of in NAnt, 30
<target> element
  code for wrapping a script task in, 88
<target> switch
  using, 41
task
  NAnt definition, 27
Task abstract class
  NAnt task inheritance from, 61–62
Task class
  reflecting over, 61–62
task contributions
  for NAnt that are not in the core NAnt
    release, 26
TaskAttribute attribute, 62
  function of in build file <mkdir>, 203
TaskName attribute
  function of in build file <mkdir>, 203
tasks
  general features of, 60–68
  important NAnt, 59–89
  running following a successful build,
    181–182
"Technical Debt"
  related to delivery implementation, 15
test databases
  setting up, 248–249

Test target
for analysis performed on compiled
assemblies, 111–116
TestDB-Development database
setting up, 248–249
TestDB-Integration database
setting up, 248–249
table Users in, 236
TestDB-Integration script
code example for testing, 235
TestDB-System database
setting up, 248–249
Test-Driven Development in Microsoft.NET
by James Newkirk, 94, 133
testing
the multi source control, 190–194
test.xml.cst
for generating a file with an XML file
input, 286–287
third-party assemblies
maintaining libraries of, 142–144
third-party components. *See* third-party
assemblies
Tidwell, Doug
XSLT (O'Reilly, 2001) by, 318
Together .NET
web site address, 347
tools
automating the organization of, 339–343
deciding on for automated delivery
process, 18
organization strategy for, 338–339
others used in this book, 346–347
selection of, 330
used to implement delivery processes,
337–347
tools and support organization
management of, 144–145
TransformationTests.cs
code example from, 258–259
Transformer application
building the web version of, 135–166
creating the deploy file for, 128–131
delivery scenario solutions, 137
examining the output, 119–127
failing NUnit tests with NUnit2Report, 114
generation of the documentation, 116–117
list of Build folders, 99
main form for, 92
maintaining a version number, 105–106
NUnit test results, 94
opportunities for refactoring, 127–128
organizing the environment, 98–100
output of versioning section, 120
projects in solution, 92

publish target output, 125–127
source code for, 91
use of publish target in, 117–118
versioning the assemblies, 106–108
viewing the correct assembly version, 123
viewing the generated assets, 122
VSS user account list for Builder
account, 99
what it does, 92–96
XML and HTML outputs in reports folder,
125
the XML document, 94–95
Transformer web application
building, 135–166
considering the delivery scenario, 136–138
TransformerEngine project
for providing transformation services, 92
TransformerGui project
for providing a Windows Forms GUI, 92
Transformer.ndoc project
code for, 95
TransformerTests project
unit tests for the application contained
in, 92
TransformXml utility method
code for, 293–294

U
/u switch
using with installutil to uninstall
VSSManager Windows service, 163
unit test configuration
pointing to the integration test instance,
261
unit testing
differences between build files, 147
practical guide for, 133
unit tests
for the Transformer application, 93–94
unit-testing task
for CodeSmith template build script after
changes, 308
unless attribute
example of use of, 49
of properties, 47
of target node, 43, 44–46
UnlessDefined property
translation to the unless attribute, 61
<unzip> [NAnt] task. *See* <zip>
[NAnt]/<unzip> [NAnt] tasks
use cases
build system, 97
deploy system, 98
function of, 96–98
user mailing lists. *See* NAnt user mailing lists

Users-AddPostcode.sql script
  for adding a new PostCode column to
    existing table, 235
Users.sql CREATE script
  for a table Users, 234–235
utilities
  installutil, 163
utility applications
  VSSManager, 158–166
utility tasks
  defined, 60
  function of, 81–83

V

value attribute
  of properties, 46
verbose attribute
  for enabling messages for actions on
    properties, 50
  of properties, 47
Verbose property
  translation to the verbose attribute, 61
-verbose, -v option, 32
version number
  maintaining information using <version>
    task, 105–106
<version> task
  for maintaining version number
    information, 105–106
  for providing updated version number to a
    property, 205
versioning
  problems with in Web projects, 141
  providing for our Transformer application
    code, 105–106
virtual directories
  configuring for published assets, 184
virtual environments
  benefits of using, 144
  pros and cons of using for development
    activities, 10
Visual SourceSafe (VSS)
  labeling, 109–110
  list of user accounts in the database, 99
  for source control tasks, 83
  for storage of core coding assets, 13–14
Visual Studio project
  for the <fxcop> task, 210
VS .NET
  documentation configuration in, 116
VS .NET settings
  as part of process standards, 140–142
VSS API dependency, 162

VSS database
  labeling, 109–110
VSS labels
  applied in Transformer application,
    121–122
<vsscheckin> [NAntContrib] task
  function of, 84
<vsscheckout> [NAntContrib] task
  function of, 84
<vssdiff> task
  using to produce a changes report, 206
<vssget> [NAntContrib] task
  function of, 84
<vsslabel> [NAntContrib] task
  function of, 84–85
VSSManager
  changes to the deployment script for,
    163–166
  function of, 158–166
  functionality diagram, 158
  packages and dependencies, 160
  remoting capabilities of, 159
VSSManager service
  example of installed, 165
VSSManager.Client
  example of it running, 166
<vssundocheckout> [NAntContrib] task
  function of, 85

W

Web build files
  vs. library build files, 147
  vs. Window build files, 146–147
web dashboard
  configurating as the ccnet virtual
    directory, 175–176
  function of in CCNet, 174–175
  setting up in IIS, 176
Web projects
  problems associated with, 141
  swapping for class libraries, 142
web site address
  for CodeSmith application, 281, 344
  for continuous integration article by
    Martin Fowler, 24
  CruiseControl.NET (CCNet), 196, 343
  Draco.NET, 196
  Enterprise Architect, 347
  FxCop, 346
  for a good independent NUnit task, 112
  Hippo.NET, 196
  for LLBLGen Pro code generation
    application, 281

for Microsoft User Interface Application Block, 136
for MSBuild information, 197
NAnt homepage, 25
NDoc, 347
for Nini configuration service, 253
NUnit, 346
NUnit2Report, 346
for Red Gate Software, Ltd., 237, 343
Refactory, 347
Reflector, 347
Resharper, 347
Together .NET, 347
web site component
function of in CCNet, 173–174
webURL element
in ccnet.config file, 178
Window build files
vs. Web build files, 146–147
Windows service
developed to allow client access to VSS databases, 159
installing for VSSManager, 162–163
workingDirectory element
in ccnet.config file, 178
WriteScript() method
in <dbAutoIntegrate> task, 247

X
xmllogger method
for publishing the log to CCNet web site and dashboards, 182–183
XmlLogger option
for IBuilderLogger, 36–39
<xmlpeek> [NAnt] task
function of, 82–83
<xmlpoke> [NAnt] task
for changing configuration files, 253
function of, 82–83
XmlSerializedFilePicker control
in CodeSmith, 285
XSLT
investigating, 292–296
using for code generation, 281
XSLT (O'Reilly, 2001)
by Doug Tidwell, 318
XSLT template
CodeSmith syntax vs. XSLT syntax, 302–304
use of curly brackets ({}) by, 309

Z
<zip> [NAnt] and <unzip> [NAnt] tasks
function of, 81–82